The CFO Guidebook

Third Edition

Steven M. Bragg

Published by AccountingTools, Inc., Centennial, Colorado.

For more information about AccountingTools® products, visit our Web site at www.accountingtools.com.

ISBN-13: 978-1-938910-91-3

Printed in the United States of America

Table of Contents

Preface

The chief financial officer (CFO) occupies the top financial position within a company. In that role, the CFO is responsible for an enormous range of activities, including accounting, fund raising, risk management, acquisitions, and strategic planning. *The CFO Guidebook* is specifically designed to give advice on all of these areas of responsibility – and in detail. In an era where the CFO is expected to be the chief advisor to the chief executive officer, the *Guidebook* can be of considerable assistance in ensuring that a company is financially viable and positioned for long-term growth.

Following an introduction to the CFO position in Chapter 1, we cover in Chapters 2 through 6 several of the more critical functions in which the CFO is heavily involved. These functions include strategic planning, risk management, control systems, performance measurement, and acquisitions. We then move on to a number of financial management topics in Chapters 7 through 11, including budgeting and forecasting, product pricing, cash management, and investment management. The book then shifts to several fund raising topics, with debt funding located in Chapter 12, equity funding in Chapter 13, and the role of credit rating agencies in Chapter 14. Chapters 15 through 19 give a thorough grounding in the concept of the publicly-held company, with discussions of going public, stock exchanges, investor relations, financial reporting, and share management. Finally, Chapter 20 notes a number of information technology issues that may be of interest to the CFO who wants to incorporate IT issues into corporate planning. The chapters include tips, podcast references, and a variety of illustrations.

You can find the answers to many questions that are of interest to the CFO in the following chapters, including:

- What types of strategies can a company pursue?
- What is the process for mitigating risks?
- How can a company operate without a budget?
- How do I construct a cash forecast?
- What are the different strategies for investing excess cash?
- What product pricing strategies are available, and which one should I use?
- What types of debt and equity funding are available?
- How do I calculate the amount to pay for an acquisition?
- What alternatives can be used to take a company public?
- How do I manage relations with the investment community?

The CFO Guidebook is designed for both professionals and students. Professionals can use it as a reference tool for improving their performance as CFOs, while it provides students with an overview of the CFO position.

Centennial, Colorado
July 2017

About the Author

Steven Bragg, CPA, has been the chief financial officer or controller of four companies, as well as a consulting manager at Ernst & Young. He received a master's degree in finance from Bentley College, an MBA from Babson College, and a Bachelor's degree in Economics from the University of Maine. He has been a two-time president of the Colorado Mountain Club, and is an avid alpine skier, mountain biker, and certified master diver. Mr. Bragg resides in Centennial, Colorado. He has written the following books and courses:

7 Habits of Effective CEOs
7 Habits of Effective CFOs
7 Habits of Effective Controllers
Accountant Ethics [for multiple states]
Accountants' Guidebook
Accounting Changes and Error Corrections
Accounting Controls Guidebook
Accounting for Casinos and Gaming
Accounting for Derivatives and Hedges
Accounting for Earnings per Share
Accounting for Inventory
Accounting for Investments
Accounting for Intangible Assets
Accounting for Leases
Accounting for Managers
Accounting for Stock-Based Compensation
Accounting Procedures Guidebook
Agricultural Accounting
Behavioral Ethics
Bookkeeping Guidebook
Budgeting
Business Combinations and Consolidations
Business Insurance Fundamentals
Business Ratios
Business Valuation
Capital Budgeting
CFO Guidebook
Change Management
Closing the Books
Coaching and Mentoring
Conflict Management
Constraint Management
Construction Accounting
Corporate Cash Management
Corporate Finance

Cost Accounting (college textbook)
Cost Accounting Fundamentals
Cost Management Guidebook
Credit & Collection Guidebook
Developing and Managing Teams
Employee Onboarding
Enterprise Risk Management
Fair Value Accounting
Financial Analysis
Financial Forecasting and Modeling
Fixed Asset Accounting
Foreign Currency Accounting
Fraud Examination
Fraud Schemes
GAAP Guidebook
Governmental Accounting
Health Care Accounting
Hospitality Accounting
How to Audit Fixed Assets
How to Run a Meeting
Human Resources Guidebook
IFRS Guidebook
Interpretation of Financial Statements
Inventory Management
Investor Relations Guidebook
Lean Accounting Guidebook
Mergers & Acquisitions
Negotiation
New Controller Guidebook
Nonprofit Accounting
Partnership Accounting
Payables Management
Payroll Management
Project Accounting
Project Management

(continued)

Public Company Accounting	The MBA Guidebook
Purchasing Guidebook	The Soft Close
Real Estate Accounting	The Statement of Cash Flows
Records Management	The Year-End Close
Recruiting and Hiring	Treasurer's Guidebook
Revenue Recognition	Working Capital Management
Sales and Use Tax Accounting	

On-Line Resources by Steven Bragg

Steven maintains the accountingtools.com web site, which contains continuing professional education courses, the Accounting Best Practices podcast, and thousands of articles on accounting subjects.

The CFO Guidebook is also available as a continuing professional education (CPE) course. You can purchase the course (and many other courses) and take an on-line exam at:

www.accountingtools.com/cpe

Chapter 1
The CFO Position

Introduction

The chief financial officer (CFO) position indirectly encompasses a broad range of activities. The CFO must have a strong knowledge of accounting issues, cash flows, investor relations, tax planning, and financial reporting. This knowledge should be coupled with the ability to communicate easily with the entire senior management team and the board of directors, as well as bankers and auditors. Thus, the ideal CFO is one with the process orientation of an engineer, the knowledge base of a librarian, and the persuasion skills of a preacher. In this chapter, we discuss the job description of the CFO and how it relates to the controller position, the nature of the CFO's organizational structure, and how the position relates to the chief executive officer (CEO), board of directors, audit committee, and audit partner.

> **Related Podcast Episodes:** Episodes 87, 123, and 194 of the Accounting Best Practices Podcast discuss the CFO position, the controller position, and the CFO career path, respectively. They are available at: **accountingtools.com/podcasts** or **iTunes**

The CFO Job Description

The job description noted in this section represents the normal set of responsibilities for a CFO, which encompasses the administrative, financial, and risk management aspects of a business. The job can be split into the following five general areas:

- *Planning.* This involves the formulation of the strategic direction of the business and the tactical plans, budgeting systems, and performance metrics required to achieve that direction.
- *Operations.* This involves the direct oversight of a number of departments, as well as coordinating the operations of those departments with other areas of the business. It can also include the selection, purchase, and subsequent integration of acquired businesses.
- *Financial information.* This involves the compilation of financial information into financial statements, and the presentation of this information to various internal and external recipients.
- *Risk management.* This involves understanding the current and potential risks to which the business is subjected and taking steps to mitigate those risks.

- *Financing.* This involves monitoring projected cash balances and arranging for either additional financing or investment options, depending on the amount of expected cash balances.

More specifically, the CFO's job includes the following tasks:

Planning

- Develop a strategic direction for the business, along with supporting tactics
- Monitor the progress of the company in meeting its strategic goals
- Oversee the formulation of the annual budget
- Develop a system of performance metrics that support the company's strategic direction

Operations

- Manage the accounting, treasury, tax, human resources, and investor relations departments
- Oversee the activities of any supplier to which functions have been out-sourced
- Participate in the functions and decisions of the executive management team
- Implement operational best practices throughout his or her areas of responsibility
- Engage in acquisition selection, purchase negotiations, and acquiree integration into the business

Financial Information

- Oversee the compilation of financial information into financial statements, with accompanying disclosures
- If the company is publicly held, certify the financial statements filed with the Securities and Exchange Commission (SEC) as part of the Forms 10-Q and 10-K
- Report financial results to management, the board of directors, and the investment community

Risk Management

- Understand the current and potential risks to which the business is subjected
- Take steps to mitigate risks, including the use of control systems, shifting risk to other parties, and insurance coverage
- Report on risk issues to the board of directors
- Ensure that the business complies with all regulatory and other legal requirements
- Monitor known legal issues involving the company, as well as legal issues impacting the entire industry

- Review and act upon the findings and recommendations of internal and external auditors

Financing

- Monitor projected cash balances
- Arrange for financing to meet future cash requirements
- Invest excess funds based on projected cash balances
- Invest funds on behalf of the company pension plan
- Maintain relationships with banks, lenders, investors, investment bankers, and outside analysts

The Controller Job Description

The controller is *the* key employee of the CFO. The controller manages all of the accounting operations within a business, which can safely be considered the single largest responsibility of the CFO. Given the critical nature of this position, we will devote more attention to it than to other positions reporting to the CFO. The controller's responsibilities can be split into the following five general areas:

- *Management.* This involves overseeing the operations of the accounting staff, as well as of any outsourced activities. There should also be a management infrastructure in place, such as policies, procedures, and calendars of activities.
- *Transactions.* This involves the proper processing of all types of business transactions, which includes supplier invoices, billings to customers, payroll, and cash receipts and disbursements. It also requires the use of a system of controls to ensure that transactions are processed properly, and a record keeping system in which transactions are recorded and archived.
- *Reporting.* This involves the preparation of the standard set of monthly financial statements, as well as a variety of management reports.
- *Planning.* This involves coordinating the creation of the annual budget, as well as the investigation and reporting of any subsequent variances between it and actual results.
- *Compliance.* This involves compliance with a variety of tax reporting requirements, government reports, debt covenants, and accounting standards.

More specifically, the controller's job includes the following tasks:

Management

- Manage the operations of the accounting department
- Oversee the activities of any supplier to which functions have been outsourced

- Oversee the accounting operations of any subsidiaries of the parent company
- Maintain a system of accounting policies and procedures

Transactions

- Verify that supplier invoices should be paid, and pay them by the designated due date, taking early payment discounts where this is economical to do so
- Issue invoices to customers as soon as goods have been sold or services delivered
- Collect accounts receivable promptly
- Process payroll information with minimal errors, and issue compensation payments to employees by scheduled pay dates
- Record cash receipts in a timely manner and deposit them promptly
- Complete bank reconciliations for all bank accounts at regular intervals
- Make scheduled debt payments as needed
- Operate an adequate accounting software package
- Maintain a chart of accounts that fulfills the record keeping needs of the business
- Maintain an orderly filing system for all paper-based accounting records, including a system of document archiving and destruction
- Maintain a comprehensive system of controls over all accounting functions

Reporting

- Compile and issue accurate financial statements on a timely basis
- If the company is publicly held, prepare reports for filing with the Securities and Exchange Commission
- Measure the financial and operational performance of the business and report this information in ongoing reports to management
- Prepare various financial analyses for management
- Assist in the preparation of the company's annual report
- Provide information needed by outside auditors to examine the company's financial statements and accounting system

Planning

- Coordinate the creation of the annual budget, as well as testing it for achievability
- Calculate variances between actual and budgeted results, and report the reasons for the variances to management

Compliance

- Monitor the company's compliance with debt covenants and warn management of covenant breaches

- Comply with any filing requirements imposed by local, state, or federal governing authorities
- Comply with all tax reporting and payment requirements

In short, most of the controller responsibilities involve detailed, "nuts and bolts" transactions and their summarization into the financial statements. In essence, this is a middle management position that involves a large amount of staff and process monitoring.

CFO and Controller Differences

Even the most cursory examination of the controller and CFO job descriptions reveals that the two positions are very different. The controller is responsible for the detailed daily operations of the accounting department, as well as for creating the financial statements and other reports. The CFO has a much broader and higher-level role, being responsible for planning, finances, risk management, and the management of a number of areas besides the accounting department.

In practice, the CFO is the supervisor of the controller, and so has the power to shift tasks between the two positions. Consequently, the controller may be placed in a more restricted or comprehensive role than what has been outlined here.

There was some duplication in the roles of the controller and CFO, as described in the preceding job descriptions. In particular:

- *Budgeting.* The controller is responsible for assembling the budget from input provided by planning participants. The CFO reviews the budget that the controller has assembled to see if it dovetails with the strategic direction of the business.
- *Financial statements.* The controller is responsible for assembling the financial statements. The CFO certifies to the SEC that the financial statements are correct, and also presents the statements to management and the investment community, along with relevant interpretations of the information.
- *Management.* The controller is directly responsible for the activities of the accounting department. The CFO supervises the controller, and so has indirect management responsibility over the accounting department.

In short, even when there appear to be duplicate responsibilities in some areas, the controller and CFO are engaged in different aspects of the same area.

The controller and CFO positions have inherently different educational and experience requirements. The controller needs a strong accounting education, and may have obtained an accounting certification. There is a much greater need for the CFO to have a strong ability to raise financing for the company, so this position is more likely to have an investment banking background, which does not necessarily call for accounting training or an accounting certification.

The CFO Organizational Structure

That part of the organization that reports to the CFO will vary by company, and may evolve over time. A new CFO may be given authority over a limited portion of the business, until he can prove to the CEO that he is worthy of taking on a broader range of work. In this section, we assume that a CFO is experienced and fully competent to take on the full range of tasks – but what are those tasks?

The organizational structure for a CFO is based on two possible ranges of authority. At a minimum, the CFO is responsible for all finance and accounting activities. A more expanded interpretation of the position also places all administrative activities under the CFO. In the following organization chart, we assume the broader interpretation of the role. In addition, note on the chart that the controllers of any subsidiaries report on at least a dotted-line basis to the corporate controller, who in turn reports to the CFO. By establishing a link between the business unit controllers and the corporate controller, it is easier to share best practices information between subsidiaries, impose standardized controls, and implement identical charts of accounts and accounting software.

As noted in the last section, the controller reports directly to the CFO. In addition, the CFO is responsible for all finance and accounting activities, which means that the treasurer and tax manager also report to the CFO. Further, it is customary for the investor relations officer (IRO) to report to the CFO. The IRO position is only required if a company is publicly-held, and therefore needs to engage in ongoing discussions with the investment community. By having an IRO-to-CFO reporting relationship, the CFO can coordinate the production of financial statements and how the information in those statements is communicated to outsiders.

One other key position that *may* report to the CFO is the human resources manager. This position is sometimes elevated to a vice president position and works alongside the CFO. However, the position typically reports to the CFO on the grounds that the CFO is responsible for all administration activities within a business, which includes human resources.

Another area that may report to the CFO is information technology (IT), on the grounds that it is part of the administrative activities of a business. However, IT can be so complex that the CFO can add little value by managing it, in which case the IT area should be administered by a vice president of IT, who reports directly to the CEO.

One position not appearing in the CFO's area of responsibility is the internal audit manager. Ideally, this position should report to the audit committee of the board of directors. Otherwise, the audit manager would find himself reporting to the CFO about systems that are under the control of the CFO – in other words, the CFO would be policing his own systems, and would therefore be more likely to quash any control problems that might reflect badly on his job performance.

CFO Organization Chart

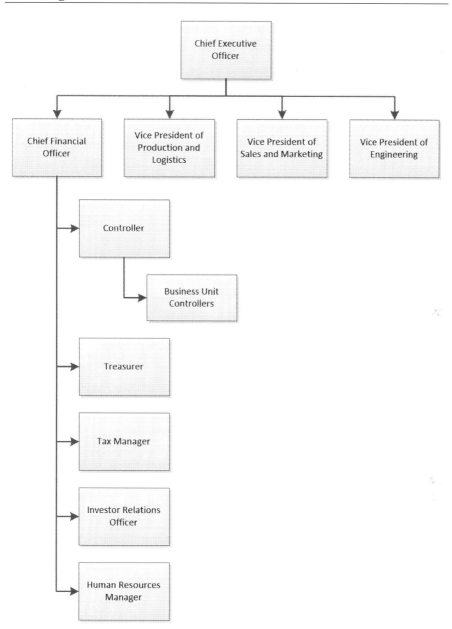

In the following organization chart, we note the specific areas of responsibility under the job titles noted in the preceding organization chart. This shows the full expanse of functional areas for which the CFO has direct or indirect responsibility.

Organizational Responsibilities

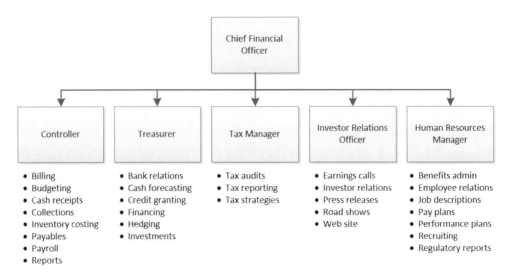

Controller	Treasurer	Tax Manager	Investor Relations Officer	Human Resources Manager
• Billing	• Bank relations	• Tax audits	• Earnings calls	• Benefits admin
• Budgeting	• Cash forecasting	• Tax reporting	• Investor relations	• Employee relations
• Cash receipts	• Credit granting	• Tax strategies	• Press releases	• Job descriptions
• Collections	• Financing		• Road shows	• Pay plans
• Inventory costing	• Hedging		• Web site	• Performance plans
• Payables	• Investments			• Recruiting
• Payroll				• Regulatory reports
• Reports				

Relations with the Chief Executive Officer

The CFO reports to the CEO. The CFO is more likely to be a highly educated person with an analytical outlook on business. The CEO is more likely to be an extrovert who thinks in terms of grand strategy, rather than the minutiae of how each individual aspect of a business operates. These differences can make the working relationship between the two a stressful one.

The differences in outlook are both a challenge and an opportunity for the CFO. Ideally, the CFO needs to fill in where the CEO is weakest, by researching the details that support the CEO's vision for the business, and by providing quantitative analyses that might suggest alternative paths for the direction of the company. However, this may appear to the CEO to be ongoing nitpicking that interferes with what he wants to achieve. To mitigate any feeling by the CEO that he is being monitored by a nanny, the CFO needs to have excellent "boss management" interpersonal skills. At times, however, it will be necessary to remember that the CEO is indeed the boss, and the CFO must do the best job possible to support the CEO's vision for the business.

The CEO can also provide an excellent growth opportunity for the CFO. Many CEOs are entrepreneurs, and they can teach the CFO a great deal about how to create and expand new lines of business. This can eventually lead to the CFO being promoted into the CEO role, or being hired away to fill the role in another company. At a minimum, business management skills learned from the CEO should give the CFO additional insights into how accounting and finance issues can be adjusted to match the realities of a growing business.

In order to achieve the optimum ongoing transfer of information between the CFO and CEO, the relationship must be extremely close. The two should discuss issues constantly, preferably multiple times per day. By doing so, the CFO can provide valuable input into strategies while the CEO is in the early stages of formulating them, while also gaining the position of trusted advisor.

In short, relations between the CFO and CEO can be a challenge, but if handled well, can result in a nearly unbeatable team that builds on each other's strengths.

Relations with the Board of Directors

The board of directors oversees the activities of a business. In that role, they are extremely interested in the financial condition of the business. The CFO should make a formal presentation of the company's financial results at every board meeting, using a standard format that can be replicated easily from meeting to meeting. By using a standardized presentation, the CFO can gradually improve the format over successive meetings.

The key presentation issue for the CFO is to report financial information at a just sufficiently aggregated level to give board members a good idea of the company's results, financial position, and cash flows, without burying them with too many details. Frequently, the CFO spends too much time going over details that should be beneath the notice of board members, to the point where they are overwhelmed with information and cannot see the "big picture" of the company's financial situation. In addition, the CFO should address key metrics, such as days receivables outstanding, but only if these metrics are useful to board members. Ideally, there will only be a few key metrics to focus on. These metrics will probably change over time as the company itself changes, though the "term in office" for each metric should be fairly long – perhaps several years.

The format of the presentation should be supplemented with trend line analysis and graphical presentations where appropriate, rather than having everyone pore over detailed financial reports. The intent is to *not* have a flashy presentation, but simply one that cogently conveys the most important information within a short period of time.

An experienced board will also be interested in the risks to which the business is subjected, and the management practices in place to deal with those risks. The CFO is in the best position to discuss these issues with the board. If the board wants to see additional risk management measures taken, they will likely expect to hear back from the CFO in regard to how their concerns have been addressed.

Whatever information the CFO shares with the board should be actively discussed with the CEO in advance. We never advocate blindsiding the CEO with *any* information in a board presentation; doing so means that the CEO may appear uninformed. The CFO needs to understand that a key part of the job is supporting the CEO, and that requires full cooperation between the two in the presentation of information.

If the CEO wants to hide information from the board, or adjust or downplay certain information being presented to the board, the CFO is clearly being placed in a difficult position. If this situation arises, the best alternative for the CFO is to express any concerns privately to the chair of the audit committee.

Relations with the Audit Committee and Auditors

The audit committee is concerned with the integrity of a company's financial reporting and controls. In a publicly-held company, the audit committee must also review and approve the quarterly financial statements before they are issued. These tasks require the audit committee to be far more knowledgeable about a company's financial statements and controls than the board of directors as a whole. Because of this difference in orientation, the CFO must interact with the committee on a much more detailed level.

Given the larger amount of detailed information being discussed, the CFO should issue a written report to the committee prior to each meeting, providing sufficient descriptive information about those agenda items over which the CFO has control. Otherwise, too much time will be spent during the meeting to educate the committee members on basic issues, which takes away time from the discussion of those issues.

The relationship between the audit committee and the CFO should be sufficiently close that the CFO does not feel constrained in discussing any issues. This can involve side meetings with individual committee members, as well as ongoing phone discussions on any number of issues. The CFO should be proactive in contacting at least the chair of the audit committee regarding issues that require immediate decisions, or items about which the committee may want to be forewarned before normally-scheduled committee meetings.

The outside auditors who audit a company's financial statements report to the audit committee, not the CFO. This means that the auditors will quite possibly report any shortcomings in the company's controls and accounting processes to the audit committee, which may not reflect well upon the performance of the CFO. Clearly, this can create some tension between the audit partner and the CFO. A well-mannered audit partner should apprise the CFO of issues found prior to audit committee meetings, so the CFO will have time to correct the issues or at least have formulated a defensible position prior to the meetings. To keep these issues to a minimum, the CFO should foster continual communications with the audit partner throughout the year, even when there is no audit or review currently under way. By doing so, the partner and CFO can discuss upcoming accounting issues, so that the company can record them in a manner that is satisfactory to the auditors, and requires no adjustment after the books have been closed.

Summary

While a large part of this chapter contained a list of CFO responsibilities, we must place strong emphasis on the role of the CFO in supporting other parts of the business. This means providing information to the CEO and other managers as needed, as well as supporting them in designing systems that will enhance the performance of the company as a whole. In other words, the best CFO is one who sees beyond the traditional recordation role of the accountant and instead sees how the position can help to transform the entire business into a competitive engine.

In this chapter, we alluded to the role of the CFO in developing strategy for a company. This is a key area that may develop into one of the larger responsibilities of the CFO. In the next chapter, we delve more deeply into the CFO's involvement in strategy.

Chapter 2
Strategic Planning

Introduction

Strategic planning is the formulation of plans to get from where the business is now to where it wants to be. The chief executive officer (CEO) is usually at the center of the strategic planning process, since this person is ultimately responsible for the direction that a company takes. As we will see in this chapter, the CFO can be a key participant in the planning process by expanding upon the CEO's general strategy, as well as by noting the financial constraints that will keep certain strategies from being viable, and by pointing out the risks associated with different strategies.

Strategy Overview

The CEO is the person ultimately responsible for the strategy that a company follows. The CEO may drive a business to take advantage of a perceived change in the marketplace, a new technology, a new market, or some other factor that the CEO believes will give the company a competitive advantage in maximizing its market share or profitability. The CEO can be very good at spotting these future changes, but is perhaps less skilled in determining how to get from here to there.

The CFO is much more knowledgeable about the finances, processes, and risk mitigation needed to achieve the CEO's strategic vision. With this knowledge, the CFO can perform the valuable role of filling in the details in the strategic plan, as well as testing the plan to see if it is viable. In some cases, the CFO may suggest alternative paths that can form the basis for an entirely new strategy. In the latter case, the CFO is the person driving strategy.

There are many books whose sole focus is the development of strategy, headed by Michael Porter's superb *Competitive Strategy*. We do not attempt to repeat or even summarize these books. Instead, we make note in passing of the general concept of strategy, and then move on in the following sections to the areas in which the CFO can most effectively participate in the formulation of strategy.

The process of developing a strategy can be grossly summarized into three steps, which are:

1. *Define the strategic goal.* This can involve a study of the competitive structure of the industry, the entrance of new competitors, regulatory changes, how the company earns a profit, and many other factors that lead the CEO to target a particular strategic direction. This step also includes consideration of the expected strategies that will be followed by competitors.
2. *Document the current capabilities of the company.* This is an inward-focused examination of the strengths and weaknesses of the business, from a competitive perspective. This analysis can throw out many issues that have

no bearing on the competitive posture of the business. For example, the ability to close the books in one day is usually not considered a competitive advantage, whereas a one-month product design cycle may be considered quite important.

3. *Develop a plan to reach the goal, starting with the company's current capabilities.* There must be a plan that states precisely how the business is to achieve its goals. This typically requires a tight focus on improvements in just a few areas. Attempting to improve all aspects of a business is usually much too difficult, and merely diverts attention and funding from the areas that really require improvement. Instead, focus on improvements only in those areas where the competitive advantage must be strengthened or supported.

At the end of the strategic planning process, there should be a written plan that states the strategic direction, the actions required to attain all designated goals, who is responsible for each action, and the date by which each action must be completed. This plan is unique to every business, since the CEO and CFO must take steps to refashion a company's unique set of strengths and weaknesses to match a future state that maximizes the company's position in relation to the strategies being pursued by competitors.

Types of Strategies

Having just stated that each business has a unique strategy, we must qualify that point by noting that strategies tend to fall into a few major categories. A business may pursue a truly unique strategy, or its strategy may incorporate elements of several major categories. Nonetheless, one of the following strategic themes will likely appear in a company's business plan:

Products Category

- *Superior products.* A business will develop products so noticeably superior to the competition that they can command premium prices. This requires a large investment in research and development, and usually results in a smaller market niche, since the majority of customers cannot afford premium products. However, this model has been pursued with great success by Apple, which occupies quite a large niche.
- *Product line extensions*. A company develops a product to fit every conceivable product niche in the market. This approach works well in a retail environment, where it is a competitive advantage to exclude competing products by filling store shelf space. The approach can also be used to combine products and services to provide a complete, end-to-end offering to customers.
- *Lowest cost products.* A business obtains the bulk of all market share by relentlessly driving down its costs, which allows it to maintain low price points. This calls for excellent production and logistics processes. The re-

sulting products must meet a reasonable quality standard, but will likely leave room on the periphery for higher quality or more innovative niche products that sell at higher prices.

- *Faster cycle time.* A company can refine its new-product development process to increase the speed of new product rollouts, thereby trumping competitor offerings with new designs on a regular basis. This approach is particularly common in the consumer products arena.

Marketing Category

- *Branding.* A company can invest heavily in advertising and other forms of marketing over a long period of time to build customer awareness of its products. This approach needs to be combined with high product quality and excellent customer support in order to arrive at a long-term, value-added strategy. The result can be a significant amount of market share, despite the presence of relatively high price points.
- *Expand the market.* A business has several alternatives for expanding the overall market in which it sells. This can include expansion into new geographic regions or marketing to new customers within existing regions. This approach may involve the development of revised products that more closely match the needs of the new customer base being pursued.
- *Distribution channel.* A company can roll out a new distribution channel that circumvents the distribution systems used by competitors. For example, Internet stores are more convenient for users than having to travel to a local bricks-and-mortar store location.

Financial Engineering Category

- *Industry roll up.* It may be possible to combine a number of companies in a highly fragmented industry, with the objective of creating economies of scale in marketing, production, and distribution. This approach is difficult, and requires a large amount of capital to achieve.
- *Accretive acquisitions.* A common approach to acquisitions is to methodically acquire smaller businesses that can be easily absorbed into the parent company, resulting in a gradual increase in overall company sales and profits. When handled correctly, this approach can offer superior returns on an ongoing basis, while also eliminating companies that might eventually grow up to become significant competitors.
- *Split up.* If a company owns several businesses that do not have mutual synergies, it may be best to spin off parts of the business or sell them outright. Doing so allows management to focus more closely on the remaining company operations.
- *Maximize cash flow.* In a staid industry where additional growth seems unlikely, a company can instead focus on generating the largest possible amount of cash, which it transfers to shareholders via dividends or stock buybacks.

- *Buyout*. New owners can buy out a business and cut costs to pay back their initial investment in the business. Alternatively, they can invest additional cash in the business in order to increase its market share.

Technology

- *Disruptive technology*. At long intervals, a company may create a technology that so completely alters the value proposition in an industry that it can rapidly take market share away from competitors. Consider the impact of electronic images on the photo processing industry, for example.
- *Licensing*. A company may be essentially a research lab, and so does not have the capability to launch its own products. Instead, it patents new technology and licenses it to other companies. These companies may also set themselves up to be acquired by a licensee that does not want the technology to be shared with other competitors.

The CFO can limit the discussion of strategic alternatives by putting boundaries around the financial capabilities of a business, which eliminates some strategy categories. For example, a cash-strapped business probably cannot afford strategies involving acquisitions, branding expenditures, or the expenditures needed to achieve low-cost producer status. However, the lack of cash does not prevent the exploration of strategic alternatives in the areas of reduced cycle times, new distribution channels, splitting up the business, or pursuing licensing arrangements. In short, knowing the types of strategic categories allows management to quickly throw out some areas that clearly will not work, and zero in on categories more likely to yield success.

Risk Analysis

The CEO is typically more concerned with expanding the business and building competitive advantages. This means that the CFO may be left with an ongoing analysis of the downside – what could go wrong with the business. The analysis of potential problems should not be a casual affair, but rather a studied one. Therefore, keep a running list of problems that other companies have encountered within the industry and in adjacent industries, and review the list at regular intervals to see if events have made any items more or less likely.

This does not mean that the CFO should be the corporate doomsayer. On the contrary, consider the reverse – identifying risks so well that the company can launch initiatives in new areas that competitors might consider excessively risky. For example, there is a general dearth of storefronts near a certain section of coastline, since it has been hit by three hurricanes in the past ten years. A real estate company is fully aware of the hurricane risk, and develops a new building design that mitigates the risk of storm damage by elevating the first floor of the building, leaving room for storm waters to flow under the building. The company successfully builds and operates these structures, which survive several additional hurricanes with minimal damage. In this case, the company is fully aware of the risks, and chooses to proceed in a manner that mitigates those risks.

Thus, the CFO can become involved in risk analysis with the intent of not only identifying risks, but also to determine ways to grow the business despite the presence of those risks. There is a lengthier discussion of risk issues in the Risk Management chapter.

A Tight Strategic Focus

Given the CFO's focus on risk, this is the position best able to say "no" to a divergence from company strategy, since it entails moving away from a known set of risks and into a new area where risks are not well defined. The CFO can be involved in tightening the strategic focus with the following techniques:

- *Agree on areas not to enter.* There are dozens of possible products and services that a company can pursue. Since each one consumes company resources, it is critical to determine which avenues *not* to pursue, thereby maintaining focus on the smaller number of projects most likely to succeed. The CFO should maintain a master list of these areas to be avoided, and point them out whenever the rest of the company appears to be in danger of pursuing them.

> **Tip:** If a company has decided not to pursue acquisitions, it is particularly important to turn away investment bankers at the door, rather than letting them overwhelm the company with acquisition opportunities. The analysis of these potential purchases can require a large amount of staff time from all over the company.

- *Make many small bets.* Within the areas that a company has determined are to be a company focus, ensure that there are many ideas being funded. Some will prove to be failures, but this is simply knowledge of the marketplace that can be used to reposition or enhance other ideas. By encouraging the continual investigation of new ideas, a business is much more likely to create its next big growth engine. The CFO can encourage this process by tracking where funds are being invested.
- *Drop unpromising projects.* It is all too common for a company to keep pouring money into a project that does not appear to have an adequate payoff, eventually resulting in a massive investment that could have been used to fund other, more promising projects. The CFO is in an excellent position to point out these situations, since he has no personal involvement in them, and so can dispassionately examine them from a purely quantitative perspective.
- *Do not let first-to-market drive the company.* The first company to bring a new product to market is by no means assured of owning the market. Instead, a short delay to examine the mistakes made by competitors, as well as to tweak a company's offerings, can yield much better customer acceptance.

Thus, the CFO needs to examine the circumstances surrounding product launches and see if product flaws are being ignored because of a first-to-market mentality.

Unfortunately, keeping the management team operating within a narrow range of strategic alternatives can give the impression that the CFO is the proverbial catholic nun who wields a large ruler. Nonetheless, this is a critical role to which the CFO is best suited.

Pacing

An immensely important strategic consideration is the pace of growth. Ideally, the CFO should advocate an extremely steady clip that allows a business to grow at a sustainable rate. By doing so, the business has the time to hire only the best people, employ the appropriate amount of training, and roll out concepts in an efficient manner. Over time, a business that uses a modest growth pace will be very likely to achieve its growth targets. Conversely, the CFO should be on the lookout for CEOs who try to grow the business by massive amounts over a short period of time, frequently by acquiring a large competitor. These massive growth spurts are difficult to incorporate into a business, can put an entire company at risk of failure, and can derail its strategic direction. Too-rapid growth can cause the following problems:

- Product shortages
- Product quality problems
- A diffused sense of company culture
- Reduced employee training
- Variations in the application of company policies and procedures
- Excessive obsolete inventory and bad debts
- An excessive amount of cash tied up in working capital

If the CEO wants to engage in such a spurt, it is up to the CFO to present a convincing argument in favor of a more restrained rate of growth.

The pacing concept means that a business must strive to attain the same growth rate in bad times. By doing so, the business can leapfrog its competitors during the slow periods, since they are probably hunkering down to conserve cash. Growth during a down cycle calls for the hoarding of cash during profitable periods, so that it can be expended in down cycles. The CFO can assist with cash hoarding by arguing in favor of liquid investments and retaining larger-than-usual cash balances at all times.

It is immensely difficult to consistently achieve a reasonable, targeted rate of growth, year after year. To do so, the CFO should lead the investigation whenever the growth target is not achieved. The management team must understand what failed, and commit to correcting the problem to bring the company back on track as soon as possible.

In short, the concept of pacing focuses the organization to a considerable extent. On an ongoing basis, everyone in the company knows the goal, and understands that they are capable of achieving the goal, irrespective of outside forces. This approach is not glamorous, but it consistently achieves results that can be formidable, if pursued consistently and over a long period of time.

What if the CEO wants to expand into an entirely new line of business? If so, the pacing concept can be applied here, too. There will be a risk associated with ramping up rapidly when the company really has no idea how well it will be accepted in the marketplace, so that a large investment may turn out to have been grossly larger than was really needed. Instead, consider smaller investments in a large number of pilot projects. After each pilot is completed, its results can be reviewed and an investment made that incorporates whatever adjustments were noted in the first pilot. This process may go on through several iterations before it is apparent that the company can reasonably expect to move into a new business area and thrive there. In this case, the pacing concept will certainly slow down the rate at which new sales are achieved, but will likely avoid excessive levels of investment.

Acquisition Strategy

The CFO is deeply involved in the analysis and justification of all acquisitions. What is sometimes lost in an acquisition investigation is why an acquisition is necessary at all. Many organizations adopt a passive stance, where they evaluate each potential acquisition as it appears, and then find a reason to justify a purchase after the fact with a "strategy." A vastly better approach is to settle upon a single acquisition strategy that works best for the business, and then aggressively follow it. Several possible strategies are noted next.

- *Diversification strategy.* A company may elect to diversify away from its core business in order to offset the risks inherent in its own industry.
- *Full service strategy.* An acquirer may have a relatively limited line of products or services, and wants to reposition itself to be a full-service provider. This calls for the pursuit of other businesses that can fill in the holes in the acquirer's full-service strategy.
- *Geographic growth strategy.* A company may want to roll out its business concept in a new region. This involves finding another business that has the support characteristics that the company needs, such as a regional distributor, and rolling out the product line through the acquired business.
- *Market window strategy.* A company may see a window of opportunity opening up in the market for a particular product or service. Its best option may be to acquire another company that is already positioned to take advantage of the window with the correct products, distribution channels, facilities, and so forth.
- *Product supplementation strategy.* An acquirer may want to supplement its product line with the similar products of another company. This is particu-

larly useful when there is a hole in the acquirer's product line that it can immediately fill by making an acquisition.

- *Roll-up strategy.* Some companies attempt an industry roll-up strategy, where they buy a number of smaller businesses with small market shares to achieve a consolidated business with significant market share.
- *Sales growth strategy.* A slow-growth company can acquire in a faster-growing niche, thereby giving the entire business a faster rate of growth. It may be possible to engage in a series of such acquisitions, continually skipping from niche to niche within an industry to position the business in the fastest-growing areas.
- *Synergy strategy.* Examine other businesses to see if there are costs that can be stripped out or revenue advantages to be gained by combining the companies. Ideally, the result should be greater profitability than the two companies would normally have achieved if they had continued to operate as separate entities. It is usually focused on similar businesses in the same market.
- *Vertical integration strategy.* A company may want to have complete control over every aspect of its supply chain, all the way through to sales to the final customer. This approach may involve buying the key suppliers of those components that the company needs for its products, as well as the distributors of those products and the retail locations in which they are sold.

The danger with acquisitions is when the result is a group of loosely-organized companies that now operate under a single parent company. These businesses have no better growth rate than they had when operating alone, their product lines overlap, their salespeople call on the same customers multiple times a month, and so on – and on top of that, the acquirer has squandered its resources to complete the acquisitions, and now has a massive debt burden. This not-uncommon scenario points out the main problem with acquisitions – growing for the sake of reporting a larger amount of total revenue does not create value.

Instead of simple growth, the CFO must understand *exactly* how an acquisition strategy will generate value. This cannot be a simplistic determination to combine two businesses, with a generic statement that overlapping costs will be eliminated. The management team must have a specific value proposition that makes it likely that each acquisition transaction will generate value (i.e., profits or cash flows) for the shareholders. Only through the consistent pursuit of profits can a business hope to be sustainable and provide shareholder value over the long term. Unfortunately, many acquirers lose sight of that goal and focus instead on simple revenue expansion, which can be disastrous.

The concepts of acquisition strategy are expanded upon in the Mergers and Acquisitions chapter.

Outsourcing

One of the larger strategy decisions that a company is routinely faced with is whether to outsource certain functions. When this decision involves the outsourcing of manufacturing, the cost per unit of the outsourced goods should not be the central factor that drives the outsourcing decision. Instead, the total cost of ownership must be considered. The following factors comprise the total cost of ownership:

- *Administration.* There can be significant costs and delays associated with maintaining a relationship that spans country borders, since this involves customs paperwork, and possibly coordination with a variety of transport services.
- *Damage.* Goods transported over long distances may be damaged in transit, or require expensive packaging to avoid damage.
- *Intellectual property risk.* Some countries, notably China, do not fully comply with intellectual property laws, so products manufactured in these countries are more likely to be illegally copied.
- *Shipping costs.* Ongoing increases in the price of fuel can make long-distance shipping prohibitively expense, especially when inventory is needed on short notice and must therefore be shipped by air freight.
- *Travel.* The company's design, production, and quality assurance staffs must routinely travel to supplier locations to monitor production. This may require some permanent on-site staffing.
- *Working capital.* A company may have to purchase in large volumes, and may have such long supply lines that it must also invest in extra safety stock to guard against unexpected delivery delays.

In many cases, a full consideration of the total cost of ownership will at least drive a decision to outsource closer to home, if not rejection of the entire outsourcing concept. Since the CFO has the best access to financial information, and probably employs most of the financial analysts in the company, the review of these outsourcing considerations will likely be a major CFO responsibility.

The Consideration of Cash in Strategy

A strategic issue that sits squarely in the area of responsibility of the CFO is how much cash to retain on an ongoing basis. The retention of cash requires the consideration of a multitude of factors. For instance:

- *Comparative returns.* If a company is earning a minimal amount on its invested cash and paying more on the after-tax cost of its debt, it may be reasonable to use cash to pay down the debt.
- *Investor demands.* Investors may want a dividend, which requires that cash be set aside at recurring intervals for these payments.
- *Pacing.* If the company is committed to growing at a steady clip through good times and bad, the CFO should retain a much higher cash reserve to

pay for this growth through poor economic cycles. Also, it may be possible to acquire assets and companies at lower cost during these periods, which also calls for a large cash reserve.

- *Work stoppage.* How long can the company last if a disaster completely halts sales? This could range from a union strike to flood damage or the destruction of a key supplier. Whatever the cause, the CFO must estimate the number of months of cash to have on hand to guard against these events.
- *Variability of results.* If a business is in an industry that continually suffers from short product life cycles, price wars, and so forth, it can make sense to retain a major cash reserve to guard against the continual downward spikes in the business cycle.
- *Lender problems.* For various reasons, the banking industry sometimes restricts its lending arrangements, to the point of putting some clients on the edge of bankruptcy. Maintaining an outsized cash reserve can keep a business running through these periods.

Of the points noted here, only investor demands and comparative returns indicate that cash levels should be drawn down. All other points made here indicate that outsized cash reserves should be considered the norm. In general, we advise that the prudent CFO hoard cash to the greatest extent possible, thereby guarding against situations where cash may be difficult to come by.

Summary

There is no perfect way to conduct strategic planning, nor is there a perfect way to force an organization to achieve the selected goals. A major problem with strategic planning is that the ultimate goal of a business is usually selected by a small number of people (or just one) who may have a flawed concept of how the business is really positioned in the marketplace, or who do not adjust the goal as the market changes over time. The result is an excessively rigid planning method that is difficult to follow.

An approach that tends to work better is for senior management to set a general target for the organization to follow, within certain guidelines, and then give employees the authority to achieve the target as they see fit. By doing so, the means by which a company evolves will vary over time to match changes in the market. The discussion of operating without a budget in the Budgeting and Forecasting chapter may be of use in formulating how to develop a strategy.

No matter how the strategic planning system evolves, the CFO will be closely associated with it, for no one else can provide a sufficient amount of input regarding prospective outcomes, how the company's systems must change to support the evolving enterprise, or how much funding will be required to achieve targeted goals.

Chapter 3
Risk Management

Introduction

A major concern of the CFO should be the risks to which a business is subjected. While minor risk events occur regularly, their financial impact on the business is small. What is of greater concern is the low-probability, high-cost risk event that can topple a business.

In this chapter, we give an overview of the types of risks, as well as how to locate, quantify, rank, and plan for them. In addition, we describe the major types of insurance that are available for offloading a portion of a company's risk, and also delve into several of the more critical risk areas. We then move on to two risk areas that are squarely under the control of the CFO – foreign currency variability and interest rate variability. Finally, we cover risk management themes, which are the overarching practices used by those organizations that are able to routinely reduce their exposure to risk.

Risk Management

A risk can be defined as an event that interferes with the ability of a business to achieve its objectives; that definition merely implies that a company's planned rate of growth could decline as the result of a risk event. In reality, some risks are so massive that they can potentially throw a business into bankruptcy, which is a far greater problem than a mere reduction in the rate of growth. The corporate planning function should have a detailed knowledge of a company's risk profile, in order to incorporate the variability and size of potential risks into future plans. Since the CFO is usually responsible for corporate planning, this person should be not only cognizant of the major risks, but also have a detailed knowledge of the associated plans to mitigate the risks.

Any company is subject to a large number of risks, many of which can lead to losses large enough to endanger the business. The CFO should periodically review these risks, if only to identify those most likely to cause trouble for the business. Examples of risks that can bring down a company are:

Hazard Risks

- Earthquake, flood, or storm damage to company facilities

Operating Risks

- Theft by an employee
- Supply chain disruption
- Computer system crashes

Financial Risks

- Changes in interest rates
- Changes in exchange rates
- Customer default on credit sales

The most dangerous type of risk is *strategic risk*, which interferes with a company's business model. A strategic risk undermines the value proposition which attracts customers and generates profits. For example, if a company's business model is to be the low-cost provider of a product and a competitor from a low-wage country suddenly enters the market, the company will find that its value proposition has been destroyed. Examples of strategic risk scenarios are:

- A new product fails catastrophically
- A major acquisition fails
- A customer gains massive market share and then has an inordinate ability to set prices
- A supplier gains monopoly control over supplies and raises raw material prices
- A key product goes off patent
- There is a sudden shift in technology that makes the company's products obsolete
- The contamination of company products with a hazardous substance leads to brand erosion
- A trade agreement reduces barriers to entry, resulting in a flood of new competitors into the market
- Regulatory changes eliminate sales or reduce profits
- Company assets are nationalized
- Terrorist attacks reduce sales or destroy property

The types of risks to which a business is subjected will vary considerably by company, since risk is based on such factors as geography, industry, product type, employee relations, and so forth. Thus, the risk mix is unique to every business. For example, a mining company is subject to the risk of a local shutdown by people who object to local pollution issues, while a business in the apparel industry may face a customer revolt over the working conditions of employees at its foreign clothing factories.

The Role of the CFO

It may appear that the absence of purely financial issues from the preceding list keeps risk management from being the responsibility of the CFO. However, risk management has traditionally been considered a non-operational area that is best tucked into the finance and accounting umbrella that is managed by the CFO. Thus, it is evident that a multitude of risks exist, and that the CFO is responsible for monitoring them. The actions of the CFO in this area can take a variety of forms, including the following (which are presented in order of increasing involvement):

1. *Financial statement disclosure.* Risks are commonly itemized in the footnotes that accompany the financial reports of public companies. However, these disclosures tend to be brief, and are intended more as a general warning to investors regarding the riskiness of their investments. Thus, these disclosures are not usually acted upon.
2. *Narrative form.* Any risk certainly requires a fair amount of narrative to make clear the nature of the issue, and how it can impact the company. However, a discussion of this type does not quantify the risk, and so tends to be ignored.
3. *Quantitative analysis.* It is usually possible to assign a range of costs and probabilities to almost any risk, even if the initial range is quite large. Over time and with additional analysis, it should be possible to refine these estimates somewhat. In particular, attempt to quantify each possible outcome of a specific risk, to see if there are some outcomes so catastrophic that they deserve additional attention.
4. *Monitoring and reporting.* There can be a system in place that tracks identified risks and reports them to management, along with the identification of newly-discovered risks and their ramifications.
5. *Risk planning.* A number of steps can be taken to either mitigate risks, or shift them to or share them with another party. It is also entirely possible that management will deliberately accept certain risks.

Ideally, risk management involves all of the preceding activities. That is, risks must be identified, clarified, ranked, and monitored aggressively enough to ensure that management can take action within a reasonable period of time.

We now turn to additional discussions of several of the topics just noted for risk management.

Risk Identification

The first step in risk analysis is to determine which risks may be most applicable to one's business. An excellent source of information is one's own industry. It is entirely possible that a competitor has been subjected to a risk that might also impact the company in the future. In some cases, these risks might be extremely rare, perhaps just a few times per century. Nonetheless, an event from a number of years ago may still be applicable to a company's risk planning – the frequency level may be low, but if the associated cost is high, the event is still worth documenting.

Another source of information is in the public filings of any competitors who are publicly held. The Securities and Exchange Commission requires that these businesses routinely state all of the risks to which they are subjected, and their attorneys can be quite comprehensive in their itemizations. If so, a perusal of these lists may uncover additional risks.

A third source of risk information is adjacent industries. Just because a company's own industry has not experienced a particular risk does not eliminate the probability of its occurrence. By casting somewhat further afield to similar industries, additional risks can be found that are applicable to a company's circumstances. For example, a car manufacturer with facilities in a foreign country might want to consider the risk of expropriation, if the assets of a car parts company in the same country have been expropriated recently.

Risk Quantification Issues

Some risks initially appear so vague that it may not seem possible to assign any value to them at all. For example, what is the cost of the loss of a company's reputation? While certainly difficult, it may be possible to estimate these costs by examining what happened to other companies that experienced the same or similar problems in the past. Examples of risks that certainly pose quantification difficulties are:

- Losses from a customer boycott
- Reduced sales from a decline in the perception of a brand
- Difficulty in hiring high-grade employees because of a reputational issue

Other risks are considerably easier to quantify, since a specific action should result in a tightly-defined cost. For example, if a factory is located in a flood plain, flooding damage will be limited to the complete replacement of the factory, along with lost profits from sales that could not be fulfilled from that factory. Similarly, asset expropriation can be tightly defined; the assets located in the at-risk country will be taken.

The cost of some risks will fall midway between the two extremes just noted, and may encompass expenditures that a business has not been accustomed to dealing with in the past. For example, a company dealing with a loss in reputation may need to factor in the cost of a lobbyist, extra security personnel to protect company property, a community relations manager, payments to the local populace, an advertising campaign, a public relations advisor, incentive packages to retain or hire employees, and so forth.

Once risks have been quantified, there may be a temptation to multiply the expected cost range by the probability of occurrence, which results in an expected value. For example, if the probability of an event is 10% and the cost of an unfavorable outcome is $1 million, we multiply the cost by the probability to arrive at an expected value of $100,000. The trouble with the expected value concept is that it tends to hide the sheer size of some risks. For example, a risk may have a cost of $100 million but a probability of only ¼%, so anyone examining the expected value report would reasonably conclude that the risk is worth only $250,000. In reality, readers should be made aware of the total projected cost of a risk, even if the risk is small, to see which risks are hefty enough to bring down a business. This means that both the probability and cost information for each risk should be presented.

Tip: It is dangerous to rely entirely upon a financial model to calculate how much a risk can impact a business, since models cannot comprehensively account for every eventuality. If the results of a model do not appear to match real-world results, distrust the model.

Risk Ranking

There may be hundreds of possible risks that could impact an organization, so they must be prioritized to focus attention on the key items. This is typically based on their frequency and severity, which can be plotted on a grid that uses frequency and severity as the axes. Severity can be measured by conducting a what-if analysis that reveals the full impact of a risk event on a business. The outcome should show the extent of losses and any reduction of cash reserves.

The ranking of risks can be difficult, for they cannot always be quantified. For example, the risk of a product recall can probably be quantified in terms of a range of product repair costs, but cannot be quantified in terms of the damage to the brand. The first figure could be reliably stated as falling somewhere between $800,000 and $1,000,000, but the cost of brand damage could extend for years and involve many lost customers who will no longer automatically turn to the company for replacement products. Consequently, an analysis of the frequency and severity of risks will require a significant amount of judgment, rather than hard numerical analysis. This hardly means that a ranking system should be ignored – judgment can be based on many years of experience, and may result in risk rankings that prove to be fairly accurate.

Given the difficulty of quantification, it can be difficult to assemble an exact ranking of which specific risks are more critical than others. Instead, it can make more sense to use a simple scale to measure a risk's frequency and severity, and concentrate attention on the cluster of risks that score the highest. We illustrate this concept in the following chart, which uses a zero-to-five scale to rate each risk.

Note in the sample table that there is a clear differentiation between three key risks (supplier damage, delivery disruptions, and bottleneck issues) and the remaining risk topics, which would certainly direct management's attention toward these items. At a lesser degree of risk, the chart shows a high frequency for commodity price swings, as well as high severity levels for hurricanes at one location and the risk of a pollution-related shutdown. The remaining risks are a combination of low severity and low frequency, and so would likely receive less management attention.

Sample Risk Rankings Chart

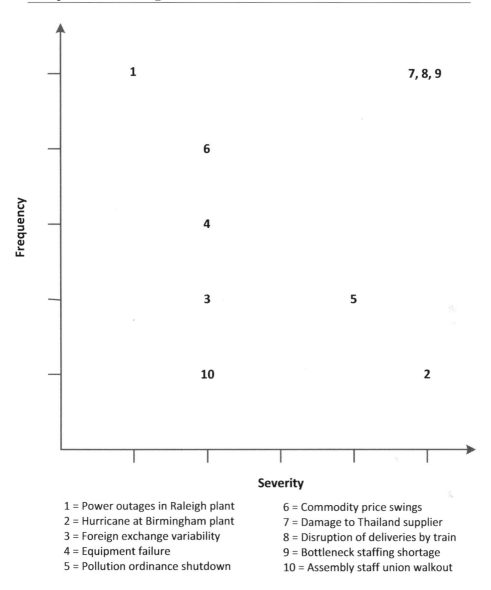

1 = Power outages in Raleigh plant
2 = Hurricane at Birmingham plant
3 = Foreign exchange variability
4 = Equipment failure
5 = Pollution ordinance shutdown
6 = Commodity price swings
7 = Damage to Thailand supplier
8 = Disruption of deliveries by train
9 = Bottleneck staffing shortage
10 = Assembly staff union walkout

The zero-to-five scale used in the sample chart can be clarified in greater detail, so that those people deriving scores for risks can set scores with a fair degree of reliability. For example, the following frequency scoring system sets ranges for each of the scores from zero to five.

Frequency Scoring Guidelines

Score	Description	Time Guideline
5	Frequent activity	Weekly
4	High activity	Quarterly
3	Normal activity	Annually
2	Modest activity	Every 2-3 years
1	Low activity	Every 5+ years
0	No activity	No historical activity whatsoever

The same approach can be applied to the severity of a risk, as described in the following severity scoring system. In the sample scoring guidelines, the table notes multiple ways in which to set a zero-to-five score, since it is not always possible to define a risk based on a single set of criteria.

Severity Scoring Guidelines

Score	Description	Sales Reduction	Expense Increase	Order Fulfillment Rate in 24 Hours
5	Potentially business threatening	Sales terminated	50% increase	0%
4	Major disruption	50% decline	25% increase	50%
3	Concerning to stakeholders	20% decline	10% increase	75%
2	Material impact	10% decline	5% increase	80%
1	Minor impact	5% decline	2% increase	90%
0	No impact	< 1% decline	< 0.5% increase	98%

Note that in the preceding severity scoring guidelines table, the percentages listed for a sales reduction are higher than the percentages used for an expense increase. The reason for the difference is that the effects of a sales reduction are reduced by the cost of goods sold, which will not occur if there is no sale. This means that the severity scoring will vary, depending on the gross margin that a company earns. For example, a potential sales reduction of 10% may be considered to have a material impact if the contribution margin is high, since most of the sale passes through to profits. Conversely, a potential sales reduction of 10% might be considered to have a minor impact if the contribution margin is relatively low, since only a small part of each sale appears in profits.

The Risk Profile

A risk profile is a categorization of the main risks that can impact an organization. A risk profile document is useful for focusing the attention of management on those risks that can cause significant turmoil for the entity, either in terms of financial losses or operational difficulties. The types of categories used can vary by organization. Here are a number of risk categories that might be used:

- *Brand.* Includes issues that can cause the perception of a company's brand to decline, such as a product recall, a marketing flop, bad publicity, negative product reviews, and public squabbles with business partners.
- *Catastrophic.* Primarily includes natural disasters, such as hurricanes, earthquakes, tornadoes, and floods.
- *Environmental.* Includes fines and remediation costs related to pollution, as well as damage to the environment.
- *Financial.* Includes the risks of customer nonpayment, foreign exchange rate variability, capital availability concerns, and employee fraud.
- *Human resources.* Includes the loss of key employees and the lack of properly directive leadership.
- *Industry risk.* Includes factors that can alter the competitive profile of the industry, such as changes in the entire size of the market that the industry serves, the rate at which the industry is consolidating, and the ability of new competitors to enter the market.
- *Information technology.* Includes factors that do not allow an organization to have responsive IT systems, such as being tied to legacy software and having a significant amount of systems downtime. Can also include system breaches that result in the loss of key data.
- *International.* Includes factors caused by doing business in other countries, such as employee kidnappings, terrorist attacks, asset expropriation, political unrest, and sanctions.
- *Legal and regulatory.* Includes new laws or regulatory requirements, such as changes in available tax credits and increased filing requirements for publicly held companies. Can also include internal legal issues, such as being unable to lock down trade secrets.
- *Operational.* Includes factors that impact the ability to produce a sufficient number of quality goods and services, such as inadequate peak capacity, low fulfillment rates, high scrap rates, and processes not being followed.
- *Strategic.* Includes risks arising from the decisions that management makes to follow certain strategic directions. Examples of these risks are bringing new products too late to market, being unable to secure key distribution channels, and selling a product mix that does not attract a sufficient number of customers.

The risk profile document can be combined with the preceding risk rankings chart to yield a good overview of the risks to which a business is subjected. This report can be used as the basis for risk planning.

Risk Planning

There are three major decisions to be made when a risk has been identified, which are:

- *To mitigate the risk.* There are a variety of internal actions that can be taken to mitigate risk, such as moving a factory away from a flood plain or selling off a subsidiary that might otherwise be nationalized. Or, if there is a risk of product failure in the marketplace, consider developing two products at the same time. As another example, the risk of expropriation can be dealt with by halting the investment in the at-risk country or even selling off facilities in that country.
- *To accept the risk.* The likely payout from a risk may be so small that the company can easily bear the risk of loss. Alternatively, the offsetting amount of profit may be so high that the company is willing to accept a sub-stantial amount of risk. For example, there could be massive profits from operations in another country, which make the risk of asset appropriation worthwhile.
- *To transfer the risk.* Many types of risk can be shifted to a third party by purchasing insurance. Of course, this comes at the cost of the insurance, which could be quite high if the insurance company expects a high rate of claims occurrence. A mid-way solution is to retain some of the risk and offload only a portion of the risk to the insurance company.

Also, risk planning should be fully integrated into a company's capital investment decisions. This means that the decision to acquire major assets should include consideration of all related risks, not just the net present values associated with those assets.

If there is a reasonable probability that a negative event will occur, it is useful to prepare a list of key action items in advance that the company can implement at once. Advance preparation of this type is particularly useful when it is obvious that the company will have to cut costs at once if the event occurs. Otherwise, the company will continue to spend money on its current cost structure while the senior management team takes weeks or months to evaluate the most appropriate set of cost reductions.

> **Tip:** When the occurrence of a negative event appears to be highly probable, it may make sense to spend extra time creating several alternative plans, so that management can more quickly evaluate the options and take action.

Insurance

Some managers seem to think that all risk can be insured, thereby leaving no risk mitigation activities for them to engage in. This is not true, because insurance is only designed for events that are infrequent and high-loss. If events are too frequent, the cost of insurance coverage will be too expensive. If an event has small losses, there is no point in obtaining insurance coverage, since self-insurance is less expensive. Thus, insurance is intended for a very specific set of situations. All other types of risks must be dealt with in other ways, as just noted under the "Risk Planning" topic. Nonetheless, there are many types of insurance available, of which the most common are noted in the following list:

- *Business interruption insurance.* This policy covers lost profits from business interruption, as well as the reimbursement of actual expenses incurred during the period when a business cannot conduct its normal operations. Some companies elect to forego this insurance.

- *Commercial automobile insurance.* This policy covers damage to the vehicles used in a business, as well as injuries to third parties caused by those vehicles. This coverage may not be necessary, if a company does not own vehicles or have employees use their own vehicles on company business.

- *Errors and omissions insurance.* This policy covers injuries to third parties that are caused by inadvertent mistakes or failures. This policy could, for example, cover losses due to delays related to missing export paperwork. Some companies elect to forego this insurance.

- *General liability insurance.* This policy can provide for a variety of exposures, including liabilities to third parties on the company's premises, injuries related to company products, and so forth.

- *Inland marine insurance.* This policy covers damage to commercial goods while in transit on dry land, as well as when the goods are in storage. This coverage may not be necessary if a company uses third-party carriers that also have this insurance.

- *Property insurance.* This policy protects against the loss of physical assets. The cost ranges from minimal for a services business with few assets to a substantial sum for an asset-intensive manufacturing facility. This is essential insurance.

- *Umbrella insurance.* This policy provides additional coverage above the limits set by other insurance policies.

- *Workers' compensation insurance.* This policy is required under state law, and compensates employees for injuries suffered in the workplace. The advantage to these mandated programs is that state law does not allow employees to sue their employers for negligence related to workplace injuries, unless there is gross negligence by the employer.

We also provide a somewhat more extensive discussion of two types of insurance that are becoming more worthy of consideration, given the critical need for data security and the extent to which companies have operations in other countries.

- *Cyber risk insurance.* Also known as network security liability insurance, this type of insurance is available but rarely considered by CFOs. It covers a valuable asset – information. Most other types of insurance coverage are designed to protect against the physical loss of or damage to tangible assets, such as buildings and machinery. This insurance is needed to cover damage to or theft of electronic information, which is arguably the most critical asset in a business. Consider the damage to a business if its customer database is stolen, client medical records are destroyed, or product design specifications are damaged. Besides recovery costs, a business may also have to deal with privacy-related class action lawsuits and the loss of customers. Further, many governments require companies to notify every person whose personal identity information was compromised.

To obtain coverage, insurance companies will want to review the network security standards and related security procedures of a business. It may be necessary to upgrade the level of security in order to obtain insurance coverage. Depending on the policy, coverage should include the following types of coverage:

- o Loss of business income
- o Data restoration expenses
- o Cyber extortion expenses
- o Litigation and regulatory defense expenses
- o Public relations and consumer notification expenses

- *Political risk insurance*. This policy reimburses a company for the loss of fixed assets, net investment values (investment plus retained earnings) and sales and supply contracts that are destroyed by civil wars, taken through expropriation, or damaged by contract repudiation or regulatory changes. Even if company management does not believe this coverage is necessary, investors or lenders may force the issue in order to protect their investments in the company, though only if it is doing business where there appears to be a reasonable degree of political risk. The policy is particularly useful for businesses contemplating overseas expansion, or which have production facilities in low-wage areas.

We pay special attention to directors and officers (D&O) liability insurance, which covers claims made against directors and officers. Examples of such claims are as follows:

- A competitor claims that the company has improperly hired away several key employees
- A shareholder claims that the company has failed to properly disclose financial information related to irregular accounting practices
- A limited partner claims that the company has diverted assets to several related parties
- Company officials are held liable in a trademark infringement case
- The owner of a nearby business claims that the demolition of a structure on company property damaged his own property
- The government claims that a company is liable for the illegal dumping of hazardous materials

D&O coverage is essential, since the personal assets of directors and officers can be pursued by aggrieved shareholders, vendors, customers, employees, government agencies, and other parties. With this insurance, directors and officers are covered for acting within the scope and capacity of their positions. Coverage includes defense costs, as well as settlements and judgments. Typical exclusions from this policy include fraud, criminal acts, known liabilities, and punitive damages.

Unlike most other types of insurance, D&O insurance is underwritten on a *claims-made* basis. This means that the policy currently in effect absorbs the liability for claims made, rather than the year in which the alleged wrongdoing took place. This aspect of D&O coverage can be a major problem for directors and officers, who have a five-year statute of limitations on alleged wrongdoing, and yet may no longer be with the company during the latter part of that period, and so have no control over the quality of the D&O coverage in subsequent years. It is possible to purchase insurance for retired directors and officers that addresses this problem. Realistically, most claims are filed against directors and officers immediately after the triggering event, so this risk may not be considered an especially large one.

Tip: An excellent supplement to D&O insurance is for a company to indemnify directors and officers in its charter or bylaws, thereby limiting their personal liability from the assertion that they acted negligently. This approach helps to retain directors and officers when a business is in difficult financial circumstances for various reasons, and is therefore more likely to be sued.

In general, when the insurance market is restricted, insurers will attempt to underwrite on a specific set of risks that they identify in the coverage; this is called *named perils* coverage. Since this type of coverage can exclude many types of risks, the CFO should instead strive for *all-perils* coverage. Realistically, the cost of all-perils coverage may be so high that it is not attainable; if so, obtaining insurance devolves into an analysis of how to obtain the largest amount of named perils coverage for the lowest price.

Tip: When purchasing insurance, be sure to review the credit rating of the insurance company, to see if it has adequate reserves to pay claims if the company experiences a loss.

If the cost of a particular type of insurance continues to rise over a period of time, this means that the insurer believes there is a high probability of loss and resultant payouts to policy holders. If so, and rather than continuing to pay the insurance, consider whether the company should restructure its business to mitigate the risk. After all, the insurer is using its pricing to tell management that a business activity is excessively risky. For example, if flood insurance rises to absurd levels, take this as a warning that the company needs to move its operations to a safer location.

One option for reducing benefit costs is to self-insure all or a portion of employee medical costs. This involves paying directly for the medical care of employees, and retaining a third-party administrator to process claims. Given the possibility of an employee incurring extremely high medical bills, a company can obtain *stop loss insurance* that provides coverage once an employee's annual medical claims exceed a certain predetermined amount. Thus, the concept of self-insurance really applies only up to a certain maximum amount. An insurance advisor can discuss whether self-insurance is cost-beneficial; the point at which this approach can be used is now considered to be as low as 100 employees.

An added benefit of self-insurance is the detailed level of information available to the company concerning what types of claims are being filed. With this information, it may be possible to create wellness programs that target the types of claims being filed.

> **Tip:** When buying stop loss insurance, avoid any contract language that allows the insurer to require a higher stop loss limit on certain employees in later years. Otherwise, a company may find itself paying out excessively large claims for those employees with a history of sickness.

We now change topics to address three specific types of risk that are particularly likely, given the level of electronic communications and widespread supplier networks now in place around the world.

Data Security Risk

If critical company records are stolen, made accessible, corrupted, or destroyed, there can be serious monetary and business repercussions. For example, if customer records are stolen, the company must notify its customers, investigate and correct the security breach that caused the theft, and possibly pay a government fine. Customers may also depart as a result of the theft. Given the magnitude of these problems, the CFO should be aware of the steps that can be taken to protect data security, which are:

- *Internal access.* Employees should only be given access to the data they need to conduct their jobs. They should be denied access to all other types of data. When employees change positions or leave the company, this should trigger an examination and revision of their data access privileges, so that unnecessary privileges are revoked. Further, databases should be encrypted. There should also be systems in place that track who is accessing information, what they are accessing, and the specific data being accessed.
- *External access.* Firewalls and password access should be mandatory for all external access to company systems. It may even be necessary to physically break any connection between a company's key databases and the outside world.
- *Portable data.* Keep close control over any data that is copied onto portable media. Track when it is taken and when the portable media are returned. All portable data should be encrypted.

Tip: Create a reporting system that shows the data access privileges of every employee, as well as their job titles. A brief perusal of this report may flag excessive data access privileges, based on employee roles.

In addition, when any company operations are outsourced, the supplier probably requires some access to company data in order to complete its assigned tasks. If so, the company must extend its own data security procedures to the supplier, and periodically verify that those procedures are being followed.

Tip: One of the best ways to deal with data security is to minimize the amount of data. This means promptly deleting data that is no longer needed, which requires an active data archiving and destruction program.

Supply Chain Risk

If a company has a far-flung group of suppliers, a major risk management issue is having an early warning system, so that the company can take immediate steps to re-route supplies from other parts of the globe. One tool for this is a subscription-based incident-monitoring service that issues e-mail alerts. A company can use this information to determine if the projected delay will impact the sales of a top-selling product. If so, a rapid response team should immediately notify a secondary supplier, and work on the logistics needed to bring in the required components on time. If there is no incident-monitoring service available, then at least make note of the locations of all major supplier facilities, and correlate these locations with events as the company becomes aware of them.

A particular quandary from the risk management perspective is whether to have multiple suppliers for some components. If a company adheres to just-in-time manufacturing concepts, it probably concentrates its buying with a single supplier for each component, and has a tightly-integrated relationship with these suppliers. However, if one of these key suppliers were to fail, the company's sourcing programs could be thrown into disarray. One option is to maintain relations with a second supplier for each key component, so that purchase orders can be shifted quickly. Another option is to set up different clusters of suppliers and manufacturing facilities by region, so that a catastrophe that impacts one region can be offset by increased production in another region.

The CFO can take a direct hand in supply chain risk issues by using such credit research firms as Moody's Analytics and Dun & Bradstreet to monitor the financial health of suppliers. If the credit information forwarded by these research firms indicates a problem, the purchasing department can bolster its planning to ramp up production with secondary suppliers, in anticipation of a default by the primary supplier. This approach can also be used to swap out secondary suppliers that appear to be having financial difficulties. This type of overview can become more detailed if the credit research firms detect a significant problem, perhaps involving an on-site team that investigates the condition of a supplier.

> **Tip:** Maintain and regularly review a supplier watch list, on which are noted all suppliers that appear to be having difficulties, and which may require replacement.

A possible solution to supply chain problems is the targeted stockpiling of some types of raw materials. Even though stockpiling increases the investment in working capital, it also protects manufacturing facilities from work stoppages. For example, if a key supplier anticipates that a labor union will walk out on strike, the company can stockpile a sufficient amount to last through the expected period of the strike. Similarly, if a raw material is in short supply, a company can stockpile a sufficient amount to last while it finds new sources of supply or finds alternative materials. A useful side benefit of a stockpiling program is that it also provides extra stock if there is an unexpected increase in demand.

A particularly difficult supply chain issue to consider is the second tier of suppliers. Most companies have no idea who supplies their suppliers – even though a disruption in the second tier will also impact the primary suppliers. At a minimum, consider discussing the next tier of suppliers with those primary suppliers who are critical to the success of the company, with an emphasis on persuading them to institute their own supply chain risk management systems.

In short, managing the risk of a supply chain means reviewing the financial, operational, and environmental risks that can impact all parts of a supply chain, and planning in advance to re-route supplies to avoid trouble spots before they happen.

Political Risk

A business may have operations in a country where there is significant political risk. For example, there may be a risk of unfavorable regulations impacting profits, or of the expropriation of assets. While political risk insurance is available, there are other alternatives. One option is to diversify the company's assets into other countries. For example, if it appears likely that capacity levels must be increased, should the company build the new production facility in another country and import the goods, rather than increasing the size of existing facilities that might be expropriated? This is a judgment that balances the incremental increase in costs from diversifying the asset base with the reduced risk of asset loss.

Another option with political risk is to integrate the company so closely with local inhabitants that the business is seen to be local, rather than foreign owned. This means giving high-paying jobs to residents, becoming involved in local charity events, and engaging in joint ventures with nearby businesses. By doing so, the local population has a good reason to intercede on behalf of the company.

The "local" tactic should extend to forcing the facility's managers to live in-country. This allows for better information gathering regarding local political conditions. In addition, the managers can build up their networks of local business and government leaders, which yields even better information about what may transpire that could impact the company.

We now turn to in-depth discussions of two major risk areas over which the CFO has a significant level of control – changes in foreign exchange rates and changes in interest rates.

Foreign Exchange Risk Overview

There are several types of foreign exchange risks that can impact a company, and which are described below.

A company may incur *transaction exposure*, which is derived from changes in foreign exchange rates between the dates when a transaction is booked and when it is settled. For example, a company in the United States may sell goods to a company in the United Kingdom, to be paid in pounds having a value at the booking date of $100,000. Later, when the customer pays the company, the exchange rate has changed, resulting in a payment in pounds that translates to a $95,000 sale. Thus, the foreign exchange rate change related to a transaction has created a $5,000 loss for the seller. The following table shows the impact of transaction exposure on different scenarios.

Risk When Transactions Denominated in Foreign Currency

	Import Goods	Export Goods
Home currency weakens	Loss	Gain
Home currency strengthens	Gain	Loss

When a company has foreign subsidiaries, it denominates the recorded amount of their assets and liabilities in the currency of the country in which the subsidiaries generate and expend cash. This *functional currency* is typically the local currency of the country in which a subsidiary operates. When the company reports its consolidated results, it converts these valuations to the home currency of the parent company, which may suffer a loss if exchange rates have declined from the last time when the financial statements were consolidated. This type of risk is known as *translation exposure*.

EXAMPLE

Hammer Industries has a subsidiary located in England, which has its net assets denominated in pounds. The home currency of Hammer is U.S. dollars. At year-end, when the parent company consolidates the financial statements of its subsidiaries, the U.S. dollar has depreciated in comparison to the pound, resulting in a decline in the value of the subsidiary's net assets.

The following table shows the impact of translation exposure on different scenarios.

Risk When Net Assets Denominated in Foreign Currency

	Assets	Liabilities
Home currency weakens	Gain	Loss
Home currency strengthens	Loss	Gain

There are also several types of economic risk related to the specific country within which a company chooses to do business. These risks include:

- *Political risk* is based on the actions of a foreign government that can impact a company, such as the expropriation of assets. Political risk can also encompass the violence that may accompany a change in government. There can be a significant risk of expropriation when a company has a large asset base within a country.
- *Convertibility risk* is the inability to convert a local currency into a foreign currency, because of a shortage of hard currencies. This tends to be a short-term problem.
- *Transfer risk* is the inability to transfer funds across a national border, due to local-country regulatory restrictions on the movement of hard currencies out of the country. Thus, a company may find that a local subsidiary is extremely profitable, but the parent company cannot extract the profits from the country.

Country-specific risks call for strategic-level decisions in the executive suite, not in the accounting or treasury departments. The senior management team must decide if it is willing to accept the risks of expropriation or of not being able to extract cash from a country. If not, the risk is eliminated by refusing to do business within the country.

Please note that the *type* of risk has a considerable impact on the time period over which a company is at risk. For example, transactional risk spans a relatively short period, from the signing date of the contract that initiates a sale, until the final payment date. The total interval may be only one or two months. However, translation risk and the various types of economic risks can extend over many years. There tends to be an inordinate focus in many companies on the short-term transactional risk, when more emphasis should be placed on hedging against these other risks that can result in substantial losses over the long term.

Foreign Exchange Risk Management

As noted in the last section, a company is at risk of incurring a loss due to fluctuations in any exchange rates that it must buy or sell as part of its business transactions. What can be done? Valid steps can range from no action at all to the active use of several types of hedges. In this section, we address the multitude of options available to the CFO to mitigate foreign exchange-related risks. While perusing these options, keep in mind that the most sophisticated response is not necessarily the best response. In many cases, the circumstances may make it quite acceptable to take on some degree of risk, rather than engaging in a hedging strategy that is not only expensive, but also difficult to understand.

Take No Action

There are many situations where a company rarely engages in transactions that involve foreign exchange, and so does not want to spend time investigating how to reduce risk. There are other situations where the amounts of foreign exchange involved are so small that the risk level is immaterial. In either case, a company will be tempted to take no action, which may be a reasonable course of action. The question to consider is, at what level of foreign exchange activity should a business begin to consider risk management alternatives?

The question cannot be answered without having an understanding of a company's *risk capacity*. Risk capacity is the maximum amount of a loss that a business can sustain before a financial crisis is triggered. The following are examples of maximum losses:

- A loss that would require the tapping of all remaining borrowing capacity
- A loss that would breach one or more debt covenants
- A loss that would reduce capital levels below those mandated by regulatory authorities

The preceding examples provide hard quantitative numbers for a firm's total risk capacity, all of which threaten the company's existence. This does not mean that management should routinely expose a business to threat levels that could destroy it. Instead, it is necessary to arrive at a much less quantitative number, which is the maximum risk tolerance that management is willing to operate under on an ongoing basis before it will take steps to reduce risk. The risk tolerance figure is likely to be far lower than total risk capacity – perhaps just 5% or 10% of a firm's risk capacity. The exact amount of risk tolerance will depend upon the willingness of managers to accept risk. A more entrepreneurially inclined group may be willing to bet the company on risky situations, while professional managers will probably begin managing risk at lower tolerance levels.

Avoid Risk

A company can avoid some types of risk by altering its strategy to completely sidestep the risk. Complete avoidance of a specific product, geographic region, or business line is an entirely reasonable alternative under the following circumstances:

- The potential loss from a risk condition is very high
- The probability of loss from a risk condition is very high
- It is difficult to develop a hedge against a risk
- The offsetting potential for profit does not offset the risk that will be incurred

For example, a company located in the United States buys the bulk of its supplies in China, and is required under its purchasing contracts to pay suppliers in yuan. If the company does not want to undertake the risk of exchange rate fluctuations in the yuan, it can consider altering its supply chain, so that it purchases within its home country, rather than in China. This alignment of sales and purchases within the same country to avoid foreign currency transactions is known as an *operational hedge*.

As another example, a company wants to sell products into a market where the government has just imposed severe restrictions on the cross-border transfer of funds out of the country. The government also has a history of nationalizing industries that had been privately-owned. Under these circumstances, it makes little sense for the company to sell into the new market if it cannot extract its profits, and if its assets in the country are subject to expropriation.

Shift Risk

When a company is either required to pay or receive payment in a foreign currency, it is taking on the risk associated with changes in the foreign currency exchange rate. This risk can be completely eliminated by requiring customers to pay in the company's home currency, or suppliers to accept payment in the company's home currency. This is a valid option when the company is a large one that can force this system of payment onto its suppliers, or when it sells a unique product that forces customers to accept the company's terms.

Tip: Never give customers a choice of currency in which to pay the company, since they will likely pay with their home currency, leaving the company to bear the risk of exchange rate changes.

Another possibility is to charge business partners for any changes in the exchange rate between the date of order placement and the shipment date. This is an extremely difficult business practice to enforce, for the following reasons:

- *Continual rebillings.* There will always be some degree of variation in exchange rates between the order date and shipment date, so it is probable that a company would have to issue an invoice related to exchange rate adjustments for every order, or at least include a line item for the change in every invoice.
- *Two-way rebillings.* If a company is going to insist on billing for its exchange rate losses, it is only fair that it pay back its business partners when exchange rates shift in its favor.
- *Purchase order limitations.* Customers routinely place orders using a purchase order that only authorizes a certain spending level. If the company later issues an incremental billing that exceeds the total amount authorized for a purchase, the customer will probably not pay the company.

To mitigate these issues, billing a business partner for a change in exchange rates should only be enacted if the change is sufficiently large to breach a contractually-agreed minimum level. The minimum level should be set so that this additional billing is a rare event.

Example: An outsourcing company enters into long-term services contracts with its customers, and so is at considerable foreign exchange risk. It offers customers a fixed price contract within a 5% currency trading band, outside of which customers share the risk with the company. If the company gains from a currency shift outside of the trading band, it discounts the contract price.

The conditions under which currency risk can be shifted elsewhere are not common ones. Most companies will find that if they insist on only dealing in their home currencies, such behavior will either annoy suppliers or drive away customers. Thus, we will continue with other risk management actions that will be more palatable to a company's business partners.

Time Compression

Large variations in exchange rates are more likely to occur over longer periods of time than over shorter periods of time. Thus, it may be possible to reduce the risk of exchange rate fluctuations by reducing the contractually-mandated payment period. For example, 30 day payment terms could be compressed to 10 or 15 days. However, delays in shipping, customs inspections, and resistance from business partners can make it difficult to achieve a compressed payment schedule. Also, a customer being asked to accept a shorter payment schedule may attempt to push back with lower prices or other benefits, which increases the cost of this option.

The time compression concept can take the form of a company policy that does not allow standard credit terms to foreign customers that exceed a certain number of days. By doing so, a company can at least minimize the number of days during which exchange rates can fluctuate.

Payment Leading and Lagging

If there is a pronounced trend in exchange rates over the short term, the accounts payable manager can be encouraged to alter the timing normally associated with payables payments to take advantage of expected changes in exchange rates. For example, if a foreign currency is becoming more expensive, it may make sense to pay those payables denominated in it as soon as possible, rather than waiting until the normal payment date to pay in a more expensive currency. Similarly, if a foreign currency is declining in value, there may be an opportunity to delay payments by a few days to take advantage of the ongoing decline in the exchange rate. The latter case may be too much trouble, since suppliers do not appreciate late payments.

Build Reserves

If company management believes that there is just as great a risk of a gain as a loss on a currency fluctuation, it may be willing to accept the downside risk in hopes of attaining an upside profit. If so, it is possible to build cash and debt reserves greater than what would normally be needed, against the possibility of an outsized loss. This may entail investing a large amount of cash in very liquid investments, or retaining extra cash that might otherwise be paid out in dividends or used for capital expenditures. Other options are to obtain an unusually large line of credit that can be called upon in the event of a loss, or selling more stock than would typically be needed for operational purposes.

Building reserves will protect a business from foreign exchange risk, but the cost of acquiring and maintaining those reserves is substantial. Cash that is kept on hand could have earned an investment, while a commitment fee must be paid for a line of credit, even if the line is never used. Similarly, investors who buy a company's stock expect to earn a return. Thus, there is a noticeable cost associated with building reserves. A less-expensive option is hedging, which we will address shortly.

Maintain Local Reserves

If the company is routinely engaging in the purchase and sale of goods and services within another country, the answer may be to maintain a cash reserve within that country, which is denominated in the local currency. Doing so eliminates the cost of repeatedly buying and selling currencies and paying the related conversion commissions. The downside of maintaining local reserves is that a company is still subject to translation risk, where it must periodically translate its local cash reserves into its home currency for financial reporting purposes – which carries with it the risk of recording a translation loss.

Hedging

When all operational and strategic alternatives have been exhausted, it is time to consider buying hedging instruments that offset the risk posed by specific foreign exchange positions. Hedging is accomplished by purchasing an offsetting currency exposure. For example, if a company has a liability to deliver 1 million euros in six months, it can hedge this risk by entering into a contract to purchase 1 million euros on the same date, so that it can buy and sell in the same currency on the same date. The ideal outcome of a hedge is when the distribution of probable outcomes is reduced, so that the size of any potential loss is reduced. The following exhibit shows the effect of hedging on the range of possible outcomes.

Impact of Hedging on Risk Outcome

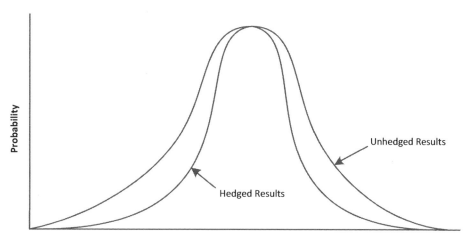

Range of Outcomes

When a company has a multi-year contract with a customer, it may be necessary to create a long-term hedge to offset the related risk of currency fluctuations. If the customer subsequently terminates the contract early, the company may have to incur a significant cost to unwind the related hedge before its planned termination date. If this scenario appears possible, or if a business has experienced such events in the past, it may make sense to include in the contract a clause stating that the customer bears the cost of unwinding the hedge if there is an early contract termination.

> **Tip:** When entering into a long-term contract for which a hedge is anticipated, be sure to estimate the cost of the hedge in advance, and include it in the formulation of the price quoted to the customer.

Summary

Clearly, there are many risk management alternatives available to a company that must deal with foreign exchange situations. We recommend avoiding active hedging strategies as long as possible, in favor of more passive methods that are easier to understand, implement, and monitor. If the risk situation is too extreme to be completely addressed by passive means, then an active hedging strategy is probably the answer. In the next section, we address several types of active hedging activities.

Types of Foreign Exchange Hedges

This section describes a number of methods for hedging foreign currency transactions. The first type of hedge, which is a loan denominated in a foreign currency, is designed to offset translation risk. The remaining hedges target the transaction risk related to the currency fluctuations associated with either specific or aggregated business transactions.

Loan Denominated in a Foreign Currency

When a company is at risk of recording a loss from the translation of assets and liabilities into its home currency, it can hedge the risk by obtaining a loan denominated in the functional currency in which the assets and liabilities are recorded. The effect of this hedge is to neutralize any loss on translation of the subsidiary's net assets with a gain on translation of the loan, or vice versa.

EXAMPLE

Hammer Industries has a subsidiary located in London, and which does business entirely within England. Accordingly, the subsidiary's net assets are denominated in pounds. The net assets of the subsidiary are currently recorded at £10 million. To hedge the translation risk associated with these assets, Hammer acquires a £10 million loan from a bank in London.

One month later, a change in the dollar/pound exchange rate results in a translation loss of $15,000 on the translation of the subsidiary's net assets into U.S. dollars. This amount is exactly offset by the translation gain of $15,000 on the liability associated with the £10 million loan.

Tip: An ideal way to create an offsetting loan is to fund the purchase or expansion of a foreign subsidiary largely through the proceeds of a long-term loan obtained within the same country, so that the subsidiary's assets are approximately cancelled out by the amount of the loan.

There are two problems with this type of hedge. First, it can be difficult to obtain a loan in the country in which the net assets are located. Second, the company will incur an interest expense on a loan that it would otherwise not need, though the borrowed funds could be invested to offset the interest expense.

The Forward Contract

A forward contract is an agreement under which a business agrees to buy a certain amount of foreign currency on a specific future date, and at a predetermined exchange rate. Forward exchange rates can be obtained for twelve months into the future; quotes for major currency pairs can be obtained for as much as five to ten years in the future. The exchange rate is comprised of the following elements:

- The spot price of the currency
- The bank's transaction fee
- An adjustment (up or down) for the interest rate differential between the two currencies. In essence, the currency of the country having a lower interest rate will trade at a premium, while the currency of the country having a higher interest rate will trade at a discount. For example, if the domestic interest rate is lower than the rate in the other country, the bank acting as the

counterparty adds points to the spot rate, which increases the cost of the foreign currency in the forward contract.

The calculation of the number of discount or premium points to subtract from or add to a forward contract is based on the following formula:

nb

$$\text{Exchange rate} \times \text{interest rate differential} \times \frac{\text{days in contract}}{360} = \frac{\text{Premium or}}{\text{discount}}$$

Thus, if the spot price of pounds per dollar were 1.5459 and there were a premium of 15 points for a forward contract with a 360-day maturity, the forward rate (not including a transaction fee) would be 1.5474.

By entering into a forward contract, a company can ensure that a definite future liability can be settled at a specific exchange rate. Forward contracts are typically customized, and arranged between a company and its bank. The bank will require a partial payment to initiate a forward contract, as well as final payment shortly before the settlement date.

EXAMPLE

Hammer Industries has acquired equipment from a company in the United Kingdom, which Hammer must pay for in 60 days in the amount of £150,000. To hedge against the risk of an unfavorable change in exchange rates during the intervening 60 days, Hammer enters into a forward contract with its bank to buy £150,000 in 60 days, at the current exchange rate.

60 days later, the exchange rate has indeed taken a turn for the worse, but Hammer's CFO is indifferent, since he obtains the £150,000 needed for the purchase transaction based on the exchange rate in existence when the contract with the supplier was originally signed.

A forward contract is designed to have a specific settlement date, but the business transaction to which it relates may not be so timely. For example, a business has a contract to sell £10,000 in 60 days, but may not be able to do so if it has not yet received funds from a customer. A *forward window contract* is designed to work around this variability in the timing of receipts from customers by incorporating a range of settlement dates. One can then wait for a cash receipt and trigger settlement of the forward contract immediately thereafter.

The primary difficulties with forward contracts relate to their being customized transactions that are designed specifically for two parties. Because of this level of customization, it is difficult for either party to offload the contract to a third party. Also, the level of customization makes it difficult to compare offerings from different banks, so there is a tendency for banks to build unusually large fees into these contracts. Finally, a company may find that the underlying transaction for which a forward contract was created has been cancelled, leaving the contract still to be settled. If so, one can enter into a second forward contract, whose net effect is to offset the first forward contract. Though the bank will charge fees for both contracts, this arrangement will settle the company's obligations.

The Futures Contract

A futures contract is similar in concept to a forward contract, in that a business can enter into a contract to buy or sell currency at a specific price on a future date. The difference is that futures contracts are traded on an exchange, so these contracts are for standard amounts and durations. An initial deposit into a margin account is required to initiate a futures contract. The contract is then repriced each day, and if cumulative losses drain the margin account, a company is required to add more funds to the margin account. If the company does not respond to a margin call, the exchange closes out the contract.

Given that futures contracts are standardized, they may not exactly match the timing and amounts of an underlying transaction that is being hedged, which can lead to over- or under-hedging. However, since these contracts are traded on an exchange, it is easier to trade them than forward contracts, which allows for the easy unwinding of a hedge position earlier than its normal settlement date.

In a forward contract, the bank includes a transaction fee in the contract. In a futures contract, a broker charges a commission to execute the deal.

The Currency Option

An option gives its owner the right, but not the obligation, to buy or sell an asset at a certain price (known as the *strike price*), either on or before a specific date. In exchange for this right, the buyer pays an up-front premium to the seller. The income earned by the seller is restricted to the premium payment received, while the buyer has a theoretically unlimited profit potential, depending upon the future direction of the relevant exchange rate.

Currency options are available for the purchase or sale of currencies within a certain future date range, with the following variations available for the option contract:

- *American option.* The option can be exercised on any date within the option period, so that delivery is two business days after the exercise date.
- *European option.* The option can only be exercised on the expiry date, which means that delivery will be two business days after the expiry date.
- *Burmudan option.* The option can only be exercised on certain predetermined dates.

The holder of an option will exercise it when the strike price is more favorable than the current market rate, which is called being *in-the-money*. If the strike price is less favorable than the current market rate, this is called being *out-of-the-money*, in which case the option holder will not exercise the option. If the option holder is inattentive, it is possible that an in-the-money option will not be exercised prior to its expiry date. Notice of option exercise must be given to the counterparty by the notification date stated in the option contract.

A currency option provides two key benefits:

- *Loss prevention.* An option can be exercised to hedge the risk of loss, while still leaving open the possibility of benefiting from a favorable change in exchange rates.
- *Date variability.* The holder can exercise an option within a predetermined date range, which is useful when there is uncertainty about the exact timing of the underlying exposure.

There are a number of factors that enter into the price of a currency option, which can make it difficult to ascertain whether a quoted option price is reasonable. These factors are:

- The difference between the designated strike price and the current spot price. The buyer of an option can choose a strike price that suits his specific circumstances. A strike price that is well away from the current spot price will cost less, since the likelihood of exercising the option is low. However, setting such a strike price means that the buyer is willing to absorb the loss associated with a significant change in the exchange rate before seeking cover behind an option.
- The current interest rates for the two currencies during the option period.
- The duration of the option.
- The volatility of the market. This is the expected amount by which the currency is expected to fluctuate during the option period, with higher volatility making it more likely that an option will be exercised. Volatility is a guesstimate, since there is no quantifiable way to predict it.
- The willingness of counterparties to issue options.

Banks generally allow an option exercise period of no more than three months. Multiple partial currency deliveries within a currency option can be arranged.

Exchange traded options for standard quantities are available. This type of option eliminates the risk of counterparty failure, since the clearing house operating the exchange guarantees the performance of all options traded on the exchange.

EXAMPLE

Hammer Industries has an obligation to buy £250,000 in three months. Currently, the forward rate for the British pound is 1.5000 U.S. dollars, so that it should require $375,000 to buy the £250,000 in 90 days. If the pound depreciates, Hammer will be able to buy pounds for less than the $375,000 that it currently anticipates spending, but if the pound appreciates, Hammer will have to spend more to acquire the £250,000.

Hammer's CFO elects to buy an option, so that he can hedge against the appreciation of the pound, while leaving open the prospect of profits to be gained from any depreciation in the pound. The cost of an option with a strike price of 1.6000 U.S. dollars per pound is $3,000.

Three months later, the pound has appreciated against the dollar, with the price having changed to 1.75 U.S. dollars per pound. The CFO exercises the option, and spends $400,000 for the requisite number of pounds (calculated as £250,000 × 1.6000). If he had not purchased the option, the purchase would instead have cost $437,500 (calculated as £250,000 × 1.7500). Thus, Hammer saved $34,500 by using a currency option (calculated as the savings of $37,500, less the $3,000 cost of the option).

Currency options are particularly valuable during periods of high currency price volatility. Unfortunately from the perspective of the buyer, high volatility equates to higher option prices, since there is a higher probability that the counterparty will have to make a payment to the option buyer.

The Cylinder Option

Two options can be combined to create a *cylinder option*. One option is priced above the current spot price of the target currency, while the other option is priced below the spot price. The gain from exercising one option is used to partially offset the cost of the other option, thereby reducing the overall cost of the hedge. In effect, the upside potential offered by one option is being sold for a premium payment in order to finance the protection afforded by the opposing option.

The cylinder option is configured so that a company can acquire the right to buy currency at a specified price (a call option) and sell an option to a counterparty to buy currency from the company at a specified price (a put option), usually as of the expiry date. The premium the company pays for the purchased call is partially offset by the premium payable to the company for the put option that it sold.

If the market exchange rate remains between the boundaries established by the two currency options, the company never uses its options and instead buys or sells currency on the open market to fulfill its currency needs. If the market price breaches the strike price of the call option, the company exercises the call option and buys currency at the designated strike price. Conversely, if the market price breaches the strike price of the put option, the counterparty exercises its option to sell the currency to the company.

A variation on the cylinder option is to construct call and put options that are very close together, so that the premium cost of the call is very close to the premium income generated by the put, resulting in a near-zero net hedging cost to the company. The two options have to be very close together for the zero cost option to work, which means that the effective currency price range being hedged is quite small.

Swaps

If a company has or expects to have an obligation to make a payment in a foreign currency, it can arrange to swap currency holdings with a third party that already has the required currency. The two entities engage in a swap transaction by agreeing upon an initial swap date, the date when the cash positions will be reversed back to their original positions, and an interest rate that reflects the comparative differences in interest rates between the two countries in which the entities are located.

Another use for a currency swap is when a forward exchange contract has been delayed. In this situation, one would normally sell to a counterparty the currency that it has just obtained through the receipt of an account receivable. If, however, the receivable has not yet been paid, the company can enter into a swap agreement to obtain the required currency and meet its immediate obligation under the forward exchange contract. Later, when the receivable is eventually paid, the company can reverse the swap, returning funds to the counterparty.

A swap arrangement may be for just a one-day period, or extend out for several years into the future. Swap transactions generally do not occur in amounts of less than $5 million, so this technique is not available to smaller businesses.

A potentially serious problem with swaps is the prospect of a default by the counterparty. If there is a default, the company once again assumes its foreign currency liability, and must now scramble to find an alternative hedge.

Netting

There are circumstances where a company has subsidiaries in multiple countries that actively trade with each other. If so, they should have accounts receivable and payable with each other, which could give rise to a flurry of foreign exchange transactions in multiple currencies that could trigger any number of hedging activities. It may be possible to reduce the amount of hedging activity through *payment netting*, where the corporate parent offsets all accounts receivable and payable against each other to determine the net amount of foreign exchange transactions that actually require hedges. A centralized netting function may be used, which means that each subsidiary either receives a single payment from the netting center, or makes a single payment to the netting center. Netting results in the following benefits:

- Foreign exchange exposure is no longer tracked at the subsidiary level
- The total amount of foreign exchange purchased and sold declines, which reduces the amount of foreign exchange commissions paid out
- The total amount of cash in transit (and therefore not available for investment) between subsidiaries declines

Tip: It is easier to create an intracompany netting system when there is already a centralized accounts payable function for the entire business, which is called a *payment factory*.

Intracompany netting will still result in some payments between subsidiaries located in different countries. Since each subsidiary may be operating its own cash concentration system, this means that cash must be physically shifted from one cash pool to another, which is inefficient. Where possible, consider creating cash pools that span international boundaries, so that there is no need for cross-border transfers between cash pools. The result is essentially free cash transfers within the company.

The same concept can be applied to payables and receivables with outside entities, though a large amount of information sharing is needed to make the concept work. In some industries where there is a high level of trade between companies, industry-wide netting programs have been established that routinely offset a large proportion of the payables and receivables within the industry. The net result is that all offsetting obligations are reduced to a single payment per currency per value date between counterparties.

A related concept is *close-out netting*, where counterparties having forward contracts with each other can agree to net the obligations, rather than engaging in a large number of individual contract settlements. Before engaging in close-out netting, discuss the concept with corporate counsel. A case has been made in some jurisdictions that close-out netting runs counter to the interests of other creditors in the event of a bankruptcy by one of the counterparties.

The only downside of netting is that the accounting departments of the participating companies must sort out how their various transactions are settled. This requires a procedure for splitting a group of netted transactions into individual payments and receipts in the cash receipts and accounts payable modules of their accounting systems.

Interest Risk Overview

Interest rate risk involves the risk of increases in interest rates on debt, as well as reductions in interest rates for investment instruments, with the attendant negative impact on profitability. This risk can take the following forms:

- *Absolute rate changes.* The market rate of interest will move up or down over time, resulting in immediate variances from the interest rates paid or earned by a company. This rate change is easily monitored.
- *Reinvestment risk.* Investments must be periodically re-invested and debt re-issued. If interest rates happen to be unfavorable during one of these rollover periods, a company will be forced to accept whatever interest rate is available.
- *Yield curve risk.* The yield curve shows the relationship between short-term and long-term interest rates, and typically slopes upward to indicate that long-term debt carries a higher interest rate to reflect the risk to the lender associated with such debt. If the yield curve steepens, flattens, or declines, these relationships change the debt duration that a company should use in its borrowing and investing strategies.

Interest risk is a particular concern for those businesses using large amounts of debt to fund their operations, since even a small increase in the interest rate could have a profound impact on profits, when multiplied by the volume of debt employed. Further, a sudden boost in interest expense could worsen a company's interest coverage ratio, which is a common covenant in loan agreements, and which could trigger a loan termination if the minimum ratio covenant is not met.

Interest Rate Risk Management

The primary objective of interest risk management is to keep fluctuations in interest rates from impacting company earnings. Management can respond to this objective in many ways, ranging from a conscious decision to take no action, passing through a number of relatively passive alternatives, and culminating in several active techniques for risk mitigation. We provide an overview of each option in this section.

Take No Action

There may be situations where a company has minimal investments that earn interest, or issues only minor amounts of debt. If so, it is certainly acceptable to not implement an aggressive risk management campaign related to interest rates. However, this state of affairs does not typically last for long, after which there will be some degree of risk related to interest rates. In anticipation of such an event, it is useful to model the amount of interest rate change that must occur before there will be a serious impact on company finances. Once that trigger point is known, the CFO can begin to prepare any of the risk mitigation alternatives noted later in this section.

Avoid Risk

The risk associated with interest rates arises between external entities and a business; it does not arise between the subsidiaries of the same business. Thus, a company can act as its own bank to some extent, by providing intercompany lending arrangements at interest rates that are not subject to fluctuations. This is particularly useful in a multi-national corporation, where cash reserves in different currencies may be scattered throughout the business, and can be lent back and forth to cover immediate cash needs.

Another way to avoid risk is to operate the business in such a conservative manner that the company has no debt, thereby eliminating the risk associated with interest rates on debt. The same result can be achieved by using invested funds to pay off any outstanding debt. The main downside of the low-debt method is that a company may be constraining its growth by not taking advantage of a low-cost source of funds (i.e., debt).

Asset and Liability Matching

A key trigger for interest rate risk is when short-term debt is used to fund an asset that is expected to be held for a long period of time. In this situation, the short-term debt must be rolled over multiple times during the life span of the asset or until the debt is paid off, introducing the risk that each successive debt rollover will result in an increased interest rate. To avoid this risk, arrange for financing that approximately matches the useful life of the underlying asset. Thus, spending $1 million for a machine that is expected to have a useful life of 10 years should be funded with a loan that also has a 10-year life.

Hedging

Interest rate hedging is the practice of acquiring financial instruments whose effects offset those of the underlying scenario causing interest rate fluctuations, so that the net effect is minimized rate fluctuations. Hedges fall into two categories:

- *Forward rate agreements and futures.* These financial instruments are designed to lock in an interest rate, so that changes in the actual interest rate above or below the baseline interest rate do not impact a business. These instruments do not provide any flexibility for taking advantage of favorable changes in interest rates.
- *Options.* These financial instruments only lock in an interest rate if the holder wants to do so, thereby presenting the possibility of benefiting from a favorable change in an interest rate.

The various types of interest rate hedges are discussed next.

Types of Interest Rate Hedges

This section describes a number of methods for hedging the variability in interest rates. These options are mostly designed for high-value transactions, and so are not available to smaller companies.

The Forward Rate Agreement

A forward rate agreement (FRA) is an agreement between two parties to lock in a specific interest rate for a designated period of time, which usually spans just a few months. Under an FRA, the parties are protecting against opposing exposures: the FRA buyer wants to protect against an increase in the interest rate, while the FRA seller wants to protect against a decrease in the interest rate. Any payout under an FRA is based on a change in the reference interest rate from the interest rate stated in the contract (the FRA rate). An FRA is not related to a specific loan or investment – it simply provides interest rate protection.

The FRA rate is based on the yield curve, where interest rates usually increase for instruments having longer maturities. This means that the FRA rate typically increases for periods further in the future.

Several date-specific terms are referred to in a forward rate agreement, and are crucial to understanding how the FRA concept works. These terms are:

1. *Contract date.* The date on which the FRA begins.
2. *Expiry date.* The date on which any variance between the market rate and the reference rate is calculated.
3. *Settlement date.* The date on which the interest variance is paid by one counterparty to the other.

Risk Management

4. *Maturity date.* The final date of the date range that underlies the FRA contract.

In essence, these four dates anchor the two time periods covered by an FRA. The first period, which begins with the contract date and ends with the expiry date, spans the term of the contract. The second period begins with the settlement date and ends with the maturity date, and spans the period that underlies the contract. This date range is shown graphically in the following example.

Relevant FRA Dates

The FRA rate is based on a future period, such as the period starting in one month and ending in four months, which is said to have a "1 × 4" FRA term, and has an effective term of three months. Similarly, a contract starting in three months and ending in six months is said to have a "3 × 6" FRA term, and also has an effective term of three months.

At the *beginning* of the designated FRA period, the interest rate stated in the contract is compared to the reference rate. The reference rate is usually a well-known interest rate index, such as the London Interbank Offered Rate (LIBOR). If the reference rate is higher, the seller makes a payment to the FRA buyer, based on the incremental difference in interest rates and the notional amount of the contract. The payment calculation is shown in the following example. If the reference rate is lower than the interest rate stated in the contract, the buyer makes a payment to the FRA seller. The payment made between the counterparties must be discounted to its present value, since the payment is associated with the FRA underlying period that has not yet happened. Thus, the discount assumes that the money would actually be due on the maturity date, but is payable on the settlement date (which may be months before the maturity date). The calculation for discounting the payment between counterparties is:

$$\frac{\text{Settlement amount}}{1 + (\text{Days in FRA underlying period}/360 \text{ Days} \times \text{Reference rate})} = \begin{array}{c} \text{Discounted} \\ \text{Payment} \end{array}$$

The reason why the contract payment is calculated at the *beginning* of the designated FRA period is that the risk being hedged by the contract was from the initial contract date until the date on which the FRA buyer expects to borrow money and lock in an interest rate. For example, a company may enter into an FRA in January, because it is uncertain of what the market interest rate will be in April, when it intends to borrow funds; the period at risk is therefore from January through April. The following example illustrates the concept.

53

EXAMPLE

Hammer Industries has a legal commitment to borrow $50 million in two months, and for a period of three months. Hammer's CFO is concerned that there may be an increase in the interest rate during the two-month period prior to borrowing the $50 million. The CFO elects to hedge the risk of an increase in the interest rate by purchasing a three-month FRA, starting in two months. A broker quotes a rate of 5.50%. Hammer enters into an FRA at the 5.50% interest rate, with 3rd National Bank as the counterparty. The notional amount of the contract is for $50 million.

Two months later, the reference rate is 6.00%, so 3rd National pays Hammer the difference between the contract rate and reference rate, which is 0.50%. At the same time, Hammer borrows $50 million at the market rate (which happens to match the reference rate) of 6.00%. Because of the FRA, Hammer's effective borrowing rate is 5.50%.

The amount paid by 3rd National to Hammer is calculated as:

(Reference rate – FRA rate) × (FRA days/360 days) × Notional amount = Profit or loss

or

(6.00% - 5.50%) × (90 days/360 days) × $50 million = $62,500

Since the payment is made at the beginning of the borrowing period, rather than at its end, the $62,500 payment is discounted and its present value paid. The discounting calculation for the settlement amount is:

$$\frac{\$62,500}{1 + (90/360 \text{ Days} \times 6.00\%)} = \$61,576.35$$

What if the reference rate had fallen by 0.50%, instead of increasing? Then Hammer would have paid 3rd National the discounted amount of $62,500, rather than the reverse. Hammer would also end up borrowing the $50 million at the new market rate of 5.00%. When the payment to 3rd National is combined with the reduced 5.00% interest rate, Hammer will still be paying a 5.50% interest rate, which is what it wanted all along.

From the buyer's perspective, the result of an FRA is that it pays the expected interest rate – no higher, and no lower.

The Futures Contract

An interest rate futures contract is conceptually similar to a forward contract, except that it is traded on an exchange, which means that it is for a standard amount and duration. The standard size of a futures contract is $1 million, so multiple contracts may need to be purchased to create a hedge for a specific loan or investment amount. The pricing for futures contracts starts at a baseline figure of 100, and declines based on the implied interest rate in a contract. For example, if a futures contract has an implied interest rate of 5.00%, the price of that contract will be 95.00. The calculation of the profit or loss on a futures contract is derived as follows:

Notional contract amount × Contract duration/360 Days × (Ending price – Beginning price)

Most trading in interest rate futures is in Eurodollars (U.S. dollars held outside of the United States), and are traded on the Chicago Mercantile Exchange.

Hedging is not perfect, since the notional amount of a contract may vary from the actual amount of funding that a company wants to hedge, resulting in a modest amount of either over- or under-hedging. For example, hedging a $15.4 million position will require the purchase of either 15 or 16 $1 million contracts. There may also be differences between the time period required for a hedge and the actual hedge period as stated in a futures contract. For example, if there is a seven month exposure to be hedged, a CFO could acquire two consecutive three-month contracts, and elect to have the seventh month be unhedged.

Tip: If the buyer wants to protect against interest rate variability for a longer period, such as for the next year, it is possible to buy a series of futures contracts covering consecutive periods, so that coverage is achieved for the entire time period.

EXAMPLE

The CFO of Hammer Industries wants to hedge an investment of $10 million. To do so, he sells 10 three-month futures contracts with contract terms of three months. The current three-month LIBOR is 3.50% and the 3 × 6 forward rate is 3.75%. These contracts are currently listed on the Chicago Mercantile Exchange at 96.25, which is calculated as 100 minus the 3.75% forward rate.

When the futures contracts expire, the forward rate has declined to 3.65%, so that the contracts are now listed at 96.35 (calculated as 100 – the 3.65 percent forward rate). By engaging in this hedge, Hammer has earned a profit of $2,500, which is calculated as follows:

$$\$10,000,000 \times (90/360) \times (0.9635 \text{ Ending price} - 0.9625 \text{ Beginning price})$$

$$= \$2,500$$

When the buyer purchases a futures contract, a minimum amount must initially be posted in a margin account to ensure performance under the contract terms. It may be necessary to fund the margin account with additional cash (a *margin call*) if the market value of the contract declines over time (margin accounts are revised daily, based on the market closing price). If the buyer cannot provide additional funding in the event of a contract decline, the futures exchange closes out the contract prior to its normal termination date. Conversely, if the market value of the contract increases, the net gain is credited to the buyer's margin account. On the last day of the contract, the exchange marks the contract to market and settles the accounts of the buyer and seller. Thus, transfers between buyers and sellers over the life of a contract are essentially a zero-sum game, where one party directly benefits at the expense of the other.

It is also possible to enter into a bond futures contract, which can be used to hedge interest rate risk. For example, a business that has borrowed funds can hedge against rising interest rates by selling a bond futures contract. Then, if interest rates do in fact rise, the resulting gain on the contract will offset the higher interest rate that the borrower is paying. Conversely, if interest rates subsequently fall, the borrower will experience a loss on the contract, which will offset the lower interest rate now being paid. Thus, the net effect of the contract is that the borrower locks in the beginning interest rate through the period of the contract.

Tip: A bond futures contract is not a perfect hedge, for it is also impacted by changes in the credit rating of the bond issuer.

When a purchased futures contract expires, it is customary to settle it by selling a futures contract that has the same delivery date. Conversely, if the original contract was sold to a counterparty, then the seller can settle the contract by buying a futures contract that has the same delivery date.

The following table notes the key differences between forward rate agreements and futures contracts. Similarities between the two instruments are excluded from the table.

Differences between a Futures Contract and FRA

Feature	Futures Contract	Forward Rate Agreement
Trading platform	Exchange-based	Between two parties
Counterparty	The exchange	Single counterparty
Collateral	Margin account	None
Agreement	Standardized	Modified
Settlement	Daily mark to market	On expiry date

The preceding table reveals two key differences between a futures contract and an FRA. First, there can be significant counterparty risk in an FRA, since the contract period can be lengthy, and financial conditions can change markedly over that time. Second, a futures contract is settled every day, which can create pressure to fund a margin call if there are significant losses on the contract.

The Interest Rate Swap

An interest rate swap is a customized contract between two parties to swap two schedules of cash flows that could extend for anywhere from one to 25 years, and which represent interest payments. Only the interest rate obligations are swapped, not the underlying loans or investments from which the obligations are derived. The counterparties are usually a company and a bank. There are many types of rate swaps; we will confine this discussion to a swap arrangement where one schedule of cash flows is based on a floating interest rate, and the other is based on a fixed interest rate. For example, a five-year schedule of cash flows based on a fixed interest rate may be swapped for a five-year schedule of cash flows based on a floating interest rate that is tied to the London Interbank Offered Rate (LIBOR).

Tip: To prevent confusion, replicate the same swap terms across all swap agreements. Replicated terms should include the reference rate, the interest calculation method, and the coupon frequency. Other terms, such as the notional amount and swap term, will probably vary by agreement.

The most common reason to engage in an interest rate swap is to exchange a variable-rate payment for a fixed-rate payment, or vice versa. Thus, a company that has only been able to obtain a floating-rate loan can effectively convert the loan to a fixed-rate loan through an interest rate swap. This approach is especially attractive when a borrower is only able to obtain a fixed-rate loan by paying a premium, but can combine a variable-rate loan and an interest rate swap to achieve a fixed-rate loan at a lower price.

A company may want to take the reverse approach and swap its fixed interest payments for floating payments. This situation arises when the CFO believes that interest rates will decline during the swap period, and wants to take advantage of the lower rates.

A swap contract is settled through a multi-step process, which is:

1. Calculate the payment obligation of each party, typically once every six months through the life of the swap arrangement.
2. Determine the variance between the two amounts.
3. The party whose position is improved by the swap arrangement pays the variance to the party whose position is degraded by the swap arrangement.

Thus, a company continues to pay interest to its banker under the original lending agreement, while the company either accepts a payment from the rate swap counterparty, or issues a payment to the counterparty, with the result being that the net amount of interest paid by the company is the amount planned by the business when it entered into the swap agreement.

EXAMPLE

Hammer Industries has a $15 million variable-rate loan outstanding that matures in two years. The current interest rate on the loan is 6.5%. Hammer enters into an interest rate swap agreement with Big Regional Bank for a fixed-rate 7.0% loan with a $15 million notional amount. The first scheduled payment swap date is in six months. On that date, the variable rate on Hammer's loan has increased to 7.25%. Thus, the total interest payments on the swap date are $543,750 for Hammer and $525,000 for Big Regional. Since the two parties have agreed to swap payments, Big Regional pays Hammer the difference between the two payments, which is $18,750.

Hammer issues an interest payment of $543,750 to its bank. When netted with the cash inflow of $18,750 from Big Regional, this means that the net interest rate being paid by Hammer is 7.0%.

Several larger banks have active trading groups that routinely deal with interest rate swaps. Most swaps involve sums in the millions of dollars, but some banks are willing to engage in swap arrangements involving amounts of less than $1 million. There is a counterparty risk with interest rate swaps, since one party could fail to make a contractually-mandated payment to the other party. This risk is of particular concern when a swap arrangement covers multiple years, since the financial condition of a counterparty could change dramatically during that time.

If there is general agreement in the marketplace that interest rates are headed in a certain direction, it will be more expensive to obtain a swap that protects against interest rate changes in the anticipated direction.

Interest Rate Options

An option gives its owner the right, but not the obligation, to trigger a contract. The contract can be either a call option or a put option. A *call option* related to interest rates protects the option owner from rising interest rates, while a *put option* protects the option owner from declining interest rates. The party selling an option does so in exchange for a one-time premium payment. The party buying an option is doing so to mitigate its risk related to a change in interest rates.

An interest rate option can be relatively inexpensive if there has been or is expected to be little volatility in interest rates, since the option seller does not expect interest rates to move enough for the option to be exercised. Conversely, if there has been or is expected to be significant interest rate volatility, the option seller must assume that the option will be exercised, and so sets a higher price. Thus, periods of high interest rate volatility may make it cost-prohibitive to buy options.

Tip: An interest rate hedge using an option may not be entirely successful if the reference rate used for the option is not the same one used for the underlying loan. For example, the reference rate for an option may be LIBOR, while the rate used for the underlying loan may be a bank's prime rate. The result is a hedging mismatch that can create an unplanned gain or loss.

An interest rate option sets a *strike price*, which is a specific interest rate at which the option buyer can borrow or lend money. The contract also states the amount of funds that the option buyer can borrow or lend (the *notional amount*). Rate increases and declines are measured using a *reference rate*, which is typically a well-known interest rate index, such as LIBOR. There is also an option expiration date, or *expiry date*, after which the option is cancelled. The buyer can specify the exact terms needed to hedge an interest rate position with a customized option.

If an option buyer wants to be protected from increases in interest rates, a *cap* (or ceiling) is created. A cap is a consecutive series of options, all having the same strike price. The buyer of a cap is paid whenever the reference rate exceeds the cap strike price on an option expiry date. For example, if a company wants to hedge its interest risk for one year with a strike price of 6.50%, beginning on January 1, it can buy the following options:

Desired Coverage Period	Option Number	Expiry Date	Option Term	Strike Price
January - March	--	Not applicable*	Not available*	N/A*
April - June	1	April 1	4 to 6 months	6.50%
July – September	2	July 1	7 to 9 months	6.50%
October - December	3	October 1	10 to 12 months	6.50%

* There is no option available for the first three-month period, since the expiry date is at the beginning of the contract period, so the expiry date will be reached immediately.

With a cap arrangement, the buyer is only subject to interest rate changes up to the cap, and is protected from rate changes above the cap if the reference rate exceeds the cap strike price on predetermined dates. If the reference interest rate is below the cap at the option expiration, the option buyer lets the option expire. However, if the reference rate is above the cap, the buyer exercises the option, which means that the option seller must reimburse the buyer for the difference between the reference rate and the cap rate, multiplied by the notional amount of the contract.

A cap may be included in a loan agreement, such that the borrower is guaranteed not to pay more than a designated maximum interest rate over the term of the loan, or for a predetermined portion of the loan. In this case, the lender has paid for the cap, and will probably include its cost in the interest rate or fees associated with the loan.

If a CFO wants to be protected from decreases in interest rates (for invested funds), a *floor* is structured into an option, so that the option buyer is paid if the reference rate declines below the floor strike rate.

EXAMPLE

Hammer Industries has a $25 million 3-month loan that currently carries a fixed interest rate of 7.00%. Hammer's bank refuses to grant a fixed-rate loan for a longer time period, so Hammer plans to continually roll over the loan every three months. Recently, short-term interest rates have been spiking, so the CFO decided to purchase an interest rate cap that is set at 7.50%, and which is comprised of two consecutive options, each with a three-month term.

At the expiry date of the first option, the reference rate is 7.25%, which is below the cap strike rate. The CFO lets the option expire unused and rolls over the short-term loan at the new 7.25% rate.

At the next option expiry date, the reference rate has risen to 7.75%, which is 0.25% above the cap strike rate. The CFO exercises the option, which forces the counterparty to pay Hammer for the difference between the cap strike rate and the reference rate. The calculation of the amount to be reimbursed is:

(Reference rate – Strike rate) × (Lending period/360 days) × Notional amount = Profit or loss

or

(7.75% - 7.50%) × (90/360) × $25 million = $15,625

Of course, the cost of the option reduces the benefits gained from an interest rate option, but still is useful for providing protection from outsized changes in interest rates.

Tip: From an analysis perspective, it is useful to include the premium on an option with the amount of interest paid on a loan and any proceeds or payments associated with an exercised option, in order to derive the aggregate interest rate on any associated debt being hedged.

The cylinder option described earlier for foreign exchange risk can also be applied to interest rates. Under this concept, a company purchases a cap and sells a floor, with the current reference rate located between the two strike rates. The gain from exercising one option is used to partially offset the cost of the other option, which reduces the overall cost of the hedge. The three possible outcomes to this *collar* arrangement are:

1. The reference rate remains between the cap and floor, so neither option is exercised.
2. The reference rate rises above the cap, so the company is paid for the difference between the reference rate and the cap strike rate, multiplied by the notional amount of the contract.
3. The reference rate falls below the floor, so the company pays the option counterparty for the difference between the reference rate and the floor strike rate, multiplied by the notional amount of the contract.

The functioning of a collar arrangement is shown in the following exhibit, where the cap is set at 5% and the floor is set at 3%. No option is triggered until the reference rate drops to 2% in one of the later quarters, and again when it rises to 6%. In the first case, the company pays the 1% difference between the 3% floor and the 2% reference rate. In the latter case, the company is paid the 1% difference between the 5% cap and the 6% reference rate.

Risk Management

The Operation of an Interest Rate Collar

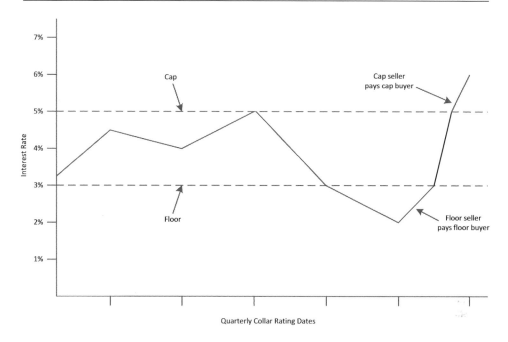

Quarterly Collar Rating Dates

From the perspective of a company using a collar arrangement, the net effect is that interest rates will fluctuate only within the bounds set by the cap and floor strike rates.

A variation on the interest rate option concept is to include a call feature in a debt issuance. A call feature allows a company to buy back its debt from debt holders. The feature is quite useful in cases where the market interest rate has fallen since debt was issued, so a company can refinance its debt at a lower interest rate. However, the presence of the call option makes investors wary about buying it, which tends to increase the effective interest rate at which they will buy the debt. Investor concerns can be mitigated to some extent by providing for a fairly long time period before the issuing company can trigger the call option, and especially if the call price is set somewhat higher than the current market price.

Interest Rate Swaptions

A swaption is an option on an interest rate swap arrangement. The buyer of a swaption has the right, but not the obligation, to enter into an interest rate swap. In essence, a swaption presents the option of being able to lock in a fixed interest rate or a variable interest rate (depending on the terms of the underlying swap arrangement). Thus, a CFO may suspect that interest rates will begin to rise in the near future, and so enters into a swaption to take over a fixed interest rate. If interest rates do indeed rise, the swaption holder can exercise the swaption. If interest rates hold steady or decline, the swaption is allowed to expire without being exercised.

61

The two types of swaption are the *payer swaption* and the *receiver swaption*, which are defined as follows:

- *Payer swaption.* The buyer can enter into a swap where it pays the fixed interest rate side of the transaction.
- *Receiver swaption.* The buyer can enter into a swap where it pays the floating interest rate side of the transaction.

There is no formal exchange for swaptions, so each agreement is between two counterparties. This means that each party is exposed to the potential failure of the counterparty to make scheduled payments on the underlying swap. Consequently, it is prudent to only enter into these arrangements with counterparties with high credit ratings or other evidence of financial stability.

Swaption market participants are primarily large corporations, banks, and hedge funds. The most likely counterparty for a corporation is a large bank that has a group specializing in swaption arrangements.

Risk Management Themes

There are several general themes that well-managed businesses usually follow, and which keep them from adopting risky behavior patterns. If the management team adheres to the following concepts, it is much less likely to experience major losses or participate in highly risky, high-return enterprises. These themes are:

- *Deep knowledge of the business.* Risky behavior is much less likely to arise when every employee of a business has a deep knowledge of his or her own responsibilities, and also how the organization as a whole operates. When there is a well-trained work force, many more people can spot anomalies that may lead to losses, and will also recognize the associated risks that accompany new business proposals. This level of detailed knowledge should cover absolutely everyone – from the board of directors down to production-line employees. This level of knowledge can only be obtained through the long-term training of all employees on all aspects of the business. It also requires basic business policies to promote employee retention, such as excellent benefits, a commitment to retain staff during business downturns, and promoting from within.
- *Infrastructure commitment.* A proper level of risk management requires deep controls in selected parts of an organization – even if those controls are expensive and/or interfere with the efficient processing of transactions. In a business that focuses excessively on streamlining operations and cutting out costs, it is likely that key controls will be removed, thereby making it more likely that high-loss incidents will occur. This issue is less likely when responsibility over processes and controls is kept away from profit center managers, so there is no temptation to reduce controls in order to increase profits. A strong commitment to infrastructure is especially important when

there is a drive to re-engineer processes, since the newly reformulated systems are likely to contain fewer controls than the predecessor systems.

- *Activity boundaries*. Many business transactions can be taken to excess, so it is necessary to set boundaries to limit them. For example, it may be acceptable to write 1,000 insurance policies for flood damage in Louisiana, but writing 100,000 of them will expose an insurer to a potentially massive loss if the Mississippi River overflows its banks. Similarly, it may be unwise to double the amount of credit available to a customer, if the amount of this increase would expose the seller to a large enough bad debt to destroy the business.
- *Performance targets*. The management team should set reasonable performance targets for a business. By doing so, employees can set a reasonable and sustainable annual pace at which to grow sales. If targets are set too high, and especially if compensation systems match the high targets, then expect employees to engage in increasingly risky behavior, if not outright fraud, in order to meet the imposed targets. The performance targets to be set depend on the stage in the life of a product or business. Early sales may increase at a prodigious growth rate until the market reaches maturity, at which point vastly lower performance targets should be set. This is also a function of the gross sales level of a business – that is, an organization with $1 million in sales may reasonably expect to double its sales in one year, but a $10 billion business is extremely unlikely to duplicate this feat.

Summary

The sheer size of this chapter should make it clear that the study of risk should be a key part of the job description of a prudent CFO. While we have spent considerable time describing the hedging of foreign exchange risk and interest rate risk, that is simply because they fall completely under the control of the CFO. Realistically, many of the other risks identified earlier in the chapter, such as supply chain disruptions and product failures, are more likely to result in major operational and financial problems that could seriously harm or even destroy a business. Since the CFO does *not* have complete control over these other areas, it will be necessary to work with the entire management team to identify and mitigate many of the identified risks. Thus, the CFO will need significant powers of persuasion to enact the changes needed to alter the risk profile of a business.

Chapter 4
The Control Environment

Introduction

Accounting controls are the means by which we gain a reasonable assurance that a business will operate as planned, that its financial results are fairly reported, and that it complies with laws and regulations. They are usually constructed to be an additional set of activities that overlay or are directly integrated into the basic operations of a business.

In this chapter, we discuss how control systems are usually introduced into a business, how to find the right balance of controls that does not overly burden operations, the main principles to consider when creating a control system, the failings of internal controls, different types of controls, how to implement a controls installation, and the impact on controls of several common business scenarios.

> **Related Podcast Episodes:** Episodes 1-15, 47, 76, 78, 135, and 169-172 of the Accounting Best Practices Podcast discuss various aspects of control systems. They are available at: **accountingtools.com/podcasts** or **iTunes**

The Genesis of Accounting Controls

From the perspective of an overburdened management team, accounting controls are simply a form of bureaucracy that interferes with their running of the business; and in a small start-up firm, they may have a point. During the start-up phase, a company is so small that nearly all business transactions are visible to the owners, who may be able to maintain a reasonable degree of control simply because they are deeply involved in every aspect of the business. Adding any type of formal control system at this point is expensive in comparison to the relatively small number of business transactions being processed, so the owners are not thrilled about what they perceive to be a waste of time and money.

However, this situation changes when a company brings in a few employees, since the owners are no longer able to keep direct tabs on operations. At this point, controls are typically added wherever errors arise in the accounting systems. Thus, an inadvertent double payment of an invoice to a supplier will then trigger a set of controls to mitigate the risk of double payments. This is a reactive approach to accounting controls, since the owners are still primarily interested in expanding the business, not in adding "bureaucracy." In short, accounting controls in this stage of a company's life cycle are typically a hodgepodge of controls that were installed in reaction to prior problems.

If a business matures sufficiently, it will encounter an event that will trigger a review of its entire system of controls, probably resulting in an overhaul of the entire system. Examples of those events are:

- *Hire senior accounting management.* The company hires a controller or CFO who has an auditing background, and who therefore has a background in control systems.
- *Engage auditors.* The company is required by an investor or lender to have its financial statements audited, and the auditors generate a considerable amount of advice regarding the inadequacy of the company's control systems.
- *Go public.* If the owners want to take the company public, then it must have a strong system of controls, and an annual audit, *and* an audit committee – all of which result in a deep, multi-layered system of controls.

Thus, the system of controls tends to begin with a scattering of controls that were created in response to specific problems, and then becomes more structured over time as a business grows.

The Proper Balance of Control Systems

A person who has been trained in control systems will likely want to install every possible control, and will then feel satisfied that he or she has saved the company from an impending failure. Those on the receiving end of these controls have a differing opinion of the situation, which is that controls slow down transactions, require more staff, and have the same general effect on a business as pouring sand into the gas tank of a car.

Because of these radically differing views of the utility of control systems, it is useful to adopt a set of controls that are based on the following points:

- *Risk – monetary.* If a control can prevent a large loss, such as one that could bankrupt a business, then it makes sense to install it, as long as the probability of the event is reasonably high. For example, having two people involved in every wire transfer transaction is a reasonable precaution, given the amount of funds that could be transferred out in a single wire transfer. Conversely, if a control can never save more than a few dollars (such as locking the office supply cabinet), it is entirely likely that the sheer annoyance caused by the control greatly outweighs any possible savings to be achieved from it.
- *Risk – financial statements.* A business must understand its performance, and it can only do so with reliable financial statements. Consequently, controls over recordkeeping should be among the most comprehensive in the company. However, this does not necessarily call for an oppressive amount of controls in those areas where the amounts involved are essentially immaterial to the financial statements.

- *Repetitiveness*. Only install comprehensive controls for those transactions that a business will engage in on a recurring basis. For example, if a company sells equipment to a foreign customer once a year, and wants to hedge the outstanding receivable, a once-a-year transaction does not require an elaborate control system (unless the receivable is for a large amount – see the preceding point about risk). Thus, it behooves a business to concentrate on a finely-tuned set of controls for the 20% of its processes that make up 80% of its business (the Pareto Principle). Of the remaining 80% of the company's processes, those items involving the most inherent risk should be the prime candidates for strong controls.
- *Offsetting controls*. It may be acceptable to have weak controls in one part of a business, as long as there are offsetting controls elsewhere. For example, it may not be necessary to have someone sign checks, as long as all purchases are initiated with an authorizing purchase order. This concept can be used to great effect if there is a good business reason to keep one business process running as smoothly as possible (i.e., without controls), with offsetting controls in a less noticeable part of the business.
- *Cost*. The cost of controls must be balanced against the expected reduction in risk. This is not a simple calculation to make, for it can be quite difficult to estimate the reduction of risk that will be achieved by implementing a control. One approach to quantifying risk is to multiply the risk percentage by the exposure to the business, which is known as the *expected loss*. See the following example.

    Conversely, it is easy enough to measure the labor cost and other factors required to implement and maintain a control, so there is a tendency for businesses to focus on the up-front cost of a control, and downplay the savings that may or may not arise from having the control. The result tends to be a control level that is lower than it should be.

EXAMPLE

Hammer Industries operates a payroll system that pays employees on a semi-monthly basis. When there are a significant number of data errors in the payroll, Hammer's payroll manager requires that the payroll be run again, at a cost of $5,000.

The payroll manager is considering the installation of an automated data validation software package that is expected to reduce the payroll data error rate from 8% to 1%, at a software rental cost of $250 per payroll. The cost–benefit analysis is:

- *No data validation*. There is an 8% chance of incurring a $5,000 payroll reprocessing cost, which is an expected loss of $400 ($5,000 exposure × 8% risk) per payroll.
- *Data validation*. There is a 1% chance of incurring a $5,000 payroll reprocessing cost, which is an expected loss of $50 ($5,000 exposure × 1% risk) per payroll. There is also a charge of $250 per payroll for the software rental cost.

Thus, there is a reduction of $350 in the expected loss if the control is implemented, against which there is a control cost of $250. This results in a net gain of $100 per payroll by using the control.

The resulting system should be one where some failures will still occur, but either in such small amounts that they do not place the business at risk, or where the probability of occurrence is very low. It is difficult to maintain this balance between controls and operational effectiveness over time, seeing that a growing business is constantly in a state of flux, expanding some lines of business, curtailing others, and installing any number of new systems. It is the job of the controller to watch the interaction of these processes with existing control systems, and know when it is an acceptable risk to pare back some controls, while introducing new ones elsewhere. The CFO should discuss this situation with the controller on a regular basis, to ensure that the control system is being monitored.

It is quite common to see a control system that lags behind the current state of its processes, usually due to inattention by the controller. This means that some controls are so antiquated as to be essentially meaningless (while still annoying the staff), while new systems are devoid of controls, and will only see new ones when a system failure occurs.

In summary, there is a balance between the system of controls and the efficient operation of a business that is difficult to manage. A good CFO will understand the needs of employees to keep operations efficient, and so should be willing to subsist in some areas on control systems that may appear rather skimpy, as long as the tradeoff is between a large improvement in efficiency and the risk of only modest losses that would have been prevented by controls.

The Nature of Risk

In the last section, we made reference to risk. What is risk, and how does it relate to controls? Risk is the probability that events will vary from expectations. Examples of risk are:

- That competitors will alter the business environment
- That new technology will alter the business environment
- That new legislation will alter the business environment
- That a product failure will lead to a product recall
- That a customer will enter bankruptcy
- That a key raw material will increase in price

Of these sample risks, the first three are caused by external factors and the last three by internal factors. Controls can be used to mitigate internal risks. For example, if there is a risk of product failure, controls can be designed to test the quality of components as they enter the production process, and of finished goods before they are shipped to customers. Similarly, the risk that a customer will enter bankruptcy can be mitigated to some extent by the imposition of strong credit controls.

No matter how thoroughly controls are laced throughout an organization, it is impossible to use them to completely eliminate risk. Instead, there will always be some residual amount of risk that a business must accept. There is usually a tradeoff between imposing a really oppressive system of controls on a business in exchange for a lowered risk level, or a lighter system of controls that makes the business easier to manage, but at the cost of accepting a higher level of risk.

Control Principles

There are a number of principles to keep in mind when constructing a system of controls for a business. These principles are frequently the difference between a robust control system and one that appears adequate on paper, but which never seems to work in practice. The principles are:

- *Separation of duties.* The separation of duties involves assigning different parts of a process to different people, so that collusion would be required for someone to commit fraud. For example, one person opens the mail and records a list of the checks received, while a different person records them in the accounting system and a third person deposits the checks. By separating these tasks, it is much more difficult for someone to (for example) remove a check from the incoming mail, record a receivables credit in the accounting system to cover his tracks, and cash the check into his own account. Unfortunately, there is a major downside to the separation of duties, which is that shifting tasks among multiple people interferes with the efficiency of a process. Consequently, only use this control principle at the minimum level needed to establish the desired level of control – too much of it is not cost-effective.
- *Process integration.* Controls should be so thoroughly intertwined with business transactions that it is impossible for employees *not* to perform them as part of their daily activities. This level of integration substantially reduces the incidence of errors and the risk of fraud. An example of proper process integration with a control is running all produced items past a fixed bar code scanning station on a conveyor belt, to ensure that all completed goods are recorded. The information is collected without the staff having to do anything. An example of minimal process integration that will likely result in frequent control problems is requiring employees to record this information by hand on a paper form.
- *Management support.* The management team must make it abundantly clear to employees that it thoroughly supports the system of controls. This does not mean that a general statement of ethics is included in the employee manual. Instead, it means that management takes the time to explain controls to employees, is highly visible in investigating control breaches, and takes sufficient remedial action to make it clear to the entire staff that controls are to be taken seriously. Management also does not override its own controls, nor does it set performance standards so difficult to attain that employees would be forced to circumvent controls in order to meet the stand-

ards. Further, there may be a code of conduct that managers actively reinforce with their direct reports.

- *Responsibility.* No control system will work unless people are made responsible for them. This means that someone should be assigned responsibility for every control, and that they receive regular updates on the status of those controls. It would also be useful if the status of their controls are noted in their compensation reviews, and have a direct impact on changes in their pay.

- *Conscientious application.* Employees cannot simply treat controls in a perfunctory manner. Instead, there should be a culture that encourages the close examination of control breaches to determine what went wrong, and how the system can be adjusted to reduce the risk that the same issue will occur again. This level of conscientious behavior must be encouraged by the management team through constant reinforcement of the message that the system of controls is important. It also requires the availability of communication channels through which employees can anonymously report suspected improprieties.

- *Systems knowledge.* It is impossible to expect employees to conscientiously inspect controls unless they already know how systems operate. This calls for the ongoing training of employees to ensure that they thoroughly understand all aspects of the systems with which they are involved. This requires not only an initial training session for new employees, but also reminder sessions that are timed to coincide with any changes in processes and related controls, as well as thorough documentation of the systems. A good level of systems knowledge may call for the use of procedures, training materials, and a core group of trainers.

- *Error reporting.* It is impossible to know if a control is functioning properly unless there is a system in place for reporting control breaches. This may be a report generated by a computer system, but it may also call for open communications channels with employees, customers, and suppliers to solicit any errors that have been found. In this latter case, error reporting is strongly supported by a management group that is clearly interested in spotting errors and correcting them in a way that does not cast blame on those reporting the information. In addition, errors should be communicated all the way up through the organization to the audit committee and board of directors, who can enforce the establishment of enhanced controls.

- *Staffing.* There must be an adequate number of employees on hand to operate controls. Otherwise, there will be great pressure to avoid manual controls, since they take too much time to complete. This is actually a profitability issue, since a business experiencing losses is more likely to cut back on staffing, which in turn impacts the control system.

- *Outlier analysis.* Most businesses create control systems to deal with problems they have seen in the past, or which have been experienced elsewhere in the industry. They rarely create controls designed to mitigate outlier issues – that is, problems that occur very infrequently. The sign of a great control system is one in which employees take the time to examine the control system from a high level, and in light of the current and future business environment, to see if there are any outlier events that present a risk of loss in sufficiently large amounts to warrant the addition of controls. This outlier analysis requires excellent knowledge of the industry and a perceptive view of the direction in which it is headed.

Of the principles just noted, management support is the most crucial. Without it, a system of controls is like a building with no supporting framework – the entire structure crashes to the ground if there is any pressure placed upon it at all. For example, the control system may appear to have proper separation of duties, but this makes no difference if the management team ignores these separations for transactions that it has an interest in ramming through the system.

The Failings of Internal Controls

A well-constructed system of internal controls can certainly be of assistance to a business, but controls suffer from several conceptual failings. They are:

- *Assured profitability.* No control system on the planet can assure a business of earning a profit. Controls may be able to detect or even avoid some losses, but if a business is inherently unprofitable, there is nothing that a control system can do to repair the situation. Profitability is, to a large extent, based on product quality, marketplace positioning, price points, and other factors that are not related to control systems.
- *Fair financial reporting.* A good control system can go a long ways toward the production of financial statements that fairly present the financial results and position of a business, but this is by no means guaranteed. There will always be outlier or low probability events that will evade the best control system, or there may be employees who conspire to evade the control system.
- *Judgment basis.* Manual controls rely upon the judgment of the people operating them. If a person engages in a control activity and makes the wrong judgment call (such as a bad decision to extend credit to a customer), then the control may have functioned but the outcome was still a failure. Thus, controls can fail if the judgment of the people operating them is poor.
- *Determined fraudulent behavior.* Controls are typically designed to catch fraudulent behavior by an individual who is acting alone. They are much less effective when the management team itself overrides controls, or when several employees collude to engage in fraud. In these cases, it is quite possible to skirt completely around the control system.

Thus, the owners, managers, and employees of a business should view its controls not as an absolute failsafe that will protect the business, but rather as something designed to *increase the likelihood* that operational goals will be achieved, its financial reports can be relied upon, and that it is complying with relevant laws and regulations.

Preventive and Detective Controls

When considering the proper balance of controls that a business needs, also consider the types of controls being installed. A *preventive control* is one that keeps a control breach from occurring. This type of control is highly prized, since it has a direct impact on cost reduction. Another type of control is the *detective control*. This control is useful, but it only detects a control breach after it has occurred; thus, its main use is in making management aware of a problem that must be fixed.

A control system needs to have a mix of preventive and detective controls. Even though preventive controls are considered more valuable, they also tend to be more intrusive in the functioning of key business processes. Also, they are installed to address specific control issues that management is already aware of. Management also needs a liberal helping of detective controls, which can be used to spot problems that management was not aware of. Thus, a common occurrence is to throw out a web of detective controls that occasionally haul in a new type of problem, for which management installs a preventive control.

In short, a mix of the two types of controls is needed, where there may be no ideal solution. There may be a range of possible configurations within which a controls auditor would consider a control system to be effective.

Manual and Automated Controls

If a control is operated by the computer system through which business transactions are recorded, this is considered to be an *automated control*. If a control requires someone to manually perform it, this is considered a *manual control*. Automated controls are always preferred, since it is impossible to avoid them. Conversely, manual controls can be easily avoided, simply by forgetting them. Examples of automated controls are:

- A limit check in a payroll data entry screen that does not allow one to enter more hours in a work week than the total number of hours in a week.
- An address reviewer in the vendor master file that does not allow one to enter an address without the correct zip code.
- An error checker in the inventory database that does not allow an inventory deduction that would otherwise result in a negative inventory balance.

Examples of manual controls are:

- Requiring a second signature on a check payment that exceeds a certain amount.
- Requiring the review of the final payroll register by a supervisor.
- Requiring the completion of a monthly bank reconciliation.

The best controls are ones that are preventive (see the preceding section) and automated, since they actively prevent errors from occurring, and are very difficult to avoid.

Constructing a System of Controls

The preceding discussion has revolved around the general concept of controls and the principles that should underlie them. But how does a company actually create a system of controls? What are the nuts and bolts of building a system? The primary steps are:

1. *Understand the new system.* Work with the systems analysts who have designed the new system to understand what it is designed to do, and each step in the process flow. This may call for the use of flowcharts and walkthroughs of test transactions. The result may be a formal report describing the system, probably including a preliminary set of procedures.
2. *Explore possible control breaches.* Work with the internal and external auditors, department managers, and systems analysts to estimate where control breaches are most likely to arise in the prospective system.
3. *Quantify possible control breaches.* Estimate the number of occurrences of each type of control breach, the maximum and most likely amounts that a control breach would cost, and their impact on customers and other key company performance metrics.
4. *Design controls.* Based on the quantification of control breaches, design controls that will cost-effectively mitigate risks and be so thoroughly integrated into the underlying process that they will be as robust as possible.
5. *Implement the controls.* Install the controls, along with all necessary documentation, forms, systems, and training, and oversee the initial rollout to ensure that it is operating as planned.
6. *Test the system.* A system of controls does not necessarily operate as planned, perhaps due to a misperception of how the underlying system operates, a bad control design, technology issues, poor employee training, and so on. To detect these issues, test the system of controls by feeding incorrect transactions into it, and see if the controls detect the transactions. If not, adjust the controls and repeat the exercise as many times as necessary.
7. *Conduct a post-implementation review.* All systems change over time, so expect control redundancy and gaps to appear as systems change. Review systems at least once a year, and more frequently if there have been major changes, to see if the existing system of controls should be adjusted. This task may be most easily handled by the internal auditing department, though the controller may want to take on this task instead.

In a larger company, it may be cost-effective to hire a controls analyst who deals with these matters on a full-time basis. In a smaller enterprise, it is more likely that this work will be handled by the controller, who might consider outsourcing it to a consultant. In this area, the CFO should oversee the work of the controller.

Special Case - Acquisitions

A particularly burdensome area from the perspective of controls is the acquisition. The CFO or controller of the acquiring company is usually responsible for determining the entire system of controls and underlying control principles at the acquired entity, and ensuring that the control environment is brought up to the standards of the acquiring entity as quickly as possible. There are a number of factors to consider in this situation:

- *Outside assistance.* The acquiring entity's accounting staff is fully occupied with integrating the operations of the two businesses, and certainly does not have time to spare for a review of controls. Accordingly, the CFO or controller should hire consultants to review the acquiree's control systems and recommend changes. This review should begin as part of the due diligence review prior to the acquisition, and should continue through the subsequent integration process.
- *Principles review.* The fundamental principles outlined earlier in the Control Principles section still apply. This means that the acquiree's control system must be reviewed for separation of duties, process integration, management support, responsibility for controls, systems knowledge, and so on. A particular concern is that the acquirer might want to cut costs by reducing headcount at the acquiree, which may impact the principle that there must be adequate staffing to operate the system of controls.
- *Impact of change.* When there are large changes in an organization, as typically happens in an acquiree immediately following an acquisition, there can be equally major morale issues which usually have a negative impact on the system of controls. Both the CFO and the controller should be aware of this problem, and expect that there will be more control breaches in the near term as a result of it.

In addition to these concerns, consider whether a standardized set of controls should be installed throughout all company locations, or if variations will be allowed. If acquisitions are infrequent and the acquirees have business models differing from that of the acquirer, it may be easier to allow local variations on the basic system of control. However, if the parent company is buying a large number of similar businesses, it may make more sense to allow minimal variation, and instead impose the same basic control structure everywhere. The level of standardization has an impact on the variability of procedure documentation and training throughout the enterprise.

Special Case – Employee Turnover

A high level of employee turnover presents a particular problem for the control environment, for the controls knowledge weakens with the departure of each successive group of employees. Eventually, employees no longer understand the full breadth of business systems, nor why controls are used. Instead, they are only aware of the particular controls for which they are responsible, and which they were instructed in as part of their abbreviated training. This problem is particularly pernicious when systems and controls are poorly documented, and when those with the most seniority (and presumed knowledge of operations) are the first to leave.

The likely result of a continuing series of employee departures is the gradual decline in the use of manual controls. Also, since employees do not know why controls are being used, they are less likely to be conscientious in pursuing any control breaches found. In addition, business processes will change over time, while controls will no longer change with them. The overall result is a control system that may appear on the surface to be reliable, but which in fact can no longer be relied upon.

The best way to resolve the control problems engendered by high employee turnover is to reduce the turnover. This may involve increased pay rates, improved benefits, less oppressive working conditions, and so forth. Though there is a cost associated with these improvements, they will hopefully be offset by the cost reductions that will occur as the control environment is strengthened.

Special Case – Rapid Growth

When a business grows at a high rate of speed, it encounters the same problems found with a high rate of employee turnover. The problem is that the knowledge of business processes and control systems is centered on the core group of original employees, and must be passed along rapidly to an ever-expanding group of employees. The risk in this situation is that controls knowledge will be so ephemeral among newer employees that the same system of controls operated by new employees will be substantially less effective than the same system operated by longer-term employees.

The reduced effectiveness of a control system in this environment can be mitigated through the following actions:

- *System replication.* When there is a high rate of growth, there is no way to accommodate local variations on the basic control system, since each one must be separately documented. Instead, management must settle upon one control system, and replicate it throughout the business in a rigid manner. This is much easier to replicate as the business continues to grow.
- *Written procedures.* When there are too many new employees to be properly trained in person, the fallback approach is to construct written procedures that are as thorough as possible. New employees can use these materials to learn more about controls, and they can also be used as training materials.
- *Training.* It is critically important to have a formal training program in a fast growth environment, since new employees can be rotated through it quickly, and they can all be taught exactly the same material. This allows for a con-siderable amount of uniformity, which is useful for replicating the same control system throughout a company.

- *Employee dispersion.* No matter how well new employees may be trained, they do not yet fully understand why the control system has been constructed in its present form. To lend credence to the current system, it may be necessary to disperse the original group of employees among the various company locations, where they can provide newer employees with a historical perspective on the control system.

Even the recommendations noted here may not be sufficient. If it becomes apparent that the incidence of control breaches is increasing over time, it may be necessary to slow the rate of company growth until the experience level of the employees has increased sufficiently to operate it in a competent manner. Thus, the level of control difficulties may control the pace of further expansion.

Special Case – Audit Committee Oversight

When a company is publicly-held, it will likely have an audit committee, which is an offshoot of the board of directors. This committee is tasked with the oversight of corporate financial reporting, the outside auditors, and internal controls. The members of this committee work on a very part-time basis and may be deluged with information; this combination leads to a low level of effectiveness, since they are not overly familiar with corporate operations or accounting issues, and do not have sufficient time to sort through all of the information provided to determine which issues are most important.

The CFO can help to make the audit committee more effective by preparing periodic reports for them that focus attention on potential problem areas. For example:

- *Alternative treatments available.* Whenever the accounting standards allow a business multiple ways in which to account for a transaction, outline the alternatives available and why the company has chosen to use a particular option. This information can be used as the basis for a discussion about the financial statement effects of the choices made by the CFO.
- *Non-standard practices.* Whenever the company uses an accounting treatment that varies from the industry-standard usage, explain the effect of the unique treatment being used, and how it alters the financial results of the business. This is a particular concern in the area of revenue recognition, where aggressive treatment can accelerate the recognition of revenue.
- *Non-standard transactions.* Outline the reasons why the company is engaging in any non-standard transactions, and the effects of these transactions on the financial statements. This type of information can spark discussions about whether the transactions are really needed, especially in cases where the effect is to bolster the financial results of the business.

The preceding reports can be extremely useful in expanding the knowledge base of the audit committee, which could lead to recommendations to follow more conservative accounting practices.

A serious issue with the preceding list of reports is that they all depend on self-reporting by the company's accounting department. If they want to hide certain accounting transactions, they will most certainly not include those items in a report to the audit committee. To guard against this problem, the committee could periodically hire an outside analyst to review the company's financial statements and disclosures. The analyst notes any unusual items and reports them to the committee, along with commentary regarding the possible presence of non-standard accounting transactions.

Control System Documentation

It is difficult to have a formal system of controls without documentation of them. After all, such documents are useful for training new staff, providing consistency in the application of controls, and proving their existence to auditors. However, this does not mean that a company has to hire a consultant to create a superlative set of interlocking documentation for every control in the company. Since controls should accommodate changes in business processes, this means that an elaborate procedures and control manual will probably need to be replaced shortly after it has been issued.

A more efficient view of documentation is to post it on a company intranet site, along with copies of all supporting forms and reports, so that individual pieces can be altered as needed, and users can download what they want.

Also, the level of control documentation should vary by the size of the business. A larger business with many employees and locations may need a detailed level of documentation, because people situated in different locations may be involved in the same process, and do not know how the entire process flows. However, a smaller business where everyone works close together requires far less documentation, since normal interaction between employees makes it relatively easy for them to understand how controls are supposed to work. Thus, an international business may produce an elaborate set of procedure manuals, while a smaller business gets by with a short checklist of controls that are reinforced by discussions among the employees.

Even at the most minimal level, documentation of controls should certainly encompass checklists that can be easily updated and posted in a business. For example, it is essential to close the books consistently every month, so that there is some assurance of having comparable financial statements from month to month. A simple checklist of closing activities can be used, which is a highly effective control over the financial statements.

If there is an audit of a company's financial statements, or if the company is making assertions to regulators about the effectiveness of its system of controls, there will need to be a sufficient level of documentation to support its assertions. This does not mean that the business must produce elaborate documentation, but it should be able to prove that the system of controls was properly designed and that it functions properly. Justifying the design of a system of controls may require something as simple as flowcharts documenting the placement and type of controls, while proof of functionality may require documenting the results of periodic tests of the system.

In summary, the level of documentation used for controls can range from simple checklists to quite elaborate productions, and may be issued electronically or in print. The exact type of documentation used will depend on the nature of the business.

Tip: A smaller business almost certainly does not have the in-house expertise to construct a system of controls. If so, consider retaining a controls consultant who can periodically visit the business and recommend controls based on the structure of its processes and subsequent changes to them.

Summary

A key point to take away from this chapter is that there is no ideal system of controls that can be inserted into any company. Instead, the control system must be fashioned to meet the risk profile of a business, while accepting minor losses in areas where it is more important to pare back on controls in favor of having more efficient business processes. Consequently, it takes a deep knowledge of a company's processes to set up and continually tweak a system of controls that yields the proper blend of risk aversion and business performance.

Even if a correct set of controls is installed and they are designed to match the risk profile of a business, this does not mean that they will work properly; excellent control implementation demands a culture of conscientious examination of controls and control breaches by the entire organization. Only through a continuing and company-wide focus on the importance of controls is it possible to have a robust set of controls. Thus, a top-notch control system involves both the controls themselves and the commitment of the organization behind them.

Chapter 5
Performance Measurement

Introduction

The CFO should focus on a small number of key performance measurements over the long term, as well as a set of more specific measurements that are unique to the corporate strategy. In this chapter, we focus on several of the more useful long-term measurements, with a particular emphasis on cash flow. This chapter does not contain several of the more commonly-used metrics, such as sales growth, gross profit margin, and the net profit margin, since elements of these measurements are flawed or can be misleading. Instead, we focus on other measurements that give a clearer picture of corporate performance.

> **Related Podcast Episode:** Episode 234 of the Accounting Best Practices Podcast discusses how to find the right metrics. The episode is available at: **accounting-tools.com/podcasts** or **iTunes**

Cash Conversion Cycle

The cash conversion cycle is the time period extending from the payment of cash for the production of goods, until cash is received from the sale of those goods to customers. The activities involved in the cash conversion cycle include the purchasing of raw materials or items to be resold, their storage, the production process, payments to employees related to the production process, and the sale of goods to customers. If a company only provides services, then the cash conversion cycle extends from the date of payments to employees to the receipt of cash from the sale of services to customers. The cash conversion cycle tends to be much shorter for the provision of services.

It is important to know the duration of the cash conversion cycle, for this is the time period over which cash is invested in a business. If the conversion cycle can be shortened, then cash can be permanently extracted from a business and made available for other purposes. The steps in the cash conversion cycle that can potentially be compressed include:

- Placement of orders for goods with suppliers
- Time required for goods to be delivered to the company
- Time required to inspect and log in received goods
- Inventory holding period
- Duration of production process
- Time required to prepare goods for shipment

- The delay incorporated into payment terms with customers
- The time required to collect overdue accounts receivable

The cash conversion cycle can be severely compressed through the use of a just-in-time "pull" system that only produces goods just as they are needed for immediate sale to customers.

To calculate the amount of the cash conversion cycle, add together the days of sales in accounts receivable and the days of sales in inventory, and subtract the days of payables outstanding. For example, a company has 60 days of sales in accounts receivable, 80 days of sales in inventory, and 30 days of payables outstanding. Its cash conversion cycle is therefore:

$$60 \text{ Days receivables} + 80 \text{ Days inventory} - 30 \text{ Days payables}$$

$$= 110 \text{ Days cash conversion cycle}$$

The calculations for days of sales in accounts receivable, days of sales in inventory, and days payables outstanding are explained next.

Days Sales in Accounts Receivable

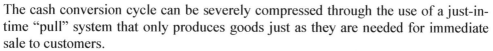

Days sales in accounts receivable is the number of days that a customer invoice is outstanding before it is collected. The measurement is usually applied to the entire set of invoices that a company has outstanding at any point in time, rather than to a single invoice. The point of the measurement is to determine the effectiveness of a company's credit and collection efforts in allowing credit to reputable customers, as well as its ability to collect from them. When measured at the individual customer level, it can indicate when a customer is having cash flow troubles, since the customer will attempt to stretch out the amount of time before it pays invoices.

There is not an absolute number of accounts receivable days that represents excellent or poor accounts receivable management, since the figure varies considerably by industry and the underlying payment terms. Generally, a figure of 25% more than the standard terms allowed may represent an opportunity for improvement. Conversely, an accounts receivable days figure that is very close to the payment terms granted to a customer probably indicates that a company's credit policy is too tight.

The formula for accounts receivable days is:

$$(\text{Accounts receivable} \div \text{Annual revenue}) \times \text{Number of days in the year}$$

For example, if a company has an average accounts receivable balance of $200,000 and annual sales of $1,200,000, then its accounts receivable days figure is:

$$(\$200,000 \text{ Accounts receivable} \div \$1,200,000 \text{ Annual revenue}) \times 365 \text{ Days}$$

$$= 60.8 \text{ Accounts receivable days}$$

The calculation indicates that the company requires 60.8 days to collect a typical invoice.

An effective way to use the accounts receivable days measurement is to track it on a trend line, month by month. Doing so shows any changes in the ability of the company to collect from its customers. If a business is highly seasonal, a variation is to compare the measurement to the same metric for the same month in the preceding year; this provides a more reasonable basis for comparison.

No matter how this measurement is used, remember that it is usually compiled from a large number of outstanding invoices, and so provides no insights into the collectability of a specific invoice. Thus, it should be supplemented with an ongoing examination of the aged accounts receivable report and the collection notes of the collection staff.

Days Sales in Inventory

Days sales in inventory (DSI) is a way to measure the average amount of time that it takes for a company to convert its inventory into sales. A relatively small number of days sales in inventory indicates that a company is more efficient in selling off its inventory, while a large number indicates that a company may have invested too much in inventory, and may even have obsolete inventory on hand.

To calculate days sales in inventory, divide the average inventory for the year by the cost of goods sold for the same period, and then multiply by 365. For example, if a company has average inventory of $1.5 million and an annual cost of goods sold of $6 million, then its days sales in inventory is calculated as:

$$(\$1.5 \text{ million inventory} \div \$6 \text{ million cost of goods sold}) \times 365 \text{ days}$$

$$= 91.3 \text{ days sales in inventory}$$

The days sales in inventory figure can be misleading, for the following reasons:

- A company could post financial results that indicate a low DSI, but only because it has sold off a large amount of inventory at a discount, or has written off some inventory as obsolete. An indicator of these actions is when profits decline at the same time that the number of days sales in inventory declines.
- A company could change its method for calculating the cost of goods sold, such as by capitalizing more or fewer expenses into overhead. If this calculation method varies significantly from the method the company used in the past, it can lead to a sudden alteration in the results of the measurement.
- The person creating the metrics might use the amount of ending inventory in the numerator, rather than the average inventory figure for the entire measurement period. If the ending inventory figure varies significantly from the average inventory figure, this can result in a sharp change in the measurement.

- A company may switch to contract manufacturing, where a supplier produces and holds goods on behalf of the company. Depending upon the arrangement, the company may have no inventory to report at all, which renders the DSI measurement useless.

Days Payables Outstanding

The accounts payable days formula measures the number of days that a company takes to pay its suppliers. If the number of days increases from one period to the next, this indicates that the company is paying its suppliers more slowly. A change in the number of payable days can also indicate altered payment terms with suppliers, though this rarely has more than a slight impact on the total number of days. If a company is paying its suppliers very quickly, it may mean that the suppliers are demanding short payment terms because they are suspicious of the company's ability to pay.

To calculate days payables outstanding, summarize all purchases from suppliers during the measurement period, and divide by the average amount of accounts payable during that period. The formula is:

$$\frac{\text{Total supplier purchases}}{(\text{Beginning accounts payable} + \text{Ending accounts payable}) \div 2}$$

This formula reveals the total accounts payable turnover. Then divide the resulting turnover figure into 365 days to arrive at the number of accounts payable days.

The formula can be modified to exclude cash payments to suppliers, since the numerator should include only purchases on credit from suppliers. However, the amount of up-front cash payments to suppliers is normally so small that this modification is not necessary.

As an example, a CFO wants to determine his company's accounts payable days for the past year. In the beginning of this period, the beginning accounts payable balance was $800,000, and the ending balance was $884,000. Purchases for the last 12 months were $7,500,000. Based on this information, the CFO calculates the accounts payable turnover as:

$$\frac{\$7,500,000 \text{ Purchases}}{(\$800,000 \text{ Beginning payables} + \$884,000 \text{ Ending payables}) \div 2}$$

$$=$$

$$\frac{\$7,500,000 \text{ Purchases}}{\$842,000 \text{ Average accounts payable}}$$

$$= 8.9 \text{ Accounts payable turnover}$$

Thus, the company's accounts payable is turning over at a rate of 8.9 times per year. To calculate the turnover in days, the CFO divides the 8.9 turns into 365 days, which yields:

$$365 \text{ Days} \div 8.9 \text{ Turns} = 41 \text{ Days}$$

Companies sometimes measure accounts payable days by only using the cost of goods sold in the numerator. This is incorrect, since there may be a large amount of administrative expenses that should also be included. If a company only uses the cost of goods sold in the numerator, this creates an excessively small number of payable days.

A significant failing of the days payables outstanding measurement is that it does not factor in all of the short-term liabilities of a business. There may be substantial liabilities related to payroll, interest, and taxes that exceed the size of payables outstanding. This issue can be eliminated by incorporating all short-term liabilities into the days payable outstanding measurement.

Free Cash Flow

Free cash flow is the net change in cash generated by the operations of a business during a reporting period, minus cash outlays for working capital, capital expenditures, and dividends during the same period. Thus, the calculation of free cash flow is:

$$\text{Operating cash flow} \pm \text{Working capital changes} - \text{Capital Expenditures} - \text{Dividends}$$

The "operating cash flow" component of that equation is calculated as:

$$\text{Net income} + \text{Depreciation} + \text{Amortization}$$

Free cash flow is important because it is an indicator of the financial health of a business, and particularly of its ability to invest in new business opportunities. The measure is also used by investors to estimate the amount of cash flow that may be available for distribution to them in the form of dividends. However, there can be a variety of situations in which a company can report positive free cash flow, and which are due to circumstances not necessarily related to a healthy long-term situation. For example, positive free cash flow can be caused by:

- Selling off major corporate assets
- Cutting back on or delaying capital expenditures
- Delaying the payment of accounts payable
- Accelerating receivable receipts with high-cost early payment discounts
- Foregoing a dividend
- Cutting back on key maintenance expenditures
- Reducing marketing expenditures
- Curtailing scheduled pay increases
- Entering into sale and lease back arrangements for key assets

In these examples, management has taken steps to reduce the long-term viability of a business in order to improve its short-term free cash flows. Other actions, such as accelerating the collection of accounts receivable through changes in payment terms or switching to just-in-time materials management systems, can be beneficial to a business while still reducing its outgoing cash flows.

Free cash flow can also be impacted by the growth rate of a business. If a company is growing rapidly, it requires a significant investment in accounts receivable and inventory, which increases its working capital investment and therefore decreases the amount of free cash flow. Conversely, if a business is shrinking, it is converting some of its working capital back into cash as receivables are paid off and inventory liquidated, resulting in an increasing amount of free cash flow.

An additional consideration is the ability of a business to repatriate cash from a subsidiary. If a subsidiary is spinning off enormous amounts of cash, the ability to do so makes little difference to the corporate parent if it cannot access the cash, due to stringent controls over cash repatriation by the government.

In short, be aware of the general condition and strategic direction of a business when evaluating whether the state of its free cash flows is beneficial or not.

Working Capital Productivity

The working capital productivity measurement compares sales to working capital. The intent is to measure whether a business has invested in a sufficient amount of working capital to support its sales. From a financing perspective, management wants to maintain low working capital levels in order to keep from having to raise more cash to operate the business. This can be achieved by such techniques as issuing less credit to customers, implementing just-in-time systems to avoid investing in inventory, and lengthening payment terms to suppliers.

Conversely, if the ratio indicates that a business has a large amount of receivables and inventory, this means that the organization is investing too much capital in return for the amount of sales that it is generating.

To decide whether the working capital productivity ratio is reasonable, compare a company's results to those of competitors or benchmark businesses.

To derive working capital productivity, divide annual revenues by the total amount of working capital. The formula is:

$$\frac{\text{Annual revenues}}{\text{Total working capital}}$$

When using this measurement, consider including the annualized quarterly sales in order to gain a better short-term understanding of the relationship between working capital and sales. Also, the measurement can be misleading if calculated during a seasonal spike in sales, since the formula will match high sales with a depleted inventory level to produce an unusually high ratio.

EXAMPLE

A lender is concerned that Pianoforte International does not have sufficient financing to support its sales. The lender obtains Pianoforte's financial statements, which contain the following information:

Annual revenues	$7,800,000
Cash	200,000
Accounts receivable	800,000
Inventory	2,000,000
Accounts payable	400,000

With this information, the lender derives the working capital productivity measurement as follows:

$$\frac{\$7,800,000 \text{ Annual revenues}}{\$200,000 \text{ Cash} + \$800,000 \text{ Receivables} + \$2,000,000 \text{ Inventory} - \$400,000 \text{ Payables}}$$

$$= 3:1 \text{ Working capital productivity}$$

This ratio is lower than the industry average of 4:1, which indicates poor management of the company's receivables and inventory. The lender should investigate further to see if the receivable and inventory figures may contain large amounts of overdue or obsolete items, respectively.

Cash Reinvestment Measurements

It may be useful to track the uses to which a company puts its cash flows. In this section, we review one ratio designed to examine *actual* cash usage, as well as another ratio that is intended to examine the usage of *expected* cash flows.

Cash Reinvestment Ratio

One of the more interesting cash flow ratios does not examine the sources of cash flow, but rather how cash flow is used. The cash reinvestment ratio focuses on the proportion of cash flow that is invested back into the business – specifically, in fixed assets and working capital. The inverse of this ratio would reveal the amount of cash flowing out of a business, such as through dividends paid to investors. If the ratio is very high, it can be indicative of a business that is rapidly growing, and which therefore needs all of its excess cash to fund further expansion. However, a high ratio can also indicate that a business is barely profitably, so all of its cash is needed to maintain operations.

To calculate the cash reinvestment ratio, aggregate the amount of any increases in the gross amount of fixed assets, as well as any changes in working capital, and then divide by net income plus non-cash expenses. The gross amount of fixed assets is used instead of the net amount, so that the effects of depreciation are excluded. The calculation is:

$$\frac{\text{Increase in gross amount of fixed assets} \pm \text{Changes in working capital}}{\text{Net income} + \text{non-cash expenses}}$$

When interpreting this ratio, it is of some importance to recognize when a business is using more assets than would be required by a lean operation. This calls for the development of turnover ratios for receivables, inventory, and fixed assets, which can then be compared to other companies in the industry. If these ratios indicate low asset turnover levels, there could be a problem with the manner in which a business is being managed.

EXAMPLE

A prospective buyer is reviewing the financial statements of Giro Cabinetry, which reveals a very high cash reinvestment ratio of 95%. However, the company is generating net profits of 20%, which indicates a high level of available cash, while sales are only increasing at a rate of 10% per year. The buyer digs further and examines the company's asset turnover ratios. Accounts receivable average 45 days old, which is normal for the industry. The proportion of fixed assets to sales is also normal. However, average inventory is 200 days old, which is far beyond the industry average. After more investigation, the buyer learns that Giro has an antiquated materials management system that results in very large amounts of excess inventory. The inventory is still usable, so the investor decides to buy the company, install a new job control system, and sell off the excess inventory.

Funds-Flow Adequacy Ratio

A key component of a corporate budgeting process is the examination of forecasted cash flows, to see if the cash flows will be sufficient for all projected company requirements, such as additions to working capital and fixed assets, as well as planned dividends to shareholders. This examination can be conducted with the funds-flow adequacy ratio. To calculate the ratio, aggregate all of the cash requirements just noted and divide this total into the projected net cash outflows from the operations of the business. The formula is:

$$\frac{\text{Net budgeted cash available from operations}}{\text{Budgeted increase in fixed assets} + \text{Budgeted increased in working capital} + \text{Expected dividends}}$$

If the outcome of this ratio is more than 1:1, the business can internally generate sufficient funds for all of its needs. If the ratio is less than 1:1, the budget can be recast to require fewer expenditures, or additional financing can be included in the budget to cover the shortfall.

The ratio can also be used to judge the historical ability of a company to fund its own cash requirements. If the company has continually suffered cash shortfalls in prior years, it is entirely likely that a more optimistic target in the budget will not be achieved.

EXAMPLE

The CFO for Camelot Construction (maker of wedding props) is reviewing the first draft of management's budget for the next year. She is suspicious of the amount of cash flow projected to be produced by the company, and decides to compare it to actual results for previous years. She does so using the funds-flow adequacy ratio, as shown in the following table:

	20X1 Actual Results	20X2 Actual Results	20X3 Budgeted Results
Cash available from operations	$250,000	$235,000	$680,000
Cash usage	$280,000	$305,000	$400,000
Funds-flow adequacy ratio	89%	77%	170%

The table reveals that the proposed budget is a fantasy. Based on its historical results, Camelot is quite unlikely to generate anywhere near the cash flow noted in the first iteration. The CFO appears before a round table of company managers to state her findings.

Contribution Margin Ratio

The contribution margin ratio is the percentage of a firm's contribution margin to its sales. Contribution margin is a product's price minus its variable costs, resulting in the incremental profit earned for each unit sold. The total contribution margin generated by an entity represents the total earnings available to pay for fixed expenses and generate a profit.

The contribution margin formula is useful for determining the proportion of profit earned from a sale. The contribution margin should be relatively high, since it must be sufficient to also cover fixed costs and administrative overhead. Also, the measure is useful for determining whether to allow a lower price in special pricing situations. If the contribution margin ratio is excessively low or negative, it would be unwise to continue selling a product at that price point, since the company would have difficulty earning a profit over the long term. The contribution margin ratio is also useful for determining the profits that will arise from various sales levels (see the example).

The contribution margin is also useful for determining the impact on profits of changes in sales. In particular, it can be used to estimate the decline in profits if sales drop, and so is a standard tool in the formulation of budgets.

86

To calculate the contribution margin ratio, divide the contribution margin by sales. The formula is:

$$\frac{\text{Sales} - \text{Variable expenses}}{\text{Sales}}$$

EXAMPLE

The Iverson Drum Company sells drum sets to high schools. In the most recent period, it sold $1,000,000 of drum sets that had related variable costs of $400,000. Iverson had $660,000 of fixed costs during the period, resulting in a loss of $60,000. The key information is:

Revenue	$1,000,000
Variable expenses	400,000
Contribution margin	600,000
Fixed expenses	660,000
Net loss	-$60,000

Iverson's contribution margin ratio is 60%, so if it wants to break even, the company must either reduce its fixed expenses by $60,000 or increase its sales by $100,000 (calculated as the $60,000 loss divided by the 60% contribution margin ratio).

Core Earnings Ratio

There are many ways in which the net profit ratio of a business can be skewed by events that have little to do with its core operating capabilities. To get to the root of the issue and concentrate on only the essential operations of a business, Standard & Poor's has promulgated the concept of core earnings, which strips away all non-operational transactions from a company's reported results.

There are a multitude of unrelated transactions that can be eliminated from net profits, some of which are so specific to certain industries that Standard & Poor's probably never thought of them. The most common of these unrelated transactions are:

- Asset impairment charges
- Costs related to merger activities
- Costs related to the issuance of bonds and other forms of financing
- Gains or losses on hedging activities that have not yet been realized
- Gains or losses on the sale of assets
- Gains or losses related to the outcome of litigation
- Profits or losses from pension income
- Recognized cost of stock options issued to employees
- Recognized cost of warrants issued to third parties
- The accrued cost of restructuring operations that have not yet occurred

Many of these special adjustments only occur at long intervals, so a company may find that its core earnings ratio is quite close to its net profit ratio in one year, and substantially different in the next year. The difference tends to be much larger when a company adds complexity to the nature of its operations, so that more factors can impact net profits.

The calculation of the core earnings ratio is to adjust reported net income for as many of the preceding items as are present, and divide by net sales. The formula is:

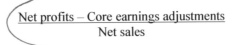

$$\frac{\text{Net profits} - \text{Core earnings adjustments}}{\text{Net sales}}$$

EXAMPLE

Subterranean Access, maker of drilling equipment, has reported a fabulous year, with profits of $10,000,000 on sales of $50,000,000. A credit analyst that rates the company's bonds is suspicious of this good fortune, and digs through the company's annual report to derive the core earnings ratio of the business. She uncovers the following items:

Profit from favorable settlement of a lawsuit	$8,000,000
Profit on earnings from pension fund	500,000
Gain on sale of a subsidiary	3,500,000
Impairment charge on acquired intangible assets	-1,000,000
Total	$11,000,000

When these adjustments are factored out of the company's net profits, it turns out that the core earnings figure is actually a $1,000,000 loss, which results in a core earnings ratio of negative 2%. Based on this information, the analyst issues a downgrade on the company's debt, on the assumption that the multitude of favorable adjustments will not continue.

Quality of Earnings Ratio

The "real" performance of a business equates to the cash flows that it generates, irrespective of the results that appear in its income statement. Any number of accruals and aggressive or conservative interpretations of the accounting standards can lead to a wide divergence between the reported amounts of cash flows and net income. The greater the divergence, the more an observer must wonder about the reliability of the information being presented. This issue is addressed by the quality of earnings ratio, which compares the reported level of earnings to the reported cash flows. Earnings are considered to be of high quality if the two figures are relatively close to each other. To calculate the quality of earnings, follow these steps:

1. Obtain the "Cash from operations" line item in the statement of cash flows.
2. Subtract the cash from operations figure from the net profit figure in the income statement.

3. Divide the result by the average asset figure for the business during the measurement period.

The formula is:

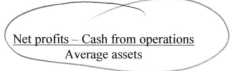

$$\frac{\text{Net profits} - \text{Cash from operations}}{\text{Average assets}}$$

An occasional spike in this ratio can be explained by a company's compliance with the accounting standards in regard to a specific issue, and can be entirely legitimate. However, if the amount of net profits is persistently higher than cash from operations for a number of reporting periods, it is likely that management is actively engaged in the inflation of the net profits figure.

EXAMPLE

The Red Herring Fish Company has been having difficulty meeting its loan covenants over the past few months, and the loan officer is beginning to suspect that something fishy is going on. She reviews the company's latest set of financial statements, and extracts the following information:

Cash from operations	$2,300,000
Net profits	4,700,000
Beginning assets	11,000,000
Ending assets	11,400,000

Based on this information, she compiles the following quality of earnings ratio:

$$\frac{\$4,700,000 \text{ Net profits} - \$2,300,000 \text{ Cash from operations}}{(\$11,000,000 \text{ Beginning assets} - \$11,400,000 \text{ Ending assets}) \div 2}$$

$$= 21\%$$

The ratio reveals quite a substantial difference between the cash flows and reported (and possibly inflated) earnings of Red Herring. The loan officer decides that it is time to send in an audit team to review the company's books.

Breakeven Point

The breakeven point is the sales volume at which a business earns exactly no money. It is mostly used for internal analysis purposes, since the CFO can use it to model the point at which various mixes of product sales and fixed costs will trigger a loss.

To calculate the breakeven point, divide total fixed expenses by the contribution margin. Contribution margin is sales minus all variable expenses, divided by sales. The formula is:

$$\frac{\text{Total fixed expenses}}{\text{Contribution margin percentage}} \quad \Rightarrow = \frac{\text{Sales} - \text{Variable costs}}{\text{Sales}}$$

A more refined approach is to eliminate all non-cash expenses (such as depreciation) from the numerator, so that the calculation focuses on the breakeven cash flow level.

EXAMPLE

A CFO is reviewing the financial statements of a customer that has a large amount of fixed costs. The industry is highly cyclical, so the CFO wants to know what a large downturn in sales will do to the customer. The customer has total fixed expenses of $3,000,000, sales of $8,000,000, and variable expenses of $4,000,000. Based on this information, the customer's contribution margin is 50%. The breakeven calculation is:

$$\frac{\$3,000,000 \text{ Total fixed costs}}{50\% \text{ Contribution margin}}$$

$$= \$6,000,000 \text{ Breakeven sales level}$$

Thus, the customer's sales can decline by $2,000,000 from their current level before the customer will begin to lose money.

Margin of Safety

The margin of safety is the reduction in sales that can occur before the breakeven point of a business is reached. The amount of this buffer is expressed as a percentage. The concept is especially useful when a significant proportion of sales are at risk of decline or elimination, as may be the case when a sales contract is coming to an end. By knowing the amount of the margin of safety, management can gain a better understanding of the risk of loss to which a business is subjected by changes in sales. The opposite situation may also arise, where the margin is so large that a business is well-protected from sales variations.

The margin of safety concept does not work well when sales are strongly seasonal, since some months will yield catastrophically low results. In such cases, annualize the information in order to integrate all seasonal fluctuations into the outcome.

To calculate the margin of safety, subtract the current breakeven point from sales, and divide by sales. The formula is:

$$\frac{\text{Current sales level} - \text{Breakeven point}}{\text{Current sales level}}$$

Here are two alternative versions of the margin of safety:

1. *Budget based.* A company may want to project its margin of safety under a budget for a future period. If so, replace the current sales level in the formula with the budgeted sales level.
2. *Unit based.* If there is a need to translate the margin of safety into the number of units sold, use the following formula instead (though note that this version works best if a company only sells one product):

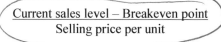

$$\frac{\text{Current sales level} - \text{Breakeven point}}{\text{Selling price per unit}}$$

EXAMPLE

Lowry Locomotion is considering the purchase of new equipment to expand the production capacity of its toy tractor product line. The addition will increase Lowry's operating costs by $100,000 per year, though sales will also be increased. Relevant information is noted in the following table:

	Before Machinery Purchase	After Machinery Purchase
Sales	$4,000,000	$4,200,000
Gross margin percentage	48%	48%
Fixed expenses	$1,800,000	$1,900,000
Breakeven point	$3,750,000	$3,958,000
Profits	$120,000	$116,000
Margin of safety	6.3%	5.8%

The table reveals that both the margin of safety and profits worsen slightly as a result of the equipment purchase, so expanding production capacity is probably not a good idea.

Return on Equity

The return on equity (ROE) ratio reveals the amount of return earned by investors on their investments in a business. It is one of the metrics most closely watched by investors. Given the intense focus on ROE, it is frequently used as the basis for bonus compensation for senior managers.

ROE is essentially net income divided by shareholders' equity. ROE performance can be enhanced by focusing on improvements to three underlying measurements, all of which roll up into ROE. These sub-level measurements are:

- *Profit margin.* Calculated as net income divided by sales. Can be improved by trimming expenses, increasing prices, or altering the mix of products or services sold.

- *Asset turnover*. Calculated as sales divided by assets. Can be improved by reducing receivable balances, inventory levels, and/or the investment in fixed assets, as well as by lengthening payables payment terms.
- *Financial leverage*. Calculated as assets divided by shareholders' equity. Can be improved by buying back shares, paying dividends, or using more debt to fund operations.

Or, stated as a formula, the return on equity is as follows:

Dupont

$$\text{Return on Equity} = \frac{\text{Net income}}{\text{Sales}} \times \frac{\text{Sales}}{\text{Assets}} \times \frac{\text{Assets}}{\text{Shareholders' equity}}$$

EXAMPLE

Hammer Industries manufactures construction equipment. The company's return on equity has declined from a high of 25% five years ago to a current level of 10%. The CFO wants to know what is causing the problem, and assigns the task to a financial analyst, Wendy. She reviews the components of ROE for both periods, and derives the following information:

	ROE		Profit Margin		Asset Turnover		Financial Leverage
Five Years Ago	25%	=	12%	×	1.2x	×	1.75x
Today	10%	=	10%	×	0.6x	×	1.70x

The information in the table reveals that the primary culprit causing the decline is a sharp reduction in the company's asset turnover. This has been caused by a large buildup in the company's inventory levels, which have been caused by management's insistence on stocking larger amounts of finished goods in order to increase the speed of order fulfillment.

The multiple components of the ROE calculation present an opportunity for a business to generate a high ROE in several ways. For example, a grocery store has low profits on a per-unit basis, but turns over its assets at a rapid rate, so that it earns a profit on many sale transactions over the course of a year. Conversely, a manufacturer of custom goods realizes large profits on each sale, but also maintains a significant amount of component parts that reduce asset turnover. The following illustration shows how both entities can earn an identical ROE, despite having such a different emphasis on profits and asset turnover. In the illustration, we ignore the effects of financial leverage.

Comparison of Returns on Equity

	ROE		Profit Margin		Asset Turnover
Grocery Store	20%	=	2%	×	10x
Custom manufacturer	20%	=	40%	×	0.5x

Usually, a successful business is able to focus on either a robust profit margin *or* a high rate of asset turnover. If it were able to generate both, its return on equity would be so high that the company would likely attract competitors who want to emulate the underlying business model. If so, the increased level of competition usually drives down the overall return on equity in the market to a more reasonable level.

A high level of financial leverage can increase the return on equity, because it means a business is using the minimum possible amount of equity, instead relying on debt to fund its operations. By doing so, the amount of equity in the denominator of the return on equity equation is minimized. If any profits are generated by funding activities with debt, these changes are added to the numerator in the equation, thereby increasing the return on equity.

The trouble with employing financial leverage is that it imposes a new fixed expense in the form of interest payments. If sales decline, this added cost of debt could trigger a steep decline in profits that could end in bankruptcy. Thus, a business that relies too much on debt to enhance its shareholder returns may find itself in significant financial trouble. A more prudent path is to employ a modest amount of additional debt that a company can comfortably handle even through a business downturn.

EXAMPLE

The president of Finchley Fireworks has been granted a bonus plan that is triggered by an increase in the return on equity. Finchley has $2,000,000 of equity, of which the president plans to buy back $600,000 with the proceeds of a loan that has a 6% after-tax interest rate. The following table models this plan:

	Before Buyback	After Buyback
Sales	$10,000,000	$10,000,000
Expenses	9,700,000	9,700,000
Debt interest expense	---	36,000
Profits	300,000	264,000
Equity	2,000,000	1,400,000
Return on equity	15%	19%

The model indicates that this strategy will work. Expenses will be increased by the new amount of interest expense, but the offset is a steep decline in equity, which increases the return on equity. An additional issue to be investigated is whether the company's cash flows are stable enough to support this extra level of debt.

A business that has a significant asset base (and therefore a low asset turnover rate) is more likely to engage in a larger amount of financial leverage. This situation arises because the large asset base can be used as collateral for loans. Conversely, if a company has high asset turnover, the amount of assets on hand at any point in time is relatively low, giving a lender few assets to designate as collateral for a loan.

> **Tip:** A highly successful company that spins off large amounts of cash may generate a low return on equity, because it chooses to retain a large part of the cash. Cash retention increases assets and so results in a low asset turnover rate, which in turn drives down the return on equity. Actual ROE can be derived by stripping the excess amount of cash from the ROE equation.

Return on equity is one of the primary tools used to measure the performance of a business, particularly in regard to how well management is enhancing shareholder value. As noted in this section, there are multiple ways to enhance ROE. However, we must warn against the excessive use of financial leverage to improve ROE, since the use of debt can turn into a major burden if cash flows decline.

A case can be made that ROE should be ignored, since an excessive focus on it may drive management to pare back on a number of discretionary expenses that are needed to build the long-term value of a company. For example, the senior management team may cut back on expenditures for research and development, training, and marketing in order to boost profits in the short term and elevate ROE. However, doing so impairs the ability of the business to build its brand and compete effectively over the long term. Some management teams will even buy their companies back from investors, so that they are not faced with the ongoing pressure to enhance ROE. In a buyback situation, managers see that a lower ROE combined with a proper level of reinvestment in the business is a better path to long-term value.

Return on Assets

A central reason why a business asks investors for money is to fund the acquisition of assets, of which there are many types – receivables, inventory, fixed assets, and so forth. Consequently, it behooves an investor to inquire into the return subsequently generated from those assets, which is called the return on assets ratio. Ideally, the assets as a group should generate a significant return, indicating that the company is capable of investing shareholder funds in an effective manner.

The return on assets measurement can be misleading, for a variety of reasons. Consider the following situations:

- *Request for additional funds.* A company has thus far generated a high return on assets, and asks investors for more funds, so that it can acquire additional equipment. In this case, investors are making the assumption that the return generated in the past will continue in the future, which may not be the case. The additional funds may be used for an entirely different purpose than the funds invested previously. Consequently, simply basing an investment on the historical return on assets is dangerous; there should also be an inquiry into how the additional funds will be used, and how this varies from previous investments.

- *Small asset base.* In some cases, a company does not require a large amount of assets in order to conduct operations. For example, it may provide services, in which case its primary asset may only be accounts receivable. In these situations, the return on assets may appear astronomical. However, because there are so few assets, it is questionable whether the measurement should even be used. Instead, use it only for asset-intensive operations.

- *Asset replenishment.* The fixed assets upon which this measurement is partially based are being continually reduced by depreciation, which makes the return on assets figure appear to increase over time as the carrying amount of the assets declines. This issue is not material if a company is continually replenishing its fixed assets with new purchases, thereby keeping the total amount of fixed assets relatively consistent from period to period. However, if management is not reinvesting in the business, then the impact of depreciation will gradually reduce the total carrying amount of assets, resulting in a higher return on assets, but also an older and less-efficient infrastructure. This issue can be spotted by reviewing the trend line of maintenance expenses; if the expense is rising over time, it could mean that an entity is spending more money to maintain older machines.

Given these issues, any measure of the return on assets should be treated with a certain amount of caution.

Next, we will address the primary return on assets calculation, followed by a variation on the concept that focuses on those assets actually being used to operate a business.

Return on Assets

The generic return on assets measurement is designed to measure the total return from all sources of income from all assets. The formula is:

$$\frac{\text{Net income}}{\text{Total assets}}$$

The measurement is certainly a simple one, but its all-encompassing nature also means that the result may not yield the type of information needed. Consider the following issues:

- *Non-operating income.* The numerator of the ratio is net income, which includes income from all sources, some of which may not be even remotely related to the assets of the business. For example, net income may include one-time gains or losses from lawsuits or hedging activities, as well as interest income or expense. This issue can be avoided by only using operating income in the numerator.

- *Tax rate*. The net income figure is net of the company's income tax liability. This liability is a result of the company's tax strategy, which may yield an inordinately low (or high) tax rate. Also, depending on the tax strategy, the tax rate could change markedly from year to year. Because of the effect of tax planning, a non-operational technical issue could have a major impact on the calculated amount of return on assets. This concern can be sidestepped by only using before-tax information in the measurement.
- *Cash basis*. The net income figure can be significantly skewed if a company operates on the cash basis of accounting, where transactions are recorded when cash is received or paid out. This issue can be avoided by only using the measurement on a business that employs the accrual basis of accounting.
- *Cash holdings*. The total assets figure in the denominator includes *all* assets; this means that a company with a significant amount of undistributed cash reserves will reveal a lower return on assets, simply because it has not chosen to employ the cash. This problem can arise not only for a successful company with a large amount of cash earned, but also for a company that has recently sold a large amount of stock, and has not yet employed the resulting cash hoard. This issue can be avoided by subtracting cash from the total assets figure in the measurement, or by using a cash amount considered sufficient to support the ongoing operation of the business.

These concerns are in addition to the asset replenishment issue already noted earlier in this section. Given these problems, we suggest an alternative measurement, which uses operating income in the numerator and subtracts all cash from the denominator. The formula is:

$$\frac{\text{Operating income}}{\text{Total assets - Cash}}$$

EXAMPLE

Bland Cabinets, a maker of mass-produced cabinets for apartment complexes, has net income of $2,000,000, which includes a one-time lawsuit settlement cost of $500,000. The company has assets of $11,000,000, of which $1,000,000 is excess cash that the board of directors intends to issue to shareholders as a dividend. For the purposes of calculating Quality's return on assets, the lawsuit settlement cost is added back to the net income figure, while the $1,000,000 of excess cash is subtracted from its total assets figure. The resulting calculation is:

$$\frac{\$2,500,000 \text{ Adjusted income}}{\$10,000,000 \text{ Assets net of excess cash}}$$

$$= 25\% \text{ Return on assets}$$

Return on Operating Assets

The general version of the return on assets just noted is based on the assumption that all of the assets recorded in a company's balance sheet are actually being used productively to generate income. This is extremely unlikely, as there are always excess amounts of receivables, inventory, and fixed assets that are not needed or should never have been acquired. For example:

- *Receivables*. A company may be allowing employees to borrow cash from the company, which are recorded as non-trade receivables. There may also be trade receivables on the books that are unlikely to be paid, and for which there is not a sufficient reserve in the allowance for doubtful accounts.
- *Inventory*. There may be a large amount of inventory on hand that is effectively obsolete, in that it will not be used for a long time, if ever. If there is not a reserve that offsets the amount of this obsolete inventory, the reported inventory asset is likely too high in comparison to the profits being generated.
- *Fixed assets*. Some fixed assets may have fallen into disuse, and so are no longer involved in the generation of income. These assets are likely to be tucked away in odd corners of the business, and are still being depreciated down to their salvage values.

An alternative format for the return on assets measurement can be used that sidesteps all of these issues. The return on operating assets measurement focuses attention on only those assets used to generate a profit. This means that all unnecessary receivables, inventory, and fixed assets are removed from the assets listed in the denominator of the return on assets calculation, yielding the theoretical return that could be achieved if a company were making optimal use of its assets. The formula is:

$$\frac{\text{Net income}}{\text{Total assets} - \text{Assets not used to generate income}}$$

The return on operating assets figure can be extremely effective if used properly. Management can use the resulting measurement as a target figure, and then determine how to eliminate the excess assets that were subtracted from the denominator. The result should be a gradual decline in the asset base of the business, which may generate extra cash that can either be returned to investors through a dividend or stock buyback, or used to invest in more productive assets.

EXAMPLE

The Hegemony Toy Company, maker of military games, has acquired a number of assets through acquisitions, and may no longer need some of the assets. The president tells the CFO to develop a return on operating assets measurement, with the intent of spotting equipment that can be disposed of. The CFO assembles the following information:

Net income	$500,000
Total assets listed on balance sheet	17,000,000
Excess assembly line	500,000
Excess plastic molding facility	1,500,000
Excess warehouse	750,000

Based on this information, the CFO suggests that the return on operating assets is:

$$\frac{\$500,000 \text{ Net income}}{\$17,000,000 \text{ Total assets} - \$2,750,000 \text{ Excess assets}}$$

$$= 3.5\%$$

The behavior that can be engendered by use of this measurement can be troubling, so it should be employed with caution. The following scenarios may arise:

- *Gaming*. Managers will realize that any assets not included in the measurement will eventually be considered excess, and therefore likely to be eliminated. Consequently, expect them to game the system by classifying unnecessary assets as necessary assets.
- *Excessive asset reduction*. Some assets may not be used frequently, but can be of value if production levels spike, when they can be used as excess capacity. This is a particular issue when assets are stripped away that were being used to maintain an even flow of goods into a bottleneck operation. The result can be foregone profits that the terminated assets might otherwise have generated.
- *Tighter credit*. Management may conclude that the accounts receivable asset can be reduced by restricting the amount of credit granted to customers. However, doing so may also reduce the amount of net income, since there may be fewer resulting sales. If this situation arises, be sure to adjust the numerator by a reasonable estimate of lost profits.

Affordable Growth Rate

The central issue for many companies is the correct rate at which a business should grow, since growing too fast can strain the financial resources of an organization. This rate of growth can be estimated by assuming that a certain proportion of assets to sales must be maintained in order to fund future growth. The assumption is valid in most cases, since a certain amount of receivables, inventory, and fixed assets are required for each dollar of revenue generated. To calculate the affordable growth rate, follow these steps:

1. Subtract dividends paid from the amount of net profits reported for the year. The result should be an approximation of the cash generated by the business, and which is still available to fund future growth.

2. Divide this amount by stockholders' equity for the preceding year that was derived from tangible assets. In other words, aggregate all tangible assets listed on the balance sheet and subtract all liabilities to arrive at tangible stockholders' equity. Intangible assets are excluded from the measurement, since these assets can be artificially manufactured through acquisitions.

The formula for the affordable growth rate is:

$$\frac{\text{Net profits} - \text{Dividends}}{\text{Tangible stockholders' equity in preceding year}}$$

The affordable growth rate is a useful metric, but must be considered in relation to several issues that could potentially vary over time, yielding different results. These issues are:

- *Asset usage.* A company may alter its business practices to reduce the amount of assets needed to support a given amount of sales. For example, production could be outsourced, thereby reducing the need for fixed assets. Similarly, a just-in-time production system could reduce the need for a large investment in inventory.
- *Borrowings.* The measurement assumes that lenders will continue to offer debt to the company in roughly the same proportion of debt to assets that they did in the past, which provides cash for growth. This assumption may be incorrect, based on the general availability of credit and the perceived ability of the company to support a certain debt load.
- *Cash flows.* Net profits are assumed to equate to cash flows, which may not be the case. The use of accrual-basis accounting may result in reported net profits that are significantly different from cash flows.
- *Dividends.* Dividends may be issued in the form of stock, which does not represent a cash outflow.
- *Equity.* The owners of the company may be willing to increase stockholders' equity by selling shares to additional investors, which gives the company a large amount of cash to use as the basis for a growth spurt.

Despite the issues noted here, the affordable growth rate is a reasonable tool for estimating the proper long-term rate of growth of a business.

EXAMPLE

The management team of Snyder Corporation is under pressure from the investment community to expand its sales in the coming year. To educate investors about the company's proper growth rate, the CFO decides to formulate the affordable growth rate. Snyder's net profits for the current year were $12,000,000, dividends issued were $4,000,000, and the company's tangible net worth in the preceding year was $80,000,000. Based on this information, the company's affordable growth rate is:

99

$$\frac{\$12,000,000 \text{ Net profit} - \$4,000,000 \text{ Dividends}}{\$80,000,000 \text{ Tangible net worth in preceding year}}$$

$$= 10\% \text{ affordable rate of growth}$$

Summary

The CFO should not rely solely upon a small set of performance measurements, however well they may have served in the past. It is also necessary to monitor indicators of future company performance. For example, there are probably a few costs that can have a major impact on company performance, and which the CFO should therefore monitor closely. Examples of these costs are:

- *Energy costs.* Situations where energy costs have a strong impact on company performance are jet fuel in the airline industry, the cost of coal for a utility, and the cost of electricity for a data center.
- *Raw material costs.* A clothing manufacturer will have a strong interest in the price of cotton, while a builder will be concerned about the price of cement, and ship builder will monitor the cost of steel.
- *Labor costs.* Any company manufacturing products that have a high labor component will constantly monitor the latest labor agreement, or trend of pay raise percentages.

The CFO should also monitor the company's backlog of customer orders on a daily basis. Backlog is the best indicator of an impending increase or decline in sales, so a considerable amount of attention should be paid to this information. Backlog analysis should extend into sales by region, store, and product, and be tracked on a trend line. By doing so, the company has advance warning of revenue changes that may call for rapid retooling or expense cutbacks by management.

> **Tip:** An excellent source of information is the sales staff. They interact directly with customers, and have the best view of customer needs. Accordingly, the CFO should routinely schedule time for salesperson meetings, to gain a better understanding of customers.

In short, the monitoring activities of the CFO should only encompass historical results to the extent that they must be investigated for remedial action and explained to the investment community. In all other respects, measurement systems should be focused upon giving early warning of the key indicators that drive future company performance.

Chapter 6
Mergers and Acquisitions

Introduction

In some organizations, the central role of the CFO is to engage in an ongoing series of acquisitions. The level of direct CFO involvement in these deals can vary, depending on the size and experience of an acquisitions team. In any case, the CFO must be cognizant of all acquisition activities, since any deal failures will likely be ascribed to him or her. In this chapter, we address the key aspects of the acquisition – strategy, due diligence, valuation, payment, legal structure, and integration. For a much more detailed discussion of mergers and acquisitions, please refer to the author's *Mergers & Acquisitions* book.

Related Podcast Episodes: Episodes 75, 80, and 88 of the Accounting Best Practices Podcast discuss acquisition valuation, due diligence, and acquisition types, respectively. They are available at: **accountingtools.com/podcasts** or **iTunes**

Acquisition Strategies

There are a multitude of reasons why a company might want to pursue an acquisition. However, a typical problem for many companies is having a passive stance, where they evaluate each potential acquisition as it appears, and then come up with a "strategy" after the fact for why they should make the purchase. A vastly better approach is to settle upon a single acquisition strategy that works best for the business, and then aggressively follow it. Several possible strategies are noted below.

- *Diversification strategy.* A company may elect to diversify away from its core business in order to offset the risks inherent in its own industry. These risks usually translate into highly variable cash flows which can make it difficult to remain in business when a bout of negative cash flows happen to coincide with a period of tight credit where loans are difficult to obtain. The trouble with the diversification strategy is that there are usually few synergies to be gained, since the businesses are so different from each other. On the contrary, it usually requires *more* expenses for an additional layer of corporate oversight to manage the disparate businesses. Thus, the main benefit of the diversification strategy is more consistent cash flows, rather than more profits.
- *Full service strategy.* An acquirer may have a relatively limited line of products or services, and wants to reposition itself to be a full-service provider. This calls for the pursuit of other businesses that can fill in the holes

in the acquirer's full-service strategy. This approach usually involves the combination of products with supporting services, which may then be extended into multiple geographic regions.

- *Geographic growth strategy.* A company may want to roll out its business concept in a new region. This can be a real problem if the company's product line requires local support in the form of regional warehouses, field service operations, and/or local sales representatives. Such product lines can take a long time to roll out, since the business must create this infrastructure as it expands. A geographical growth acquisition strategy involves finding another business that has the support characteristics that the company needs, such as a regional distributor, and rolling out the product line through the acquired business.

- *Market window strategy.* A company may see a window of opportunity opening up in the market for a particular product or service. It may evaluate its own ability to launch a product within the time during which the window will be open, and conclude that it is not capable of doing so. If so, its best option is to acquire another company that is already positioned to take advantage of the window with the correct products, distribution channels, facilities, and so forth. Such an acquisition will allow the acquirer to gain market share in an area where it otherwise would have had no chance of competing at all. The downside of the market window strategy is that correctly-positioned target companies know they are valuable commodities, and so may be entertaining offers from multiple bidders.

- *Product supplementation strategy.* An acquirer may want to supplement its product line with the similar products of another company. This is particularly useful when there is a hole in the acquirer's product line that it can immediately fill by making an acquisition. This approach is particularly useful when customers want to progress from an introductory model to a more complex model, and a company does not offer the more complex version. This can be a difficult strategy to pursue, because acquired products must be rebranded and properly distributed and serviced.

- *Roll-up strategy.* Some companies attempt an industry roll-up strategy, where they buy up a number of smaller businesses with small market shares to achieve a consolidated business with significant market share. While attractive in theory, this is not that easy a strategy to pursue. In order to create any value, the acquirer needs to consolidate the administration, product lines, and branding of the various acquirees, which can be quite a chore. There is a further risk in that a roll-up involves multiple acquisitions within a relatively short period of time, which makes the integration goals even harder to achieve. Further, an acquirer that is good at the legal aspects of buying many other businesses may not have an equivalent level of expertise in integrating them, which leads to more of a conglomeration of companies than a seamless, well-oiled business machine.

- *Sales growth strategy.* It is very difficult for a business to grow at more than a modest pace through internal (*organic*) growth, because it must overcome a variety of obstacles, such as bottlenecks, hiring the right people, entering new markets, opening up new distribution channels, and so forth. Conversely, it can massively accelerate its rate of growth with an acquisition. The sales growth strategy is especially plausible when the expansion rate of a business is slowing down or has stalled, possibly because it is located in a market niche that has a slow rate of growth. A company could acquire a business located in a faster-growing niche, thereby giving the entire business a faster rate of growth. It may be possible to engage in a series of such acquisitions, continually skipping from niche to niche within an industry to position the business in the fastest-growing areas.

- *Synergy strategy.* One of the more successful acquisition strategies is to examine other businesses to see if there are costs that can be stripped out or revenue advantages to be gained by combining the companies. Ideally, the result should be greater profitability than the two companies would normally have achieved if they had continued to operate as separate entities. This is the synergy strategy, and it is usually focused on similar businesses in the same market, where the acquirer has considerable knowledge of how businesses are operated. It may also be termed a *bolt-on acquisition*, since the acquired business is typically added directly onto the acquirer's existing business lines. If a business continues to acquire companies without engaging in thorough integration efforts, it may find that it must hire more staff to administer an ungainly set of disparate businesses. If so, rather than achieving synergies, it has attained *diseconomies of scale*, where it must spend more money to coordinate the various businesses than would be the case if they were operating as separate entities.

- *Vertical integration strategy.* A company may want to have complete control over every aspect of its supply chain, all the way through to sales to the final customer. This approach may involve buying the key suppliers of those components that the company needs for its products, as well as the distributors of those products and the retail locations in which they are sold. A company does not normally engage in a comprehensive vertical integration strategy, but instead focuses on those suppliers who control key raw materials and production capacity, as well as those sales channels that generate the most profit.

The Failings of Acquisition Strategy

A business located in a moribund industry may see an acquisition strategy as its road to glory – more sales must equate to more shareholder value, right? Instead, when an acquirer assembles a group of companies in the same industry, all it may achieve is a group of companies that now operate under a single parent company. These businesses have no better growth rate than they had when operating alone, their product lines overlap, their salespeople call on the same customers multiple times a month, and so on – and on top of that, the acquirer has squandered its resources to complete the acquisitions, and now has a massive debt burden. So where was the value in the acquisition strategy?

This not-uncommon scenario points out the main problem with acquisitions – growing for the sake of reporting a larger amount of total revenue does not generate value. Instead, it may *destroy* value, since all of the businesses now sheltering under the umbrella of the corporate parent may no longer have an incentive to compete against each other through innovation or cost reductions.

Instead of simple growth, the acquirer must understand *exactly* how its acquisition strategy will generate value. This cannot be a simplistic determination to combine two businesses, with a generic statement that overlapping costs will be eliminated. The management team must have a specific value proposition that makes it likely that each acquisition transaction will generate value for the shareholders. Here are several examples of properly-designed acquisition strategies:

- The acquirer only wants to buy the patents of a target company, which it can then use to pursue licensing deals.
- The acquirer already sells to a major national retail chain, and plans to introduce the products of the target company to that chain.
- The acquirer has several large contracts with the federal government, and can slot the consultants working for a target company directly into those contracts.

In all of the examples just noted, the ultimate goal of the acquirer is not solely to increase its revenue, but primarily to increase its profits. Only through the consistent pursuit of profits can a business hope to be sustainable and provide shareholder value over the long term. Unfortunately, many acquirers lose sight of that goal and focus instead on simple revenue expansion, which can be disastrous.

Acquisition Due Diligence

An essential part of any acquisition is due diligence, which is the investigation of all aspects of the target company. It is addressed immediately after the parties have agreed in principle to a deal, but before a binding agreement has been signed. Doing so tells the acquirer if there are any issues that might alter its valuation of the business, or which might scuttle the deal entirely. It also produces useful information for the eventual integration of the business into the acquirer.

There may be several hundred due diligence issues to investigate, especially when a target company has multiple locations, product lines, and legal entities. In the following bullet points, we address the general areas to investigate as part of due diligence. For a more complete listing, please refer to the author's *Mergers & Acquisitions* book.

- *Overview discussion.* There should be a series of questions regarding why the target company is willing to sell, whether it has attempted to sell before, and the competitive positioning of the business. Though these questions may appear excessively high-level, they can reveal issues about the target company that are so deep-rooted that any possibility of an acquisition must be thrown out.

- *Corporate culture*. Corporate culture is the manner in which a company does its business. It begins with the general concept of how the senior management team wants to operate the company, and percolates down through the organization in the form of management structure, how decisions are made, policies and procedures, the types of people hired, and even its marketing efforts. In particular, there can be serious problems with an acquisition if the corporate culture of the acquirer is of the command-and-control variety and the target company practices localized responsibility. The typical result is a large initial surge in employee turnover. If the reverse situation arises, employees of the target company will not be used to having responsibility thrust upon them, which can result in a prolonged period of confusion, reduced operating results, and employee turnover.

- *Management*. There may be a few members of the target company's management team that form of the core of the business, and whose absence might have a major negative impact on the business. Conversely, some companies would operate substantially better *without* certain managers. The due diligence team must investigate these intangibles, as well as any inordinate ego levels, excessive focus on compensation, and the quality of the subordinates of key managers.

- *Employees*. There is a tendency for the due diligence involving employees to be a simple review of pay levels and employment agreements, which are the two most easily quantifiable topics related to employees. The due diligence team should dig deeper, to understand how the employees work together, which ones are closely associated with customers, the extent of nepotism, union issues, discrimination claims, and so forth. This greater level of detail can yield clues about how to manage the company, and how employees will react to the acquirer.

- *Benefits*. Benefits would be of concern to the due diligence team if only because they are such a large expense. In addition, they can present a problem if there is a large disparity between the benefits granted to the employees of the acquirer and the target company, especially if the acquirer is intent upon standardizing benefits across the entire organization. In addition, look for undocumented benefits, and unusual benefits that are inordinately expensive.

- *Financial results*. The team should investigate the target company's financial statements to determine its profitability, cash flows, and financial position. However, the financial statements are presented at an aggregate level, so it is only possible to draw general conclusions from them. The team must dig deeper to arrive at a thorough understanding of the financial aspects of a business. The investigation should include analyses of fixed and variable costs, profits by business segment, one-time expenses that can be eliminated, and any assets that appear to be overvalued (as indicated by obsolete inventory or bad debts).

- *Revenue.* One of the most important due diligence areas is the future revenue stream, since this is the foundation upon which most acquirers construct their expectations for a business. The investigation should address the size of the order backlog, the proportion of sales that are recurring, customer turnover, the credit granting process, the age of accounts receivable, and similar matters.
- *Expenses.* A key area of concern is the cost structure of the target company. The team should review the trend line for all major expenses, as well as cost containment programs, to see if the target company has its costs under control. Also, see if the company is spending enough to support its core business areas, or if the buyer will need to invest additional funds to bring the target up to a competitive level. Further, look for questionable expenses, such as payments to family members, and excessive travel and entertainment expenses, which can be curtailed.
- *Intellectual property.* In some industries, the majority of the price paid for a business is based on its intellectual property (IP). This asset is usually not listed on a company's balance sheet, so the due diligence team needs to conduct an investigation to determine what types of IP are owned by the business, and what it might be worth. Be particularly careful to determine ownership of patents and copyrights, as well as the amount of licensing income that can potentially be earned.
- *Fixed assets and facilities.* Fixed assets and facilities can be an enormously important topic in an asset-intensive industry, or only of passing interest in more service-oriented businesses. If the first situation is the case, determine the market value of the more expensive items, how well key assets have been maintained, and how much maintenance may be needed to correct any remedial situations. Also estimate the amount of capacity utilization, to see if additional assets should be acquired.
- *Liabilities.* At a minimum level, verify the amount and payment dates of all larger liabilities, as well as whether any debts can be accelerated by a change in control of the target company. In addition, conduct a search for any missing liabilities. Also note the extent to which assets have been assigned to various debts as collateral.
- *Equity.* The attorneys who create acquisition purchase agreements are very particular about the target company's shareholding information, since they must incorporate it into the document. Consequently, be very certain of the numbers of shares and owners stated on the shareholder list, the classes and amounts of stock authorized and outstanding, conversion rights, and the existence of any options and warrants. Further, verify whether there are any declared but unpaid dividends.
- *Taxes (general).* The buyer does not want to acquire any undocumented tax liabilities, so verify that the target company has been paying all normal taxes, such as sales taxes, payroll taxes, and income taxes. It is also possible that some taxes have never been paid, such as franchise taxes in states where the target does business; it can require considerable investigation to uncover

these issues. Also investigate any tax disputes that the target currently has with any government entities, and the likely outcomes of those disputes.

- *Tax loss carry forwards.* Tax loss carry forwards were generated by a company in previous years, and can be applied against the earnings (if any) of that business in future years. The IRS strictly limits the uses to which these tax loss carry forwards can be used by an acquiring business with its Section 382 limitation. In essence, an acquirer can only use the carry forwards in very small amounts per year, and then only if the acquired entity earns a profit against which the carry forwards can be offset. The calculation of the tax loss carry forward that can be used by an acquirer is the value of the acquired entity immediately before the change in ownership, multiplied by the highest of the federal long-term tax-exempt interest rates (based on the average market yield on obligations of the United States with remaining periods to maturity of over nine years). The following example illustrates the concept:

EXAMPLE

Hammer Industries is conducting due diligence on Holbein Hammers, and learns that it has $840,000 of tax loss carry forwards. The price that Hammer expects to pay for Holbein is $2,500,000, and the interest rate on the highest of the United States treasury bonds is 4.2%. The annual amount of the tax loss carry forward that can be used by Hammer to offset any future profits generated by Holbein is calculated as:

$2,500,000 company valuation × 4.2% interest rate = $105,000 carry forward usable per year

Thus, it will take eight years for Hammer to use up the tax loss carry forward, assuming that it continues to operate Holbein as a separate entity and that Holbein generates at least enough profits each year to offset the carry forwards.

The due diligence team should communicate to Hammer's management the amount of the tax loss carry forward and the amount that Hammer could probably use each year if the company were to proceed with the acquisition. This information may alter the valuation assigned to Holbein, as well as the decision to continue operating it as a separate entity.

> **Tip:** If an acquired business has a large tax loss carry forward, it must continue to operate the acquired business under its existing employer identification number in order to take advantage of the carry forwards at a later date. If the acquirer elects to dissolve the business and move its various components into the rest of its operations, then it will lose the carry forwards.

- *Accounting policies.* The financial results of a company may be skewed by its accounting policies to such an extent that they are misleading to the acquirer. This is a particular problem if the financial statements provided by the company have not been audited. The due diligence team can detect these

107

issues by discussing accounting policies with the accounting department. In particular, investigate the policies for revenue recognition, inventory valuation, the recognition of bad debts, and the amount at which purchases are capitalized as assets.

- *Product development.* Product development is one of the most difficult areas in which to conduct due diligence, for the team is being asked to render opinions on incomplete products that are still in the development pipeline. Since these projects are not yet complete and have no related sales information, it is only possible to render an educated guess about the performance of the process and the resulting products. At a minimum, investigate development expenditure levels, any delays in product launches, the types of technology being incorporated into new products, and the amount of warranty claims and product recalls associated with recent product launches.
- *Selling activities.* A key focus of due diligence in the sales department is the efficiency with which sales are made. Accordingly, investigate which salespeople and stores are the most and least effective, as well as the amount of experience and training needed for a salesperson. Make note of any bottlenecks in the selling area that prevent the target from generating additional sales.
- *Marketing activities.* Marketing activities can be critical, particularly in the retail sector. Accordingly, the due diligence team may find it necessary to investigate how well the target company markets its products and services in relation to the efforts of competitors, the level of product branding in use, and how well this appears to be translating into repeat business from customers.
- *Production operations.* The manufacturing area is a difficult one to judge based on just operational or financial metrics. Instead, consider conducting a visual review of the company's facilities. Assign an experienced group of production personnel to these tours, with each person assigned to look for specific issues. The group then assembles immediately after each tour to document their findings. They should document such factors as space usage, scrap left on-site, the use of feedback regarding employee performance, the work flow system being used, equipment maintenance, and so forth.
- *Materials management.* If the target company purchases a large amount of raw materials from suppliers, the review team should investigate whether the business can be impacted by raw material shortages, issues with an overly long supply chain, the amount of sole sourcing used, freight costs, and whether there is a system in place for certifying suppliers to work with the company. There should also be an extensive investigation of how well the company tracks its inventory, and whether inventory is promptly disposed of if it is not to be used in the manufacturing process.
- *Information technology.* The amount of due diligence needed for information technology (IT) depends upon the amount of in-house resources devoted to this area. In many companies, such baseline systems as accounting, payroll, and sales management are outsourced, so there are few IT is-

sues to address. However, there are other situations where custom-designed IT systems form a key part of the competitive stance of a company, and so are worthy of a considerable amount of investigation. In the latter case, document the systems in place, licensing used, the total system cost, the need for imminent system upgrades, the extent to which the company has developed its own legacy systems, and the amount of maintenance required for those systems.

- *Treasury.* The buyer wants to know if it will need to pump more cash into the target company, or if it can reliably extract cash from the business. To understand the situation, the team should drill down into the construction of the target's cash forecast to ensure that it is generating correct information. Also, see if any funds are tied up in long-term investments from which the buyer may have difficulty extracting cash. If the company has operations in other countries, document the amount of cash in countries that do not allow the repatriation of cash back to the parent company.

- *Risk management.* The level of risk to which a company is subjected could be so high that a proposed acquisition is out of the question. Accordingly, investigate the types and amounts of risk, the extent to which risks are being hedged, the amount of insurance, and the size of any remaining risks that are uncovered. Problems with insurance may not be a problem if the acquirer intends to substitute its own insurance coverage for coverage currently used by the target company.

- *Legal issues.* As was the case with risk issues, the presence of a particularly pernicious legal problem can shut down what might otherwise have been considered a promising acquisition. Pay particular attention not only to the size of settlements and injunctions likely to arise from current lawsuits, but also the target's lawsuit history and the probability of there being additional lawsuits in the future. Also review contracts to see if the company might be in violation of any contract terms.

- *Regulatory compliance.* Regulatory compliance is one of the areas in which an acquirer can find itself in trouble if it did not conduct a thorough due diligence investigation. Some issues can have such severe ramifications that they could bankrupt the acquirer and even extend personal liability to its officers. For example, investigate the possibility of any liabilities for hazardous waste remediation, and pay particular attention to any warnings received from regulatory agencies. Also investigate whether regulatory licenses are current, or are in danger of not being renewed. If a company product is waiting for regulatory approval, some estimate should be made of whether the approval will be forthcoming.

A significant concern with any due diligence investigation is the limited amount of time allowed for it. The senior management team probably has a target closing date in mind, which gives the due diligence team only a limited time period in which to conduct its investigation. This can be a real problem if the target is a large, diversified business with multiple locations, since there is no way to complete the work within a tight timeline. Instead, it is the job of the due diligence manager to push back at senior management and clarify the time needed to complete the work. The amount of time needed will be hazy at first and become clearer over time, as the team works its way through the list of items to investigate. Eventually, the team will have a short list of areas that may contain significant risk, which the due diligence manager will advocate investigating before the team is recalled from the field. There is also likely be a larger number of lesser investigations in areas where the risk level is considered minimal, and which can safely be abandoned if the team runs out of time.

The due diligence team is likely to find at least one issue significant enough to halt the acquisition. In the author's experience with dozens of due diligence investigations, there was always such an issue, and it was usually so severe that senior management elected to walk away from the deal. In fact, the mindset of the review team became an assumption that the deal would probably *not* work, and that it needed to be convinced that an acquisition *should* proceed.

This mindset may seem unusually conservative, but anyone who has engaged in a sufficient number of due diligence investigations understands the severity of the problems hiding in many companies. If an acquirer purchases a company without a proper due diligence investigation, it is at risk of buying into a business whose problems are comparable to those of a toxic waste dump.

Indicators of a Strong Acquisition Candidate

A typical due diligence effort will result in a mound of paperwork, from which the due diligence manager must somehow extract those key nuggets of information on which to base a recommendation to senior management. Which items are the most important? The following are indicators of a strong, stable business:

- Employees: Low employee turnover, caused by a favorable work environment and competitive pay and benefits
- Employees: Stable management team with a history of promotion from within
- Financial: A history of producing revenues and earnings from operations
- Financial: Audited financial statements
- Financial: Conservative accounting policies
- Financial: Evidence of a strong system of controls
- Financial: No special charges or history of extraordinary gains or losses
- Complexity: A simple, uncomplicated business model that is easy to understand
- Legal: An uncomplicated legal structure with a minimal number of subsidiaries
- Legal: No litigation, or litigation unlikely to yield significant judgments against the company
- Markets: A strong, defensible position in either a long-term or fast-growing market

- Markets: Sales are spread among many customers, with no dominant customers whose absence would seriously impair the business
- Markets: Long-term investment in branding the company's products and services
- Products: Long-term investment in research and development, with a history of regular product releases

While there may be other issues that could cause a prospective deal to dissolve, the preceding factors should favorably dispose an acquirer toward proceeding with an acquisition.

It is also useful to understand the key indicators of a business that an acquirer may want to steer clear of. If there is a cluster of the following issues in an acquisition candidate, it is a likely indicator of deep-seated problems that will lead to a difficult acquisition:

- The outside auditor has resigned from the annual audit engagement
- Recent changes in accounting methods, particularly when the new methods are not considered to be the standards used in the industry
- Transactions designed primarily to avoid income taxes
- A complex organizational structure when there is no discernible reason for it
- One or more people in key positions with criminal records
- The company has attempted to sell itself in the past, and failed to do so
- There is an extraordinary focus on meeting revenue and profit targets
- There is a command-and-control management structure, under which access to information is restricted

Acquisition Valuation

There are many ways to value a business, which can yield widely varying results, depending upon the basis of each valuation method. Some methods assume a valuation based on the assumption that a business will be sold off at bankruptcy prices, while other methods focus on the inherent value of intellectual property and the strength of a company's brands, which can yield much higher valuations. There are many other valuation methods lying between these two extremes.

We need all of these methods, because no single valuation method applies to all businesses. For example, a rapidly-growing business with excellent market share may produce little cash flow, and so cannot be valued based on its discounted cash flows. Alternatively, a company may have poured all of its funds into the development of intellectual property, but has no market share at all. Only through the application of multiple valuation methods can we discern what the value of a business may be. The most common valuation methods are:

- *Liquidation value*. Liquidation value is the amount of funds that would be collected if all assets and liabilities of the target company were to be sold off or settled. Generally, liquidation value varies depending upon the time allowed to sell assets. If there is a very short-term "fire sale," then the assumed amount realized from the sale would be lower than if a business were permitted to liquidate over a longer period of time. The liquidation value concept is based on the assumption that a business will terminate, so that it no longer generates additional earning power from its intellectual property, products, branding, and so forth. Thus, liquidation value sets the lowest possible valuation for a business.

- *Enterprise value.* This is a theoretical compilation of value that is based on the concept of buying all of the shares of a target company on the open market, paying off its debt, and keeping any residual cash. This calculation tends to result in a low valuation, since it does not include the impact of a control premium. In addition, the current market price may not be indicative of the real value of the business if the stock is thinly traded, since a few trades can substantially alter the market price.
- *Multiples analysis.* It is quite possible to derive the value of a business by comparing it to the financial information and stock prices of comparable publicly-held companies. The usual multiples analyses are based on either the revenues or EBITDA of a business. The following example illustrates the concept.

EXAMPLE

Hammer Industries routinely acquires other businesses within the hand tools industry, and so conducts an annual review of the revenue and EBITDA multiples associated with the smaller publicly-held companies in the same industry. Accordingly, the acquisitions staff prepares the following multiples analysis.

Multiples Analysis
Hand Tools Industry
As of January 10, 20xx
(000s)

Name	Market Capitalization	One Year Revenues	One Year EBITDA	Revenue Multiple	EBITDA Multiple
Arbuckle Anvils	$145,000	$174,000	$19,300	0.8x	7.5x
Chase Cutters	90,000	117,000	11,500	0.8x	7.8x
Holbein Hammers	128,000	160,000	24,200	0.8x	5.3x
Morton Multi-Tools	210,000	210,000	30,000	1.0x	7.0x
Pennsylvania Pliers	52,000	24,000	3,900	2.2x	13.2x
Ralston Rivet	360,000	240,000	42,400	1.5x	8.5x
Visual Vise	76,000	19,000	3,200	4.0x	24.0x
Totals	$1,061,000	$944,000	$134,500	1.1x	7.9x

Thus, the review shows a weighted-average revenue multiple of 1.1x and a weighted-average EBITDA multiple of 7.9x.

One month later, Hammer is engaged in a valuation analysis of a prospective acquisition, which has annual sales of $6.8 million and EBITDA of $400,000. Based on the multiples analysis, Hammer arrives at the following possible valuations for the company:

	Revenue	EBITDA
Target company results	$6,800,000	$400,000
× Industry average multiple	1.1x	7.9x
= Valuation based on multipliers	$7,480,000	$3,160,000

The results suggest quite a broad range of possible valuations, from a low of $3,160,000 to $7,480,000. It is possible that the target company has unusually low EBITDA in comparison to the industry, which is causing its EBITDA-based multiplier to be so low. This means that Hammer might want to push for a lower valuation if it proceeds with the acquisition.

It is most common to multiply the valuation multiples by the revenue and EBITDA information for the target company for its last 12 months. This is known as *trailing revenue* or *trailing EBITDA*. This is the most valid information available, for it represents the actual results of the business in the immediate past. However, if a target company expects exceptional results in the near future, then it prefers to use *forward revenue* or *forward EBITDA*. These measurements multiply expected results for the next 12 months by the valuation multipliers. While the use of forward measurements can create a good estimate of what a business will be worth in the near future, it generally incorporates such optimistic estimates that it tends to result in excessively high valuations.

- *Discounted cash flows.* One of the most detailed and justifiable ways to value a business is through the use of discounted cash flows (DCF). Under this approach, the acquirer constructs the expected cash flows of the target company, based on extrapolations of its historical cash flow and expectations for synergies that can be achieved by combining the two businesses. A discount rate is then applied to these cash flows to arrive at a current valuation for the business. There can be a considerable amount of manipulation involved in adjusting the items to be included in a discounted cash flow analysis. The seller invariably wants to exclude selected expenses from the calculation, on the grounds that they were one-time events that the acquirer will not experience in the future. The seller will also identify a large number of expense exclusions that are based on presumed synergies. The result, according to the seller, is likely to be startlingly high cash flows that the target would be unlikely to ever achieve in practice. It is the task of the acquirer to sort through these alleged expense reductions and verify which ones may actually be achieved. The following example illustrates the compilation of cash flows for a target company, as well as their reduction to net present value using a discount rate.

EXAMPLE

The CFO of Hammer Industries is constructing a discounted cash flow forecast for Ralston Rivet. The CFO begins with the cash flow for the preceding 12-month period, which was $5,800,000. The Ralston management team claims that the following items should be added back to the cash flow figure:

- One-time charge of $200,000 related to a lawsuit judgment
- One-time bonus payment of $120,000 made to the management team
- Elimination of $60,000 for CEO travel and entertainment expenses that would go away once the CEO is terminated
- Reduction of $400,000 in salary and payroll taxes related to the CEO, who will be terminated
- Reduction of $92,000 for a leased warehouse that the management team had not quite gotten around to terminating on its own

The CFO does not exclude the $200,000 lawsuit judgment, on the grounds that Ralston has incurred a series of similar judgments from similar lawsuits in the past, and there is a significant possibility that it will continue to do so in the future. The CFO also does not exclude the $120,000 bonus payment, since further investigation reveals that this was a performance-based bonus, and there is an expectation in the industry for this type of bonus to be paid; further, the amount is not unreasonable. The CFO accepts the combined $460,000 expense reduction related to the CEO, since that expenditure will not be required in the future. Finally, the CFO elects not to exclude the $92,000 warehouse lease, on the grounds that there is no evidence yet that the company can operate without the additional warehouse space.

In addition, the CFO's due diligence team comes up with the following suggestions, which are added back to the cash flow report for valuation purposes:

- $200,000 for duplicated corporate staff who can be terminated
- $80,000 from volume purchasing discounts
- $320,000 from the consolidation of leases
- $38,000 from the elimination of duplicated software maintenance charges

The due diligence team also notes that Ralston's fixed assets are very old, and will require $2,000,000 of expenditures in years two, three, and four to bring them up to standard.

Finally, the due diligence team prudently recommends that Hammer assume that Ralston's cash flow will likely drop 5% in the year following the merger, as uncertainty causes some customers to switch to competitors. Cash flow growth thereafter should be 5% per year.

The CFO combines this information into the following table, in which he estimates the most likely cash flow scenario for the next five years. Hammer has a cost of capital of 9%, which is used to derive the discount rates noted in the table.

	Year 1	Year 2	Year 3	Year 4	Year 5
Beginning* cash flow	$5,800,000	$6,608,000	$6,938,000	$7,285,000	$7,649,000
Base level % change	-290,000	+330,000	+347,000	+364,000	+382,000
CEO expense reduction	+460,000				
Fixed asset replacements		-2,000,000	-2,000,000	-2,000,000	
Duplicate staff	+200,000				
Volume discounts	+80,000				
Lease consolidation	+320,000				
Software maintenance	+38,000				
Net cash flow	$6,608,000	$4,938,000	$5,285,000	$5,649,000	$8,031,000
Discount rate	0.9174	0.8417	0.7722	0.7084	0.6499
Present value of cash flows	$6,062,000	$4,156,000	$4,081,000	$4,002,000	$5,219,000
Present value grand total	$23,520,000				

* Considered to be the cash flow for the year, based on prior year results, not including fixed asset replacements

- *Replication value.* An acquirer can place a value upon a target company based upon its estimate of the expenditures it would have to incur to build that business "from scratch." Doing so would involve building customer awareness of the brand through a lengthy series of advertising and other brand building campaigns, as well as building a competitive product through several iterative product cycles. It may also be necessary to obtain regulatory approvals, depending on the products involved. There is also the prospect of engaging in a price war in order to unseat the target company from its current market share position. Here is a summary of the more likely expenditures to include in the derivation of replication value:
  - o Product development
  - o Production design and investment in new production equipment
  - o Working capital to support new product line
  - o Startup scrap and spoilage costs
  - o Branding expenditures
  - o Expenditures to set up and support a new distribution channel
  - o Cost of additional sales force or retraining of existing sales force
- *Comparison analysis.* A common form of valuation analysis is to comb through listings of acquisition transactions that have been completed over the past year or two, extract those for companies located in the same industry, and use them to estimate what a target company should be worth. The

comparison is usually based on either a multiple of revenues or cash flow. In rare instances, the analysis may be based on recurring (contract) sales. Information about comparable acquisitions can be gleaned from public filings or press releases, but more comprehensive information can be obtained by paying for access to any one of several private databases that accumulate this information.

- *Strategic purchase.* The ultimate valuation strategy from the perspective of the target company is the strategic purchase. This is when the acquirer is willing to throw out all valuation models and instead consider the strategic benefits of owning the target company. For example, an acquirer can be encouraged to believe that it needs to fill a critical hole in its product line, or to quickly enter a product niche that is considered key to its future survival, or to acquire a key piece of intellectual property. In this situation, the price paid may be far beyond the amount that any rational examination of the issues would otherwise suggest. The downside of a strategic purchase is that the buyer is more likely to dismantle the target company and fully integrate it into its own operations, on the grounds that the strategic value gained must be maximized by rolling it into the acquirer's business to the greatest extent possible.

When investors purchase stock in a business, they gain the right to dividends, any appreciation in the market price of the stock, and any final share in the proceeds if the business is sold. If an investor buys at least a 51% controlling interest in a business, then it also obtains the right to redirect the business in any way it chooses. Consequently, obtaining a controlling interest is worth an additional price, which is known as the *control premium*. Historical evidence shows that control premiums for healthy businesses can range from 30% to 75% of the market price of a company's stock.

A significant problem for the acquirer is a seller that insists upon a valuation that is based on future expectations for the business. For example, the target company may be "just a few months" away from landing a major new contract, or launching a new product, or opening up a new distribution channel. The seller may believe that these prospective changes will have immense value, while the acquirer rightfully feels that these future prospects are entirely unproven, and may never occur or generate additional cash flow. These differences of opinion can cause major differences in the assumed valuation of the business.

A solution that bridges the valuation gap between the two parties is the *earnout*. An earnout is a payment arrangement under which the shareholders of the target company are paid an additional amount if the company can achieve specific performance targets after the acquisition has been completed. It has the following advantages:

- *Payment source.* The improvements generated by the target company will likely generate sufficient cash flow to pay for all or a portion of the earnout, so the acquirer may be cash flow neutral on the additional payment.

- *Target achievement.* The shareholders of the target company will push for the completion of the performance targets, so that the acquirer pays the earnout. This helps the acquirer, too (despite having to pay the earnout), since the results of the target company will have been improved.
- *Tax deferral.* The shareholders of the target company will be paid at a later date, after the earnout is achieved, which means that the income tax related to the earnout payment is also deferred for the payment recipients.

Despite these advantages, an earnout is generally not a good idea. The trouble is that, even after purchasing it, the acquirer must leave the target company as a separate operating unit, so that the target's management group has a chance to achieve the earnout. Otherwise, there is a risk of a lawsuit in which there is a complaint that the acquirer's subsequent actions to merge it into the rest of the company impair any chance of completing the earnout conditions. It is risky for the acquirer to leave a newly acquired company alone in this manner, since doing so means that it cannot engage in any synergistic activities designed to pay for the cost of the acquisition – such as terminating duplicate positions or merging the entire business into another part of the acquirer.

Further, the management of the acquired business will be so focused on achieving the earnout that they ignore other initiatives being demanded by the acquirer – and the acquirer may not be able to fire them for insubordination until the earnout period has been completed. In short, agreeing to an earnout clause subjects the acquirer to an uncomfortable period when it cannot achieve its own goals for the target company.

Finally, it is entirely possible that a buyer will be caught up in the excitement of the chase, especially if there is a bidding war with another company, and bid too high a price for a target company. To avoid this problem, go over the valuation calculations for a target company with the board of directors before entering into final price negotiations with the seller. If the negotiated price ends up being higher than the valuation information previously given to the board, they should not authorize the deal. A variation on this approach is for the board to give approval for a deal up to a certain maximum price, above which additional approval must be given. Thus, obtaining the active involvement of the board in acquisition valuations can prevent overbidding.

Forms of Acquisition Payment

There are a number of ways to pay for an acquired business, including a stock-for-stock exchange, debt, and cash. In this section, we cover the essentials of each form of acquisition payment.

The Stock-for-Stock Exchange

In a stock-for-stock exchange, the shareholders of the selling entity swap their shares for the shares of the acquirer. A stock-for-stock exchange is useful for the seller when its shareholders do not want to recognize taxable gains in the near term.

Instead, they pay income taxes only when they sell the shares paid to them by the acquirer. They will pay taxes only on the difference between their cost basis in the stock of the acquiree and the price at which they sell the stock of the acquirer. However, this also means that shareholders will not have liquid investment positions in the short term.

In a stock-for-stock exchange, the seller shares with the acquirer the risk that the benefits of the acquisition are not realized. Thus, if the acquirer derives a purchase price based on the realization of synergy gains and those gains are not achieved, it is quite possible that the market will then force down the price of its shares. If the seller's shareholders now own some of those shares, the value of the payment to them will decline.

When the buyer is a privately-held business, the stock-for-stock exchange will probably be unpalatable to the seller, since there will be no way to sell the shares. Even if the buyer is publicly-held, the seller must ensure that the shares will be registered with the SEC for sale, and that there is a sufficient market for the acquirer's stock to ensure that the shares can be sold within a reasonable period of time. If the seller decides to proceed with the deal despite a lack of stock registration or an illiquid market for the acquirer's shares, the seller should at least impose a sharp discount on the value of the acquirer's stock in comparison to what it would have accepted in cash.

A stock-for-stock exchange is accomplished through the derivation of an *exchange ratio*. The exchange ratio is the number of shares of the acquirer that it is offering to exchange for each share of the seller. This calculation is based on the market price of the shares of the acquirer and the price offered for the seller.

EXAMPLE

The shares of Hammer Industries are currently trading at $14 per share. It is contemplating the acquisition of Chase Cutters for $4,000,000. Chase has 500,000 shares of common stock outstanding, so each share is valued at $8 per share.

Based on this information, Hammer offers an exchange ratio of 0.57143 shares of Hammer stock for each share of Chase stock. The exchange ratio calculation is:

$8 Chase share price ÷ $14 Hammer share price = 0.57143 exchange ratio

Thus, the Chase shareholders receive a total of 285,715 shares of Hammer stock. At the current trading price of $14 per share, the Hammer shares issued to the Chase shareholders are worth $4,000,000.

The derivation of the exchange ratio can be quite a contentious one when the shares of the acquirer are not publicly traded. If so, there is no market to independently value the shares, resulting in a value that is largely based on opinion.

There are two ways in which a stock-for-stock deal can be structured. They are:

- *Fixed share count.* Under this method, the exact number of shares to be paid is incorporated into the purchase agreement. This introduces some risk to the seller, in that the market value of the acquirer's shares could change in the days leading up to the purchase date. However, it also gives the seller a fixed percentage of ownership in the acquirer, irrespective of changes in the stock price.
- *Fixed price.* Under this method, the total price to be paid is incorporated into the purchase agreement. The actual payment is based on the market price of the acquirer's stock on the effective date of the agreement. This method reduces the risk to the seller that the value of the underlying shares will decline in the days leading up to the acquisition.

The problem with stock price variability and its impact on the purchase price is sometimes resolved through the use of a *collar* agreement, where the number of shares paid to the shareholders of the seller will be adjusted if the market price of the acquirer's shares trade above or below certain predetermined levels, which are usually 10-20% above and below the midpoint stock price. The collar agreement is particularly important in two situations:

- *Volatility.* Stock prices in some industries are unusually volatile, making it difficult to pin down a price to use for the exchange ratio.
- *Time to close.* If regulatory approval is required, it will lengthen the time required to close the purchase transaction. This means there is some risk that the acquirer's share price will gradually drift away from the amount at which the exchange ratio was first calculated. For these longer closing transactions, it is customary to adopt fairly wide collars.

In short, the collar agreement is useful for preserving the value of the compensation that the seller receives, at least for the time period covered by the collar agreement.

The Debt Payment

The acquirer may include debt in the structure of its deal to buy the acquiree. This can be beneficial to the seller's shareholders, since they do not pay income taxes until they receive the debt payments. Payment in debt also means that the acquirer is in a position to profit from 100% of any stock appreciation caused by the acquisition, while the seller is locked into a fixed payment plan.

The acquirer is more likely to offer debt, if only because it can then conserve its cash. The use of debt may be the only alternative when it is difficult for the acquirer to obtain credit from lenders. It is an especially useful tool when the acquirer can force the seller to accept a junior debt position behind its other lenders, thereby effectively placing the seller's shareholders in a position not much better than that of its general creditors.

The seller should not accept this form of payment unless it is very certain of the financial condition of the acquirer. Otherwise, if the acquirer were to enter bankruptcy, the seller's shareholders would simply be categorized among other creditors to be paid out of any remaining assets. Also, now that they are debt holders, rather than shareholders, they have no ability to vote for a new board of directors, and so have no control over the business that owes them money.

In short, despite the favorable tax impact of debt payments, payment in debt is the worst alternative for the seller. On the flip side of the deal, it is usually the best alternative for the acquirer. Thus, the two sides are quite likely to dicker over the presence of debt in a deal, the terms associated with the debt, and its convertibility into the acquirer's stock.

The Cash Payment

The form of payment generally preferred by shareholders is cash. It is particularly appreciated by shareholders who are unable to sell their stock by other means, which is the case for most privately-held companies. In addition, they no longer have to worry about the future performance of their company impacting the amount that they will be paid. The degree to which cash is preferred is indicated by the extent to which sellers are generally willing to accept a smaller amount of cash rather than a larger payment in stock or debt. However, a cash payment also means that the selling shareholders must pay income taxes on any gains immediately.

From the perspective of the acquirer, a cash payment presents both pluses and minuses. One advantage is that, in a competitive bidding situation, the bid of the buyer willing to pay cash is more likely to be accepted by the seller. Also, not paying in stock means that any future upside performance generated by the acquisition accrues solely to the existing shareholders of the acquirer – the shareholders of the acquiree are taking cash instead, so they are blocked from the gains.

The main disadvantage of paying with cash is the availability of cash to the acquirer. If the purchase will use up the bulk of its cash on hand, and the borrowing environment is difficult, the acquirer could place itself in a tenuous financial position. However, using cash places greater financial discipline on an acquirer, who may therefore be more prudent in setting an offer price than a company that is willing to pay with vast amounts of stock.

Summary

When negotiating a deal structure, the two parties must take into account their respective financial positions, expectations for future gains, and tax requirements. The following table shows the respective issues of both parties.

Deal Structure	Acquirer	Acquiree
Stock	• Shares future stock gains • Preserves cash	• No immediate liquidity • Defers income taxes
Debt	• Takes all future stock gains • Preserves cash • Accepts liens on some assets	• No share of future stock gains • At risk of non-payment • Defers income taxes
Cash	• Takes all future stock gains • More likely to win in bidding war • At risk of not having sufficient cash • Requires more discipline	• Gains liquidity • No share of future stock gains • Immediate tax liability

However, if there is only one possible buyer, and that buyer is having trouble obtaining financing for the deal, then all of the various permutations just noted do not factor into the deal structure. Instead, the acquirer simply assembles the only available funding package and presents it to the seller for approval; there is no negotiation of structure, for the acquirer cannot negotiate. Instead, the seller is faced with a binary solution – to either accept or reject the deal as offered.

The Acquisition Legal Structure

There are a number of legal structures available for combining the businesses of the acquirer and the acquiree. The structure chosen will have a direct impact on whether the income tax on the seller's gain can be deferred, on the ability of the acquirer to avoid liabilities, on the types of payment made, and several other factors. Consequently, both parties must be cognizant of the advantages and shortfalls of the legal structure they select. This section discusses the merits and failings of the most common legal structures for an acquisition.

Tax Issues

The seller wants to delay the taxation of any gains it may realize through an acquisition transaction. Delaying taxes has value, since income taxes paid in the future have a smaller present value than taxes paid now. The tax treatments of the various forms of compensation are as follows:

- *Stock-for-stock.* In a stock-for-stock exchange, income taxes are deferred until such time as the recipient of the stock of the acquirer sells that stock (which could be years in the future).
- *Cash.* A cash payment requires the immediate recognition of income taxes.
- *Debt.* Debt payments are taxable when received. Thus, there is a tax deferral aspect to this type of payment.
- *Other consideration.* If some other form of consideration is paid, the recipient is likely to owe income taxes at once if the recipient realizes a gain

on the difference between the value of the consideration received and the cost basis of the stock given up.

If the consideration received in an acquisition is a combination of the preceding elements, then some elements will be taxable and others will have deferred taxation.

Tax issues have a much smaller impact on the acquirer than the acquiree. Nonetheless, the acquirer should certainly be aware of the following issues:

- *Asset step up*. The acquirer wants to step up the recorded value of any assets it acquires to their fair market values, which allows it to use a higher level of depreciation expense to shield more profits from taxation. This is allowable in a taxable transaction, and not allowed in a tax-free transaction. However, if the fair market value of acquired assets is *less than* their net book values, the acquirer has no opportunity to engage in a step up transaction.
- *Net operating loss carry forwards*. The acquirer can gain access to unused net operating losses (NOLs) incurred by the seller, which the acquirer can use to shield the profits of the acquiree. However, these losses can only be recognized over lengthy periods, and so do not play a major role in the acquisition decision or how it is structured. Ultimately, an acquisition should be based primarily on other factors than the use of an NOL.

Issues with Stock Purchases

Buying shares means that the acquirer will then own the seller's business entity, rather than just its assets. This has the following ramifications:

- *Contracts*. Since the seller's business is presumably going to continue in operation as a subsidiary of the acquirer, the acquirer also obtains both the customer and supplier contracts of the seller. This can be useful if the seller has a large backlog of customer orders. However, some business partners include a "change of control" clause in their contracts, under which they have the option to terminate a contract if there is a change of control of the business. This does not necessarily mean that those business partners will terminate the contracts, but the acquirer will probably have to negotiate new contracts.
- *Liabilities*. The downside of purchasing an entire business is that the acquirer is now responsible for all of its liabilities, even those that are not documented. It may have the right to obtain reimbursement from the seller for undocumented liabilities, but nonetheless, this presents a risk to the acquirer.
- *Net operating loss carry forwards*. Since a stock purchase shifts ownership of the seller entity to the acquirer, the acquirer also gains any NOLs owned by the seller.
- *Goodwill amortization*. When the acquirer buys the stock of the seller, it cannot amortize any goodwill associated with the transaction for tax purpos-

es. Since goodwill can comprise a large part of the amount paid, this can substantially increase the amount of income taxes that the acquirer pays.

Gain Recognition Avoidance Rules

The Internal Revenue Service (IRS) stipulates in its Internal Revenue Code a number of acquisition structures that can allow the deferral of gain recognition. A proposed transaction must incorporate all three of the following concepts into an IRS-approved acquisition structure before gain deferral will be allowed:

- *Bona fide purpose.* The proposed transaction must have a genuine business purpose other than the deferral or complete avoidance of taxes.
- *Continuity of business enterprise.* The acquirer must continue to operate the acquired entity, or at least use a large proportion of the acquired assets in a business.
- *Continuity of interest.* The shareholders of an acquired business must receive a sufficient amount of stock in the acquiring entity (generally considered to be at least 50% of the purchase price) to have a continuing financial interest in it.

Type "A" Acquisition

An acquisition transaction can be designed to follow the IRS guidelines for a Type "A" acquisition. This acquisition has the following characteristics, and must also comply with the IRS gain recognition avoidance rules:

- At least 50% of the payment must be in the stock of the acquirer
- The selling entity is liquidated
- The acquirer acquires all assets and liabilities of the seller
- It must be approved by the boards of directors of both entities, plus the shareholders of the selling entity

This transaction type is among the more flexible alternatives available, since it allows for a mix of payment types. It also allows selling shareholders to defer the recognition of income taxes related to those shares exchanged for acquirer stock. However, shareholders must recognize income on all non-equity payments made to them. Also, because the acquired entity is liquidated, this terminates any acquiree contracts that had not yet expired, which could cause problems for the acquirer.

The Type "A" acquisition is most useful in situations where the seller wants to receive a mix of cash and stock from the acquirer, which allows it to defer a portion of the related taxable income. Acquirers tend to be less enamored of this approach, since they run the risk of losing any contracts held by the acquired entity when it is liquidated.

Type "B" Acquisition

An acquisition transaction can be designed to follow the IRS guidelines for a Type "B" acquisition. This acquisition has the following characteristics, and must also comply with the IRS gain recognition avoidance rules:

- Cash cannot exceed 20% of the total consideration
- At least 80% of the acquiree's stock must be acquired with the acquirer's voting stock
- The acquirer must buy at least 80% of the acquiree's outstanding stock
- Acquiree shareholders cannot be given the option of being paid in cash instead of stock, if the result could potentially be that less than 80% of the acquiree's stock is acquired with the acquirer's voting stock; even having this option available disallows the use of the Type "B" acquisition
- The selling entity becomes a subsidiary of the acquirer
- It must be approved by the boards of directors of both entities, plus the shareholders of the selling entity

The Type "B" acquisition is most useful when the seller needs to keep operating the seller's business and its contracts. However, it forces the seller to accept nearly all acquirer stock in payment for the acquisition.

Type "C" Acquisition

An acquisition transaction can be designed to follow the IRS guidelines for a Type "C" acquisition. This acquisition has the following characteristics, and must also comply with the IRS gain recognition avoidance rules:

- The acquirer must buy at least 80% of the fair market value of the acquiree's assets
- The acquirer can use cash only if it uses its voting stock to buy at least 80% of the fair market value of the acquiree's assets
- The selling entity must be liquidated
- The acquirer may not have to gain the approval of its shareholders for the transaction, since this is an asset purchase. The acquired entity must gain the approval of its shareholders for the transaction.

A problem with the Type "C" acquisition is that dissenting shareholders can demand that their shares be appraised and paid for in cash. If the resulting cash payments are more than 20% of the total compensation paid, this violates the Type "C" requirements and invalidates its use as a tax-deferral method for those shareholders receiving stock.

The Type "C" acquisition is most useful when the acquirer wants to treat the transaction as an asset purchase, and the seller wants to be paid primarily in stock in order to defer the recognition of income taxes.

Triangular Merger

In a triangular merger, the acquirer creates a wholly-owned subsidiary, which in turn merges with the selling entity. The selling entity then liquidates. The acquirer is the sole remaining shareholder of the subsidiary. The characteristics of the transaction are the same as those for a Type "A" acquisition, which are:

- At least 50% of the payment must be in the stock of the acquirer
- The selling entity is liquidated
- The acquirer acquires all assets and liabilities of the seller
- It must be approved by the boards of directors of both entities

This is a merger transaction, rather than the acquisition format presented for the earlier legal structures. In a merger, all shareholders are required to accept the price offered by the acquirer, if the seller's board of directors approves the deal. This alternative avoids the risk of having dissenting shareholders.

Reverse Triangular Merger

A reverse triangular merger is the same as a triangular merger, except that the subsidiary created by the acquirer merges into the selling entity and then liquidates, leaving the selling entity as the surviving entity, and a subsidiary of the acquirer. Its characteristics are:

- At least 50% of the payment must be in the stock of the acquirer
- The subsidiary created by the acquirer is liquidated
- The acquirer acquires all assets and liabilities of the seller
- It must be approved by the boards of directors of both entities

The reverse triangular merger is used much more frequently than the triangular merger, because the reverse version retains the seller entity, along with any business contracts it may have. It is also useful when there are a large number of shareholders and it is too difficult to acquire their shares through a Type "A" acquisition.

Asset Purchase

The preceding legal structures were based on the assumption that the acquirer wants to control the business entity of the seller. What if that is not the case, and the acquirer only wants to purchase the assets of the seller? Doing so has the following ramifications:

- *Contracts*. If the acquirer only buys the assets of the seller, it is not acquiring any contracts with the business partners of the seller.
- *Liabilities*. An asset acquisition actually means that the acquirer buys only those assets *and liabilities* specifically stated in the purchase agreement. It will not include undocumented or contingent liabilities; this is the main reason for an asset acquisition.

- *Asset step-up*. The acquirer records any assets acquired at their fair market values, and depreciates these (presumably) stepped-up values for tax purposes. In addition, the acquirer can amortize any goodwill associated with the acquisition for tax purposes.
- *Net operating loss carry forwards*. Since the acquirer is not purchasing the seller's business entity, it does not obtain the NOLs associated with that entity.

Tip: If an acquirer elects to purchase the assets of an acquiree, this means that it must obtain the title to each individual asset that it purchases – which can involve a substantial amount of legal work if there are many fixed assets. Also, it may be necessary to have liens removed from the acquired assets, which may call for negotiations with the creditors of the acquiree.

It may not be possible to disassociate the liability for environmental cleanup from an asset purchase. In some situations, environmental regulations state that the cost of future hazardous waste remediation can attach to assets, as well as legal entities. Consequently, if the acquirer is planning to buy real estate as part of an asset purchase, it should engage in significant due diligence for environmental problems.

In summary, an acquirer may insist on an asset acquisition if it believes that the risk of acquiring additional liabilities is too great. It may also be a useful method if the acquirer only wants to pluck a specific "crown jewel" asset out of the seller, such as a key patent.

Summary

There are many types of legal structures available to the buyer and seller, each offering a different mix of features. The legal structure selected will be the result of negotiations between the parties, and perhaps an alteration of the mix and amount of compensation paid in order to match the structure selected. The party that stands to gain the most from a particular legal structure is the seller, which can defer taxes on the sale. The acquirer has less need to engage in a specific legal structure, but may be able to enforce its requirements on the seller if there is no other bidder or if the seller is in difficult financial circumstances.

Acquisition Integration

Once the acquirer has decided to buy a company and its offer has been accepted, the next step is to integrate the two organizations. This can be a difficult process, for the acquirer needs to enact all of the synergies that it already identified in order to make the acquisition a financial success. Depending upon the extent of the synergies, this may result in a considerable amount of upheaval within the acquired business, though proper management of the integration team can mitigate problems to some degree. In this section, we discuss a variety of integration topics.

General Integration Concepts

When a company has just been acquired, the productivity of its employees will nosedive, and is not likely to recover until the integration process has been completed. In addition, any employee interested in self-preservation is likely to test the employment market; the departure of multiple employees is likely, if not certain. The acquirer can mitigate both issues by integrating quickly and keeping employees fully informed regarding integration efforts.

The integration process must begin the moment the purchase has been completed, and should progress as hard and fast as possible. By doing so, the integration team has a better chance of completing its integration goals and achieving the synergies needed to make the acquisition a financial and operational success. The longer the integration takes, the more likely it is that the simple passage of time, combined with resistance from the acquiree's employees, will eventually halt the integration effort before all of its goals have been achieved.

There is no point in hiding any layoffs from employees. If the integration effort goes as fast as it should, everyone will know about the layoffs within a few weeks or months – so tell them as soon as the integration team has decided which positions are redundant. If subsequent events alter the integration plans, then keep employees apprised of the changes as soon as there is some certainty concerning future actions.

Function-Specific Integration Issues

There are a multitude of areas in an acquired business that may require integration work – and sometimes in the acquirer, too. The following bullet points touch upon the more critical integration issues to be aware of, by functional area or special topic:

- *Accounting.* If the acquirer elects to fully integrate the accounting area, this involves the development of a common chart of accounts, notifying suppliers that they should send invoices to a central processing facility, shifting bank accounts to the acquirer's bank, installing a company-standard set of policies and procedures, verifying that controls are adequate, switching to a single accounting software package, and adopting a common payroll period for all employees. There are a multitude of smaller issues beneath the general ones noted here, which can result in a full-year conversion process.
- *Customer service.* There are some integration opportunities in customer service, but only if the underlying products are approximately the same. For example, the acquirer may sell high-end products that are supported by intensive field service operations, while the acquiree sells low-end products that are simply replaced if they break. In such a situation, there is little room for integration. Possible opportunities are to combine inbound call centers and field service systems.
- *Employees.* A massive issue is to decide which employees work in which positions. This involves the evaluation of key employees, developing proper relations with those employees who are opinion leaders, relocating employ-

ees as necessary, developing retention plans, and terminating those whose services are no longer needed.

- *Human resources.* The control over benefit expenses resides in the human resources area. The benefits of both companies must be compared to determine which benefits are to be retained or altered. Alternatively, it may be necessary to retain different benefit plans in different parts of the company, depending on local cost structures and the needs of the local employees. Changes to employee manuals may also be required.
- *Information technology.* There can be a number of opportunities for improvement in consolidating IT systems. However, many acquirers only treat them as opportunities, and never take the time to actually complete any of the more in-depth synergy projects. This is caused by the great difficulty of standardizing on the same technology platforms, which is not only expensive, but may also require several years to complete. Nonetheless, the results can be rewarding, so the acquirer should at least consider the option of centralizing IT facilities, standardizing on certain software packages, eliminating legacy systems, and standardizing on a small number of approved types of computer hardware.
- *Marketing.* Marketing is sometimes ignored by acquirers, on the grounds that its activities are so specific that they cannot be easily aggregated at the parent company level to reduce costs. This is not entirely the case, since advertising spending can be consolidated to gain volume discounts, some product lines can be combined for advertising purposes, and trade show attendance can be combined, along with other efficiencies.
- *Materials management.* Depending upon the level of integration that the acquirer wants to achieve, the integration team may find itself completely ignoring the materials management function, or engaging in a massive systems replacement and upgrade. The latter is usually the case if the acquirer believes that it can achieve a major reduction in the inventory investment of the acquiree. If so, possible improvements include combining distribution systems and consolidating purchases.
- *Production.* It can be difficult to successfully engage in any integration activities in the production area, for an acquiree's production facilities are designed specifically for the manufacture of its own products; thus, moving production elsewhere is not always an option, at least in the short-term. Nonetheless, the integration team might review production facilities to see if throughput can be maximized, reconfigure fixed asset usage, outsource some production, and/or use a different production flow system (such as the just-in-time methodology).
- *Risk management.* It may be worthwhile to extend the better hedging strategies and insurance programs of one company to the other, so that both entities benefit from better risk management.
- *Selling.* The typical company targets a very specific slice of the market, and trains its sales force to deal with that niche. If the two sales departments have different training, deal with different customers, and use different sell-

ing strategies, then combining them may fail. If it still seems reasonable to attempt some integration, then consider cross-training the sales staffs on the products of both companies, reconfiguring sales territories, and targeting new customers who may be more willing to deal with the newly combined company.

- *Treasury*. Consider installing a comprehensive cash centralization system that encompasses the acquiree's bank accounts, so that cash can be centrally invested at optimal interest rates. A major factor can be the shift to new bank accounts, which is a time-consuming process.

Integration for the Serial Acquirer

The strategies of some businesses are built around the ongoing acquisition and integration of other businesses. If so, they likely have full-time integration teams who move from one acquisition to the next. These teams have developed a standard set of integration topics to address, which are based on their experience with similar acquirees in the same industry. Assuming that most acquirees are roughly similar, this means that the teams have a good idea not only of what issues they will find, but also which synergies will work, and how long it will take to complete the bulk of the integration work.

A well-managed serial acquirer realizes that it can only acquire companies at a certain pace, because its integration teams are only able to complete *their* integration activities at a certain pace. If the acquirer were to buy companies at an excessively fast pace, the most recent acquisitions would receive little management attention until an integration team became available; this means that no synergies or other integration activities would be completed in the meantime. From the perspective of an outside observer, this pacing issue should highlight those businesses acquiring at a torrid pace, for they are unlikely to achieve outsized profits from their acquisition activities. If anything, the sheer weight of the problems introduced by their undigested acquisitions may bring them down over the long term.

Acquisitions are, by their nature, unpredictable – one cannot determine exactly when a purchase will be completed, or if it will fall through. Thus, it is impossible to have a perfectly-timed series of acquisitions to which integration teams can be neatly assigned. Given this issue, it is better to schedule excess "free" time for integration teams than to over-schedule them. Doing so gives them more time to tie up loose ends on their current projects before moving to the next one.

Summary

The acquisition integration process is a difficult one, which calls for the services of a full-time, committed integration team that works on-site for as long as it takes to achieve the primary integration goals. It is of great importance for this group to complete its tasks as rapidly as possible, while communicating its changes to all and sundry. However, the team should not leave behind an outraged workforce; it requires great delicacy to negotiate through the maze of local relationships and viewpoints to make changes function properly.

Acquisition integration always meets with some degree of resistance. The manager of the integration team needs to determine the extent to which he is willing to modify the integration plan to mitigate resistance. However, it never makes sense to alter the plan to a massive extent (thereby foregoing valuable synergies) in order to please everyone. Instead, the manager needs to understand that there will be a disaffected minority who *cannot* be placated unless the bulk of the integration efforts are abandoned. Thus, there is a continuum of trade-offs, with the achievement of all integration objectives at one end and a happy workforce at the other. The integration manager needs to select a spot on that continuum that represents a reasonable tradeoff between the two extremes.

Summary

A CFO will likely engage in acquisitions at some point, either for an occasional purchase or as part of an ongoing program that routinely targets a certain number of deals per year. In either case, the CFO will likely be deeply involved in the inspection of each prospective purchase, negotiating a reasonable price, structuring deals, and ensuring that each acquired entity is integrated with a minimum of fuss. Even the most skilled CFO will periodically be involved in a failed acquisition for which the invested funds must be written off. Whenever these failures occur, determine the underlying problems and treat them as a learning experience for the acquisition team. In many cases, the causes of failure could have been foreseen prior to closing a deal, and probably relate to issues in the areas of overpayment, acquiring outside of the company's core strategy, and/or conflicts with personnel at the acquired business. The inevitable result of these failures will be a heightened sense of caution when reviewing target companies, probably yielding a reduced number of purchase offers.

The key point to take away from this chapter is that all target companies have problems – the key to success is identifying the issues and making a reasoned judgment regarding whether the problems can be mitigated or eliminated. If not, the CFO must advocate walking away from a deal.

Chapter 7
Budgeting and Forecasting

Introduction

The corporate budget is one of the principal documents used by a CFO to gain an understanding of where a company is supposed to go, and how to get there. However, the budget has also fallen into some disrepute, since it can lead to a variety of negative outcomes, and can diverge so wildly from actual results that it is essentially ignored. In this chapter, we explore the advantages and disadvantages of budgeting, the main elements of a budget (if the decision is made to construct one) and how to operate without a budget. We also describe the concept of a rolling forecast, which can take the place of a budget.

For a detailed discussion of budgeting and its alternatives, consider the author's *Budgeting: A Comprehensive Guide*. The book shows how to construct a budget, and presents several alternative budgeting methods, including flexible budgeting and the zero-base budget.

Related Podcast Episodes: Episodes 71, 76, 130, 131, and 144-145 of the Accounting Best Practices Podcast discuss budget model improvements, budgeting controls, problems with budgeting, operating without a budget, and capital budgeting, respectively. They are available at: **accountingtools.com/podcasts** or **iTunes**

The Advantages of Budgeting

Budgeting has been with us a long time, and is used by nearly every large company. They would not do so if there were not some perceived advantages to budgeting. These advantages include:

- *Planning orientation.* The process of creating a budget takes management away from its short-term, day-to-day management of a business and forces it to think longer-term. This is the chief goal of budgeting, even if management does not succeed in meeting its goals as outlined in the budget - at least it is thinking about the company's competitive and financial position and how to improve it.
- *Model scenarios.* If a company is faced with a number of possible paths down which it can travel, one can create a set of budgets, each based on different scenarios, to estimate the financial results of each strategic direction.
- *Profitability review.* It is easy to lose sight of where a company is making most of its money, during the scramble of day-to-day management. A

properly structured budget points out which aspects of a business generate cash and which ones use it, which forces management to consider whether it should drop some parts of the business or expand in others. However, this advantage only applies to a budget sufficiently detailed to describe profits at the product, product line, or business unit level.

- *Assumptions review.* The budgeting process forces management to think about why the company is in business, as well as its key assumptions about its business environment. A periodic re-evaluation of these issues may result in altered assumptions, which may in turn alter the way in which management decides to operate the business.
- *Performance evaluations.* Senior management can tie bonuses or other incentives to how employees perform in comparison to the budget. The accounting department then creates budget versus actual reports to give employees feedback regarding how they are progressing toward their goals. This approach is most common with financial goals, though operational goals (such as reducing the scrap rate) can also be added. We will address a countervailing argument in the Command and Control System section later in this chapter.
- *Predict cash flows.* Companies that are growing rapidly, have seasonal sales, or which have irregular sales patterns have a difficult time estimating how much cash they are likely to require in the near term, which results in periodic cash-related crises. A budget is useful for predicting cash flows in the short term, but yields increasingly unreliable results further into the future.
- *Cash allocation.* There is only a limited amount of cash available to invest in fixed assets and working capital, and the budgeting process forces management to decide which assets are most worth investing in.
- *Cost reduction analysis.* A company that has a strong system in place for continual cost reduction can use a budget to designate cost reduction targets that it wishes to pursue.
- *Shareholder communications.* Large investors may want a benchmark against which they can measure the company's progress. Even if a company chooses not to lend much credence to its own budget, it may still be valuable to construct a conservative budget to share with investors. The same argument holds true for lenders, who may want to see a budget versus actual results comparison from time to time.

These advantages may appear to be persuasive ones, and indeed have been sufficient for most companies to implement budgeting processes. However, there are also serious problems with budgets that we will outline in the following sections.

The Disadvantages of Budgeting

There are a number of serious disadvantages associated with budgeting. This section gives an overview of the general issues, while the following sections address the particular problems associated with capital budgeting, as well as the use of budgets within a command and control management system. The disadvantages of budgeting include:

- *Inaccuracy*. A budget is based on a set of assumptions that are generally not too far distant from the operating conditions under which it was formulated. If the business environment changes to any significant degree, then the company's revenues or cost structure may change so radically that actual results will rapidly depart from the expectations delineated in the budget. This condition is a particular problem when there is a sudden economic downturn, since the budget authorizes a certain level of spending that is no longer supportable under a suddenly reduced revenue level. Unless management acts quickly to override the budget, managers will continue to spend under their original budgetary authorizations, thereby rupturing any possibility of earning a profit. Other conditions that can also cause results to vary suddenly from budgeted expectations include changes in interest rates, currency exchange rates, and commodity prices.

- *Rigid decision making*. The budgeting process only focuses the attention of the management team on strategy during the budget formulation period near the end of the fiscal year. For the rest of the year, there is no procedural commitment to revisit strategy. Thus, if there is a fundamental shift in the market just after a budget has been completed, there is no system in place to formally review the situation and make changes, thereby placing a company at a considerable disadvantage to its more nimble competitors.

- *Time required*. It can be very time-consuming to create a budget, especially in a poorly-organized environment where many iterations of the budget may be required. The time involved is lower if there is a well-designed budgeting procedure in place, employees are accustomed to the process, and the company uses budgeting software. The work required can be more extensive if business conditions are constantly changing, which calls for repeated iterations of the budget model.

- *Gaming the system*. An experienced manager may attempt to introduce budgetary slack, which involves deliberately reducing revenue estimates and increasing expense estimates, so that he can easily achieve favorable variances against the budget. This can be a serious problem, and requires considerable oversight to spot and eliminate.

- *Blame for outcomes*. If a department does not achieve its budgeted results, the department manager may blame any other departments that provide services to it for not having adequately supported his department.

- *Expense allocations*. The budget may prescribe that certain amounts of overhead costs be allocated to various departments, and the managers of those departments may take issue with the allocation methods used. This is a particular problem when departments are not allowed to substitute services provided from within the company for lower-cost services that are available elsewhere.

- *Use it or lose it.* If a department is allowed a certain amount of expenditures and it does not appear that the department will spend all of the funds during the budget period, the department manager may authorize excessive expenditures at the last minute, on the grounds that his budget will be reduced in the next period unless he spends all of the authorized amounts. Thus, a budget tends to make managers believe that they are entitled to a certain amount of funding each year, irrespective of their actual need for the funds.
- *Only considers financial outcomes.* The nature of the budget is numeric, so it tends to focus management attention on the quantitative aspects of a business; this usually means an intent focus on improving or maintaining profitability. In reality, customers do not care about the profits of a business – they will only buy from the company as long as they are receiving good service and well-constructed products at a fair price. Unfortunately, it is quite difficult to build these concepts into a budget, since they are qualitative in nature. Thus, the budgeting concept does not necessarily support the needs of customers.

The disadvantages noted here are widely prevalent and difficult to overcome. Unfortunately, we have not yet presented all of the problems with budgeting. There are additional issues with capital budgeting, as well as the use of budgeting within the command and control style of management. We describe these problems in the next two sections.

Capital Budgeting Problems

The traditional budgeting system has an especially pernicious impact on capital budgeting. Under capital budgeting, managers apply for funding for whichever fixed assets they feel are needed in their areas of responsibility. A significant amount of detailed analysis is needed for these requests, since the amount of funding requested can be quite large. The problem is that the budgeting timeline forces most capital budgeting requests to be submitted within a short time period each year, after which additional funds are only grudgingly issued. In effect, this means that the corporate "bank" is only open for business for a month or two every year! Thus, someone may spot an excellent business opportunity for the company, but not be able to take advantage of it for many months, when the "bank" is again open for business. This can be a massive impediment to the continuing growth of a business.

Given the "bank" issue just noted, managers fight hard for the maximum amount of funding as soon as the "bank" opens – and they spend *all* of it. In addition, many managers receive their annual allocation of capital expenditure funds and then push for *more* funds throughout the budget year for additional projects. In short, the capital budgeting process really creates a *minimum* funding level, above which a company is very likely to go as the year progresses. It is a rare company that only spends what it initially budgets for fixed assets.

In summary, the budgeting process creates two capital budgeting problems. First, it is unusually difficult to obtain funds outside of the budget period, even for deserving projects. And second, managers tend to game the system, so that the capital budgeting process nearly always ends up absorbing more funds than senior management originally intended.

The Command and Control System

The single most fundamental problem underlying the entire concept of a budget is that it is designed to control a company from the top. The basic underpinning of the system is that senior management forces managers throughout the company to agree to a specific outcome (that portion of the budget for which they are responsible), which senior management then monitors to control the activities of the managers. This agreement is usually a formal agreement under which each manager commits to achieve a fixed target in exchange for receiving a bonus. Examples of target commitments are:

- A revenue target, which may be defined for a specific product, product line, or geographic region.
- An expense target, which may be a single block expense for an entire department or expenditures for individual line items.
- A profit target, which a manager may achieve by any combination of revenue increases or expense reductions.
- A cash flow target, such as producing a specific amount of net positive cash flow.
- A metrics target, such as return on assets or return on equity.

These targets may be combined to further control the actions of managers. For example, there may be a combination geographic revenue target and profit target, so that a manager is forced to commit resources to sales in a new sales region while still maintaining overall profitability. When there are many targets to achieve, managers find that their actions are entirely constrained by the budget – there is no time or spare funding for any other activities. Thus, the combination of the budget and a bonus system create an extremely tight command and control system.

Formal performance agreements are the source of an enormous amount of inefficiency within a company, and can also reduce employee loyalty to the company. They require a great deal of time to initially negotiate, and may be altered over time as changing conditions give managers various excuses to complain about their agreements. Further, if the recipient of a bonus agreement misses out on a substantial bonus, how does he feel about the company? He may complain bitterly that the bonus system was rigged against him, and leave to work for a competitor.

In short, when budgeting is used within a command and control management system it imposes a rigid straightjacket on the actions of any managers who want to earn their designated bonuses. This level of rigidity makes it particularly difficult for a company to react quickly to changes in its competitive environment, since managers are constrained by their performance plans from proceeding in new directions.

Behavioral Impacts

The command and control nature of the budget results in an immediate behavioral change in the management team before the budget has even been completed, because managers understand that they can influence their bonus plans in advance by negotiating the amount of improvement that they will be required to achieve. This calls for fierce protection of their existing funding levels, as well as committing to the lowest possible improvement levels in their areas of responsibility. They will have an excellent chance to earn maximum bonuses, because their performance commitments under the budget are so minimal. In short, the concept of the budget forces managers to fight for *minimal* improvements.

The marketplace may change with alacrity, so that a manager struggling to meet his budgeted targets must also somehow meet competitive pressures by altering products and services, changing price points, opening and closing locations, cutting costs, and so forth. This means that a manager is faced with the choice of either earning a bonus (or a promotion) by meeting his budget, or of improving the company's competitive position. A manager's willingness to work in the best interests of a company's competitive position is further hampered by the sheer bureaucratic oppressiveness of the budgeting system, where a manager has to obtain multiple approvals to achieve a reorientation of funding. It is simply easier to not deviate from the budget. Therefore, the budget priority wins out and a company finds that its competitive position has declined specifically because of a tight focus on achieving its budget.

The pressure to meet a budgeted target can cause managers to engage in unethical accounting and business practices in order to control their reported results. Examples of such practices are:

- Recording revenue that was shipped after the month-end deadline
- Using a discount offer to stuff sales into a sales channel during a bonus period
- Overbilling customers
- Not entering supplier invoices in the accounting system during a bonus period
- Taking unwarranted discounts from supplier invoices
- Firing employees and using contractors to avoid headcount targets

Unethical behavior is a poison that can spread through an organization rapidly; unsullied managers may leave, while the remainder engages in increasingly egregious behavior to meet their performance commitments.

There are other actions caused by the budget that are not precisely unethical, but which result in behavior by managers that does not properly support the company. Here are several examples:

- *Expenditure deferral.* When the amount of budgeted funds is running low, managers delay spending any more money until the next budget year. But what if they need funds right now to meet a golden business opportunity, or to avoid a much larger expense later? They still defer the expenditure in order to remain within their budgeted expense goals and earn their bonuses, even though the expenditure should be made right now from the perspective of the entire business.

- *Bloated budget requests.* Managers request more funding than they actually need, so that any future expense cuts will still allow them to run their departments, as well as more easily meet their performance targets.

Bureaucratic Support

Once the budget and bonus plan system takes root within a company, a bureaucracy develops around it that has a natural tendency to support the status quo. Here are several such areas:

- *Human resources.* Bonus agreements may include specific budget-based goals, due dates, and resources to be allocated; this can be one of the largest tasks of the human resources department.
- *Accounting.* The accounting staff routinely loads the budget into its accounting software, so that all income statements it issues contain a comparison of budgeted to actual results. Thus, the accounting staff incorporates the budget into its system of reports.
- *Analysts.* The budget may be used as a baseline for cost controls, where financial analysts investigate why costs are higher or lower than the budgeted amounts. These analysts report to the CFO, who will therefore want to retain the budget in order to keep tight control over costs.
- *Investment community.* If a company is publicly held, the investor relations officer or CFO may routinely issue press releases, stating how the company performed in comparison to its budget. The investment community may rely on this information to estimate a share price for the company's stock, and will want the same information to be reported to it in the future.

Consequently, there are many constituencies, both inside and outside of a company, that have a vested interest in retaining the budget and bonus plan system.

Information Sharing

A related issue in a command and control environment is that senior management has a propensity to only release financial information pertinent to the operations of each manager. This means that there is a great deal of information available at the top of the organization, but very little at the bottom. In addition, managers have a tendency to massage information as they pass it down to their subordinates. The result is a paltry amount of actionable information in the hands of front line employees.

We can only presume that managers engage in this information filtering because they assume that employees below them in the corporate hierarchy are not capable of making their own decisions. Instead, the system is designed to hoard information with those people authorized to make decisions. Therefore, by default, those people receiving a *minimum* amount of information are *not* authorized to make decisions.

This type of restricted information sharing has a profound impact on the budget, because most employees never know what their budgets are, or how they are performing in relation to the budget. Since there is no knowledge of the budget, there can be no acceptance of it by employees, and therefore little chance that it will be achieved.

The System of Budgets

After having perused the preceding discussions of budgeting advantages and disadvantages, one may conclude that having a budget is still useful. If so, read this section to gain an understanding of the components of a typical corporate budget. For a detailed analysis of how each budgeting component is derived, see the author's *Budgeting* book.

The key driver of any budget is the amount of revenue that is expected during the budget period. Revenue is usually compiled in a separate revenue budget. The information in this budget is derived from estimates of which products or services will sell, and the prices at which they can be sold. Forecasted revenue for this budget cannot be derived just from the sales staff, since this would limit the information to the extrapolation of historical sales figures into the future. The chief executive officer provides additional strategic information, while the marketing manager addresses new-product introductions and the purchasing staff provides input on the availability of raw materials that may restrict sales. Thus, a group effort from many parts of a company is needed to create the revenue budget.

Once the revenue budget is in place, a number of additional budgets are derived from it that relate to the production capabilities of the company. The following components are included in this cluster of budgets:

- *Ending inventory budget*. As its name implies, this budget sets the inventory level as of the end of each accounting period listed in the budget. Management uses this budget to force changes in the inventory level, which is usually driven by a policy to have more or less finished goods inventory on hand. Having more inventory presumably improves the speed with which a company can ship goods to customers, at the cost of an increased investment in working capital. A forced reduction in inventory may delay some shipments to customers due to stockout conditions, but requires less working capital to maintain. The ending inventory budget is used as an input to the production budget.
- *Production budget*. This budget shows expected production at an aggregated level. The production budget is based primarily on the sales estimates in the revenue budget, but it must also take into consideration existing inventory levels and the desired amount of ending inventory, as stated in the ending inventory budget. If management wants to increase inventory levels in order to provide more rapid shipments to customers, the required increase in production may trigger a need for more production equipment and direct labor

138

staff. The production budget is needed to derive the direct labor budget, manufacturing overhead budget, and direct materials budget.

- *Direct labor budget.* This budget calculates the amount of direct labor staffing expected during the budget period, based on the production levels itemized in the production budget. This information can only be generally estimated, given the vagaries of short-term changes in actual production scheduling. However, direct labor usually involves specific staffing levels to crew production lines, so the estimated amount of direct labor should not vary excessively over time, within certain production volume parameters. This budget should incorporate any planned changes in the cost of labor, which may be easy to do if there is a union contract that specifies pay increases as of specific dates. This budget provides rough estimates of the number of employees needed, and is of particular interest to the human resources staff in developing hiring plans. It is a key source document for the cost of goods sold budget.

- *Manufacturing overhead budget.* This budget includes all of the overhead costs expected to be incurred in the manufacturing area during the budget period. It is usually based on historical cost information, but can be adjusted for step cost situations, where a change in the structure or capacity level of a production facility strips away or adds large amounts of expenses at one time. Even if there are no changes in structure or capacity, the manufacturing overhead budget may change somewhat in the maintenance cost area if management plans to alter these expenditures as machines age or are replaced. It is particularly important to adjust this budget if management contemplates running a production facility at close to 100% utilization, since doing so requires a large incremental increase in many types of expenditures. This budget is a source document for the cost of goods sold budget.

- *Direct materials budget.* This budget is derived from a combination of the manufacturing unit totals in the production budget and the bills of material for those units, and is used in the cost of goods sold budget. The bills of material must be accurate if this budget is to be remotely accurate. If a company produces a large variety of products, this can become an excessively detailed and burdensome budget to create and maintain. Consequently, it is customary to estimate material costs in aggregate, such as at the product line level. It may also be necessary to state expected scrap and spoilage levels in this budget, especially if management plans to improve its production practices to reduce scrap and spoilage below their historical levels.

- *Cost of goods sold budget.* This budget contains a summarization of the expenses detailed in the direct material budget, manufacturing overhead budget, and direct materials budget. This budget usually contains such additional information as line items for revenue, the gross margin, and key production statistics. It is heavily used during budget iterations, since management can consult it to view the impact of various assumptions on gross margins and other aspects of the production process.

Once the revenue and production-related budgets have been completed, there are still several other budgets to assemble that relate to other functions of the company. They are:

- *Sales and marketing budget.* This budget is comprised of the compensation of the sales and marketing staff, sales travel costs, and expenditures related to various marketing programs. It is closely linked to the revenue budget, since the number of sales staff (in some industries) is the prime determinant of additional sales. Further, marketing campaigns can impact the timing of the sales shown in the revenue budget.
- *Administration budget.* This budget includes the expenses of the executive, accounting, treasury, human resources, and other administrative staff. These expenses are primarily comprised of compensation, followed by office expenses. A large proportion of these expenses are fixed, with some headcount changes driven by total revenues or other types of activity elsewhere in the company.

A budget that is not directly impacted by the revenue budget is the research and development budget. This budget is authorized by senior management, and is set at an amount that is deemed appropriate, given the projected level of new product introductions that management wants to achieve, and the company's competitive posture within the industry. The size of this budget is also influenced by the amount of available funding and an estimate of how many potentially profitable projects can be pursued.

Once these budgets have been completed, it is possible to determine the capital budgeting requirements of the company, as well as its financing needs. These two topics are addressed in the capital budget and the financing budget:

- *Capital budget.* This budget shows the cash flows associated with the acquisition of fixed assets during the budget period. Larger fixed assets are noted individually, while smaller purchases are noted in aggregate. The information in this budget is used to develop the budgeted balance sheet, depreciation expense, and the cash requirements needed for the financing budget.
- *Financing budget.* This budget is the last of the component budgets developed, because it requires the cash inflow and outflow information from the other budgets. With this information in hand, the financing budget addresses how funds will be invested (if there are excess cash inflows) or obtained through debt or equity financing (if there is a need for additional cash). This budget also incorporates any additional cash usage information that is typically addressed by the board of directors, including dividends, stock repurchases, and repositioning of the company's debt to equity ratio. The interest expense or interest income resulting from this budget is incorporated into the budgeted income statement.

Once the capital budget and financing budget have been created, the information in all of the budgets is summarized into a master budget. This master budget is essentially an income statement. A more complex budget also includes a balance sheet that itemizes the major categories of assets, liabilities, and equity. There may also be a statement of cash flows that itemizes the sources and uses of funds.

The complete system of budgets is shown in the following exhibit.

Exhibit: The System of Budgets

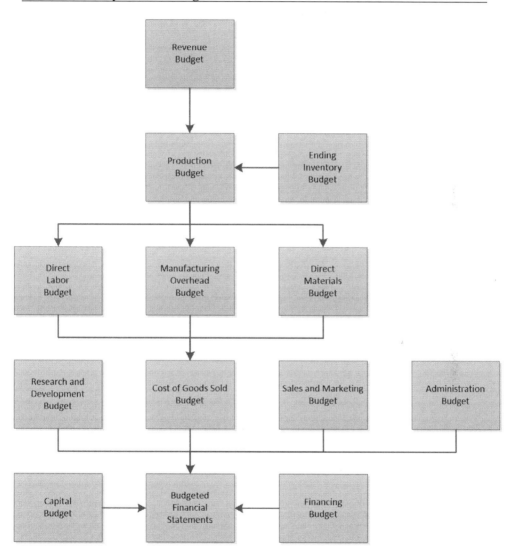

Employee staffing levels are usually included in each of the various budgets, so that employee compensation is fully integrated into the expenses in each budget. However, since compensation comprises a major proportion of all company expenses, it may be useful to also create a staffing budget that summarizes headcount and compensation for all areas of the business. This information is useful for determining whether there will be a sufficient number of employees to support planned revenue levels, as well as to provide guidance for the recruiting and layoff plans of the human resources department.

The system of budgets frequently includes another activity that is not officially a part of the budget – compensation plans. These plans are prepared by the human resources department for selected individuals within the company, and define exactly which budgeted targets a person must attain in exchange for a bonus payment. There is a separate compensation plan for each person, so they are not mentioned in the system of budgets, other than as a budgeted amount of additional compensation.

In summary, the system of budgets ultimately depends upon the revenue budget and the amount of planned ending inventory. These two budgets directly or indirectly influence the amounts budgeted in many other parts of the corporate budget.

The System of Budgets for a Multi-Division Company

The same system of budgets just noted also applies to a company that has multiple operating divisions, with the following differences:

- *Corporate budget.* There will be a separate budget for the corporate headquarters group, which may include such additional items as directors and officers insurance, and the treasury and internal audit departments, which may not be found at the subsidiary level. This budget can usually be constructed independently of the subsidiary budgets.
- *Corporate allocation.* Each subsidiary may be asked to shoulder a portion of the cost of the corporate overhead group, in the form of an overhead allocation. This allocation is not recommended, since the subsidiaries have no control over the amounts allocated.
- *Financing feedback.* Financing needs are generally handled at the corporate level, so there may be capital rationing by the corporate headquarters group that reduces the expenditures for fixed assets that are itemized in the budgets of the subsidiaries. Thus, the corporate financing budget is used as input for the various capital budgets.
- *Cash repatriation.* If some subsidiaries are located in countries that restrict the outflow of cash back to the parent company (known as "cash repatriation"), this issue must be integrated into the budget, so that the company does not mistakenly allocate cash from such locations to other parts of the company. This can have a significant impact on local financing needs.

Thus, there are additional levels of budgeting complexity in larger businesses. This complexity usually extends the budget preparation process into a multi-month endeavor that can be so complicated that there is a dedicated budgeting staff whose work continues throughout the year.

Operating Decisions Impacting the System of Budgets

As senior management oversees the construction of the system of budgets each year, it must be mindful of how certain operating decisions can impact the results of the budget. If management does not incorporate the trickle-down effects of these decisions into the budget, it will likely see variances from the budget in the near future. Some of the operating decisions that may have multiple impacts on the budget include:

- *Increase prices.* If management decides to increase the price of the company's goods or services, this may trigger a decline in demand. This decline may result in a reduced need for overtime in the direct labor budget. Also, a demand reduction may reduce machine utilization levels, so there will be less need for additional investments in fixed assets.

- *Lower prices.* If management lowers prices, it can expect increased utilization of production equipment, which in turn may call for increased maintenance expenditures, as well as the purchase of more fixed assets in the production area. Also, lower prices may result in significantly lower cash flow per customer if sales volume does not increase to offset the price reduction, so verify that there is sufficient cash or debt available to offset any negative cash flow issues.

- *Add new sales territory.* If the company is moving into a new sales territory, this may require a significant increase in distribution costs into that area (especially if warehousing facilities are needed). Also, the travel and entertainment expenditures by the sales staff assigned to this area may be disproportionately high, as they travel to meet with prospective customers. Further, be prepared for higher-than-normal marketing expenditures to build brand awareness in the region. Finally, it is possible that a business may have to reduce prices in the region, due to price wars initiated by competitors in that area.

- *Relax credit terms.* When management approves the use of relaxed credit terms to customers, the obvious intention is to increase sales. However, doing so will very likely increase the amount of bad debts, so there should be a corresponding increase in the allowance for doubtful accounts in the budget. This may also call for the hiring of additional collections staff, as well as budgeting for additional fees payable to outside collection agencies. Relaxing credit terms also creates the issues already noted when management lowers prices.

- *Increase inventory levels.* Management may want to keep more inventory in stock in order to increase the speed with which it can fill customer orders. This change is made to the ending inventory budget. The change can cause a ripple effect throughout the budget, since doing so may require expenditures for additional production equipment, more direct labor staff, overtime, and inventory storage space. It will also increase the amount of budgeted working capital, and may increase the reserve for obsolete inventory.

- *Reduce inventory levels.* Management may want to reduce the company's investment in working capital by shrinking the amount of inventory on hand. There are a number of implications to this. First, there may be an increase in freight expenses, since some items may go out of stock and require overnight delivery. Second, the obsolete inventory expense may increase, since drawing down stocks will be more likely to reveal any items that are not in usable condition. Third, fewer inventories may equate to longer intervals before customer orders are shipped, which may result in some cancelled customer orders and therefore reduced revenues.

The operating decisions noted here are only a few of the multitude that can impact a budget. Management should examine any prospective change in its current operating policies to determine how alterations to them can impact the budget, and then incorporate those changes in the budget as appropriate.

The Reasons for Budget Iterations

There are several very good reasons why the first version of a corporate budget is sent back for additional work. We do not refer to the requirement by an egotistical senior manager to create "better" numbers, irrespective of the ability of the company to achieve such numbers. Instead, there are other serious issues that must be considered in depth to ensure that a budget is realistic. These issues are:

- *Constraints.* If there are bottlenecks within the company that interfere with its ability to generate additional sales, does the budget provide sufficient funding to impact these bottlenecks? If not, the company can budget whatever results it wants, but it has virtually no chance of achieving them. For example, a machine in the production area may be a bottleneck that keeps a company from producing any more products – if the bottleneck is not dealt with, sales will not increase, irrespective of improvements anywhere else in the company. See the author's *Constraint Management* book for more information.
- *Pacing.* If a company intends to expand operations in new geographical areas, or to open new distribution channels, or to offer entirely new products, it should build into the budget an adequate amount of time to ramp up each operation. This issue of pacing should include consideration of the sales cycle of customers, which may be extremely long. For example, expanding the customer base to include municipal governments may be an excellent idea, but may require a sales cycle of greater than a year, given the advance notice needed by governments to budget for purchases.
- *Financing.* If a company has a hard cap on the amount of funding that it will have available during the budget period, then the requirements of the budget must not exceed that funding limitation. This is one of the more common reasons for budget iterations, especially in small companies, where it may be difficult to obtain new funding.

- *Historical metrics.* If a company has been unable to achieve certain performance benchmarks in the past, what has changed to allow it to do so now? The chances are good that the company will still have trouble improving beyond its historical ability to do so, which means that the budget should be adjusted to meet its historical metrics. For example, if a business has historically been unable to generate more than $1 million of sales per salesperson, the preliminary budget should continue to support a similar proportion of sales to salespeople. Similarly, a historical tendency for accounts receivable to be an average of 45 days old prior to payment should probably be reflected in the preliminary budget, rather than a more aggressive collection assumption.

This section has highlighted the need to conduct a close examination of preliminary versions of a budget to see if it meets a number of reasonableness criteria. This usually calls for a number of adjustments to the budget, which typically begins with excessively optimistic assumptions, followed by a certain amount of retrenching.

Alternatives to the Budget

There are so many downsides to the entire concept of a budget that a business may not want to have one at all. If so, how can an entity operate without one? It is quite possible to do so if there is a willingness to change several systems and the corporate approach to managing employees. We will briefly address both issues in this section, and then expand on the concepts in the following sections.

In order to have a properly functioning organization that operates without a budget, it is necessary to alter three systems. They are:

- *Forecast.* The forecast is a rolling forecast that is updated at frequent intervals, and especially when there is a significant event that changes the competitive environment of the business. The forecast is simply the expected outcome of the business in the near term, and is intended to be an early warning indicator of both threats and opportunities. It is completely detached from any compensation plans. The rolling forecast is covered later in this chapter.
- *Capital budgeting.* Requests for funds to buy fixed assets are accepted at all times of the year. Funding allocations are based on expected results and the needs of the requesting business unit. There is no longer a formal once-a-year capital budgeting review.
- *Goal setting.* Employees jointly set targets that are relative to the performance of other business units within the company, and against other benchmark organizations. If there is a bonus plan, it is based on these relative results.

A key point is that the forecast and capital budget are not related to targets. By separating these processes from any corporate targets, there is no incentive for employees to fudge their forecasts or fixed asset funding applications in order to earn bonuses.

From the management perspective, it is critical that senior managers step away from the traditional budget-based command and control system and replace it with a great deal of local autonomy. This means that local managers can make their own decisions as long as they stay within general guidelines imposed by senior management. The focus of the organization changes from short-term budgets to medium-term to long-term financial results. There is no emphasis on budget variances, since there is no budget.

Also, senior management must trust its employees to spend money wisely. The expectation is that an employee is more likely to question the need for any expenditure, instead of automatically spending all funds granted under a budget allocation.

From a more general perspective, if a company abandons budgeting, how does it maintain any sort of direction? The answer depends upon the structure of the business and the environment within which it operates. Here are several examples of how to maintain a sense of direction:

- *Margin focus.* If a business has a relatively consistent market share, but its product mix fluctuates over time, it may be easier to focus the attention of managers on the margins generated by the business, rather than on how they achieve those margins. This eliminates the structural rigidity of a budget, instead allowing managers to obtain revenues and incur expenses as they see fit, as long as they earn the net profit margin mandated by senior management.

- *Key value drivers.* If senior management believes that the company will succeed if it closely adheres to specific value drivers, then it should have the company focus its attention on those specific items, and not hold managers to overly-precise revenue or profit goals. For example, the key to success in an industry may be an overwhelming amount of customer support; if so, focus the entire company on maximizing that one competitive advantage.

- *Few products and very competitive environment.* If a business relies upon only a small number of products and is under constant competitive pressure, then decisions to change direction must be made quickly, and the organization must be capable of reorienting its direction in short order. This calls for a centralized management environment where a small team uses the latest information to reach decisions and rapidly drive change through the organization. In this case, a budget is not only unnecessary, but would interfere with making rapid changes. Thus, keeping employees focused on the operational direction given by senior management is vastly more important than meeting revenue or expense targets; taken to an extreme, employees may never even see the financial results of their areas of responsibility, because the focus is on operations, not financial results.

We have described in general terms how to operate without a budget. In the following sections, we will address various aspects of the no-budget environment in more detail.

Forecasting without a Budget

A good replacement for a budget is the rolling forecast. This is a simple forecast that contains information only at an aggregate level, such as:

- Revenues by product line
- Expenses aggregated into a few line items
- Customer order backlog
- Cash flow

The intent is to create a system that is easily updated, and which gives the organization a reasonable view of what the future looks like for at least the next few months. A key reason for having a rolling forecast is to bring up issues as soon as possible, so that a company can initiate corrective actions to deal with them. Thus, the goal of a rolling forecast is not to attain a specific target, but rather to provide early notice of problems and opportunities.

Employees should update their parts of the rolling forecast about once a month, and should only spend a short time doing so – a fine level of detail is not expected. Since the forecast is updated regularly, it does not have a great deal of impact on the organization if the forecast proves to be incorrect – after all, a new version will replace it shortly, so there is very little time during which a bad forecast can impact the business.

While it is customary to update a forecast at fixed periodic intervals, an alternative approach is to update it whenever there is a significant event that impacts the business. There may be events that trigger a forecast update only for a local business unit, and not for the entire company, while other events may be so significant that they warrant a complete review of the forecast. Such events should be rare, but should trigger an immediate response from the company, so that employees know what to expect.

The rolling forecast is accompanied by a rough work plan that is adjusted as frequently as the forecast. No one has to submit the work plan to a higher authority for approval. Instead, employees formulate their direction, document it in the work plan, and adjust it to compensate for both current and expected future events.

The rolling forecast is covered in more detail in the Rolling Forecast section.

Capital Budgeting

As noted earlier in this chapter, the process of reviewing and approving capital expenditures can be lengthy and complex. How does this mesh with an environment in which there is no formal budget? Even if there is no budget, there should still be a rolling forecast. Given the presence of a rolling forecast, three prospects for dealing with capital expenditures suggest themselves:

- *Fast track approvals.* Many capital budgeting proposals are positioned at the lower end of the range of possible dollar amounts, and so require both fewer funds and less analysis. For these items, senior management should maintain a pool of funds at all times, and fast track the review process for any capital budget proposals submitted. This process is designed to support the bulk of all capital expenditures needed by front-line teams.
- *Near-term projections.* The treasury staff should maintain a short-term forecast of available cash flow, so that managers can see if cash will be available for capital budget requests. If the forecast indicates a cash flow problem, then projects can be delayed until more funds are available.
- *Long-term projections.* Senior management should maintain a rolling five-year forecast. This can be quite a brief document, showing general estimates of where the market will be, and the company's position within it. Based on this forecast, the company can determine its long-term capital expenditure plans for high-cost items.

Those capital expenditures designated as fast track approvals require no attention from senior management, since the funds involved are not large. However, the largest expenditures should be labeled as strategic commitments, and therefore fall within the responsibility of senior management.

If a business has cash constraints that do not allow it to give appropriate funding to all capital projects, then senior management will likely have to become involved in more approvals. If so, they should use the following criteria when making funding choices:

1. *Legal requirements.* If the company is required to make a capital investment in order to comply with a legal or regulatory requirement, then fund it.
2. *Strategic direction.* If a lack of funding will prevent a profit center from completing a key activity that meshes with the corporate strategic direction, then fund it.
3. *Throughput.* If the overall throughput of a system can be increased by making a capital investment, and there is sufficient demand to use the extra capacity, then fund it.
4. *Return on investment.* Once all projects falling under the preceding categories have been funded, allocate funding to the remaining projects based on their returns on investment.

A good way to limit profit centers from demanding an excessive amount of funds for capital projects is to designate them as investment centers and charge them the corporate cost of capital for all invested funds. This arrangement should keep them from requesting funds for projects whose returns are below the cost of capital. If the availability of funds to the company as a whole becomes restricted, the cost of capital can be increased, which should reduce the flow of capital budgeting requests.

When the annual budget is eliminated, this also means that the annual review of existing projects is eliminated. Instead, it is far better to engage in more frequent reviews of project status. Doing so will reveal problem areas where it makes sense to terminate a project entirely, thereby making more funds available for use in other capital projects. These more frequent reviews should not be excessively detailed, or else they will consume too much time. Instead, there should be a brief review of the time to completion in comparison to the original estimate, as well as of the funds expended to date in comparison to the original projection. If either of these metrics reveals a significant negative variance, then more analysis is called for.

Goal Setting without a Budget

The senior management team typically integrates its corporate goals into the budget – so what happens to the goals when the budget is terminated? The answer is to use continual improvement goals that will place the company in the top quartile of those companies or internal profit centers against which it measures itself. For example, a retail chain can measure the profitability of its stores, and have the lowest-performing stores attempt to match the performance already reported by the top 25 percent of stores. Further, the same company can benchmark the performance of other "best in class" companies and have its top-ranking stores attempt to attain benchmarked performance levels.

For large companies having many similar profit centers, tracking performance against peers within the company can be the best basis for such goal setting, for several reasons:

- *Internal support.* Everyone works for the same company, so employees of the top-performing profit centers should be willing to assist other profit centers to improve their performance.
- *Similar environment.* The various profit centers presumably work within the same industry, and deal with similar customers and suppliers, so their results should not only be quite comparable with each other, but their business practices should be readily transferable to other profit centers.
- *Been done.* Employees may baulk at the idea of being measured against the performance of another company that may not even operate in the same industry; but this objection does not apply if the benchmark originates within the company – the benchmark has already "been done," and within the same industry.

The tracking of internal peer performance can result in an extensive reporting system where employees can readily access the results of profit centers by geographical region, or store size, or product line, or customer. The result can be an exceptional internal database that reveals who conducts business the best, and how to contact them for advice.

EXAMPLE

Mr. Dennis Houlihan has just opened a new branch of the Hammer Outlet Stores in Boston. As a new branch, the results of the Boston branch will likely initially rank among the worst of the 150 outlets operated by the company. Mr. Houlihan consults the company's internal database of profit centers to find comparable locations, and finds that the New York and Atlanta branches perform exceptionally well. He contacts their managers for advice regarding how to improve the performance of his operations.

The trick to goal setting in this environment is to not make such goals appear to be fixed targets that are agreed upon in advance, but rather goals to aspire to achieve, with compensation being paid on the extent to which they *are* achieved.

Strategy without a Budget

The traditional approach to budgeting is that strategy is finalized before the beginning of the budget year, and is not revised until the same period in the following year. Also, strategy is debated and settled among the top management team, perhaps allowing for some input from others lower in the corporate hierarchy. This approach may be suitable in a monopolistic industry, such as electrical power generation. However, most industries experience a vastly more robust amount of competition, and so would benefit from two key changes in the formulation of strategy, which are:

- *Timing.* When the competitive environment changes constantly, corporate strategy needs to change at the same pace. This may require minor tweaks to the strategy every few months, and possibly a major change as soon as a structural shift in the industry becomes apparent. Thus, strategy development must change from an annual event to an ongoing process.
- *Formulation authority.* Senior management still needs to ultimately manage the overall direction of the company. However, this must truly be at a strategic level, not tactical. Lower-level managers and teams must focus on how the strategy is to be implemented at a tactical level and on a continuous basis, and give feedback to senior management regarding the practicality of the plan. There should also be a clear set of decision authorizations that allow profit centers to make most decisions with no further interference from senior management; however, clear divergences from the corporate strategy should require the approval of senior management.

EXAMPLE

Hammer Industries has lumber yards in 30 states, all under local management. Hammer's senior management team has adopted a decentralized management structure, under which local managers are allowed to make all operational decisions as long as they follow these guidelines:

- Annual cash flow is above the median for a peer group of competitors
- Capital purchases are pre-authorized up to $3 million per year
- The business is focused on serving the needs of independent contractors

The staff of the Albuquerque branch of Hammer sees an opportunity to open a new location near a vast subdivision that has just sold out. The investment will be under $3 million, but the focus of the location would be on homeowners, rather than independent contractors, so this decision is bumped up to senior management for resolution.

Both of the proposed changes in strategy development are necessary offshoots from the concept of shifting responsibility as far down in the organization as possible. Thus, if expenditure authority is shifted down to employees, then it may be necessary to shift some elements of strategy down as well.

In short, when there is no budget, it does not mean that there is no strategy. On the contrary, senior management must still formulate it, and lower levels of the organization must interpret their key objectives and performance indicators based on that strategy. Ultimately, a company must have a system where everyone is clear about the overall direction of the business, as well as their roles in it.

Management Guidelines

Managers throughout a no-budget business must have a clear understanding of the company's overall strategy, and how they are expected it implement it within their areas of responsibility. Further, they must understand how decisions are made within the company, including:

- Which decisions they are expected to make
- Which decisions must be shifted to senior management
- The extent to which they can re-direct the activities of their areas of responsibility without the approval of senior management
- When they should give feedback to management regarding how local conditions are impacting the corporate strategy

When decisions are being forcefully shifted down into the corporate hierarchy, employees must know the answers to these questions in order to succeed in their jobs.

The Role of Senior Management

If decision making is being pushed deep into the ranks of an organization, what role remains for the members of senior management? They no longer have a budget to control, so what is their role?

First, there will be fewer senior managers, simply because there is almost no "command" work left. The elimination of the budget will likely thin the ranks of management considerably, especially those positioned in the middle of the corporate hierarchy who were most involved in monitoring performance. For those that remain, the role will encompass the following responsibilities:

- *Monitor performance.* It is still necessary to monitor the performance of the company, though senior managers should only interfere in an operation when its results are clearly falling well below expectations.
- *Exception detection.* An offshoot of the preceding point is that senior management should review all types of information to see if there are any changes in trends or other unusual patterns that could signal a need for a change in strategic direction. These changes may be too subtle to be noticed by a front-line employee, and can only be seen when viewed at a more aggregate level. Spotting these issues early can be critical to the long-term health of a business, and so is an appropriate task for senior managers.
- *Strategy.* The high-level strategy of the company remains under the control of the senior management team. They set the general direction of the company, and then let the rest of the company work on the tactical aspects of implementing it.
- *Financial analysis.* Senior managers, or at least the corporate staff, can assist profit center employees with a variety of issues to help them obtain better performance. The people providing this assistance essentially become in-house consultants. Examples of some analyses that they might be engaged in are:
  - Which products and services create the largest and smallest profit?
  - Should we drop a product or product line?
  - Should we drop a customer?
  - Can we increase prices?
  - Should any functional areas be outsourced?
- *Acquisitions.* The purchase of another company or its assets is a highly specialized activity that is best handled by a core team of experts. Even if an acquisition is requested from lower down in the corporate hierarchy, the actual transaction will likely be handled by corporate management.
- *Acquisition integration.* The senior management team can be involved in some coordination of the acquisition integration process, but most of the integration team will be drawn from the more high-performing profit centers. These people are best able to transfer knowledge to the employees of the acquiree. Still, there may be a need for a coordinator from senior management to ensure that adequate resources are allocated to the acquiree.
- *Coaching.* Especially during the early years of a conversion to a no-budget environment, senior managers must be deeply involved in training the rest of the organization to take on the roles and responsibilities once held by senior managers. This is a gradual process, as senior managers provide training, hand off selected functions, evaluate the results, and decide when to push more responsibility down into the organization.
- *Rapid response.* The reduced number of senior managers will likely create an extremely broad span of control (if any). This means that in the rare cases where a decision must be escalated to senior management, it can reach the

apex of the company almost immediately and be sent back with a decision within a very short period of time.

Since senior managers are accustomed to much more direct action than the preceding list of activities implies, it will be necessary to completely restructure not only their job descriptions, but also the job descriptions of everyone else in the company to formally shift responsibilities downward in the organization.

Compensation without a Budget

If a company's budget is eliminated and along with it the traditional bonus contract, how are employees to be compensated? Here are the key issues to consider when designing a new method of compensation:

- *Baseline.* The foundation for the traditional bonus contract is the baseline from which performance during the measurement period is to be tracked. This number is usually a negotiated figure, which means that it is subject to a great deal of politicking. An excellent alternative is to use one of the following options as a replacement baseline:

    o *Historical trend line.* Base changes in compensation on improvements in performance from prior years. However, if earlier performance was substandard, employees may be overly compensated for achievements that are better than the prior year, but not necessarily at the level of the competition. Also, if the company needs to reorient its business, focusing on improvements from the last year may not be sufficient.

    o *Peer group performance.* The company can benchmark its performance against other "best in class" companies, and compensate employees based on their performance against this "gold standard." Another option is to divide the company into a multitude of profit centers, and use the performance of the best profit centers as the baseline. This latter approach may work best, since performance is derived from the company's specific competitive situation, rather than from the performance of another company that may operate in a different market.

- *Unit of measure.* The unit of measure for a traditional bonus plan is probably profitability, but that does not have to apply to a situation where management wants to focus the attention of employees on other key success factors. For example, in a rapidly-expanding market, the most important issue may be revenue growth, even if there are no profits. Or, if a company has gone through a leveraged buyout, debt reduction (and therefore cash flow) may be the most important concern. Or, a niche strategy may mandate a high level of customer support. The central point in the selection of the unit of measure is that it provides a measure of progress toward the company's strategic objectives.

153

- *Team basis*. The traditional model favors bonuses for individuals. However, when longer-term goals are paramount, it requires the ongoing efforts of a large team to achieve above-average performance. Thus, it makes more sense to eliminate individual bonus plans in favor of group-based bonuses. Ideally, there should be one bonus plan, and it should include *every* person in the company. With one bonus plan, every employee has an incentive to help everyone else to optimize their performance. Conversely, if there were to be localized bonus plans, it is more likely that employees in different bonus plans would not assist each other, since they would have no economic reason for doing so. The worst situation is to only have individual bonuses for a small number of managers, since the rest of the company has no reason to work hard so that someone else can earn a large bonus.

- *Bonus calculation*. The calculation of a bonus can be a nefariously difficult and arcane formula under a traditional budget plan which sometimes results in no bonus at all, despite the best efforts of an employee, or an inordinately large bonus because the circumstances were just right. In a no-budget situation, it makes more sense to not establish a detailed compensation plan in advance. Instead, use one of the options just noted to create a baseline for measurement, and pay out an appropriate amount based on changes from that baseline. In general, this approach means limiting bonus payments to a certain percentage of profits or cash flow, so that the company is not crippled by inordinately large payments. Also, paying all bonuses from existing profits or cash flow means that compensation will always be supportable, since the company has already earned the money.

- *Nature of the bonus*. A company that wants to *really* focus the attention of its employees on long-term performance should consider *not* immediately paying out the bonuses that it grants to employees. A better alternative is to pay all or a portion of the bonus into a fund, which in turn invests at least some of the money in the company's shares. The fund then pays out both the accumulated bonuses and any earnings to employees when they retire. By taking this approach, a company is ensuring that employees have a significant interest in the performance of the company's stock, which in turn is driven by their ability to improve its earnings and cash flow over time.

- *Comprehensive evaluation*. A traditional bonus contract focuses on the achievement of very few targets – perhaps just profits – in order to trigger a bonus. This can lead to "gaming" to twist the system to achieve only the specified targets, perhaps to the long-term detriment of the business. A better approach is to establish a large group of performance factors that an evaluation committee can use to ascertain the improvement (or decline) of the business during the measurement period. Such a comprehensive system may start with profitability, but then go on to measure (for example) backlog, customer turnover, employee turnover, absentee levels, average accounts receivable outstanding, the debt level, and new product launches to obtain a more well-rounded view of how the organization has changed.

EXAMPLE

Mr. Jones is a traditional manager who is accustomed to moving heaven and earth to meet his profit target and earn a bonus. For the past year, he made the designated profit bonus, but ignored the company's move to a more comprehensive evaluation system. The committee discovered that he only achieved the budget by eliminating training and maintenance expenditures, which seriously impact staff knowledge and machine downtime. The committee therefore awarded Mr. Jones a minimal bonus for the year.

Compensation under this system should be based on *relative* improvement, rather than performance against a fixed target. This is a key concept, for it does not tie employees to a number or other metric that may be increasingly irrelevant over time. Thus, if there is a steep economic decline, it may still be quite reasonable to issue a bonus to the members of a profit center even if their profits dropped, because the profit decline was less than the median rate of decline for other parts of the company. Conversely, if the market is expanding rapidly, it may not make sense to issue bonuses to the members of a profit center that earned fewer profits than the median rate of profit increase for the company.

It is extremely useful to base all bonus compensation on a single company-wide profit sharing pool. By doing so, the members of the various profit centers will have a strong incentive to work together to create more profits. If the employees in profit centers were to instead be paid just on their own performance, then they would be far less likely to assist other parts of the company. Another effect of this arrangement is that a poorly-performing profit center may even receive unsolicited offers of help from other profit centers, because its poor performance is adversely affecting the compensation of other employees.

One type of compensation that has no place in a no-budget company is the stock option. A stock option generates a return for its holder if the price of the underlying stock increases. However, there is not necessarily a relationship between the price of the stock and the actual performance of the company. A stock price may go up due to general price volatility, speculation regarding a takeover, or simply because the valuation of the entire stock market is increasing due to an improvement in general economic conditions. None of these scenarios are impacted by the performance of the person to whom a stock option is granted. Indeed, the reverse can be the case – a person could engender phenomenal company performance, while a variety of factors *decrease* the value of his or her stock options. Consequently, it is better to use compensation devices that only provide increased pay if the company performs better than its peer group.

Behavioral Norms

Senior managers may point to specific individuals within a company who might take advantage of the situation if a tight budgeting system were not imposed; however, this justification is based on the concept of imposing a command and control system on an entire company in order to prevent possible deleterious activities by just a few

155

people. It would certainly be easier to only restrict the behavior of those few people, or even encourage them to work elsewhere, rather than impose a repressive level of control on the entire company. Thus, a reasonable alternative to the command and control system is to imbue the organization with a strong sense of ethics and limits to acceptable behavior, and then act decisively when one of the few miscreants in the company breaks those boundaries.

Another argument by senior management in favor of strong controls over expenditures is that there are always a few employees who add improper expenditures to their expense reports, which only detailed cost reviews will find. This certainly does happen from time to time, but only a few employees engage in this sort of behavior. In most cases, it seems odd that a company will entrust its employees with expensive assets, design products, and deal with important customers, and yet assume that they will run a few unwarranted expenses through their expense reports. In reality, nearly all employees can be trusted within a framework of a modest number of controls. Instead, it is certainly worth considering the use of well-defined behavioral norms, and coming down hard on any employees who step outside of those norms. Doing so means that the company is acting forcefully against a small number of employees, while not punishing all other employees with an oppressive set of controls.

Profit Knowledge

If there is to be no budget, then the entire organization requires more knowledge of how the company makes money, so that they can contribute to making more of it. This calls for company-wide education by the accounting staff of how the company earns money, where it loses money, and the profit that the company earns from specific transactions. Thus, the sales and marketing staff should know how much profit the company makes on each product, so that it can increase sales of those items. Similarly, the engineering staff must be encouraged to use target costing to create products that generate acceptable returns. Further, the customer service department must know which customers generate the most profit for the company, so they will pay particular attention to them.

Ultimately, the amount of information transparency should be so great that it is nearly impossible for someone to hide an inappropriate expenditure.

Information Exchange

A great deal of responsibility is shifted down to the front lines of a business when there is no budget. In this situation, employees need to discuss alternatives with each other for how to run their profit centers, as well as where to find solutions to their problems, and cast around for ideas regarding how to improve their operations. None of these requirements can be met in the traditional work silos that are part of a traditional organization. Instead, employees need new ways to communicate with each other. This may involve company-sponsored blogs, newsletters, more formal gatherings, and so forth, with the goal of creating a massive number of connections amongst employees. This approach is completely at odds with the traditional view of restricting information to a select few within each department, and so can be a wrenching change for those employees who used to control all of the corporate information.

Accounting Reports

When responsibility is shifted into the depths of an organization, information needs to flow along with it. This means that the accounting staff must create and issue reports at great speed to the entire organization, thereby creating a rapid feedback loop from which the company can take corrective action.

The information provided by the accounting staff may encompass more than financial information. Indeed, such information may be downplayed if senior management wants to encourage employees to focus on other key performance indicators.

EXAMPLE

The management information systems manager of Hammer Industries is creating feedback reports for various people within the company. His reports include the following:

Title	Information Provided
Customer service manager	Customers gained; customers lost
Engineering manager	Engineering change orders; warranty claims
Maintenance manager	Downtime at bottleneck operation
Sales manager	Sales discounts granted; Days sales outstanding

A more balanced approach is to issue a complete package of financial and operating information throughout the company, which usually includes the following:

- *Rolling forecast.* This is a general-level forecast that requires little time to update, and may cover a period of as little as three months. See the Rolling Forecast section for more information.
- *Leading indicators.* This is a very limited set of leading indicators that strongly indicate the direction of the market in which the company operates.
- *Performance comparisons.* This is the operational and financial performance of the various profit centers, and is presented only for the key information that the company is most interested in. The various profit centers use this information to compare their results. It is intended to be both a spur for more action and the source document for the eventual payment of performance-based bonuses.
- *Benchmark comparisons.* If the company chooses to benchmark performance against that of one or more outside companies, it can compare the

recent performance of the company against that of the benchmark. This information can be used to calculate performance-based bonuses.

- *Financial results.* This information should be issued at the level of responsibility of the recipient, and should be formatted to show the results for each of the last 12 months in order to present a trend line, and preferably aggregated so that readers are not overwhelmed with detail. There are several ways to present financial information. A general format follows.

Sample Presentation of Financial Results

Cost Center	Current Month	Same Month Last Year	Current Y-T-D	12-Month Average/Month	Quarterly % Change
Accounting department	$50,000	$58,000	$163,000	$52,500	-4%
Engineering department	125,000	137,000	490,000	131,000	-3%
Maintenance department	72,000	55,000	160,000	60,000	+11%
Power plant	150,000	147,000	440,000	153,000	+1%

The preceding report shows that the accounting and engineering departments appear to be successfully pruning their costs, while the maintenance department has experienced a significant expense surge that is worthy of further investigation.

A variation on the trend line report is to include a percentage change line, which may be more useful to report users. Whether this feature is used is entirely up to recipients. Some people find that a percentage change number provides better information than the raw numbers upon which it is based.

There are a few reports that may still be needed by senior management, and which the rest of the company does not need to see. For example, there may be cash flow forecasts needed by the treasurer to anticipate cash borrowing and investments. There may also be transfer pricing reports needed by the tax manager to predict future tax payments. Generally, these reports are intended for specialists, and so are of no interest to the rest of the company.

The Rolling Forecast

A rolling forecast is a recasting of a company's financial prospects on a frequent basis. The frequency of forecasting means that the forecast could potentially occupy a central role in a company's planning activities. In this and the following section we address several aspects of that role – the timing of updates, the updating method, the time period covered, and the format of the forecast.

Ideally, a rolling forecast could be created as soon as a company issues its financial statements for the most recent reporting period. By doing so, management can update the existing forecast based in part on the information contained in the most recent financial statements. The forecast could be updated on a monthly basis, but do so only if the resulting information is useful to management – which is usually only the case in a volatile market. In most situations, a quarterly update to the forecast is sufficient, and is not looked upon as quite so much of a chore by the management team. An alternative view of when to update a forecast is whenever there is a significant triggering event. This may be a change in the business environment, the release of a new product, the loss of a key employee, and so forth. If updates only occur after a triggering event, the revision of a rolling forecast may be quite sporadic.

The rolling forecast is usually considered to be a much more frequent creation than the annual budget, so there should be a revision process that minimizes the amount of updating effort. Here are several ways to construct a rolling forecast, beginning with the simplest approach:

1. *Adjust recent results.* Copy forward the company's most recent actual financial results, and then adjust revenues and expenses based on any changed expectations for the forecasting period. This method is essentially based on historical results. It requires the input of very few people, and can be created very quickly.
2. *Block revision.* Only forecast at a very high level, where there is essentially a single line item block for the expenses of an entire department. There may be somewhat more detail for the revenue portion of the forecast, since this is the most critical area. This information will likely be extracted from the most recent historical results, but may be subject to more revision than the method just discussed. This approach can also be constructed quickly, with input from just a few people.
3. *Detailed revision.* Forecast every line item in the financial statements "from scratch." This approach takes substantially more time and requires broad-based input. Few companies are willing to expend the time needed for this level of forecasting.

Tip: Consider supplementing the rolling forecast with a brief summarization of risks and opportunities that can impact revenue and cost estimates, thereby allowing users of the information to form their own opinions about how likely the company is to achieve projections.

Of the preceding methods, either the first or second should work well, because they require little time to create. When forecasting requires little time, it is more likely to be accepted on a long-term basis by employees. Ideally, it should take no more than one day to update a rolling forecast.

Another issue with the rolling forecast is the time period to be covered by it. There is no universally correct period. Instead, the time period covered depends on the nature of the business. Here are several examples of situations calling for different forecast periods:

- *Software development.* A business creates software and launches it through the Internet. Its investment in fixed assets is low. In this case, competing products can appear at any time, and the market can pivot in a new direction at a moment's notice. If so, management probably does not need a forecast that extends more than three months into the future.
- *Market leading manufacturer.* A business is the dominant low-cost provider of industrial goods in its market niche, thanks to its heavy investment in fixed assets and production technology. The market is steady and changes little, so management can get by with a quarterly forecast update that extends over a two-year period.
- *Government contractor.* A company has a backlog of long-term contracts with the federal government. Its cost structure is easily predicted, and revenues are based largely on contracts that are already in hand. Management probably only needs a quarterly forecast update, with particular emphasis on the revenues generated by specific contracts. The forecast duration should match the duration of key contracts.
- *Retail business.* A company sells highly fashion-oriented retail goods from multiple stores. Sales levels are highly variable, so management probably needs a monthly forecast that has a particular emphasis on sales by product line and by store.

Another way to view the duration of the forecast period is whether extending it further into the future will alter any management decision making. If not, there is no point in creating the extended forecast. A good way to determine the correct duration is to start with a rolling 12-month forecast and adjust the duration after a few months to more closely fit the needs of management. It is quite common to have a forecast duration of at least one year, and rarely more than two years.

The Rolling Forecast Format

What should a rolling forecast look like? As just noted, keep it relatively short in order to make the updating task as easy as possible. However, this does not mean that the entire forecast should be encompassed within just a few lines. Instead, consider structuring the forecast to address the key variables in the business, so that managers focus on changes in just those areas that will make a difference to the business.

The following sample format is designed for a manufacturing business that produces roughly the same items every year and in predictable quantities. There is a focus on the cost of commodities and managing the bottleneck operation, which leads to more detail on those specific items.

Sample Rolling Forecast for Manufacturing Operation

	Quarter 1	Quarter 2	Quarter 3	Quarter 4
Sales	$8,200,000	$8,225,000	$8,290,000	$8,320,000
Cost of goods sold	5,330,000	5,593,000	5,720,000	5,741,000
Gross margin	$2,870,000	$2,632,000	$2,570,000	$2,579,000
Gross margin percentage	35%	32%	31%	31%
Other expenses	2,510,000	2,535,000	2,550,000	2,565,000
Net profit or loss	$360,000	$97,000	$20,000	$14,000
Bottleneck utilization	92%	98%	105%	108%
Platinum cost/pound	$1,700	$1,750	$1,775	$1,775
Palladium cost/pound	$700	$705	$710	$715

The rolling forecast for the manufacturing operation reveals a decline in gross margins and net profits over time, which appears to be caused by an increase in the cost of platinum, which is listed on the report as a key commodity. Also, note that the forecast is in quarters, not months – the company has a sufficiently stable product line and marketplace that it does not need to update its forecast every month. Finally, the forecast reveals that there is a growing problem with the overutilization of the company's bottleneck operation, which management needs to address.

What about if a company has minimal fixed costs and is located in a highly volatile marketplace – such as software development for smart phone apps? In this environment, a product may have a short life span or highly variable revenues, so the focus tends to be more on detailed revenue information and the rollout dates for new products. The following sample format could be applied to such a situation:

Sample Rolling Forecast for a Software Developer

	January	February	March	April
Revenue:				
App – Geolocator	$80,000	75,000	60,000	45,000
App – Find my car	55,000	65,000	65,000	40,000
App – Family tracker	160,000	160,000	100,000	80,000
Total revenue	$295,000	$300,000	$225,000	$165,000
Expenses	165,000	175,000	175,000	180,000
Net profit or loss	$130,000	$125,000	$50,000	-$15,000

	January	February	March	April
Product release dates:				
App – Backcountry locator	1/21/xx			
App – Wildlife tagger			3/5/xx	
App – Urban locator				4/4/xx

The rolling forecast for the software developer makes it clear that revenues decline rapidly, so revenues must be the key focus of the organization. There is also considerable emphasis on the release dates of new products, which will hopefully drive renewed revenue growth. Note that the preceding example format is expressed in months, rather than quarters. In a volatile marketplace, a quarterly update may be far too long an interval to show the rapid changes in sales that will likely occur.

What about a situation where a company relies upon a number of large contracts with its customers? In this case, the key focus must be on the revenue stream associated with each contract, as well as on the dates when contracts will terminate. The following sample format could be applied to such a situation:

Sample Rolling Forecast for a Contractor

	Quarter 1	Quarter 2	Quarter 3	Quarter 4
Revenue:				
Air Force contract	$1,700,000	$1,720,000	$1,690,000	$850,000
Marine Corp contract	2,400,000	2,350,000	130,000	0
USGS contract	850,000	875,000	430,000	0
Total revenue	$4,950,000	$4,945,000	$2,250,000	$850,000
Expenses	4,300,000	4,290,000	1,950,000	830,000
Net profit or loss	$650,000	$655,000	$300,000	$20,000
Contract terminations:				
Air Force contract				11/20/xx
Marine Corps contract			7/11/xx	
USGS contract			8/15/xx	

The rolling forecast for the contractor is driven entirely by revenues. The company can easily cut back on staffing when there is no work, so its expenses are not a concern. The non-financial information in the forecast keeps management aware of the truly critical item – when customer contracts are scheduled to expire.

Summary

The discussion of budgeting in this chapter has cast serious doubts on the need for a detailed and rigorously-enforced budgeting system, especially one that integrates the budget model with bonus plans. There are cases where pure corporate inertia still mandates the use of a budget – it has been used in the past, so we will continue to use it in the future. However, it is useful to at least review the no-budget arguments and concepts made in this chapter, to see if perhaps a modified budgeting system can be developed that yields a more flexible system that responds faster to changes in the market.

The rolling forecast is an ideal way to give employees the best possible estimate of what will probably occur in the near future. The forecasting process is specifically designed not to be elaborate, on the grounds that a simple update is more likely to be accepted by a company than a lengthy, bureaucratic budgeting production. And by keeping the model simple, managers can focus on the key drivers of success, rather than being bogged down in the details. It is possible to run a rolling forecast in conjunction with an annual budgeting process, but many companies find that the higher short-term accuracy of a rolling forecast makes it sufficient for their needs, and so dispense with the annual budget entirely.

Chapter 8
Product Pricing

Introduction

Ultimately, the likelihood of long-term business profitability is based on revenues. CFOs traditionally review total sales and unit volumes, and so have knowledge of the sources of revenue at an aggregate level. However, a deeper understanding of revenue requires an understanding of how a business develops prices. In this chapter, we delve into the different types of pricing strategies, which tend to fall into the following categories:

- *Cost based pricing*. Prices are derived from the costs of the underlying products.
- *Strategic pricing*. Pricing is set to drive away competitors or position the business within a market.
- *Teaser pricing*. Prices on a few items are kept low to attract customers.
- *Value based pricing*. Prices are based on customer perceptions of the value of products.

In this chapter, we discuss the more important pricing concepts in separate sections, along with the advantages and disadvantages of each one. We also provide summary descriptions of several additional pricing strategies, and introduce the concepts of price elasticity of demand and cross price elasticity of demand.

Psychological Pricing

We begin the discussion of pricing with the concept of psychological pricing, which is a general pricing concept that can be applied to many of the following strategies as a pricing adjustment. Psychological pricing is the practice of setting prices slightly lower than rounded numbers, in the expectation that customers do not round up these prices, and so will treat them as lower prices than they really are. This practice is based on the belief that customers tend to process a price from the left-most digit to the right, and so will tend to ignore the last few digits of a price. This effect appears to be accentuated when the fractional portion of a price is printed in smaller font than the rest of a price.

An example of psychological pricing is setting the price of an automobile at $19,999, rather than $20,000. This type of pricing is extremely common for consumer goods.

EXAMPLE

Hammer Industries has created an all-electric miniature backhoe. Upon investigation of competing price points, Hammer finds that there is a cluster of similar vehicles priced at $29,999. Also, many backhoe buyers use on-line price shopping services to evaluate backhoes, and those services present choices to buyers in $10,000 pricing bands. Thus, Hammer decides to price the backhoe at $29,999, not only to match the competition, but also to position itself within the $20,001 - $30,000 pricing band.

The following are advantages of using the psychological pricing method:

- *Control.* It is much more difficult for an employee to create a fraudulent sales transaction and remove cash when product prices are set at fractional levels, since it is more difficult to calculate the amount of cash to steal.
- *Discount pricing.* If a company is having a sale on selected goods, it can alter the ending digits of product prices to identify them as being on sale. Thus, any product ending with a ".98" price will receive a 20% discount at the checkout counter.
- *Non-rational pricing.* If customers are swayed by the incremental price reductions advocated under psychological pricing (which is a debatable premise) then sales should increase.
- *Price bands.* If a customer is accessing information about product prices that are segregated into bands, the use of fractional pricing can shift the price of a product into a lower price band, where customers may be more likely to make a purchase. For example, if a customer only wants to consider automobiles that cost less than $20,000, pricing a vehicle at $19,999 will drop it into the lower price band and potentially increase its sales.

The following are disadvantages of using the psychological pricing method:

- *Calculation.* It can be difficult for cashiers to calculate the total amount owed when fractional prices are used, as well as to make change for such purchases. This is less of a problem when credit cards and other types of electronic payments are used.
- *Rational pricing.* If customers are more rational than psychological pricing gives them credit for, then they will ignore fractional pricing and instead base their purchases on the value of the underlying products.

The overwhelming use of psychological pricing makes it clear that, whether or not the underlying concept is flawed, businesses are setting prices in this manner in order to compete with each other. Thus, to use the earlier example, setting a price a fraction higher than the prices charged by competitors might indeed lead to an incremental drop in unit sales volume, so a company probably has to use psychological pricing in order to remain competitive.

Cost plus Pricing

Cost plus pricing is a price-setting method under which the direct material cost is added to the direct labor cost and overhead cost for a product, after which a markup percentage is added in order to derive the price of the product. It can also be used under a contract with a customer, where the customer reimburses the seller for all costs incurred and also pays a negotiated profit in addition to the costs incurred.

EXAMPLE

Hammer Industries has designed a product that contains the following costs:

- Direct material costs = $20.00
- Direct labor costs = $5.50
- Allocated overhead = $8.25

The company applies a standard 30% markup to all of its products. To derive the price of this product, Hammer adds together the stated costs to arrive at a total cost of $33.75, and then multiplies this amount by (1 + 0.30) to arrive at the product price of $43.88.

The following are advantages to using the cost plus pricing method:

- *Assured contract profits.* Any contractor is willing to accept this method for a contractual agreement with a customer, since it is assured of having its costs reimbursed and of making a profit. There is no risk of loss on such a contract.
- *Justifiable.* In cases where the supplier must persuade its customers of the need for a price increase, the supplier can point to an increase in its costs as the reason for the price increase.
- *Simple.* It is quite easy to derive a product price using this method, though the overhead allocation method should be defined in order to be consistent in calculating the prices of multiple products.

The following are disadvantages of using the cost plus method:

- *Contract cost overruns.* From the perspective of any government entity that hires a supplier under a cost plus pricing arrangement, the supplier has no incentive to curtail its expenditures - on the contrary, it will likely include as many costs as possible in the contract so that it can be reimbursed. Thus, a contractual arrangement should include cost-reduction incentives for the supplier.
- *Ignores competition.* A company may set a product price based on the cost plus formula and then be surprised when it finds that competitors are charging substantially different prices. This has a huge impact on the market share and profits that a company can expect to achieve. The company either ends

up pricing too low and giving away potential profits, or pricing too high and achieving minor revenues.

- *Product cost overruns.* Under this method, the engineering department has no incentive to prudently design a product that has the appropriate feature set and design characteristics for its target market. Instead, the department simply designs what it wants and launches the product.

This method is not acceptable for deriving the price of a product that is to be sold in a competitive market, primarily because it does not factor in the prices charged by competitors. Thus, this method is likely to result in a seriously overpriced product. Further, prices should be set based on what the market is willing to pay - which could result in a substantially different margin than the standard margin typically assigned to a product.

Cost plus pricing is a more valuable tool in a contractual situation, since the supplier has no downside risk. However, be sure to review which costs are allowable for reimbursement under the contract; it is possible that the terms of the contract are so restrictive that the supplier must exclude many costs from reimbursement, and can potentially incur a loss.

Dynamic Pricing

Dynamic pricing is a partially technology-based pricing system under which prices are altered to different customers, depending upon their willingness to pay. Several examples of dynamic pricing are:

- *Airlines.* The airline industry alters the price of its seats based on the type of seat, the number of seats remaining, and the amount of time before the flight departs. Thus, many different prices may be charged for seats on a single flight.
- *Electricity.* Utilities may charge higher prices during peak usage periods.
- *Hotels.* The hotel industry alters its prices depending on the size and configuration of its rooms, as well as the time of year. Thus, ski resorts increase their room rates over the Christmas holiday, while Vermont inns increase their prices during the fall foliage season, and Caribbean resorts reduce their prices during the hurricane season.

Some industries, such as airlines, use heavily computerized systems to alter prices constantly, while other industries institute pricing changes at longer intervals. Thus, dynamic pricing can be adopted along a broad continuum, ranging from constant to infrequent pricing changes.

Dynamic pricing works best in the following situations:

- When it is used in concert by all of the major players in an industry. Thus, if a single hotel were to keep its prices low during the peak tourist season, it could likely steal business away from competitors.

- When demand fluctuates considerably in comparison to a relatively fixed amount of supply. In this situation, sellers reduce prices as demand falls and increase it as demand increases.

The following are advantages of using the dynamic pricing method:

- *Profit maximization.* If a seller constantly updates its prices with dynamic pricing, it will likely maximize its potential profits.
- *Clear out slow-moving inventory.* Dynamic pricing involves in-depth inventory monitoring, with price reductions in response to higher inventory levels. This approach tends to eliminate excess inventory quickly.

The following are disadvantages of using the dynamic pricing method:

- *Competitor monitoring.* If the entire industry adopts dynamic pricing, then a company must invest in competitor price monitoring systems, to see if its prices are similar to those offered by competitors.
- *Customer confusion.* If prices change constantly, customers can become confused by the situation and be attracted to those sellers who do not use dynamic pricing. Thus, it can result in a loss of market share.
- *Increased marketing activity.* An expanded marketing presence may be required to communicate pricing changes to customers.
- *Inventory management.* Sudden changes in price can alter the demand for goods, which makes it difficult to plan for inventory replenishment.
- *Printed price changes.* If used in a retail environment, it requires considerable activity to physically update prices on products as soon as the computer system alters prices.

This approach can be an annoying one for customers, but its proven ability to maximize profits means that it will likely continue to be used in many markets.

Freemium Pricing

Freemium pricing is the practice of offering a basic set of services for free, and enhanced features and/or content for a fee. This approach has had notable success on the Internet, where services can be provided by the seller at close to a zero variable cost. Thus, a company can scale its customer base rapidly with little or no incremental cost for each additional customer gained (assuming no incremental marketing expenses), and then charge for additional services. This approach will result in a larger proportion of customers using the company's offerings for free, and a smaller proportion paying for additional services.

A key point with freemium pricing is that the initial "free" price in essence is the marketing that the provider uses, since word of the zero price point will likely spread quickly among users.

Freemium pricing can be applied to the following circumstances:

- Customers can use a service for a certain amount of time for free, after which they will be charged for any continuing provision of services.
- Customers have access to a version of the service that has few features, and can scale to an expanded version by paying a price.
- Only students are allowed the free service, with corporations paying the full price. This approach assumes that students will become addicted to the service, and later demand that companies they work for buy it.
- Only allow a certain amount of usage per time period, such as one download per month, without paying extra.

The following are advantages of using the freemium pricing method:

- *Low marketing cost.* The absence of a price becomes the key marketing tool of the company, which relies upon word of mouth to spread news about the company.
- *Potential paying customer base.* There will likely be a large pool of users of the free service at all times, any of whom represent the obvious sales funnel for additional paid customers.

The following are disadvantages of using the freemium pricing method:

- *Competition.* The freemium model is one that any number of competitors can also use, which may increase price competition for the premium version of the service provided.
- *Fixed cost coverage.* Any business has a certain amount of fixed costs, and if the premium-priced packages do not generate enough revenue to offset the fixed costs, the business will fail.
- *Value perception.* Since the basic package offered by the seller is free, customers might get the perception that all versions offered by the seller are worth very little. The perception of value can also be a problem when deciding which features to give away for free. If too few or the wrong features are offered, the user base may not expand. Conversely, if there are many users but few have upgraded to the premium version, it is entirely likely that too many free features are being offered. However, if the company begins to charge for features that had been free, it may face a serious decline in its active user base.

A considerable amount of tweaking may be required to maximize profits under the freemium strategy. For example, if half of all users are converting to the premium service, this may not be good, since it implies that the initial set of free services are too limited, which may be reducing the total number of users. In this case, it could make more sense to offer additional services for free, so that the total number of users is increased; doing so expands the pool from which premium users can be drawn. However, this may not work in situations where the total market niche being addressed is relatively small; in this case, the company may have no choice but to restrict the number of free offerings, and focus on a higher conversion rate in order to generate sufficient sales to offset its costs.

> **Tip:** When projecting future sales for a freemium pricing system, expect the proportion of conversions to the premium plan to decline over time. This is because early adopters are less price sensitive, and so are more likely to buy the premium version.

High-Low Pricing

High-low pricing is the practice of setting the price of most products higher than the market rate, while offering a small number of products at below-market prices. By doing so, a retail or web store location hopes to attract customers with its low-price offerings, at which point they will also buy some of the high-price items.

The low-price items are not usually set permanently at a lower price. Instead, coupons and other promotions are used to reduce prices to low levels for short periods of time. By doing so, management can shift low pricing among different products, which may attract different customers or attract the same customers to shop at the store multiple times. Thus, the use of low prices is an ongoing marketing technique that should be in continual use.

Grocery stores routinely issue a continuing stream of advertisements that feature low prices for specific items. The advertised items are usually located far back in the stores, so that shoppers must pass an array of other products before finding the low-priced items that are on sale. Since most grocery shoppers need to buy a large number of items every time they enter the store, the business is nearly guaranteed to sell a number of high-priced items along with the low-priced item(s).

The following are advantages of using the high-low pricing method:

- *Marketing.* The high-low method essentially becomes the marketing method for the business, since it must constantly advertise a selection of low-price items.
- *Profit increase.* When properly implemented, the high-low technique can yield substantial profits; but only if customers buy multiple additional items that are fully priced.

The following are disadvantages of using the high-low pricing method:

- *Customer loyalty.* If customers become aware that the bulk of the products offered by a business are higher than the market rate, they will be more likely to shift their spending loyalties elsewhere.
- *Marketing cost.* It can be expensive to run a perpetual series of marketing campaigns to tout the latest low prices.
- *Risk of loss.* If a business does not place its low-price items properly, or is dealing with price-sensitive shoppers, it may find that it loses money on its low-price promotions.

In short, the high-low pricing method is widely used, but discerning shoppers in the Internet era are more capable of spotting lower-priced items elsewhere, and so will only buy the low-price items and will avoid the high-price items. Also, a business that persistently offers high prices on the bulk of its products will not garner much customer loyalty.

Premium Pricing

Premium pricing is the practice of setting a price higher than the market price, in the expectation that customers will purchase it due to the perception that it must have unusually high quality or reputation. In some cases, the product quality is not better, but the seller has invested heavily in the marketing needed to give the impression of high quality. Premium pricing works best in the following circumstances:

- There is a perception among consumers that the product is a "luxury" product, or has unusually high quality or product design.
- There are strong barriers to entry. These barriers may include such factors as a large marketing expenditure to gain notice among consumers, a large field service operation to support the product, a reputation for product durability, a reputation for being "fashion forward," and/or a strong replacement warranty policy.
- The seller can restrict the amount of product sold, thereby giving its products an aura of exclusivity.
- There are no substitutes for the product. The company can create this situation by taking aggressive legal action against anyone attempting to copy its products.
- The product is protected by a patent, and the company is aggressively maintaining its rights under that patent.

EXAMPLE

Hammer Industries has developed a patented titanium pen that stores ink at high pressure, thereby allowing it to store four times the normal amount of ink. The company uses metal etching craftsmen to etch custom designs into the metal of the pens. Because of the customized nature of the product and its unique ink storage system, as well as the legal protection provided by its patent, Hammer elects to price each pen at $2,000, which is substantially greater than its $200 cost. To enhance the image of the product, Hammer invests heroically in advertising the pen in premium magazines, and also supports it with a lifetime warranty.

The following are advantages of using the premium pricing method:

- *Entry barrier.* If a company invests heavily in its premium brands, it can be extremely difficult for a competitor to offer a competing product at the same price point without also investing a large amount in marketing.

171

- *High profit margin.* There can be an unusually high gross margin associated with premium pricing. However, a company engaging in this strategy must attain sufficient volume to offset the hefty marketing costs associated with it.

The following are disadvantages of using the premium pricing method:

- *Branding cost.* The costs required to establish and maintain a premium pricing strategy are massive, and must be maintained for as long as this strategy is followed. Otherwise, the premium brand recognition by consumers will falter, and the company will have difficulty maintaining its price points.
- *Competition.* There will be a continual stream of competitors challenging the top tier pricing category with lower-priced offerings. This can cause a problem, because it increases the perception in the minds of consumers that the entire product category is worth less than it used to be.
- *High unit costs.* Because the company using this strategy is restricting itself to low sales volume, it can never generate the cost reductions that a high-volume producer would be able to achieve.
- *Sales volume.* If a company chooses to follow a premium pricing strategy, it will have to confine its selling efforts to the top tier of the market, which limits its overall sales volume. This makes it difficult for a company to pursue aggressive sales growth and premium pricing at the same time. The strategy can be followed as long as the company is expanding into new geographic regions, since it is still pursuing the top tier in these new markets.

This approach is a difficult one to create and maintain, requiring an organization experienced in creating, presenting, and supporting products that give the user a premium experience. Companies aspiring to enter the top pricing tier may flounder in this market and lose a great deal of money while they try to establish themselves. For those entities already succeeding with premium pricing, they must be aware that a continual, daily emphasis on the premium strategy is the only way to continually charge the highest prices for what they offer.

Time and Materials Pricing

Time and materials pricing is used in service industries to bill customers for a standard labor rate per hour used, plus the actual cost of materials used. The standard labor rate per hour being billed does not necessarily relate to the underlying cost of the labor; instead, it may be based on the market rate for the services of someone having a certain skill set. Thus, a computer technician may bill out at $100 per hour, while costing $30 per hour, while a cable television mechanic may only bill out at $80 per hour, despite costing the same amount per hour. The cost of materials charged to the customer is for any materials actually used during the performance of services for the customer. This cost may be at the supplier's actual cost, or it may be a marked-up cost that includes a fee for the overhead cost associated with ordering, handling, and holding the materials in stock.

Under the time and materials pricing methodology, a single hourly rate may be charged irrespective of the experience level of the person performing the services, but usually there are different rates for different experience levels within the company. Thus, an associate consultant will have a lower billing rate than a consulting manager, who in turn has a lower billing rate than a consulting partner.

Industries in which time and materials pricing are used include:

- Accounting, auditing, and tax services
- Consulting services
- Legal work
- Medical services
- Vehicle repair

If a company chooses to base its labor rate under time and materials pricing on its underlying costs, rather than the market rate, it can do so by adding together the following:

- The cost of compensation, payroll taxes, and benefits per hour for the employee providing billable services
- An allocation of general overhead costs
- An additional factor to account for the proportion of expected unbillable time

---

EXAMPLE

Hammer Industries has an equipment repair group that charges out its staff at a level that covers the cost of labor, plus a profit factor. In the past year, Hammer incurred $2,000,000 of salary expenses, plus $140,000 of payroll taxes, $300,000 of employee benefits, and $500,000 of office expenses; this totaled $2,940,000 of expenses for the year. In the past year, the company had 30,000 billable hours, which is roughly what it expects to bill out in the near future. Hammer wants the division to earn a 20% profit. Based on this information, the division charges $122.50 per hour for each of its repair personnel. The calculation of the labor price per hour is:

$2,940,000 annual costs / (1 - 20% profit percentage) = $3,675,000 revenue needed

$3,675,000 revenue needed / 30,000 billable hours = $122.50 billing rate

---

The following are advantages to using the time and materials pricing method:

- *Assured profits*. If a company can keep its employees billable, this pricing structure makes it difficult *not* to earn a profit. However, the reverse situation can arise if the proportion of billable hours declines (see below).

- *High risk situations.* This pricing method is excellent in situations where the outcome of the work is in such doubt that the supplier will only take on the work if it can be properly reimbursed.

The following are disadvantages of using the time and materials pricing method:

- *Cost basis ignores market prices.* If a company sets its time and materials prices based on its internal cost structure, it may be setting prices lower than the market rate, thereby potentially losing profits. The reverse situation may also occur, where market prices are lower than internally-compiled prices. If so, a business will find itself unable to generate much business.
- *Customers will not allow.* This pricing format allows a company to potentially run up its hours billed and charge more than the customer expects. Thus, customers prefer a fixed price to time and materials pricing.
- *Lost profits.* A company that provides highly value-added services could potentially use value based pricing, where prices are set based on the perceived value delivered to the customer. Not using this approach could result in lost profits.
- *Low billable hours situations.* The basis of the time and materials pricing system is that a company will be able to bill enough hours to offset its fixed costs (usually the salaries of its employees). If the number of billable hours declines and headcount does not decline in proportion, then the company will lose money.
- *Price negotiations.* More sophisticated customers will negotiate reductions in the billable rate per hour, eliminate any mark-up on materials, and impose a "not to exceed" clause in any time and materials contract, thereby limiting profits.

Time and materials pricing is a standard practice in many services businesses, and works well, as long as the business sets sufficiently competitive prices and maintains a high rate of billable hours. Otherwise, the amount of revenue generated will not offset the fixed costs of the business, resulting in losses.

Value Based Pricing

Value based pricing is the practice of setting the price of a product or service at the perceived value to the customer. This approach does not take into account the cost of the product or service, nor market prices. Value based pricing tends to result in very high prices and correspondingly high profits for those companies that can convince their customers to agree to it.

Value based pricing is usually applied to very specialized services. For example, an attorney experienced in defense against criminal charges can charge a very high price to his or her clients, since the value to them of not being incarcerated is presumably quite high. Similarly, an attorney skilled in initial public offerings can use value pricing, since clients might not otherwise raise millions of dollars without their services. Other areas where value based pricing may be possible include:

- Bankruptcy work outs
- Cost reduction analysis
- Lawsuit defense
- Pharmaceuticals
- Product design

Value based pricing is also more applicable to situations where customer approval is made at the executive level, rather than by the procurement department. The purchasing staff is more skilled in evaluating supplier prices, and so would be less likely to allow such pricing.

EXAMPLE

Hammer Industries has built up a tool design service that assists its clients with the creation of tunnel boring equipment. The internal cost for Hammer to provide this service is usually about 1,000 hours of staff time at a cost of $100 per hour, or $100,000 in total. The typical consulting charge is $500,000. There is no relationship between the fee charged and the cost incurred by Hammer. Thus, Hammer earns $400,000 on $100,000 of internal costs. The company's clients do not complain, because they are passing through this fee to the governments commissioning the tunnel bores.

The following are advantages to using the value based pricing method:

- *Customer loyalty.* Despite the high prices charged, a business can achieve extremely high customer loyalty for repeat business and referrals, but only if the service or product provided justifies the high price. This advantage tends to also derive from the nature of the sales relationship, which needs to be both close and trusting before value based pricing can even be contemplated.
- *Increases profits.* This method results in the highest possible price that an organization can charge, and so maximizes profits.

The following are disadvantages of using the value based pricing method:

- *Competition.* Any company that persistently engages in value based pricing is leaving a great deal of room for competitors to offer lower prices and take away market share.
- *Labor costs.* Assuming that a service is being provided, a business is likely offering such a high-end skill set that the employees needed to provide the service will be quite expensive. There is also a risk that they may leave to start competing firms.

- *Niche market.* The very high prices to be expected under this method will only be acceptable to a small number of customers. It may even alienate some prospective customers.
- *Not scalable.* This method tends to work best for smaller organizations that are highly specialized. It is difficult to apply to larger businesses where employee skill levels may not be so high.

This method is exceptionally profitable in those niche areas where a company can offer premium services that are highly valued by their customers. Many attorneys and investment bankers have engaged in value based pricing for decades, so it is clearly a viable method. However, it is not applicable in most businesses, where normal competitive pressures make it impossible to use value based pricing.

Other Pricing Strategies

We have thus far analyzed the most common pricing strategies, but have by no means exhausted the full range of pricing alternatives. The following bullet points make note of additional pricing strategies that can be of use in more limited circumstances:

- *Breakeven pricing* is the practice of setting a price point at which a business will earn zero profits on a sale. The intention behind the use of breakeven pricing is to gain market share and drive competitors from the marketplace. By doing so, a company may be able to increase its production volumes to such an extent that it can reduce costs and then earn a profit at what had been the breakeven price. Alternatively, once it has driven out competitors, the company can raise its prices sufficiently to earn a profit, but not so high that the increased price is tempting for new market entrants.
- *Limit pricing* is the practice by a competitor engaging in monopolistic behavior of setting a product or service price at a level just low enough to deter potential market entrants from competing in the market. This limit price may not be the price point at which the existing competitor earns the largest profit, but it does keep other companies out of the market.
- *Marginal cost pricing* is the practice of setting the price of a product at or slightly above the variable cost to produce it. This may be done when a company has a small amount of remaining unused production capacity available that it wishes to use to maximize its profits, or when it is unable to sell at a higher price. In either case, the sales are intended to be on an incremental basis; this is not intended to be a long-term pricing strategy.
- *Predatory pricing* is the practice of deliberately setting prices so low that competitors are driven from the marketplace. Predatory pricing can also act as a strong barrier to entry, since potential competitors will steer clear of any company sending such a strong competitive signal. A predatory price is considered to be one that is lower than the incremental marginal cost of manufacturing a product.

- *Price leadership* is a situation where one company, usually the dominant one in its industry, sets prices which are closely followed by its competitors. This firm is usually the one having the lowest production costs, and so is in a position to undercut the prices charged by any competitor who attempts to set its prices lower than the price point of the price leader. Competitors could charge higher prices than the price leader, but this would likely result in reduced market share, unless competitors could sufficiently differentiate their products.
- *Price skimming* is the practice of selling a product at a high price, usually during the introduction of a new product when the demand for it is relatively inelastic. This approach is used to generate substantial profits during the first months of the release of a product, usually so that a company can recoup its investment in the product. However, by engaging in price skimming, a company is potentially sacrificing much higher sales than it could garner at a lower price point. Eventually, a company that engages in price skimming must drop its prices, as competitors enter the market and undercut its prices. Thus, price skimming tends to be a short-term strategy.

Internet Pricing

Thus far, we have addressed several types of pricing, treating them as separate concepts. It is also useful to consider the different approach to pricing that can be taken when a business has an Internet store. All of the following advantages are available to the CFO who wants to explore profit maximization:

- *Promotions.* It is quite easy to rapidly cycle through a number of promotional approaches on the Internet, since each one can be launched and terminated at low cost and within short time frames. For example, a 20%-off coupon can be launched that is only good for one day. Management can measure the response by product category, and re-launch the coupon shortly thereafter with a more refined targeting for only certain products, sales regions, or customer profiles. Similarly, different discounting formulas can be experimented with, such as giving away a free product when two other units are bought. These alternatives are not unique to the Internet, but they are much less expensive to launch and monitor.
- *Customer demand.* It is easier to monitor customer demand on the Internet, where data can be extracted on a real-time basis. In this case, it is relatively easy to boost prices when demand spikes, as well as to selectively reduce prices when there is a risk of having too large an investment in inventory. Increasing prices is easier on the Internet, since the company is accessing a larger pool of potential customers than it can reach by other means. Short-term price increases are particularly valuable in industries that are known for having short-term supply constrictions, since a seller could potentially boost prices for just a few days, until supplies return to normal.

- *Customer segmentation.* The purchasing histories of customers can be easily tracked through an Internet store, whereas this information is extremely difficult to obtain in a traditional retail environment. A company may be able to discern which customers only buy when there is a coupon offer, which ones only buy at certain times of the year, which ones buy certain combinations of products, which ones demand overnight delivery service, and so forth. This level of segmentation allows a company to precisely target its sales efforts at particular groups of customers, thereby increasing its total return.

- *Sales progression monitoring.* It is possible to track the proportion of customers that only look at a product on a web page, the proportion moving these items to a shopping cart, and the proportion actually making purchases. If a high proportion of the customers looking at a product page also purchase the item, this may signal strong demand, and trigger a price increase. If the reverse is true, it may be necessary to offer a temporary discount to offset flagging demand.

The alternatives noted here can be considered tactical avenues to be pursued, rather than an entirely new strategic approach to pricing. In essence, the Internet store allows for greater data gathering capabilities and a faster feedback loop, so that prices can be altered to more precisely match customer demand.

Price Elasticity of Demand

Price elasticity is the degree to which changes in price impact the unit sales of a product or service. The demand for a product is considered to be *inelastic* if changes in price have minimal impact on unit sales volume. Conversely, the demand for a product is considered to be *elastic* if changes in price have a large impact on unit sales volume. This concept can be a key determinant of the underlying profitability of a business. In particular, a high level of price elasticity can directly correlate with low profit margins.

A product is more likely to have inelastic demand if customers buy it for reasons other than price. This typically involves high-end luxury goods, or the "latest and greatest" products that are impacted by style considerations, where there are no obvious substitutes for the product. Thus, altering the price of a custom-made watch may not appreciably alter the amount of unit sales volume, since roughly the same number of potential customers will still be interested in buying it, irrespective of the price.

A product is more likely to have elastic demand when it is a commodity that is offered by many suppliers. In this situation, there is no way to differentiate the product, so customers only buy it based on price. Thus, if a business were to raise prices on a product that has elastic demand, unit volume would likely plummet as customers go elsewhere to find a better deal. Examples of products having elastic demand are gasoline, corn, wheat, and cement.

The key considerations in whether a product will have elastic or inelastic demand are:

- *Duration.* Over time, consumers will alter their behavior to avoid excessively expensive goods. This means that the price for a product may be inelastic in the short term, and increasingly elastic over the long term. For example, the owner of a fuel-inefficient vehicle will be forced to pay for higher gasoline prices in the short term, but may switch to a more fuel-efficient vehicle over the long term in order to buy less fuel.
- *Necessity.* If something must be purchased (such as a drug for a specific medical condition), then the consumer will buy it, irrespective of price.
- *Payer.* People who can have their purchases reimbursed by someone else (such as the company they work for) are more likely to exhibit price inelastic behavior. For example, an employee is more likely to stay at an expensive hotel if the company is paying for it.
- *Percent of income.* If something involves a significant proportion of the income of the consumer, the consumer is more likely to look for substitute products, which makes a product more price elastic.
- *Uniqueness.* If there is no ready substitute for the product, it will be more price inelastic. This is particularly true where intensive marketing is used to make the product appear indispensable in the minds of consumers.

The elasticity or inelasticity of demand is a consideration in the pricing of products. Clearly, inelastic demand gives a business a great deal of room in price setting, whereas elastic demand means that the appropriate price is already defined by the market. Products having inelastic demand tend to have smaller markets, whereas products with elastic demand can involve much larger sales volume. Thus, a company pursuing a strategy of only selling products with inelastic demand may be limiting its potential sales growth.

From a practical perspective, companies are most likely to set prices based on what competitors are charging for their products, modified by the perceived value of certain product features. Price elasticity can also be used to fine-tune prices, but it is still more of a theoretical concept than one that has practical applicability.

The formula for the price elasticity of demand is the percent change in unit demand as a result of a one percent change in price. The calculation is:

$$\frac{\text{\% Change in unit demand}}{\text{\% Change in price}}$$

A product is said to be price inelastic if this ratio is less than 1, and price elastic if the ratio is greater than 1. Revenue should be maximized when one can set the price to have an elasticity of exactly 1.

EXAMPLE

Hammer Industries wants to test the price elasticity of demand for two of its products. It alters the price of its steel construction hammer by 3%, which generates a reduction in unit volume of 2%. This indicates some inelasticity of demand, since the company can raise prices and experience a smaller offsetting reduction in sales.

Hammer then tests the price inelasticity of its home screwdriver set by altering its price by 2%. This results in a reduction in unit volume of 4%. The result indicates significant elasticity of demand, since unit sales drop twice as fast as the increase in price.

It can be useful to engage in a formal price elasticity study, to determine the degree to which a business can alter its prices. However, a formal study can be both time-consuming and expensive. An easier alternative is to establish a company website, from which products are sold. Price points can be altered on the website quite easily, while resulting sales levels are monitored. This approach can yield almost immediate insights into pricing behavior, while costing the company very little.

> **Tip:** One way to conduct a price elasticity study is to quote an altered price to a certain proportion of the visitors to the company website, and then compare the resulting sales to the results from unmodified prices.

Cross Price Elasticity of Demand

Cross price elasticity of demand is the percentage change in the demand for one product when the price of a different product changes. This concept is useful for many companies that sell a multitude of products and services, since what at first may appear to be an isolated price change can have a ripple effect on other parts of the business. The CFO should be aware of these interrelationships, and how they can impact profits. The cross price elasticity formula is:

$$\frac{\text{Percentage change in demand of one product}}{\text{Percentage change in price of a different product}}$$

If there is no relationship between the two products, then this ratio will be zero. However, if a product is a valid *substitute* for the product whose price has changed, there will be a positive ratio - that is, a price increase in one product will yield an increase in demand for the other product. Conversely, if two products are typically purchased together (known as *complementary* products), then a price change will result in a negative ratio - that is, a price increase in one product will yield a decrease in demand for the other product.

Here are examples of different ratio results for the cross price elasticity of demand:

- *Positive ratio.* When the admission price at a movie theater increases, the demand for downloaded movies increases, because downloaded movies are a substitute for a movie theater.
- *Negative ratio.* When the admission price at a movie theater increases, the demand at the nearby parking garage also declines, because fewer people are parking there to go to the movie theater. These are complementary products.
- *Zero ratio.* When the admission price at a movie theater increases, the demand at a nearby furniture store is unchanged, because the two are unrelated.

A company can use the concept of cross price elasticity of demand in its pricing strategies. For example, the food served in a movie theater has a strong complementary relationship with the number of theater tickets sold, so it may make sense to drop ticket prices in order to attract more movie viewers, which in turn generates more food sales. Thus, the net effect of lowering ticket prices may be more total profit for the theater owner.

A business can also use heavy branding of its product line to mitigate the substitution effect. Thus, by spending money on advertising, a business can make customers want to buy its products so much that a price increase will not send them out to buy substitute products (at least not within a certain price range).

Non-Price Determinants of Demand

We have spent this entire chapter describing a variety of pricing strategies and theories. But what if customers have other reasons for buying products or services? The following list enumerates several non-price determinants of demand. These factors are important, because they can change the number of units sold, irrespective of their prices. As such, they can provide great value to a company, and so should be a factor in ongoing company planning and pricing discussions. The determinants are:

- *Available income.* If the amount of available buyer income changes, it alters their propensity to purchase. Thus, if there is an economic boom, someone is more likely to buy, irrespective of price.
- *Branding.* Sellers can use advertising, product differentiation, customer service, and so forth to create such strong brand images that buyers have a strong preference for their goods.
- *Complementary goods.* If there is a price change in a complementary item, it can impact the demand for a product. Thus, a change in the price of popcorn in a movie theatre could impact the demand for movies.
- *Demographics.* A change in the proportions of the population in different age ranges can alter demand in favor of those groups increasing in size (and

vice versa). Thus, an aging population will increase the demand for arthritis drugs.

- *Future expectations*. If buyers believe that the market will change in the future, such as may happen with an anticipated constriction of supplies, this may alter their purchasing behavior now. Thus, an expected constriction in the supply of rubber might increase the demand for tires now.
- *Market size*. If the market is expanding rapidly, customers may be compelled to purchase based on other factors than price, simply because the supply of goods is not keeping up with demand.
- *Seasonality*. The need for goods varies by time of year; for example, there is a strong demand for lawn mowers in the spring, but not in the fall.

These determinants will alter the demand for goods and services, but only within certain price ranges. For example, if non-price determinants are driving increased demand, but prices are very high, it is likely that buyers will be driven to look at substitute products.

Summary

Clearly, there are a multitude of methods available for pricing products. Of the pricing strategies noted here, there is no "best" method. Instead, the overall positioning of a business in the marketplace will likely dictate the type of pricing to be employed. Thus, a business that is positioned to provide high-end luxury goods that are well differentiated would almost certainly use value based pricing – no other pricing method would maximize profits. Conversely, a company deadlocked in a price war over the sale of commodity-level products would be completely unable to follow the same strategy. The CFO should therefore be aware of the overall company strategy, and how product pricing dovetails into that strategy. In particular, be aware of instances where proposed pricing diverges from the normal pricing strategy. These situations may represent pricing flaws that should be corrected at once, or they could signal a new strategic direction for the company, or just for a particular subsidiary or product line.

Chapter 9
Capital Budgeting

Introduction

Capital budgeting is a series of analysis steps used to evaluate whether a fixed asset should be acquired, usually including an analysis of the costs, related benefits, and impact on capacity levels of the prospective purchase. In this chapter, we will address a broad array of issues that the CFO should consider when deciding whether to acquire a fixed asset, as well as the lease versus buy decision, the outsourcing alternative, and post-acquisition auditing.

> **Related Podcast Episodes:** Episodes 45, 144, and 145 of the Accounting Best Practices Podcast discuss capital budgeting from a throughput perspective, evaluating capital budget proposals, and capital budgeting with minimal cash. The episodes are available at: **accountingtools.com/podcasts** or **iTunes**

CFO Responsibilities

In a capital-intensive business, one of the most important responsibilities of the CFO is to review proposals to acquire fixed assets. The amount of funding involved may comprise a large part of company cash flows, so an incorrect purchase decision could seriously harm the liquidity of the business. In these situations, the CFO may find that capital budgeting is the most critical task of all.

The following issues are valid CFO concerns to be addressed in the capital budgeting process, any of which may result in the delay, modification, or cancellation of a capital expenditure:

- *Strategic matching.* If the management team has decided upon a certain strategic direction, capital expenditures should roughly follow that direction. Thus, there should be fewer expenditures in areas that are being de-emphasized, leaving more cash available for investments in areas where the company wants to increase its market presence.
- *Asset usage.* It is possible that the assets being proposed will have more capacity than the company is reasonably expected to need. If there is a history of usage spikes that require extra capacity, can outsourcing be used to address these situations? If so, it may be possible to acquire less-expensive assets with reduced capacity levels. The result may be reductions in utility costs, installation costs, maintenance, and floor space requirements.
- *Asset commoditization.* Wherever possible, avoid custom-designed machinery in favor of standard models that are readily available. By doing so, it is

easier to obtain repair parts, and there may even be an aftermarket for disposing of the asset when the company no longer needs it.

- *Asset features.* Managers have a habit of wanting to buy new assets with all of the latest features. Are all of these features really needed? If an asset is being replaced, then it is useful to compare the characteristics of the old and new assets, and examine any differences between the two to see if they are required. If the asset is the only model offered by the supplier, would the supplier be willing to strip away some features and offer it at a lower price?

- *Asset standardization.* If a company needs a particular asset in large quantities, then adopt a policy of always buying from the same manufacturer, and preferably only buying the same asset every time. By doing so, the maintenance staff becomes extremely familiar with the maintenance requirements of several identical machines, and only has to stock replacement parts for one model.

- *Bottleneck analysis.* As noted later in this chapter, assets that improve the amount of throughput in a production operation are usually well worth the investment, while those not impacting the bottleneck require substantially more justification, usually in the direction of reducing operating expenses.

- *Extended useful life.* A manager may be applying for an asset replacement simply because the original asset has reached the end of its recommended useful life. But is it really necessary to replace the asset? Consider conducting a formal review of these assets to see if they can still be used for some additional period of time. There may be additional maintenance costs involved, but this will almost certainly be lower than the cost of replacing the asset.

- *Facility analysis.* If a capital proposal involves the acquisition of additional facility space, consider reviewing any existing space to see if it can be compressed, thereby eliminating the need for more space. For example, shift storage items to less expensive warehouse space, shift from offices to more space-efficient cubicles, and encourage employees to work from home or on a later shift. If none of these ideas work, at least consider acquiring new facilities through a sublease, which tends to require shorter lease terms than a lease arranged with the primary landlord.

- *Monument elimination.* A company may have a large fixed asset around which the rest of the production area is configured; this is called a *monument*. If there is a monument, consider adopting a policy of using a larger number of lower-capacity assets instead of the monument asset. By doing so, one can avoid the risk of having the monument asset go out of service and stopping all production, in favor of having multiple units among which work can be shifted if one unit fails.

Tip: Despite all of the preceding concerns, it is possible that a capital proposal must be accepted if there a project interdependency – that is, a project must be completed in order to increase the probability of success of another project.

In addition, there may be situations with larger capital expenditures where the CFO can conduct reviews at various milestones during the installation process. Occasionally, one of these analyses may reveal that the cost of a project is running well over budget, or that the resulting asset will not generate the return that was originally anticipated. If so, the CFO should be deeply involved in what to do with the project. Any of the following options may be a valid alternative:

- *Abandonment.* The decision is whether to invest additional funds in a project or to scrap it. For this decision, all funds already invested should be considered sunk costs. The primary concern of the CFO is to avoid spending additional funds for which the return on investment appears to be subpar or nonexistent.
- *Deferral.* It may make sense to delay additional expenditures until the circumstances are clarified. For example, the price of a mineral may have to increase to a certain minimum level before a mining company is willing to re-open a mine. When making a deferral decision, be sure to consider the cost of maintaining the incomplete project during the deferral period.
- *Modification.* Additional information gained during the construction process may indicate that the project should be modified in order to improve its return on investment. For example, it may become apparent that the market is smaller than expected, so a smaller-capacity fixed asset should be sufficient.

Changes made as a result of a milestone review can be particularly difficult to enact, because there is a considerable amount of bureaucratic momentum built into a project that is already underway. Consequently, it may not be worth the effort to force through a change in plans unless the projected impact of the change is both significant and irrefutable.

Overview of Capital Budgeting

The normal capital budgeting process is for the management team to request proposals to acquire fixed assets from all parts of the company. Managers respond by filling out a standard request form, outlining what they want to buy and how it will benefit the company. A financial analyst then assists in reviewing these proposals to determine which are worthy of an investment. Any proposals that are accepted are included in the annual budget, and will be purchased during the next budget year. Fixed assets purchased in this manner also require a certain number of approvals, with more approvals required by increasingly senior levels of management if the sums involved are substantial.

These proposals come from all over the company, and so may not be related to each other. Also, the number of proposals usually far exceeds the amount of funding available. Consequently, management needs a method for ranking the priority of projects, with the possible result that some proposals are not accepted at all. The traditional method for doing so is net present value (NPV) analysis, which focuses on picking proposals with the largest amount of discounted cash flows.

The trouble with NPV is that it does not account for how an investment might impact the profit generated by the entire *system* of production; instead, it tends to favor the optimization of specific work centers, which may have no particular impact on overall profitability. Also, the results of NPV are based on the future projections of cash flows, which may be wildly inaccurate. Managers may even tweak their cash flow estimates upward in order to gain project approval, when they know that actual cash flows are likely to be lower. Given these issues, we favor constraint analysis over NPV, though NPV is also discussed in this chapter.

Constraint analysis focuses on how to maximize use of the bottleneck operation. The bottleneck operation is the most constricted operation in a company; to improve the overall profitability of the company, concentrate all attention on management of that bottleneck. This has a profound impact on capital budgeting, since a proposal should have some favorable impact on that operation in order to be approved.

There are two scenarios under which certain project proposals may avoid any kind of bottleneck or cash flow analysis. The first is a legal requirement to install an item. The prime example is environmental equipment, such as smokestack scrubbers, that are mandated by the government. In such cases, there may be some analysis to see if costs can be lowered, but the proposal *must* be accepted, so it will sidestep the normal analysis process.

The second scenario is when a company wants to mitigate a high-risk situation that could imperil the company. In this case, the emphasis is not on profitability at all, but rather on the avoidance of a situation. If so, the mandate likely comes from top management, so there is little additional need for analysis, other than a review to ensure that the lowest-cost alternative is selected.

A final scenario is when there is a sudden need for a fixed asset, perhaps due to the catastrophic failure of existing equipment or a strategic shift. These purchases can happen at any time, and so usually fall outside of the capital budget's annual planning cycle. It is generally best to require more than the normal number of approvals for these items, so that management is made fully aware of the situation. Also, if there is time to do so, they are worthy of an unusually intense analysis, to see if they really must be purchased at once, or if they can be delayed until the next capital budgeting approval period arrives.

Once all items are properly approved and inserted into the annual budget, this does not end the capital budgeting process. There is a final review just prior to actually making each purchase, with appropriate approval, to ensure that the company still needs each fixed asset.

The last step in the capital budgeting process is to conduct a post-implementation review, in which the actual costs and benefits of each fixed asset are summarized and compared to the initial projections included in the original application. If the results are worse than expected, this may result in a more in-depth review, with particular attention being paid to avoiding any faulty aspects of the original proposal in future proposals.

In the following sections, we provide additional detail about bottleneck analysis, net present value, and the less-rigorous payback method.

Bottleneck Analysis

Under bottleneck analysis, the key concept is that an entire company acts as a single system, which generates a profit. Under this concept, capital budgeting revolves around the following logic:

1. Nearly all of the costs of the production system do not vary with individual sales; that is, nearly every cost is an operating expense; therefore,
2. Management needs to maximize the throughput (revenue minus totally variable expenses) of the *entire* system in order to pay for the operating expense; and
3. The only way to increase throughput is to maximize the throughput passing through the bottleneck operation.

Consequently, give primary consideration to those capital budgeting proposals that favorably impact the throughput passing through the bottleneck operation.

This does not mean that all other capital budgeting proposals will be rejected, since there are a multitude of possible investments that can reduce costs elsewhere in a company, and which are therefore worthy of consideration. However, throughput is more important than cost reduction, since throughput has no theoretical upper limit, whereas costs can only be reduced to zero. Given the greater ultimate impact on profits of throughput over cost reduction, any non-bottleneck proposal is simply not as important.

See the author's *Constraint Management* book for a more complete treatment of this subject.

Net Present Value Analysis

Any capital investment involves an initial cash outflow to pay for it, followed by a mix of cash inflows in the form of revenue, or a decline in existing cash flows that are caused by expense reductions. We can lay out this information in a spreadsheet to show all expected cash flows over the useful life of an investment, and then apply a discount rate that reduces the cash flows to what they would be worth at the present date. This calculation is known as *net present value*.

Net present value is the traditional approach to evaluating capital proposals, since it is based on a single factor – cash flows – that can be used to judge any proposal arriving from anywhere in a company. However, the net present value method can be a poor evaluation method if there is a suspicion that the cash flows used to derive an analysis are incorrect.

EXAMPLE

Hammer Industries is planning to acquire an asset that it expects will yield positive cash flows for the next five years. Its cost of capital is 10%, which it uses as the discount rate to construct the net present value of the project. The following table shows the calculation:

Capital Budgeting

Year	Cash Flow	10% Discount Factor	Present Value
0	-$500,000	1.0000	-$500,000
1	+130,000	0.9091	+118,183
2	+130,000	0.8265	+107,445
3	+130,000	0.7513	+97,669
4	+130,000	0.6830	+88,790
5	+130,000	0.6209	+80,717
		Net Present Value	-$7,196

The net present value of the proposed project is negative at the 10% discount rate, so Hammer should not invest in the project.

In the "10% Discount Factor" column in the preceding example, the factor becomes smaller for periods further in the future, because the discounted value of cash flows are reduced as they progress further from the present day. The discount factor is widely available in textbooks, or can be derived from the following formula:

$$\text{Present value of a future cash flow} = \frac{\text{Future cash flow}}{(1 + \text{Discount rate})^{\text{squared by the number of periods of discounting}}}$$

To use the formula for an example, if we forecast the receipt of $100,000 in one year, and are using a discount rate of 10 percent, then the calculation is:

$$\text{Present value} = \frac{\$100,000}{(1+.10)^1}$$

Present value = $90,909

A net present value calculation that truly reflects the reality of cash flows will likely be more complex than the one shown in the preceding example. It is best to break down the analysis into a number of sub-categories, to see exactly when cash flows are occurring and with what activities they are associated. Here are the more common contents of a net present value analysis:

- *Asset purchases.* All of the expenditures associated with the purchase, delivery, installation, and testing of the asset being purchased.
- *Asset-linked expenses.* Any ongoing expenses, such as warranty agreements, property taxes, and maintenance, that are associated with the asset.

- *Contribution margin.* Any incremental cash flows resulting from sales that can be attributed to the project.
- *Depreciation effect.* The asset will be depreciated, and this depreciation shelters a portion of any net income from income taxes, so note the income tax reduction caused by depreciation.
- *Expense reductions.* Any incremental expense reductions caused by the project, such as automation that eliminates direct labor hours.
- *Tax credits.* If an asset purchase triggers a tax credit (such as for a purchase of energy-reduction equipment), then note the amount of the credit.
- *Taxes.* Any income tax payments associated with net income expected to be derived from the asset.
- *Working capital changes.* Any net changes in inventory, accounts receivable, or accounts payable associated with the asset. Also, when the asset is eventually sold off, this may trigger a reversal of the initial working capital changes.

Tip: Mandate the use of a net present value procedure that requires inclusion of all the preceding items in every analysis. Cash flows for all projects can then be reviewed on a consistent basis.

We give priority to bottleneck analysis over net present value as the preferred method for analyzing capital proposals, because bottleneck analysis focuses on throughput. The key improvement factor is throughput, since there is no upper limit on the amount of throughput that can be generated. This does not mean that net present value should be eliminated as a management tool. It is still quite useful for operating expense reduction analysis, where throughput issues are not involved.

The Payback Method

The simplest and least accurate evaluation technique is the payback method. This approach is still heavily used, because it provides a very fast "back of the envelope" calculation of how soon a company will earn back its investment. This means that it provides a rough measure of how long a company will have its investment at risk before earning back the original amount expended. Thus, it is a rough measure of risk. There are two ways to calculate the payback period, which are:

1. *Simplified.* Divide the total amount of an investment by the average resulting cash flow. This approach can yield an incorrect assessment, because a proposal with cash flows skewed far into the future can yield a payback period that differs substantially from when actual payback occurs.
2. *Manual calculation.* Manually deduct the forecasted positive cash flows from the initial investment amount from Year 1 forward, until the investment is paid back. This method is slower, but ensures a higher degree of accuracy.

EXAMPLE

The Hammer Industries CFO has received a proposal from a manager, asking to spend $1,500,000 on equipment that will result in cash inflows in accordance with the following table:

Year	Cash Flow
1	+$150,000
2	+150,000
3	+200,000
4	+600,000
5	+900,000

The total cash flows over the five-year period are projected to be $2,000,000, which is an average of $400,000 per year. When divided into the $1,500,000 original investment, this results in a payback period of 3.75 years. However, the briefest perusal of the projected cash flows reveals that the flows are heavily weighted toward the far end of the time period, so the results of this calculation cannot be correct.

Instead, the CFO runs the calculation year by year, deducting the cash flows in each successive year from the remaining investment. The results of this calculation are:

Year	Cash Flow	Net Invested Cash
0		-$1,500,000
1	+$150,000	-1,350,000
2	+150,000	-1,200,000
3	+200,000	-1,000,000
4	+600,000	-400,000
5	+900,000	0

The table indicates that the real payback period is located somewhere between Year 4 and Year 5. There is $400,000 of investment yet to be paid back at the end of Year 4, and there is $900,000 of cash flow projected for Year 5. The CFO assumes the same monthly amount of cash flow in Year 5, which means that he can estimate final payback as being just short of 4.5 years.

The payback method is not overly accurate, does not provide any estimate of how profitable a project may be, and does not take account of the time value of money. Nonetheless, its extreme simplicity makes it a perennial favorite in many companies.

The Outsourcing Decision

It may be possible to avoid a capital purchase entirely by outsourcing the work to which it is related. By doing so, the company may be able to eliminate all assets related to the area (rather than acquiring more assets), while the burden of maintaining a sufficient asset base now shifts to the supplier. The supplier may even buy the company's assets related to the area being outsourced. This situation is a well-established alternative for high technology manufacturing, as well as for information technology services, but is likely not viable outside of these areas.

> **Tip:** Retain assets in areas where the company has proprietary technology, and concentrate on outsourcing assets in those areas where there is no proprietary technology, or where suppliers are clearly more cost-effective due to higher production volumes.

If outsourcing is a possibility, then the cash flows resulting from doing so will be highly favorable for the first few years, as capital expenditures vanish. However, the supplier must also earn a profit and pay for its own infrastructure, so the cost over the long term will probably not vary dramatically from what a company would have experienced if it had kept a functional area in-house. There are three exceptions that can bring about a long-term cost reduction. They are:

- *Excess capacity*. A supplier may have such a large amount of excess capacity already that it does not need to invest further for some time, thereby potentially depressing the costs that it would otherwise pass through to its customers. However, this excess capacity pool will eventually dry up as the supplier gains more business, so it tends to be a short-term anomaly.
- *High volume*. There are some outsourcing situations where the supplier is handling such a massive volume of activity from multiple customers that its costs on a per-unit basis decline below the costs that a company could ever achieve on its own. This situation can yield long-term savings to a company.
- *Low costs*. A supplier may locate its facility and work force in low-cost countries or regions within countries. This can yield significant cost reductions in the short term, but as many suppliers use the same technique, it is driving up costs in all parts of the world. Thus, this cost disparity is useful for a period of time, but is gradually declining as a long-term option.

There are risks involved in shifting functions to suppliers. First, a supplier may go out of business, leaving the company scrambling to shift work to a new supplier. Second, a supplier may gradually ramp up prices to the point where the company is substantially worse off than if it had kept the function in-house. Third, the company may have so completely purged the outsourced function from its own operations that it is now completely dependent on the supplier, and has no ability to take it back in-house. Fourth, the supplier's service level may decline to the point where it is impairing the ability of the company to operate. And finally, the company may have entered into a multi-year deal, and cannot escape from the arrangement if the business arrangement does not work out. These are significant issues, and must be weighed as part of the outsourcing decision.

The cautions noted here about outsourcing do not mean that it should be avoided as an option. On the contrary, a rapidly growing company that has minimal access to funds may cheerfully hand off multiple operations to suppliers in order to avoid the up-front costs associated with those operations. Outsourcing is less attractive to stable, well-established companies that have better access to capital.

In summary, outsourcing is an attractive option for rapidly growing companies that do not have sufficient cash to pay for capital expenditures, but also carries with it a variety of risks involving shifting key functions to a supplier over which a company may not have a great deal of control.

The Lease versus Buy Decision

Once the asset acquisition decision has been made, management still needs to decide if it should buy the asset outright or lease it. In a leasing situation, a lessor buys the asset and then allows the lessee to use it in exchange for a monthly fee. Depending on the terms of the lease, it may be treated in one of two ways:

- *Capital lease.* The lessee records the leased asset on its books as a fixed asset and depreciates it, while recording interest expense separately.
- *Operating lease.* The lessor records the leased asset on its books as a fixed asset and depreciates it, while the lessee simply records a lease payment.

The decision to use a lease may be based on management's unwillingness to use its line of credit or other available sources of financing to buy an asset. Leases can be easier to obtain than a line of credit, since the lease agreement always designates the asset as collateral.

There are a multitude of factors that a lessor includes in the formulation of the monthly rate that it charges, such as the down payment, the residual value of the asset at the end of the lease, and the interest rate, which makes it difficult to break out and examine each element of the lease. Instead, it is much easier to create separate net present value tables for the lease and buy alternatives, and then compare the results of the two tables to see which is the better alternative.

EXAMPLE

Hammer Industries is contemplating the purchase of an asset for $500,000. It can buy the asset outright, or do so with a lease. Its cost of capital is 8%, and its incremental income tax rate is 35%. The following two tables show the net present values of both options.

192

Buy Option

Year	Depreciation	Income Tax Savings (35%)	Discount Factor (8%)	Net Present Value
0				-$500,000
1	$100,000	$35,000	0.9259	32,407
2	100,000	35,000	0.8573	30,006
3	100,000	35,000	0.7938	27,783
4	100,000	35,000	0.7350	25,725
5	100,000	35,000	0.6806	23,821
Totals	$500,000	$175,000		$360,258

Lease Option

Year	Pretax Lease Payments	Income Tax Savings (35%)	After-Tax Lease Cost	Discount Factor (8%)	Net Present Value
1	$135,000	47,250	$87,750	0.9259	$81,248
2	135,000	47,250	87,750	0.8573	75,228
3	135,000	47,250	87,750	0.7938	69,656
4	135,000	47,250	87,750	0.7350	64,496
5	135,000	47,250	87,750	0.6806	59,723
Totals	$675,000	$236,250	$438,750		$350,351

Thus, the net purchase cost of the buy option is $360,258, while the net purchase cost of the lease option is $350,351. The lease option involves the lowest cash outflow for Hammer, and so is the better option.

The Post Installation Review

It is important to conduct a post installation review of any capital expenditure project, to see if the initial expectations for it were realized. If not, the results of this review can be used to modify the capital budgeting process to yield better results.

Another reason for having a post installation review is that it provides a control over those managers who fill out the initial capital budgeting proposals. If they know there is no post installation review, they can wildly overstate the projected results of their projects with impunity, just to have them approved. Of course, this control is only useful if it is conducted relatively soon after a project is completed. Otherwise, the responsible manager may have moved on in his career, and can no longer be tied back to the results of his work.

If the post implementation review results in the suspicion that a project proposal was unduly optimistic, this brings up the question of how to deal with the responsible manager. At a minimum, the proposal reviews can flag any future proposals by this reviewer as suspect, and worthy of especially close attention.

EXAMPLE

Hammer Industries has just completed a one-year project to increase the amount of production capacity at its primary tool machining facility. The original capital budgeting proposal was for an initial expenditure of $290,000, resulting in additional annual throughput of $100,000 per year. The actual result is somewhat different. The post-installation report includes the following text:

> **Findings:** The proposal only contained the purchase price of the equipment. However, since the machinery was delivered from Germany, Hammer also incurred $22,000 of freight charges and $3,000 in customs fees. Further, the project required the installation of a new concrete pad, a breaker box, and electrical wiring that cost an additional $10,000. Finally, the equipment proved to be difficult to configure, and required $20,000 of consulting fees from the manufacturer, as well as $5,000 for the raw materials scrapped during testing. Thus, the actual cost of the project was $350,000.

> Subsequent operation of the equipment reveals that it cannot operate without an average of 20% downtime for maintenance, as opposed to the 5% downtime that was advertised by the manufacturer. This reduces throughput by 15%, which equates to a drop of $15,000 in throughput per year, to $85,000.

> **Recommendations:** To incorporate a more comprehensive set of instructions into the capital budgeting proposal process to account for transportation, setup, and testing costs. Also, given the wide difference between the performance claims of the manufacturer and actual results, to hire a consultant to see if the problem is caused by our installation of the equipment; if not, we recommend not buying from this supplier in the future.

Summary

This chapter addressed a variety of issues a CFO should consider when deciding whether to acquire a fixed asset. The level of analysis should increase in proportion to the amount of funding required for a capital proposal, not only to ensure that a massive purchase receives an appropriate amount of review, but also to keep a minor purchase proposal from being unduly delayed. It may be practical from an efficiency perspective to impose fewer reviews below a specific monetary cutoff level, and impose vastly more stringent analyses above a certain point. This more refined level of differentiation will keep the capital budgeting process from becoming excessively bureaucratic, and will focus the CFO's attention on the larger expenditures.

Chapter 10
Cash Management

Introduction

The management of cash begins with a cash forecast. The forecast is designed to give the CFO insights into the state of cash inflows and outflows over the next few weeks and months. In addition, it is useful to have a system in place for collecting and concentrating incoming cash as quickly as possible, so that it can be made available for operational and investment purposes. The ability to forecast and concentrate cash is central to a system of cash management. In this chapter, we describe how to create and enhance a cash forecast, as well as the two methods for concentrating cash.

> **Related Podcast Episode:** Episode 187 of the Accounting Best Practices Podcast discusses cash forecast accuracy. The episode is available at: **accounting-tools.com/podcasts** or **iTunes**

The Cash Forecast

The CFO needs to know the amount of cash that will probably be on hand in the near future, in order to make fund raising and investment decisions. This is accomplished with a cash forecast, which should be sufficiently detailed to show projected cash shortfalls and excess funds on at least a weekly basis. This section covers the details of how to create and fine-tune a cash forecast.

The cash forecast can be divided into two parts: near-term cash flows that are highly predictable (typically covering a one-month period) and medium-term cash flows that are largely based on revenues that have not yet occurred and supplier invoices that have not yet arrived. The first part of the forecast can be quite accurate, while the second part yields increasingly tenuous results after not much more than a month has passed. It is also possible to create a long-term cash forecast that is essentially a modified version of the company budget, though its utility is relatively low. The following exhibit shows the severity of the decline in accuracy for short-term and medium-term forecasts. In particular, there is an immediate decline in accuracy as soon as the medium-term forecast replaces the short-term forecast, since less reliable information is used in the medium-term forecast.

Variability of Actual from Forecasted Cash Flow Information

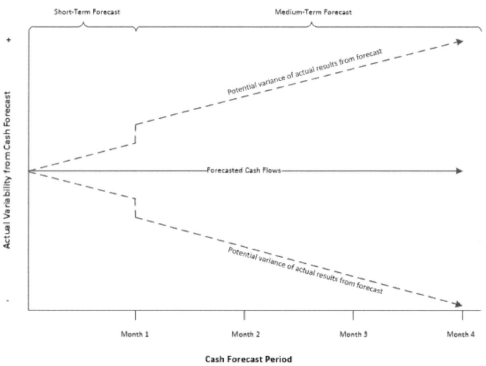

Through the remainder of this section, we will deal separately with how to construct the short-term and medium-term portions of the cash forecast, along with related topics.

The Short-Term Cash Forecast

The short-term cash forecast is based on a detailed accumulation of information from a variety of sources within the company. The bulk of this information comes from the accounts receivable, accounts payable, and payroll records. Since this forecast is based on detailed itemizations of cash inflows and outflows, it is sometimes called the *receipts and disbursements method*.

The forecast needs to be sufficiently detailed to create an accurate cash forecast, but not so detailed that it requires an inordinate amount of labor to update. Consequently, include a detailed analysis of only the *largest* receipts and expenditures, and aggregate all other items. The detailed analysis involves the manual prediction of selected cash receipts and expenditures, while the aggregated results are scheduled based on average dates of receipt and payment (see the comments at the end of this section about the use of averaging).

Tip: Use detailed analysis of cash items in the cash forecast for the 20% of items that comprise 80% of the cash flows, and use aggregation for the remaining 80% of items that comprise 20% of the cash flows.

The following table notes the treatment of the key line items in a cash forecast, including the level of detailed forecasting required.

+/-	Line Item	Discussion
+	Beginning cash	This is the current cash balance as of the creation date of the cash forecast, or, for subsequent weeks, it is the ending cash balance from the preceding week. Do not include restricted cash in this number, since it cannot be used to pay for expenditures.
+	Accounts receivable	Do not attempt to duplicate the detail of the aged accounts receivable report in this section of the forecast. However, it is useful to itemize the largest receivables, stating the period in which cash receipt is most likely to occur. All other receivables can be listed in aggregate.
+	Other receivables	Only include this line item if there are significant amounts of other receivables (such as customer advances) for which cash is expected to be received within the forecast period.
-	Employee compensation	This is possibly the largest expense item, so be especially careful in estimating the amount. It is easiest to base the compensation expense on the amount paid in the preceding period, adjusted for any expected changes.
-	Payroll taxes	List this expense separately, since it is common to forget to include it when aggregated into the employee compensation line item.
-	Contractor compensation	If there are large payments to subcontractors, list them in one or more line items.
-	Key supplier payments	If there are large payments due to specific suppliers, itemize them separately. It may be necessary to change the dates of these payments in the forecast in response to estimated cash positions.
-	Large recurring payments	There are usually large ongoing payments, such as rent and medical insurance, which can be itemized on separate lines of the forecast.
-	Debt payments	If there are significant principal or interest payments coming due, itemize them in the report.
-	Dividend payments	If dividend payments are scheduled, itemize them in the forecast; this tends to be a large expenditure.
-	Expense reports	If there are a large number of expense reports in each month, they are probably clustered near month-end. Include an estimate of the amount likely to be submitted.

+/-	Line Item	Discussion
=	Net cash position	This is the total of all the preceding line items.
+/-	Financing activities	Add any new debt, which increases cash flow, or the reduction of debt, which decreases cash flow. Also add any investments that mature during the period.
	Ending cash	This is the sum of the net cash position line item and the financing activities line item.

The following example illustrates a cash forecast, using the line items described in the preceding table.

EXAMPLE

The CFO of Hammer Industries constructs the following cash forecast for each week in the month of September.

+/-	Line Item	Sept. 1-7	Sept. 8-14	Sept. 15-22	Sept. 23-30
+	Beginning cash	$50,000	$30,000	$2,000	$0
+	Accounts receivable				
+	Apollo Cabinetry	120,000		60,000	
+	Charleston Construction		85,000		52,000
+	French Furniture Designs	29,000		109,000	
+	Other receivables	160,000	25,000	48,000	60,000
+	Other receivables	10,000		5,000	
-	Employee compensation	140,000		145,000	
-	Payroll taxes	10,000		11,000	
-	Contractor compensation				
-	Bryce Contractors	8,000		8,000	
-	Johnson Contractors	14,000		12,000	
-	Key supplier payments				
-	Kinder Knives	100,000		35,000	
-	Smith Sharpeners	20,000	80,000	29,000	14,000
-	Other suppliers	35,000	40,000	30,000	48,000
-	Large recurring payments				
-	Medical insurance				43,000
-	Rent				49,000
-	Debt payments		18,000		
-	Dividend payments			20,000	
-	Expense reports	12,000	0	0	21,000

+/-	Line Item	Sept. 1-7	Sept. 8-14	Sept. 15-22	Sept. 23-30
=	Net cash position	$30,000	$2,000	-$66,000	-$63,000
+/-	Financing activities			66,000	63,000
=	Ending cash	$30,000	$2,000	$0	$0

The forecast reveals a cash shortfall beginning in the third week, which will require a cumulative total of $129,000 of additional financing if the company wants to meet its scheduled payment obligations.

The format is designed with the goal of giving sufficient visibility into cash flows to reveal the causes of unusual cash shortfalls or overages, without burying the reader in an excessive amount of detail. To meet this goal, note the use of the "Other receivables" and "Other suppliers" line items in the exhibit. They are used to aggregate smaller projected transactions that do not have a major impact on the forecast, but which would otherwise overwhelm the document with an excessive amount of detail if they were listed individually.

A possible addition to the cash forecast is the use of a *target balance*. This is essentially a "safety stock" of cash that is kept on hand to guard against unexpected cash requirements that were not planned for in the cash forecast. All excess cash above the target balance can be invested, while any shortfalls below the target balance should be funded. If a target balance had been incorporated into the preceding cash forecast example in the amount of $10,000, the amount would have been listed for the week of September 1-7 as a deduction from the ending cash position, leaving $20,000 of cash available for investment purposes.

The model we have outlined in this section requires a weekly update. It only covers a one-month period, so its contents become outdated very quickly. Ideally, block out time in the department work schedule to complete the forecast at the same time, every week. Unless there is an extremely tight cash flow environment, we do not recommend daily updates of cash forecasts – the time required to create these forecasts is excessive in comparison to the additional precision gained from the more frequent updates.

> **Tip:** Do not schedule an update of the cash forecast on a Monday or Friday, since too many of these days involve holidays. Instead, schedule the forecast update on any other business day, thereby increasing the odds of completing a new forecast every week.

The very short-term portion of the cash forecast may be subject to some tweaking, usually to delay a few supplier payments to adjust for liquidity problems expected to arise over the next few days. To incorporate these changes into the forecast, the CFO may use a preliminary draft of the forecast to coordinate changes in the timing of payments with the controller, and then record the delays in the forecast before issuing the final version.

The Medium-Term Cash Forecast

The medium-term cash forecast extends from the end of the short-term forecast through whatever time period the CFO needs to develop investment and funding strategies. Typically, this means that the medium-term forecast begins one month into the future.

The components of the medium-term forecast are largely comprised of formulas, rather than the specific data inputs used for a short-term forecast. For example, if the sales manager were to contribute estimated revenue figures for each forecasting period, then the model could derive the following additional information:

- *Cash paid for cost of goods sold items*. Can be estimated as a percentage of sales, with a time lag based on the average supplier payment terms.
- *Cash paid for payroll*. Sales activity can be used to estimate changes in production headcount, which in turn can be used to derive payroll payments.
- *Cash receipts from customers*. A standard time lag between the billing date and payment date can be incorporated into the estimation of when cash will be received from customers.

The concept of a formula-filled cash forecast that automatically generates cash balance information breaks down in some parts of the forecast. In the following areas, manual updates to the forecast should be made:

- *Fixed costs*. Some costs are entirely fixed, such as rent, and so will not vary with sales volume. Be aware of any contractually-mandated changes in these costs, and incorporate them into the forecast.
- *Step costs*. If revenues change significantly, the fixed costs just described may have to be altered by substantial amounts. For example, a certain sales level may mandate opening a new production facility. A more common step cost is having to hire an overhead staff position when certain sales levels are reached. Thus, it is useful to be aware of the activity levels at which these step costs will occur.
- *Seasonal / infrequent costs*. There may be expenditures that only arise at long intervals, such as for the company Christmas party. These amounts are manually added to the forecast.
- *Contractual items*. Both cash inflows and outflows may be linked to contract payments, as may be the case with service contracts. If so, the exact amount and timing of each periodic payment can be transferred from the contract directly into the cash forecast.

The methods used to construct a medium-term cash forecast are inherently less accurate than the much more precise information used to derive a short-term forecast. The problem is that much of the information is derived from the estimated revenue figure, which rapidly declines in accuracy just a few months into the future. Because of this inherent level of inaccuracy, do not extend the forecast over too long a time period. Instead, settle upon a time range that provides useful information for planning purposes. Any additional forecasting beyond that time period will be a waste of time to create, and may yield misleading information.

The Long-Term Cash Forecast

There can also be a long-term cash forecast that extends for an additional one or two years past the end of the medium-term forecast. It can be extremely difficult and time-consuming to develop and maintain a sales forecast for this period, so the most common approach is to instead adapt information from the corporate budget, and update it regularly to coincide with management's best estimates of long-term results.

The cash flows indicated by a long-term cash forecast should be considered only approximate values, so you would probably be justified in not using it as the basis for any investment activities having specific maturity dates. However, the long-term forecast may be of more use in dealing with projected cash shortfalls. For lack of any better information, use it to obtain approximations of how much cash may be needed, and to plan on acquiring debt or selling stock to meet the shortfall.

The Use of Averages

There can be a temptation to use averages for estimated cash flows in the cash forecast. For example, it may seem reasonable to divide the average cash collections for receivables in a month by four, and then enter the resulting average cash receipts figure in each week of the forecast. This is not a good idea in the short-term portion of the forecast, since there are a number of timing differences that will make actual results differ markedly from average results. The following bullets contain several cash flow issues that can have sharp spikes and declines in comparison to the average:

- The receipt of payment for an unusually large invoice
- The designation of a large invoice as a bad debt
- Once-a-month payments, such as rent and medical insurance
- Sporadic payments, such as for dividends and property taxes

It is particularly dangerous to use averaging to estimate accounts receivable. In many companies, there is a disproportionate amount of invoicing at the end of each month, which means that there is a correspondingly large amount of cash receipts one month later (assuming 30-day payment terms). In short, it is quite common to have billing surges cause payment surges that vary wildly from average cash receipt numbers.

If a CFO were to rely upon an averages-based cash forecast, there would be a high risk of routinely having cash shortfalls and overages. After all, the CFO is responsible for ensuring liquidity *every day*, not just on average. Thus, we strongly recommend against the use of averages when forecasting the larger items in a short-term cash forecast.

The situation is different in a medium-term forecast, since the time period is sufficiently far into the future to make it impossible to predict cash flows with any degree of precision. In this case, it is reasonable to estimate based on averages, though with three enhancements:

- Insert specific cash flows that you are sure of, such as contractually-mandated payments or receipts.
- Insert specific cash flows that have historically proven to be reliable. For example, if a customer has proven to be consistent in paying on a certain day of the month, assume that these payments will continue with the same timing.
- It may be possible to substitute actual cash flow information for averages in the least-distant time periods. This is particularly likely for cash outflows, such as payroll, where there is not a significant amount of change in the amount paid from period to period.

The Use of Clearing Dates in a Forecast

The overall intent of the cash forecast is to give the CFO the best possible estimate of the amount of cash that is *available for use* on certain dates. This is an important issue, since a company may receive a check payment from a customer on one date, but not have use of the cash until several additional business days have passed. Similarly, the cash represented by an accounts payable check sent to a supplier may still be available to the company for a week or more, since there will be a delay associated with the transit time of the check to the supplier (mail float), as well as any in-house recordation delays at the supplier, and the time required for the check to clear the bank.

These delays in cash availability should be built into the cash forecast, but only if it is possible to reliably predict the amount of cash that will be delayed and the duration of the delay. For example, it may be possible to predict the following distribution of checks expected to clear on the days following check issuance, where the distribution is built into the amount of cash disbursed through a check run:

Sample Forecast of Expected Check Clearing

Amount of Checks Issued	Business Days After Check Issuance	Percent Expected to Clear	Amount Expected to Clear	Day
$100,000				Monday
	1	5%	$5,000	Tuesday
	2	25%	25,000	Wednesday
	3	30%	30,000	Thursday
	4	20%	20,000	Friday
	5	15%	15,000	Monday
	6	5%	5,000	Tuesday
		100%	$100,000	

It is easiest to predict a standard number of days delay before deposited cash is made available. It is more difficult to predict the delay for accounts payable checks, since it involves the actions of the postal service and the payee; a conservative approach is to apply a minimum number of days delay to all payments issued.

The timing difference between the clearing date and recordation date is declining, since many companies have turned to electronic payments. In particular, the use of direct deposit for payroll payments means that there is essentially no delay in payments made to employees.

> **Tip:** If it is too complicated to incorporate clearing dates into the cash forecast, at least consider doing so for the largest individual cash inflows and outflows, so that a small amount of additional forecasting effort will still result in better timing accuracy for a significant part of the forecast.

Cash Forecast Reconciliation

No matter how perfectly a cash forecast has been assembled, the result will never exactly match actual results. Either the amount or timing of actual cash inflows and outflows will differ from the prediction. Because of these differences, conduct a forecast reconciliation. The reconciliation should encompass the following activities:

- Investigate items that were expected to occur, but which did not
- Investigate items that were entirely unanticipated, or which were accelerated
- Investigate items that occurred in unanticipated amounts

The result can be a formal reconciliation document, but the main point is for the cash forecast preparers to gain experience with any permutations in the company's cash flows. The gradual accumulation of knowledge about such matters as the speed with which certain business partners pay the company or cash its checks is key to the improvement of cash forecasts.

> **Tip:** The best time to conduct a cash forecast reconciliation is immediately prior to generating the next forecast, so that any identified issues can be immediately incorporated into the next forecast.

There may be rare cases where the reconciliation process uncovers a check payment that was fraudulently issued. Though these occasional discoveries may qualify the cash forecast reconciliation as a weak detective control, it is not designed to be a control. Consequently, do not incorporate into the reconciliation a detailed investigation of the nature of every check paid by the business. Instead, the focus should be on improving the accuracy of the forecast.

The Need for Cash Concentration

Many organizations have a large number of highly dispersed locations that collect or disburse cash. The classic example is a chain of retail stores, each of which collects cash and checks every day, and forwards them to a local bank account. If the CFO were to leave the cash in these accounts untouched, they would not earn any interest income for the company. In these situations, it is necessary to find a way to concentrate the balances in the various accounts in order to maximize use of the cash.

There is a temptation *not* to concentrate cash balances, for concentration requires either an automated bank system (for which the fees are not inconsiderable) or the ongoing daily monitoring and movement of cash balances. However, the cost of unused cash can be quite substantial. Follow these steps to determine the cost of cash that remains in non-interest-bearing bank accounts:

1. *Determine the average account balance.* This information is available as an end-of-day account balance on the most recent bank statement. Add up the end-of-day balances for all days in the month and divide by the number of reported days.
2. *Determine the interest rate.* If the company has debts that it could pay down with the excess cash, then use the interest rate that the company is paying on this debt. If there is no debt, use the interest rate that the company is currently earning on its short-term investments (which is usually lower than the debt interest rate).
3. *Calculate lost earnings.* Multiply the average account balance by the interest rate to arrive at the cost of unused cash.

In most cases, it is prudent to have access to residual cash to cover periodic spikes in the demand for cash. This means that the interest rate on short-term investments is the most reasonable rate to use for determining the cost of residual cash, rather than the interest rate on debt; the staff would never actually use the cash to pay down debt, since doing so creates a risk of not having enough cash on hand.

Another way of looking at the cost of a widely-dispersed set of bank accounts is the cost of overdrafts charged by the bank when an account balance turns negative. In the current market conditions, a company is lucky to obtain 2% interest on its short-term investments, but will be charged at least 10% interest on any bank overdrafts. If there is no cash concentration system in place, the bank is entitled to charge interest on all overdraft situations. Conversely, a cash concentration system will set all account balances to no worse than zero, so that overdraft charges are no longer possible. Thus, if a company has a history of debit balances in some of its bank accounts, the elimination of expensive overdraft interest charges may justify the cost of a cash concentration system.

EXAMPLE

Hammer Industries has four subsidiaries, all of which are allowed to manage their funds locally. Subsidiary D has a history of having negative cash balances, which has led to a significant amount of bank overdraft charges. In the past year, the average account balance and interest income or expense associated with each subsidiary is noted in the following table, where interest income is earned at 2% and overdrafts are charged at 10%:

Subsidiary	Average Cash Balance	Applicable Interest Rate	Annual Interest Income / Expense
A	$82,000	2%	$1,640
B	30,000	2%	600
C	17,000	2%	340
D	-45,000	10%	-4,500
Totals	$84,000		-$1,920

In short, the 5x difference between the interest income paid by the bank and its bank overdraft charge virtually eliminates all interest income that the company might otherwise earn.

The CFO investigates the possibility of a cash concentration system, and finds that a key benefit is the automatic cross-funding of accounts with negative balances from those accounts with credit balances, thereby eliminating the overdraft charge. For the past year, the result would have been a 2% rate of income on the entire $84,000 company-wide average cash balance, which is $1,680. Thus, there would have been a net increase of $3,600 in interest income by switching to a cash concentration system, where Hammer goes from $1,920 of net interest expense to $1,680 of interest income. This increase in interest income is calculated prior to the imposition of any bank fees related to running the cash concentration system.

Yet a third benefit of cash concentration is the reduction in investment fees. When a single large investment is made from a concentration account, a company pays only a single transaction fee to initiate the transaction. If, however, cash is invested locally from many accounts, a transaction fee will be imposed for each investment made from every account. Thus, investment costs can be radically reduced when cash is pooled into a single location.

Cash Sweeping

A cash sweeping system (also known as physical pooling) is designed to move the cash in a company's outlying bank accounts into a central concentration account, from which it can be more easily invested. Cash sweeps are intended to occur at the end of every business day, which means that quite a large number of sweep transactions may arise over the course of a year.

Cash sweeping can be fully automated as long as a company keeps all of its bank accounts with a single bank, where the bank can monitor account balances. Since several banks now span entire countries, it is not especially difficult to locate banks that can provide comprehensive sweeping services across broad geographic regions.

The Zero Balance Account

One way to implement a cash sweeping system is the *zero balance account* (ZBA). A ZBA is usually a checking account that is automatically funded from a central account in an amount sufficient to cover presented checks. To do so, the bank calculates the amount of all checks presented against a ZBA, and pays them with a debit to the central account. Also, if deposits are made *into* a ZBA account, the amount of the deposit is automatically shifted to the central account. Further, if a subsidiary account has a debit (overdrawn) balance, cash is automatically shifted from the central account *back* to the subsidiary account in an amount sufficient to bring the account balance back to zero. In addition, subsidiary account balances can be set at a specific target amount, rather than zero, so that some residual cash is maintained in one or more accounts.

There are three possible ZBA transactions, all of which occur automatically:

- Excess cash is shifted into a central account
- Cash needed to meet payment obligations is shifted from the central account to linked checking accounts
- Cash needed to offset debit balances is shifted from the central account to linked accounts

The net result of a ZBA is that a company retains most of its cash in a central location, and only doles out cash from that central account to pay for immediate needs.

EXAMPLE

Hammer Industries has a ZBA arrangement where three accounts used by local facilities are linked to a cash concentration account. At the end of Monday, the three accounts have the following balances, along with associated transfer activity:

Account	Ending Balance	To/From Concentration Account	Transferred Amount	Ending Account Balance
A	$45,000	To	-$45,000	$0
B	-12,000	From	+12,000	0
C	39,000	To	-39,000	0
	$72,000		-$72,000	$0

The ZBA system has extracted funds from accounts A and C to bring their balances down to zero, and added funds to account B in order to bring its balance *up* to zero.

A company's bank will charge a monthly service fee to manage a ZBA, and may add additional charges for each individual automated transaction to move cash into or out of a ZBA.

A ZBA may transfer cash across national boundaries, which can cause tax issues that the tax department should monitor. If there is a national prohibition on cash transfers across borders, it may not be possible to create a cross-border ZBA.

Multiple Sweep Arrangements

An alternative to sweeping in cash from outside a bank's system is to have a separate sweeping system for each bank that the company uses. Thus, it may have one bank servicing its stores in the western half of a country, and design a system that sweeps cash from those accounts into a concentration account that is still within the same bank. The same approach could be used for each of a company's banks. This approach minimizes sweeping costs, but does require that more concentration accounts be monitored for investment purposes.

Multiple sweeping arrangements may be necessary when there are accounts within different countries. Depending on the situation, cross-border transfers can be time-consuming, and may even be restricted by government rules. If so, a reasonable alternative is to conduct sweeps within each country. This may mean that the funds concentrated through each sweeping system are also invested within the same country.

In situations where there is no prohibition on cross-border cash concentrations, but cash is administratively difficult to move across borders, it is still possible to plan for occasional transfers that are manually initiated. These moves should be coordinated with the company's tax planning staff, to ensure that the company is complying with all local tax laws when shifting funds into or out of a country.

Manual Sweeping

There may be situations where the bank operating a cash sweep cannot automatically initiate a sweep for an account located outside of its system. If so, a more manual approach is possible, where the person responsible for the account notifies the treasury staff of the most recent deposit amount or account balance; this triggers an ACH debit transaction by the treasury staff to move the funds out of the outlying account and into an account located within the sweep system. For those parts of the world where ACH debits are not available, a more expensive alternative is to move the funds with a wire transfer. Given the high cost of a wire transfer, it may be more cost-effective to let cash pile up and then initiate wire transfers at longer intervals.

> **Tip:** A manual deposit reporting system is subject to error, which can trigger an overdraft charge if a company withdraws an excessive amount from an account. Consequently, review all overdraft notices in detail, to determine what problem caused them to occur.

Sweeping Rules

A number of rules can be set up in a cash sweeping system to fit the cash requirements of the business entity using each account, as well as to minimize the cost of the system. Rules usually address:

- *Frequency.* Cash can be swept from some accounts at longer intervals than for other accounts. Some accounts accumulate cash very slowly, and only require an occasional sweep.
- *Threshold sweeps.* Cash can be swept only when the cash balance in an account reaches a certain level. This minimizes the cost of initiating sweeps for very small amounts of cash.
- *Target balances.* A designated amount of cash can be left in an account to ensure that a certain balance is always available. This may require that cash be sent *into* an account, rather than the usual outbound sweep. Target balances are useful when day-to-day operating needs are being met locally through an account. For example, a local bank may automatically extract its monthly service fee from an account, and will charge an overdraft fee if the account contains no cash with which to pay the service fee.

Sweep Problems

Cash sweeping is not to be engaged in lightly when cash is being moved among the accounts of multiple business entities, and especially when cash is being moved across national boundaries. Cash sweeping can cause all of the following problems:

- *Thin capitalization.* The automated extraction of cash from a subsidiary may result in a covenant breach with a lender, since the subsidiary has replaced cash with a loan receivable.
- *Recognition of interest income.* Some local tax jurisdictions will take exception if a business recognizes all of its interest income at the corporate level, since the cash that generated the interest income is located at the subsidiary level. To offset this problem, all interest earned should be allocated back to the subsidiaries based on the amount of their cash that was used to generate the income.
- *Recognition of interest expense.* As was the case with interest income, some tax jurisdictions want to see an interest charge recorded against those subsidiaries that required a cash infusion to avoid an overdraft situation. The interest charge should be based on the interest rate paid by the company for its debt; in the absence of any debt, use the market interest rate.

- *Sweep timing.* Cash is swept from an account near the end of each business day. Depending on sweep timing, it is possible that a late deposit into an account will not be swept into the concentration account until the following day, so that one day of interest income is lost.

Tip: Always document how interest income and expense is allocated back to and recorded by subsidiaries, since tax auditors may want to review this information.

Sweep Costs

Banks charge high service fees for cash sweeps, which should be factored into whether the service should be used. For example, a typical monthly sweep charge is $150 (which is $1,800 per year), while the interest income earned from sweeps is relatively low. The following table notes the cash balance breakeven point for different interest rates, assuming the $1,800 annual bank fee.

Cash Sweeping Breakeven Analysis

Annual Bank Fee	Interest Rate	Cash Required to Breakeven
$1,800	1.0%	$180,000
1,800	1.5%	120,000
1,800	2.0%	90,000
1,800	2.5%	72,000
1,800	3.0%	60,000
1,800	3.5%	51,000
1,800	4.0%	45,000
1,800	4.5%	40,000
1,800	5.0%	36,000

At the low interest rates that frequently apply in today's credit markets, the preceding table shows that a company probably needs to have an average cash balance of at least $100,000 on an ongoing basis before it should even consider using a bank's cash sweeping service.

EXAMPLE

A subsidiary of Hammer Industries is located in a country that does not allow the transfer of cash outside of its borders, so the subsidiary's CFO investigates the use of a cash sweep for the 10 Hammer bank accounts located within the country. In the past three months, these accounts averaged an aggregate cash balance of $127,000. The subsidiary can earn 2.2% on its short-term cash investments. The company will be charged $2,000 per year by its bank for cash sweeping services. Thus, if the company were to create an in-country cash sweep, the result would be:

($127,000 Cash balance × 2.2%) - $2,000 Annual fee = $794 Net profit

The profits from the prospective sweep arrangement are quite small but are still positive, so the CFO elects to proceed with the arrangement.

The cost of individual sweeps is minimal if all of the accounts are administered by the same bank, since the bank can simply shift the funds with an entry in its own accounting records. However, if an account is being swept that is *not* within the bank's system, the cost of doing so over time can be substantial. An ACH debit transaction is the least expensive alternative, but this method is not available in many parts of the world, and also involves a one-day lag. A wire transfer will work, but is much more expensive than an ACH debit.

EXAMPLE

Hammer Industries' CFO learns that a $150,000 wire transfer has just been made into an outlying account that is not automatically swept by the company's primary bank. If the CFO initiates a $20 wire transfer, the funds will be shifted into the company's concentration account the same day, and so will be available for investment in a bond that yields 4% interest. Alternatively, he can initiate the transfer by ACH, which costs only $0.50, but which requires a one-day delay. If the cash remains in its existing account overnight, it will earn a 1% earnings credit that will offset bank fees charged against the account.

The difference between the interest rates that can be earned from the two investment options is 3%, which is worth the following amount of interest income for a single day of investment:

($50,000 Cash × 3%) ÷ 365 Days = $4.11

Since the incremental difference in earnings from the two investment options is so small, the most cost-effective sweeping arrangement is to initiate an ACH to move the funds with a one-day delay.

Summary

Cash sweeping is a rather expensive way to move cash into a central concentration account for investment purposes. Given the minimal interest rates now available on short-term investments, the decision to use cash sweeping mandates a detailed cost-benefit analysis. If a company does not expect to maintain a reasonably large aggregate cash balance across all of its accounts, it is entirely possible that a sweeping arrangement will actually *lose* money for a company. Also, and due to the same low interest rates, it is rarely cost-effective to use wire transfers to sweep in cash from outlying accounts. Instead, consider using less expensive alternatives that may require one or more days to centralize the excess cash.

Notional Pooling

Cash sweeping can be considered an intrusive cash concentration system, since it moves cash among accounts. Local managers may complain that they do not have control over their cash, since it is being moved out from under their control. An alternative is to allow cash to remain where it is and under local control, but to record it at the bank as though the cash has been centralized. This is called *notional pooling*. If a bank offers notional pooling, it simply combines the ending balances in all of a company's accounts to arrive at an aggregate net balance. If the result is a positive cash balance, the bank typically invests the funds automatically and pays the company interest income on the amount invested. If the result is a negative cash balance, the bank charges interest on the net negative amount.

The notional pooling concept is particularly useful when individual accounts are owned by subsidiaries that want control over their cash, and do not want to see it commingled in a central concentration account.

Another advantage of notional pooling is that a few banks offer pooling across currencies. This means that interest is earned on cash holdings denominated in multiple currencies, without ever having to engage in any foreign exchange conversions into a single investment currency.

Some banks offer the automated allocation of interest income back to the accounts where cash is stored, based on the actual amount of interest earned and the relative proportions of cash in the various accounts included in the pooling arrangement.

Notional Pooling Problems

Though notional pooling initially may appear to be an ideal solution, there are some problems that limit its use. These issues are:

- *Availability*. Notional pooling systems are prohibited in some countries, and are impractical in others where banking systems are not sufficiently integrated to allow for the virtual aggregation of funds. The reason for the prohibition is that some governments believe that such pooling constitutes a co-mingling of funds from different entities. Notional pooling is allowed in most European countries, but is not allowed in the United States.
- *Legal restrictions*. Even when notional pooling is allowed, some countries restrict its use to wholly-owned subsidiaries. Other countries do not allow notional pooling to include accounts located in other countries.
- *Single bank network*. The approach only works within the account network of a single bank, since the bank must have the capability to "see" all account balances. If a company uses multiple banks, it can instead employ a separate notional pooling arrangement with each bank, or a mix of notional pooling and cash sweeps.
- *Recognition of interest income and expense*. A notional pooling system awards interest income to the corporate parent. As was the case with cash sweeping, this means that some tax jurisdictions will want that interest in-

211

come to be allocated back to the subsidiary level. The same allocation is needed for interest expense, if an account carries a debit balance. These allocations should be fully documented, since they may be perused by tax auditors.

For the first three reasons just noted, notional pooling tends to be a partial solution that works well in some areas, and is not available or allowed in others. Consequently, and despite the attractiveness of the concept, it is more likely to be implemented in a patchwork manner, with different systems installed in different parts of the world.

Notional Pooling Costs

The cost of notional pooling is lower than for cash sweeps, since no transactions are used to move cash between accounts. Also, the time that might be required to manually move funds is eliminated. Finally, the bank overdraft expense that might otherwise be charged on accounts having negative balances is eliminated, since the debit and credit positions in all accounts are merged through notional pooling; ideally, credit positions will exceed the amount of any debit account balances.

Summary

When it is available, notional pooling is administratively simple and allows for the retention of cash in accounts at the local level. However, the system is not allowed in some countries, and cannot be used as a single system where accounts are being administered by multiple banks. The latter issue is addressed in the next section, Multi-Tiered Banking.

Multi-Tiered Banking

There may be situations where a company has long-standing relationships with certain local banks that it wants to maintain, perhaps due to connections with local business partners. It is quite possible that these local banks cannot be linked into a company's worldwide cash concentration system on an automated basis. If so, an alternative is to have the company's primary bank open an account on behalf of the company within every country where the company does business, and then periodically shift funds from the local bank accounts into the designated accounts of the primary bank.

The result is a two-tiered structure, where the lowest level of banks is responsible for the local receipt and payment of day-to-day operating transactions. Excess cash is siphoned off to the higher tier of banks, which are then used to concentrate the cash on either a sweep or notional pooling basis for investment purposes. Cash transfers between the two tiers of banks may have to be manually initiated, in which case it may be more cost-effective to concentrate cash at longer intervals.

The two-tiered structure is certainly subject to local banking regulations, and so may not be universally applicable. Nonetheless, the concept can bring additional centralization to a dispersed system of accounts that might at first appear to resist centralization.

Cash Concentration Best Practices

Irrespective of the type of cash concentration system being used, periodically review a number of structural issues involving a company's use of bank accounts. These issues are:

- *Examine low-usage accounts.* Review accounts having extremely low transaction volumes to see if the transaction activity can be shifted into a more active account. This can eliminate account servicing fees, and makes it easier to concentrate cash for investment purposes.
- *Review the accounts of acquired businesses.* Include on the company's acquisition checklist a reminder to review the bank accounts of every acquired business. There are likely to be opportunities for account reduction within these inherited accounts.
- *Mandate deposit cutoff times.* Review the company's procedures for depositing cash, to ensure that cash is deposited by a certain cutoff time each day. If deposits are made late, they may not be picked up by a bank's automated cash sweep, and so will not earn interest income until the following business day.
- *Administration charges.* Charge back a reasonable amount of corporate expenses to the company subsidiaries if there are significant expenses traceable to cash concentration activities. By doing so, the company can realize tax savings when its subsidiaries are located in high-tax regions. The strategy is less useful when subsidiaries are located in low-tax regions where there is little benefit to be gained from an expense allocation.

EXAMPLE

The CFO of Hammer Industries is conducting a routine review of open bank accounts and notices that an account from a recent acquisition is still open. The account contains a balance of $5,000, and has essentially no activity. The bank is charging $50 per month to keep the account open. Hammer is currently earning 3% on its short-term investments. Based on this information, the annual cost of the account is:

$$(\$5{,}000 \text{ Account balance} \times 3\% \text{ Earnings rate}) + (\$50/\text{Month fee} \times 12 \text{ Months})$$

$$= \$750$$

Thus, the cost of maintaining this stray account balance is 15% of its current account balance. The CFO decides to close the account at once and move the funds into a more heavily-used account.

The ongoing concentration of accounts has an additional benefit, which is that the smaller number of remaining banks will see that more cash is being stored in their accounts, which may give a company slightly more bargaining power with its banks.

Cash Concentration Alternatives

A cash concentration system is not a requirement. It is extremely helpful in situations where there are many scattered accounts that are not under central control, but is not cost-effective where that specific scenario does not arise. In particular, consider alternatives to or modifications of cash concentration under the following circumstances:

- *Small local balances.* There may be a number of small accounts in which modest credit balances are maintained. This scenario is most common where there are small-scale retail operations at the local level. It is too expensive to use cash sweeps for such a large number of accounts. Notional pooling may not be possible if there are a number of accounts operated by different banks. In short, this scenario probably calls for locally controlled accounts.
- *Independent subsidiaries.* Senior management may have implemented a corporate structure that is essentially "hands off," allowing local managers great leeway to conduct operations as they see fit. If so, instituting any type of cash concentration system may be seen as the first step in the redistribution of power to the corporate staff, and so will not be allowed. A possible alternative is to use notional pooling, where cash concentration is essentially invisible at the local level.
- *Slow cash buildup.* What if the amount of cash in some accounts only builds up over a long period of time? It could be overkill to continually extract small-dollar balances from these accounts on a daily or even weekly basis. Instead, consider a manual review of these accounts at very long intervals, such as quarterly or semi-annually, with a manually-initiated cash sweep at that time.
- *Country restrictions.* A company may operate within a country that imposes severe restrictions on cash flows into or out of the country. If so, cash concentration systems can still be attempted within the country, as long as cash is never shifted to pools outside of the country.

Summary

It can take several months to achieve a forecasting process that generates reliable cash forecasts. It is not sufficient to reach this level of success and then move on to other projects. Instead, build review systems that constantly monitor forecasts to see if accuracy levels start to decline, and use this information to correct the forecasting model at once. This high level of watchfulness is needed in every company, since the alteration of company systems that is triggered by new lines of business, new software, acquisitions, and so forth will eventually alter the inputs to the cash forecast, making its results less reliable.

Cash Management

The need for a cash concentration system depends upon the structure of a business. If the organization is designed to be top-down, with close management by a corporate group, then there will probably be a cash concentration system that is managed from above. Conversely, if senior management goes to great lengths to diffuse responsibility down into an organization and keep the corporate group lean, then the management philosophy of the company may keep it from ever installing a cash concentration system – irrespective of any cost-benefit analysis.

If the decision is made to engage in cash concentration, consider the level of automation that will be used. Any system that requires the ongoing, detailed attention of the treasury staff on a frequent basis is likely to fail, simply because there are so many accounts to be monitored every day. Instead, the best solutions are either those handled automatically by the company's bank, or only at long intervals on a manual basis.

Finally, there are distinct differences between the cash sweeping and notional pooling methods of cash concentration. Consider using the following table to determine which one is the better alternative for an organization's specific circumstances:

Comparison of Cash Sweeping and Notional Pooling

	Cash Sweeping	Notional Pooling
Administrative effort	Considerable effort is needed to track intercompany loans arising from sweep activities	Minimal, since there are no cash transfers or intercompany loans
Interest allocation to subsidiaries	The calculation can be automated	The calculation can be automated
Cross-border transactions	Foreign currency conversions are required	Foreign currency conversions not required
Prohibitions on cross-border cash transfers	Can keep cash sweeps from taking place	Is not a limitation, since cash is not moved
Accounts with multiple banks	Can still be accomplished, though manually-initiated transactions may be required	Generally not possible for accounts located outside of the bank providing notional pooling services
Local control of cash	Not possible, since cash is being physically centralized	Possible, since cash is not being moved
Legality	Generally allowed in most countries	Prohibited or restricted in some countries

The preceding table shows that notional pooling is the generally preferred approach for most decision points involving cash concentration systems. However, since it only works for accounts administered by a single bank and is not allowed in some countries, it is quite possible that a business will need to install a mix of the two systems.

215

Chapter 11
Investment Management

Introduction

Any company will have occasional surges in cash flow, while wealthier ones may have substantial cash reserves. The CFO should have a system in place for investing this cash, as defined by a number of restrictions that are primarily designed to protect the cash and make it readily accessible. In this chapter, we discuss the guidelines used for investing, various investment strategies, the investment instruments most commonly used, and several formulas related to investments.

Investment Guidelines

Though this chapter is entirely concerned with investments, we must emphasize that cash management is primarily about keeping cash reserves available for operational use; it is not about maximizing return on investment. The following guidelines are designed to meet this cash availability goal:

- *Protect the cash.* Above all, do not lose the cash. No investment should be so risky that the company is unable to recover the cash that it initially placed in the investment. This is a particularly important consideration in situations where a company has a short-term operational need for the cash, and is only parking it in an investment for a short time in order to gain some assured income.
- *Ready conversion to cash.* It should be easy to convert an investment into cash on little notice. The CFO must be able to satisfy any short-term operational need for cash, even if it was not planned for in the cash forecast. This means that there should be an active secondary market for all investments, where someone else can readily be found to acquire an investment instrument held by the company.
- *Earn a return.* After the preceding two factors have been dealt with, the CFO may optimize the return on investment. This means that, if there are two possible investments that have identical risk profiles and liquidity, pick the one having the greater return on investment.

The interplay between these guidelines changes in relation to the duration of an investment. For example, a portfolio of investments that all have long-term maturities usually have returns associated with them that are locked in (assuming they are held to maturity), so there is a reduced risk related to the return that will be earned. Conversely, and depending upon the existence of a secondary market, it may be more difficult to liquidate these longer-term investments. For comparison purposes, a short-term investment is at considerable risk of a change in the rate of return, for the company is constantly buying new investments, each reflecting the most recent market rate of return; however, the shorter associated maturity makes it easier to liquidate these investments to meet short-term cash needs.

We must make it clear that the CFO should be exceedingly risk averse when investing company cash. All but the largest and wealthiest corporations will be harmed by an investment loss, so do not even attempt to gain outsized returns on investment when the accompanying risk level is too high.

> **Tip:** There should be a formal investment policy that confines the CFO to a narrow range of possible investments that are considered to be at low risk of default. A sample policy is listed later in this section.

There are several steps that can be taken to reduce the risk of losing invested funds, and which the CFO should keep in mind when engaging in investment activities. They are:

- *Diversification*. Only invest a limited amount of cash in the securities of a single entity, in case that entity defaults on its obligations. Similarly, only invest a limited amount in securities originating within one industry, in case economic circumstances lead to multiple defaults within the industry.
- *FDIC insurance*. The Federal Deposit Insurance Corporation (FDIC) protects depositors of insured banks against the loss of their deposits and accrued interest if an insured bank fails. This coverage includes deposits in checking accounts, savings accounts, money market deposit accounts, and certificates of deposit. The coverage does not include cash invested in stocks, bonds, mutual funds, life insurance proceeds, annuities, or municipal securities. The amount of this coverage is limited to $250,000 per depositor, per insured bank. Consequently, it may be worthwhile to monitor account balance levels and shift funds above the insurance cap to accounts in other banks. By doing so, a company can achieve an FDIC coverage level that is substantially higher than $250,000.
- *Sweep structure*. When a company elects to have cash automatically swept out of an account and into an interest-earning investment, it should insist on a *one-to-one sweep*, where its cash is used to acquire a specific investment instrument. If the bank handling the transaction were to enter bankruptcy, the company would have title to the acquired investment. A worse alternative is to engage in a *one-to-many sweep*, where the funds of multiple businesses are used to acquire an investment instrument. In this case, the bank handling the transaction has title to the investment instrument, which means that the company would be reduced to filing a creditor claim that may eventually result in compensation for an amount less than its original investment.

All three of these risk reduction steps are to guard against admittedly unusual circumstances that a business may never experience. Nonetheless, if a counterparty were to fail, the potential loss could be quite large. Consequently, give strong consideration to these options when engaging in investment activities.

To ensure that investment guidelines are followed, they should be codified in a formal investment policy that is approved by the board of directors. The internal audit department should monitor compliance with this policy. A sample policy follows.

EXAMPLE

Hammer Industries' board of directors adopts the following investment policy.

General

In general, investments in securities with low liquidity levels shall be restricted to 15% of the company's total investment portfolio. There must be an active secondary market for all other investments.

Debt Investments

Debt investments are subject to the following restrictions:

- May only be made in high-quality intermediate or long-term corporate and Treasury bonds
- No more than 20% of the total debt investment can be made in a single industry
- Investments cannot comprise more than 5% of the debt issuances of the investee
- The average term to maturity cannot exceed __ years
- An investment must be terminated within one month if its Standard & Poor's credit rating drops below BBB
- Any bank acting as a counterparty shall have a capital account of at least $5 billion
- Short-term investments shall be pre-qualified by the investment advisory committee for the placement of funds

Equity Investments

Equity investments are subject to the following restrictions:

- May only be made in the common stock of companies trading on the New York Stock Exchange
- No more than 20% of the total equity investment can be made in a single industry
- Investments cannot comprise more than 5% of the capitalization of the investee

Control of Securities

All securities over which the company has physical control shall be consigned to an accredited third party.

Prohibitions

The company is prohibited from investing in any of the following types of investments without the prior approval of the board of directors:

- Commodities

- Foreign equity investments and commercial paper
- Leveraged transactions
- Real estate
- Securities with junk ratings
- Short sales or purchases on margin
- Venture capital

It is useful to periodically compare the company's investment policy to the actual structure and performance of its investment portfolio over the past few months, for the following reasons:

- *Compliance.* To ensure that the CFO is following the guidelines set forth in the policy.
- *Performance.* To see if the company might have achieved better returns if the policy had been somewhat less restrictive.
- *Risk management.* To determine whether the company avoided or mitigated risks by adhering to the policy.
- *Liquidity.* To see if adherence to the policy allowed the company to routinely meet its liquidity requirements.

This analysis should be conducted by someone not reporting to the CFO, in order to avoid any bias in the results.

Investment Strategy

Within the preceding guidelines, what strategy should a company follow when investing cash? Several possibilities are noted in the following bullet points. When considering the options, please note that the more active ones require accurate cash forecasts, which may not be available.

- *Earnings credit.* The simplest investment option of all is to do nothing. Cash balances are left in the various bank accounts, where they accrue an earnings credit that is offset against the fees charged by the bank for use of the accounts. If cash balances are low, this can be an entirely acceptable strategy, since more active management of a small amount of cash will probably not glean a significantly larger return.

EXAMPLE

Hammer Industries has an African division that is in startup mode, and so has little excess cash. Currently, the division maintains an average of only $20,000 in its sole bank account. Its bank offers a 1.5% earnings credit on retained cash balances, which is $25 per month that can be offset against account fees. The best alternative is a money market fund that earns 2%, but which requires the manual transfer of funds several times per month.

Given the minor amount of the balance and the low return on other investment alternatives, the CFO elects to accept an earnings credit, rather than taking any more aggressive investment actions.

- *Automated sweeps.* Sweep all excess cash into a central account, and shift the funds in that account to an overnight investment account. This strategy requires no staff time, but yields a low return on investment, since banks charge significant fees to manage this process.
- *Laddering.* The laddering strategy involves making investments of staggered duration, so that the company can take advantage of the higher interest rates typically associated with somewhat longer-term investments. For example, a CFO can reasonably forecast three months into the future, so it invests in a rolling set of investments that mature in three months. To begin this strategy, it invests a block of funds in an investment having a one-month maturity, another block in an investment with a two-month maturity, and yet another block in an investment with a three-month maturity. As each of the shorter investments matures, they are rolled into new investments having three-month maturities. The result is an ongoing series of investments where a portion of the cash is made available for operational use at one-month intervals, while taking advantage of the higher yields on three-month investments.
- *Match maturities.* An option requiring manual tracking is to match the maturities of investments to when the cash will be needed for operational purposes. This method calls for a highly accurate cash forecast, both in terms of the amounts and timing of cash flows. To be safe, maturities can be planned for several days prior to a forecasted cash need, though this reduces the return on investment.
- *Tiered investments.* If a business has more cash than it needs for ongoing operational requirements, the CFO can conduct an analysis to determine how much cash is never or rarely required for operations, and use this cash in a more aggressive investment strategy. For example:
  - *Continual cash usage.* Cash usage levels routinely flow within a certain range, so there must be sufficient cash available to always meet these cash requirements. The investment strategy for the amount included in this investment tier should be concentrated in highly liquid investments that can be readily accessed, with less attention to achieving a high rate of return.
  - *Occasional cash usage.* In addition to cash usage for daily operating events, there are usually a small number of higher cash-usage events that can be readily predicted, such as a periodic income tax or dividend payment. The strategy for this investment tier should focus on maturity dates just prior to the scheduled usage of cash, along with a somewhat greater emphasis on the return on investment. There should be a secondary market for these types of investments.

o *No planned cash usage.* If cash usage levels have never exceeded a certain amount, all cash above this maximum usage level can be invested in longer-term instruments that have higher returns on investment, and perhaps with more limited secondary markets.

EXAMPLE

The CFO of Hammer Industries wants to adopt a tiered investment strategy. He finds that the company routinely requires a maximum of $200,000 of cash for various expenditures on a weekly basis. In addition, there are scheduled quarterly dividend payments of $50,000 per quarter, and quarterly income tax payments of $100,000, which fall on the same date. There have not been any instances in the past three years where cash requirements exceeded these amounts. Currently, Hammer maintains cash reserves of $850,000 on a weekly basis. Based on the preceding information, the company could invest the cash in the following ways:

Investment Tier	Amount	Investment Type
Continual cash usage	$200,000	Money market
Occasional cash usage	150,000	Certificates of deposit, commercial paper
No planned cash usage	500,000	Bonds
Total	$850,000	

The tiered investment strategy requires close attention to the cash forecast, particularly in regard to the timing and amount of the occasional cash usage items. Otherwise, there is a risk of being caught with too much cash in an illiquid investment when there is an immediate need for the cash.

- *Ride the yield curve.* An active CFO can buy investments that have higher interest rates and longer maturity dates, and then sell these investments when the cash is needed for operational purposes. Thus, a company is deliberately buying investments that it knows it cannot hold until their maturity dates. If the yield curve is inverted (that is, interest rates are lower on longer-maturity investments), the logical approach is to continually re-invest in very short-term instruments, no matter how far in the future the cash is actually needed again by the company.

EXAMPLE

The CFO of Hammer Industries has $300,000 available to invest for the next 90 days. He notes that the interest rate on 3-month T-Bills is 2.0%, while the rate on 6-month T-Bills is 2.25%. He elects to take advantage of this 0.25% difference in interest rates by investing the $300,000 in 6-month-T-Bills, and then selling them on a secondary market in 90 days, when he needs the cash for operational purposes.

The following investment strategies require significant investing expertise and the incurrence of more risk, in exchange for the possibility of higher investment returns. These strategies should not be followed unless the CFO has specialized expertise in the indicated areas, and spends enough time modeling probable outcomes to understand the risks being undertaken. The strategies are:

- *Credit rating anticipation.* If the CFO expects that the credit rating of a debt issuer is about to be revised upward, it may make sense to acquire those debt securities to which the rating change would apply. If anticipated correctly, this means that the company buys securities at a reduced price and later sells them at the higher price associated with the higher credit rating. This is a difficult game to play, since it is not easy to anticipate a credit upgrade, much less the timing of the upgrade. Also, an investment in the securities of a low-grade entity is at greater risk of suffering from a default, where the company loses its entire investment. Credit rating anticipation also requires a considerable amount of analysis time, which is usually not available in smaller companies.

- *Leveraged investing.* A larger organization may be able to issue debt at quite a low interest rate, and then invest the borrowed funds in higher-yielding investments, resulting in an incremental financing gain to the business. This behavior is not recommended, since it diverts attention from the management of operations. It is particularly risky when the maturities of the company's investments are shorter than those of its borrowings, since the return on investment may suddenly decline below the cost of its borrowings, resulting in losses.

A variation on all of the preceding strategies is to outsource the investment task to an experienced third party money manager. This option works well if a company is too small or has too few cash reserves to actively manage its own cash. If outsourcing is chosen, be sure to set up guidelines with the money manager for exactly how cash is to be invested, primarily through the use of lower-risk investments that mitigate the possibility of losing cash. A variation on the outsourcing concept is to invest primarily in money market funds, which are professionally managed.

Repurchase Agreements

A repurchase agreement is a package of securities that an investor buys from a financial institution, under an agreement that the institution will buy it back at a specific price on a certain date, typically the next business day. The repurchase price incorporates the interest rate paid to the investor during the investor's holding period. It is most commonly used for the overnight investment of excess cash from a company's cash concentration account, which can be automatically handled by a company's primary bank.

The interest rate earned on this investment is equal to or less than the money market rate, since the financial institution takes a transaction fee that reduces the rate earned. Despite the low return, the automated nature of repurchase agreements makes them a popular investment choice for CFOs who might otherwise not want to spend the time manually entering into a short-term investment for residual funds.

Time Deposits

A time deposit is a bank deposit that pays a fixed interest rate, and requires an investment for a specific period of time, usually anywhere from one week to one year. This is essentially a loan from the company to a bank, with interest set at a level close to the interbank rate. Time deposits have the advantage of being set at fixed interest rates, so there is no risk of an interest rate decline. However, the interest rate is typically quite low.

Certificates of Deposit

A certificate of deposit (CD) is an interest-bearing certificate that is issued by a bank as a receipt for deposits invested with it. A CD can have a maturity of as little as a few weeks to several years. There is a secondary market for some CDs, so this type of investment can be liquidated relatively quickly. CDs are available in multiple currencies. In particular, two variations on the concept are:

- *Eurodollar CDs*. Denominated in U.S. dollars, and issued by entities outside the United States.
- *Yankee CDs*. Denominated in U.S. dollars, and issued by foreign entities with operations in the United States.

A CD is issued at its face value, with additional interest due to the investor in addition to the face amount. A shorter-term CD is usually issued at a fixed interest rate, with interest being paid at the end of each year or the maturity of the instrument.

A longer-term CD may instead use a floating interest rate that is based on a major benchmark interest rate, such as LIBOR. If so, the interest rate is usually re-set every three or six months.

Bankers' Acceptances

A banker's acceptance arises when a bank guarantees (or accepts) corporate debt, usually when it issues a loan to a corporate customer, and then sells the debt to investors. These acceptances are sold at a discount, and redeemed upon maturity at their face value. Because of the bank guarantee, a banker's acceptance is viewed as an obligation of the bank. If the bank has a good reputation, the acceptance can be re-sold in an open market, at a discount to its face value. A banker's acceptance is considered to be a very safe asset, and is used extensively in international trade. A banker's acceptance usually has a term of less than 180 days.

Commercial Paper

Commercial paper is a promissory note issued by a corporation, usually with a maturity of less than 180 days; thus, it is a short-term bond. The short maturity is designed to avoid the extra cost of registration with the Securities and Exchange Commission that would be required if the term were to exceed 270 days. Typical issuers of commercial paper include:

- Financial entities
- Industrial companies
- Insurance companies
- Public utilities

Entities issuing commercial paper have usually obtained a credit rating from one of the major credit rating agencies, such as Standard & Poor's, Moody's Investors Service, or Fitch Ratings. If the credit rating of an issuer were to decline, then the value of its commercial paper would decline as well (and vice versa), which can impact the value of investments if they are to be sold on a secondary market.

Commercial paper is usually sold at a discount from its face value, which means that the investor buys it at a discounted price, and is repaid on the maturity date at its face value. Most commercial paper is unsecured, which means that this type of investment carries a higher interest rate to reflect the increased level of risk associated with it – though the rate is still quite low. Commercial paper can be acquired directly from the issuing companies, but is also commonly available through banks that act as dealers.

There is essentially no secondary market for commercial paper, so the investing entity must hold it to maturity.

Money Market Funds

A money market fund is a pool of short-term financial instruments operated by a fund manager, for which investors can purchase shares. A money market fund usually invests solely in federal government debt issuances, such as T-Bills and T-Notes. It is quite easy to invest in and move cash out of a money market fund, so it is ideal for extremely short-term investments. To attract investors, many of these funds offer late cutoff times for new investments, which allow the CFO to wait until later in the day to concentrate cash positions before making an investment in a fund.

There are some discernible differences in the risk associated with different money market funds, which is caused by some fund managers taking risks in order to outperform the market. Conversely, other fund managers do an excellent job of investment diversification in order to reduce risk. Some funds may also be able to defer redemptions under certain conditions. For these reasons, be sure to examine the stated objectives and rules of a fund before investing in it.

U.S. Government Debt Instruments

Despite the continuing increases in the debt of the United States government, its debt instruments are still considered among the lowest-risk in the world. The ones most commonly used by corporations for investment are Treasury Bills (T-Bills) and Treasury Notes (T-Notes). T-Bills have 3, 6, and 12-month maturities. T-Bills having maturities of 3 and 6 months are auctioned on a weekly basis, while T-Bills with 12-month maturities are auctioned once a month. T-Bills are sold at a discount, and redeemed upon maturity at their face value. There is a very active secondary market in T-Bills, so it is extremely easy to sell them prior to their maturity dates.

The maturities of T-Notes range from 1 to 10 years. Two-year T-Notes are issued on a monthly basis, while T-Notes with other maturities are issued on a quarterly basis. T-Notes are available as both inflation-indexed and fixed-rate investments. Interest on T-Notes is paid semi-annually. T-Notes are traded on secondary markets at premiums or discounts to their face values, to reflect the current market interest rate (see the Effective Interest Rate section).

Treasury Bonds are also available. Bonds have similar characteristics to T-Notes, but have longer maturities. Maturities are generally in the range of 10 to 30 years.

Paradoxically, the trouble with U.S. government debt instruments is their safety – the United States government can obtain the lowest possible interest rates, so there is little return on funds invested in these instruments.

State and Local Government Debt

An interesting investment option is the debt obligations issued by a variety of state and local governments. These debt instruments are usually issued in conjunction with the revenue streams associated with large capital projects, such as airport fees and tolls from toll roads. Other instruments are based on general tax revenues. The maturities of these obligations are typically multi-year, so a company in need of cash must rely upon a vigorous aftermarket to liquidate them prior to their maturity dates. The returns on state and local debt obligations are higher than the yields on federal government issuances, and income from these investments are usually exempt from federal taxation.

Though it is rare for a state or local government to default on its debt, such cases are not unknown, so be mindful of the reliability of the cash flows supporting debt repayment.

Bonds

A bond is an obligation to pay a fixed amount to the bond holder, usually in the amount of $1,000 per bond, as of one or more dates specified in a bond agreement. The maturities of bonds can be extremely long, sometimes extending to 30 or even 40 years in the future.

There are many variations on the bond concept, but the two key types are based on differing methods for paying the bond holder. They are:

- *Coupon bond.* Each bond comes with a set of coupons, which are submitted to the issuer for payment of interest at regular intervals. The company does not track bond holder contact information for coupon bonds.
- *Registered bond.* The company maintains an updated list of the holders of its bonds, and sends interest payments to them at regular intervals.

The coupon bond is designed to be more easily transferrable between bond holders. This is of some importance, since there is an active secondary market in many bonds. The presence of a secondary market is critical for investors, especially when the maturity date is many years in the future, and the holder is uncertain of how long it wants to retain possession of a bond.

Several variations on bonds are noted below:

- *Secured/unsecured.* Some bond instruments provide specific collateral against which bondholders have a claim if the bonds are not paid. If the CFO is working under a guideline to protect cash, then the only investment should be in secured bonds.
- *Convertible.* This is a bond that can be converted to stock using a pre-determined conversion ratio. This option is usually only available at set intervals, and conversion is at the discretion of the bondholder. The presence of conversion rights typically reduces the interest rate on a bond, since investors assign some value to the conversion privilege. If the CFO is primarily interested in obtaining a high return on investment, then avoid convertible bonds, since they tend to have somewhat lower returns.
- *Callable.* This is a bond that the issuer can buy back prior to its maturity, usually because there has been a decline in interest rates since the issuance of the bond, and the issuer wants to refinance at a lower rate. The existence of a call provision tends to reduce the value of a bond, so CFOs usually avoid this type of bond.

The Primary and Secondary Markets

A primary market refers to the original sale of a security to an investor. Whenever a security is sold thereafter among investors and market makers, it is referred to as the secondary market. The existence of a secondary market is critical to the investment operations of a CFO, since it allows for the liquidation of an investment prior to its maturity date. If there were no secondary market, the CFO would have to limit investment activities to the most short-term investments, in order to ensure the availability of cash.

The secondary market is comprised of financial institutions and dealers. These entities can act as brokers, taking a commission on the transfer of an investment from a seller to a buyer. Alternatively, they can hold an inventory of investments on their own behalf, and sell them directly to buyers for a profit.

Secondary markets are particularly important when a company is aggressively investing in longer-term investments that generate higher interest rates. This activity, known as "riding the yield curve," is only possible if a business can promptly liquidate an investment well before its maturity date.

The Discounted Investment Formula

Some investments, such as T-Bills and T-Notes, are sold at a discount and redeemed at their face value. The calculation used to determine the correct discount to pay for one of these instruments is:

$$\text{Face value} \times \text{Discount rate} \times \frac{\text{Day count}}{\text{Annual basis}} = \text{Amount of discount}$$

For example, a company wants to buy a 90-day $10,000,000 T-Bill at a discount of 2.5%. The calculation is:

$$\underset{\text{Face value}}{\$10,000,000} \times \underset{\text{Discount rate}}{0.025} \times \underset{\text{360 Days}}{\frac{\text{90 Days}}{\text{360 Days}}} = \underset{\text{Discount}}{\$62,500}$$

When the discount is subtracted from the face value of the T-Bill, the amount to be paid is:

$10,000,000 Face value -$62,500 Discount = $9,937,500 Purchase price

The Effective Interest Rate

If an entity buys or sells a financial instrument for an amount other than its face amount, this means that the interest rate it is actually earning or paying on the investment is different from the stated interest paid on the financial instrument. For example, if a company buys a bond for $95,000 that has a face amount of $100,000 and which pays interest of $5,000, then the actual interest it is earning on the investment is $5,000 ÷ $95,000, or 5.26%.

The effective interest rate exactly discounts estimated future cash payments or receipts over the expected life of a financial instrument. In essence, interest income or expense in a period is the carrying amount of a financial instrument multiplied by the effective interest rate.

EXAMPLE

Hammer Industries acquires a debt security having a stated principal amount of $100,000, which the issuer will repay in three years. The debt has a coupon interest rate of five percent, which it pays at the end of each year. Hammer acquires the debt for $90,000, which is a discount of $10,000 from the principal amount of $100,000. Hammer classifies the investment as held-to-maturity, and records this entry:

	Debit	Credit
Investments: Held-to-maturity debt securities	90,000	
Cash		90,000

Based on a cash outflow of $90,000 to acquire the investment, three interest payments of $5,000 each, and a principal payment of $100,000 upon maturity, Hammer calculates an effective interest rate of 8.95 percent. Using this interest rate, the CFO of Hammer calculates the following amortization table:

Year	(A) Beginning Amortized Cost	(B) Interest and Principal Payments	(C) Interest Income [A x 8.95%]	(D) Debt Discount Amortization [C – B]	Ending Amortized Cost [A + D]
1	$90,000	$5,000	$8,055	$3,055	$93,055
2	93,055	5,000	8,328	3,328	96,383
3	96,383	105,000	8,617	3,617	100,000

Using the table, Hammer makes the following entries at the end of each of the next three years:

Year 1	Debit	Credit
Cash	5,000	
Investments: Held-to-maturity debt securities	3,055	
Interest income		8,055

Year 2	Debit	Credit
Cash	5,000	
Investments: Held-to-maturity debt securities	3,328	
Interest income		8,328

Year 3	Debit	Credit
Cash	105,000	
Investments: Held-to-maturity debt securities		96,383
Interest income		8,617

The effective interest method is preferable to the straight-line method of charging off premiums and discounts on financial instruments, because it is considerably more accurate. However, it is also more difficult to compute than the straight-line method.

Summary

While there are many investment alternatives available, it is entirely likely that an efficient CFO will elect to concentrate all attention on just a few alternatives, and probably on those that are transactionally most efficient to engage in on a regular basis. For example, a business with modest cash balances may enter into an automated overnight repurchase arrangement with its primary bank, and essentially forget about any additional investment activities. An alternative where there is more investable cash on hand is to make all investments through an investment portal that conveniently links participants with a specific cluster of available investment instruments (usually limited to time deposits and money market funds), such as 360T and FXall. Thus, convenience may prove to be the key reason for continually investing excess cash in the same types of investments.

If the CFO is willing to look beyond the most convenient investments and explore other options, the next most critical element of the investment decision will likely be the presence of an active secondary market. If there is such a market, it is much easier to liquidate an investment before its maturity date. The result can be a broader range of choices when cash is available for investment even over a relatively short period of time.

Chapter 12
Fund Raising with Debt

Introduction

There will be times when the CFO must procure additional funding to meet short-term or long-term cash requirements. In this chapter, we describe a number of options for raising cash through the use of debt financing. We touch upon not only the most common sources of funds – the line of credit and leases – but also less common alternatives, such as invoice discounting and inventory financing.

> **Related Podcast Episodes:** Episodes 124, 125, and 143 of the Accounting Best Practices Podcast discuss lender relations, refinancing debt, and supply chain financing, respectively. The episodes are available at: **accounting-tools.com/podcasts** or **iTunes**

When reviewing the various debt alternatives, keep in mind that the total cost of these borrowings is not just the periodic interest charge, but also annual servicing fees, periodic lender audits, and possibly the cost of a full annual audit. The types of additional costs will vary by type of financing, so be sure to itemize all of them when deciding upon the most cost-effective form of financing to use.

Overview of Debt Funding

A large part of the cash management task is ensuring that there is sufficient cash on hand to fund company operations. While some of this cash may come from company sales and maturing investments, it is also entirely possible that the CFO must raise cash from outside parties. A major source of funding is debt financing, which falls into these categories:

- *Asset-based financing.* Company assets are used as collateral for this type of debt. Examples are the line of credit, invoice discounting, factoring, inventory financing, and leases.
- *Unsecured financing.* No company assets are used as collateral. Instead, lenders rely upon the cash flows of the business to obtain repayment. Examples are long-term loans and floating-rate notes.
- *Guaranteed financing.* A third party guarantees debt payments by the company. Government entities, such as the Export-Import Bank, usually provide these guarantees.

Examples of these types of debt financing are noted through the remainder of this chapter.

If a company obtains financing, it must pay interest on the amount borrowed. The interest percentage may be variable, with the rate adjusting in accordance with a benchmark rate at regular intervals. If the rate is variable and may rise suddenly, a company is at some risk of incurring much higher interest expenses. These costs are mitigated by the tax deductibility of interest expense. For example, if a company incurs $100,000 of interest expense and is in the 35% incremental income tax bracket, it can use the $100,000 interest deduction to reduce its income tax liability (if any) by $35,000.

There may also be a fee for an annual audit of the company's books by a bank-designated auditor, as well as an annual facility fee for keeping open a line of credit.

When reviewing the following types of debt, take note of any administrative charges that may also be billed to the company. This is a particularly large issue for financings involving accounts receivable or inventory as collateral, and can noticeably increase the total borrowing cost.

The Line of Credit

A line of credit is a commitment from a lender to pay a company whenever it needs cash, up to a pre-set maximum limit. A line of credit is generally secured by company assets, which the lender can take if the company is unable to pay back the line of credit. The lender will not allow a drawdown against a line of credit if the total amount lent will then exceed the amount of assets pledged as collateral against the line (known as the *borrowing base*). Any debt made available under a line of credit can be accessed multiple times over the course of the debt agreement. The lender may also block out a portion of a line of credit for letter of credit transactions where the borrower is committing to pay a supplier a predetermined amount on a future date. A line of credit is a highly useful form of financing for a business that does not have sufficient cash reserves to fund its day-to-day needs.

A larger and more credit-worthy business may be able to avoid any collateral; if so, the lender is relying on the general credit quality of the company. The usual agreement under which a line of credit is granted requires the company to pay an annual fee in exchange for the lender's commitment to keep a certain amount of debt available for the company's use; this is called a *committed* line of credit. It is also possible to have a less formal arrangement at a lower cost, where the lender is not obligated to make funds available to the company. This latter arrangement is called an *uncommitted* line of credit, and is useful for rare lending needs when a company has several sources of funds from which to choose.

When a bank offers a line of credit, it is typically under the agreement that the bank will also handle the company's other banking business, such as its checking accounts and lockboxes. This arrangement can be useful, since the treasury staff can monitor cash balances and routinely transfer borrowed funds back to the bank through an inexpensive intrabank transfer transaction. Doing so on a frequent basis minimizes the interest cost of the line of credit.

When entering into a line of credit arrangement, be sure to also obtain separate debt funding to handle all of the company's long-term debt needs. The reason is that a line of credit is intended to be a source of short-term funding *only*, which means that the line of credit balance is expected to drop to zero at some point each year. Otherwise, it will appear that the company is using the line as part of its long-term borrowing arrangements.

The Borrowing Base

A borrowing base is the total amount of collateral against which a lender will lend funds to a business. This typically involves multiplying a discount factor by each type of asset used as collateral. For example:

- *Accounts receivable*. 60% to 80% of accounts receivable less than 90 days old may be accepted as a borrowing base. Receivables from related parties and foreign entities are excluded.
- *Inventory*. A smaller percentage of finished goods inventory may be accepted as a borrowing base. Raw materials and work-in-process, as well as custom-made goods and slow-moving finished goods are usually not allowed, since they are more difficult to liquidate.

It is also common for a lender to only use the accounts receivable of a borrower as collateral - it may not accept *any* inventory as part of the borrowing base.

If the business is a small one, the lender issuing a line of credit will probably also want a personal guarantee from the owner of the business, in addition to the underlying collateral.

EXAMPLE

Hammer Industries enters into a line of credit arrangement that has a maximum lending limit of $6 million. The amount of the accounts receivable to be used in the borrowing base is limited to 80% of all trade receivables less than 90 days old. The amount of the inventory to be used is limited to finished goods. The amount of finished goods to be used in the borrowing base is limited to 65%.

At the end of March, there are $4.8 million of accounts receivable outstanding, of which $200,000 are more than 90 days old. Hammer also has $6.5 million of inventory on hand, of which $3.5 million is finished goods. The amount of debt that has been drawn down on the line of credit is $5 million. Based on this information, the CFO of Hammer constructs the following borrowing base certificate.

Hammer Industries	
Borrowing Base Certificate	as of 3/31/20x3
Total accounts receivable	$4,800,000
Less: Receivables > 90 days old	-200,000
Eligible accounts receivable	$4,600,000
× Advance rate	80%
= Collateral value of accounts receivable	$3,680,000
Total finished goods inventory	$3,500,000
× Advance rate	65%
= Collateral value of finished goods inventory	$2,275,000
Total collateral	$5,955,000
Total debt outstanding	5,000,000
Excess collateral	$955,000

A business that borrows money under a borrowing base arrangement usually fills out a *borrowing base certificate* at regular intervals, in which it calculates the applicable borrowing base. A company officer signs the certificate and submits it to the lender, which retains it as proof of the available amount of collateral. If the borrowing base stated on the certificate is less than the amount that the company is currently borrowing from the lender, then the company must pay the difference to the lender at once.

A lender may want to protect its borrowing base by requiring the borrower to obtain credit insurance for all of its outstanding accounts receivable. The cost of this insurance is essentially an additional borrowing cost for the borrower.

Careful monitoring of the borrowing base is of particular importance in seasonal businesses, since the inventory portion of the base gradually builds prior to the selling season, followed by a sharp increase in the receivable asset during the selling season, and then a rapid decline in all assets immediately after the season has been completed. It is necessary to balance loan drawdowns and repayments against these rapid changes in the borrowing base to ensure that a company does not violate its loan agreement.

Invoice Discounting

Invoice discounting is the practice of using a company's unpaid accounts receivable as collateral for a loan, which is issued by a finance company. Invoice discounting essentially accelerates cash flow from customers, so that instead of waiting for customers to pay within their normal credit terms, cash is received almost as soon as the invoice is issued.

This is an extremely short-term form of borrowing, since the finance company can alter the amount of debt outstanding as soon as the amount of accounts receivable collateral changes. The amount of debt issued by the finance company is less than the total amount of outstanding receivables (typically 80% of all invoices less than 90 days old).

The finance company earns money both from the interest rate it charges on the loan (which is well above the prime rate), and a monthly fee to maintain the arrangement. The amount of interest that it charges the borrower is based on the amount of funds loaned, not the amount of funds available to be loaned.

Invoice discounting is impossible if another lender already has blanket title to all company assets as collateral on a different loan. In such cases, the other lender needs to waive its right to the accounts receivable collateral, and instead take a junior position behind the finance company.

From an operational perspective, the borrower sends an accounts receivable report to the finance company at least once a month, aggregating receivables into the categories required by the finance company. The finance company uses this information to adjust the amount of debt that it is willing to loan the borrower. The borrower retains control over the accounts receivable, which means that it is responsible for extending credit to customers, invoicing them, and collecting from them. There is no need to notify customers of the discounting arrangement.

Invoice discounting works best for companies with relatively high profit margins, since they can readily absorb the higher interest charges associated with this form of financing. It is especially common in high-profit businesses that are growing at a rapid rate, and need the cash flow to fund additional growth. Conversely, this is not a good form of financing for low-margin businesses, since the interest on the debt may eliminate any prospect of earning a profit.

Invoice discounting tends to be a financing source of last resort, because of the substantial fees associated with it. It is normally used only after most other forms of financing have been attempted.

Factoring

Another type of asset-based lending is *factoring*. A company that engages in factoring sells its accounts receivable to a third party, known as the *factor*. As was the case with invoice discounting, factoring is only an option if a company has not allowed other parties to attach its receivables as collateral on other loans.

The pricing arrangement for a factoring deal includes the following components:

- *Advance*. This is a proportion of the face amount of the invoices that the factor pays to the company at the point of sale.
- *Reserve*. This is the remaining proportion of the face amount of the invoices, which the factor retains until collections have been completed.
- *Fee*. This is the cost of the factoring arrangement, which is deducted from the reserve payment.

Once the factor owns a company's receivables, customers are notified to send their payments to a lockbox controlled by the factor. Payments made into the lockbox are retained by the factor. If the factoring arrangement is *with recourse*, the factor can pursue the company for any unpaid customer invoices. If the arrangement is *without recourse*, the factor absorbs any bad debt losses. A without recourse arrangement is more expensive, to compensate the factor for bad debt losses.

The total amount of fees associated with a factoring arrangement can be substantial, so this is generally considered a fund-raising arrangement of last resort.

Inventory Financing

The preceding two sections discussed how to use accounts receivable as collateral for different types of loan arrangements. The same approach can be applied to inventory. To make this arrangement work to the satisfaction of the lender, the inventory being used as collateral is placed in a controlled area and under the supervision of a third party that only releases inventory with the approval of the lender. The lender is paid from the proceeds of inventory sales. Under a less controlled environment, the lender may agree to periodic inventory reports by the borrower, with occasional inspections of the inventory to ensure that the counted amounts match the borrower's reports.

There must be a sufficient amount of insurance in place to ensure that the lender will be paid back if the inventory is destroyed or damaged. Also, depending on state laws, it may be necessary to post notices around the collateralized inventory, stating that a lien has been imposed on the inventory. Further, the inventory cannot be used as collateral on any other loans, unless they are subordinate to the arrangement with the inventory financing company.

If the amount of inventory being used as collateral drops below the amount of the loan associated with it, the borrower must immediately pay the lender the difference.

Because of the cost of third party monitoring, inventory financing is one of the more expensive forms of financing available and can also be quite intrusive, so it is used only after less-expensive alternatives have been explored. The sole advantage of this form of financing is that the lender relies exclusively on the inventory asset to ensure that it is repaid; it does not impose covenants on the borrower.

Purchase Order Financing

Purchase order financing is applicable when a company receives an order from a customer that it cannot process with its existing working capital. A lender accepts the purchase order as collateral, which allows the borrower to obtain sufficient funds to buy the materials and labor required to complete the order. This arrangement is risky for the lender, since the borrower must perform under the contract in order to receive payment from the customer. Given the extra risk, the borrowing cost is higher for purchase order financing.

Leases

When cash is needed to acquire a fixed asset, an excellent choice is to do so with a lease, rather than using cash from other sources. A lease is an agreement under which the lessee makes a number of incremental payments to the lessor, rather than a lump sum payment, while the lessor owns the asset associated with the lease. A lease can be structured so that the lessee owns the asset at the end of the lease term, which is called a *capital lease*. If the lessor continues to own the asset at the end of the lease, then the lease is called an *operating lease*.

Leases are especially useful under the following circumstances:

- *Cash flow.* Lease payments are spread out over the term of a lease, thereby keeping a business from having to deal with large one-time cash outflows to purchase assets.
- *Covenants.* A lessor does not impose any covenants on a company as a whole, since it is only concerned with the specific asset it is leasing to the company. Thus, a company wanting to avoid covenants should consider leases.
- *Specific collateralization.* When a company has pledged its other assets under a blanket collateralization agreement for another loan, a lease essentially segregates a single asset as collateral for a new loan (the lease).

There are two problems with leases. First, the company is committing to a minimum set of lease payments, which can be quite expensive to terminate early. Second, it can be difficult to ascertain the interest rate used to compile lease payments, so be sure to manually derive the interest rate before agreeing to a lease.

The Long-Term Loan

When a company finds that it is unable to draw its line of credit down to zero at any point during the year, this means that its funding needs have become more long-term. If so, it should apply to a lender for a long-term loan that will be paid off over a number of years.

The following points may clarify whether it is even possible to obtain such a loan, and whether doing so would be the correct action to take:

- *Banking services.* The provider of a long-term loan may insist on providing a complete package of banking services, to maximize its profits. If so, expect to shift all bank accounts, lines of credit, lockboxes, and other services to the lender.
- *Cash flow.* The lender is particularly sensitive to the historical and projected performance of the business, since the loan must be repaid from continuing cash flows. If positive cash flows have been a rare event, it will be very difficult to obtain a long-term loan. The lender may also want to see a budget for at least the next year.

- *Covenants.* The lender will probably impose covenants on the company that are designed to keep it from disbursing cash outside of the normal course of business. In particular, dividends may be restricted.
- *Creditor positioning.* A lender willing to commit to a long-term loan will certainly want to be designated as having the senior position among all creditors of the company, so that it will be more likely to be paid back in the event of a loan default by the company. This positioning is necessary, because the lender is committing a large amount of funds to the company over a long period of time, during which the company's financial results may change dramatically.
- *Personal guarantee.* In a smaller business where there are few owners, and especially where historical cash flow has been uncertain, the lender may insist on personal guarantees that allow the lender to pursue the owners for repayment.

A long-term loan can be configured as a series of fixed payments, or as interest-only payments with a large balloon payment due at the end of the loan. While the balloon payment option may appear tempting from a short-term cash flow perspective, it introduces the risk that credit conditions may have changed by the time it is due for payment, making it difficult to refinance.

Tip: If there is a loan with a balloon payment, begin watching trends in interest rates and credit availability well before the payment is due, and roll over the loan into a new debt instrument early, if reduced interest rates warrant such action.

The conditions associated with a long-term loan might leave management less inclined to pursue this option. However, a long-term loan allows a business to lock in debt for an extended period of time, without having to worry about the vagaries of the short-term credit markets. Thus, it can make sense to assign a portion of a company's debt to longer-term loans.

Agency Financing

When a company needs to finance the export or import of goods, this can constitute a large surge in borrowings that cannot be supported by its line of credit. A good alternative is to use agency-backed financing for these transactions. An "agency" is a government-sponsored export credit agency, such as the Export-Import Bank (Ex-Im Bank) of the United States. These agencies provide financial packages for the export or import of goods. A typical financing arrangement is for a commercial bank to supply credit to the borrowing entity, with the agency providing a credit guarantee to the bank. Alternatively, an agency may directly provide credit, thereby eliminating the need for an intermediary bank.

    Agencies are not in the business of losing money on their financing packages, so minimum standards apply to all applications. For example, a first-time applicant to the Ex-Im Bank of the United States must meet the following criteria:

- Has been in the same line of business for at least three years
- Has at least one year of exporting experience
- Had an operating profit in the most recent fiscal year
- Has a Dun & Bradstreet Paydex score of at least 50, as well as no derogatory information
- Has signed financial statements for the last fiscal year that shows positive net worth
- Has no material adverse issues

In addition, the Ex-Im Bank may require corporate guarantees, personal guarantees, and/or collateral. Thus, agencies do not gratuitously give away funds; a company must qualify for financing under specific standards, and may be turned down. Nonetheless, this is a viable alternative when other sources of funds are not available.

Other Lending Alternatives

In this section, we note two alternatives that may apply in less-common circumstances. The first alternative is not strictly defined as debt, since it merely uses a line of credit to delay payments to suppliers. The latter alternative is only available to large corporations.

Improving Upon Prepayment Terms

A company may have abused a supplier relationship in the past, to the point where the supplier will only accept prepayment terms for any new orders by the company. If so, consider offering the supplier payment under a letter of credit instead. By doing so, the supplier is essentially assured of being paid, while the company shifts from paying in advance to paying somewhat later, depending on the terms of the letter of credit. Another option is to negotiate for credit terms where there is a standby letter of credit, so that the company's bank will pay the supplier in the event of default by the company. Either arrangement is designed to obtain better payment terms, while assuaging the non-payment fears of the supplier.

Floating-Rate Notes to Individuals

A possible option for raising short-term funds is to issue floating-rate demand notes to individual investors, for which the interest rate is updated regularly by the issuer. The floating-rate notes do not have a stated maturity date, and are not traded on a secondary market. Instead, investors are allowed to cash out of the notes at any time. There is no initial sales fee or departure penalty paid by investors. These notes yield higher interest rates than can be achieved with investments in money market funds and bank savings accounts, which make them attractive to investors.

This type of debt favors the issuer, which benefits from reasonably low interest rates. The investor, however, is not protected from default by the Federal Deposit

Insurance Corporation, so the small increase in return is offset by a substantial increase in risk.

To sell floating-rate notes, a company can post a notice on its website, which links investors to a page on which they can purchase the notes. It can also advertise the note program to the general public, and can offer it to employees as an investment option.

Debt Covenants

Lenders routinely require borrowers to sign off on debt covenants, which are conditions related to company operations and practices. If a borrower breaches a covenant, the lender may be able to terminate the borrowing arrangement and accelerate payment of the loan. Consequently, the CFO should have a detailed understanding of all debt covenants currently in force, and monitor the company's compliance with them. In particular, consider the following techniques to reduce the risk of covenant breaches:

- Before agreeing to a covenant, create a model of the company's expected future performance, and create several worst-case scenarios to see if the company is at risk of a breach. If so, negotiate for covenants that fall outside of a reasonable worst-case scenario. This may include modeling for expected acquisitions that may require additional debt or working capital.

Tip: Integrate loan covenants directly into the company's budget model, so that budget changes causing covenant breaches will be flagged at once by the model.

- Include on the checklist of month-end closing activities a comparison of preliminary results to covenants, to obtain early warning of a possible breach.
- Every time a loan renewal is negotiated, work on a relaxation of the existing covenants.
- If there are several loans with the same bank, review the covenants in all of these agreements to see if any conflict with each other or may have unintended consequences, and negotiate changes to those covenants.
- See if the lender will accept a somewhat higher interest rate in exchange for a particularly odious covenant.

Tip: If covenants are required as part of a loan agreement, make sure that there is a grace period during which the company is allowed to cure any covenant breach.

A lender may impose covenants that are specifically tailored to the borrower. However, most covenants are of the boilerplate variety, and will be found in any loan agreement. Common covenants include:

- Dividends cannot be paid

- Shares cannot be repurchased
- Net worth must exceed $___
- Capital expenditures shall not exceed $___ per year
- Asset sales are not allowed unless the proceeds are used to pay down the loan
- The net worth to total liabilities ratio must exceed ___
- The current ratio must exceed ___
- The interest coverage ratio must exceed ___
- There shall be no major change in the company's business activities

A loan agreement may also include a material adverse changes clause, under which the lender can terminate the loan if the company's financial condition takes a significant turn for the worse. If the lender insists on including this clause, be sure to integrate numeric minimums that the company must breach before the clause can be invoked. Otherwise, the clause is too judgmental, and can be invoked at the whim of the lender.

The number and severity of covenants tend to increase when a company has a large amount of borrowings, because lenders want to keep the company on a tighter leash. If so, it may be useful to determine the debt level at which additional covenants will be imposed, and then give management the alternative of accepting the additional covenants along with more debt, or backing away from some growth plans to avoid the additional debt.

If a company breaches a covenant, it does not automatically mean that the lender will demand immediate loan repayment. The lender may waive any rights triggered by a breach, or it may require that the borrower agree to additional covenants or other requirements. For example, the lender may require more collateral, a penalty payment, a higher interest rate or shorter maturity on the loan, or a smaller loan. If the penalty for a covenant breach appears to be unusually severe, it is certainly worthwhile to attempt to negotiate a lesser penalty. If the lender is unresponsive to pleas for clemency, then you have at least learned how the bank treats its customers, and can begin the process of moving company business to a different lender.

In short, lenders like to impose covenants. They have the ability to do so during periods of restricted credit when borrowers have few other options. Given the risk of loan acceleration posed by covenants, borrowers always want to loosen or eliminate covenants to the greatest extent possible, and should be particularly aggressive in doing so when they have multiple lenders available, and especially during periods when credit is broadly available.

Tip: If the company's current lender appears to be requiring unusually restrictive covenants, consider discussing the company's loan situation with other lenders, to see if there are better alternatives available.

Lender Relations

It is extremely important to avoid the breach of a debt covenant, particularly if the breach comes as a surprise to the lender. A surprise announcement may leave a lender wondering if it would be better to call the loan, rather than issuing a waiver. Also, a surprised lender will be less likely to grant a request for an increase in the amount loaned, or an extension to the existing loan. The obvious solution is to maintain a high level of communication with the lender, which should involve the following activities:

- Review covenants as part of the monthly financial statement review process. This means not only comparing covenants to reported results, but also comparing covenants to a rolling forecast of what the company expects over the next few months.
- Compare asset sales to lien agreements. It is possible that a lender should be notified when an asset is sold, and possibly also paid the proceeds from the asset sale. This means that the CFO should be informed whenever a significant asset is sold.
- Ensure that accounts receivable are collected within 90 days. Otherwise, the lender does not allow the receivables to be included in the borrowing base calculation on any asset-based loans, thereby reducing the amount of available debt.
- Communicate expected expenditures to the lender. If the company expects to make large cash outlays for fixed asset purchases or make alterations to its operations that call for larger amounts of working capital, make sure that the lender understands the reasons for these changes. Otherwise, unusual borrowing spikes may trigger frantic calls from the lender.
- Communicate any changes in control. Many lending agreements state that the associated loan is callable upon a change in control. Thus, if the company plans to issue shares or enter into a merger or acquisition, the lender should be aware of what this will do to the ownership percentages of the business.

Above all, keep constant track of short-term projections to see if the company is in any danger of running afoul of its loan agreements. If so, discuss matters with the lender as early as possible. By doing so, the lender is more likely to work with the company through any subsequent lending issues. Even if the company's performance improves and a lending crisis is averted, the lender will at least gain confidence that the CFO is doing everything possible to keep everyone apprised of the condition of the company.

Debt Risk Issues

How much debt should a company have? How hard should lenders be pushed for better terms? And when should debt be renewed? These questions and other factors are impacted by a variety of risks associated with debt. In a simplistic universe, a

CFO only borrows enough to meet forecasted needs, bargains hard with a single lender for the best rates, and rolls over debt agreements shortly before they are scheduled to terminate. From a risk perspective, this simplistic view can result in serious problems, of which the most important is the lender suddenly backing out of a loan renewal for reasons that have nothing to do with the company. It is entirely possible that there has been a general tightening of credit, and the lender is no longer rolling over debt. A CFO who wants to guard against debt risk should consider all of the following options:

- *Arrange for extra debt.* Even if the company does not need it, consider setting up a multi-year debt arrangement. The long-term nature of the agreement is crucial, since it makes cash available to the company even during periods when credit would not otherwise be available. Since the excess cash made available through such an arrangement can be invested, the net effect on interest expense of having extra debt is not especially high.
- *Ensure that the lender earns a profit.* Though it may be tempting to squeeze lenders to keep fees low, it makes sense to deliberately allow them a reasonable profit, as well as to make all scheduled payments on time. By doing so, lenders will be more inclined to continue offering the company credit when they might not otherwise do so.

> **Tip:** Periodically compile a listing of the fees the company pays to each of the banks with which it does business. The company will have more lending leverage over those banks to which it pays the most fees.

> **Tip:** If the company has a procurement card program, source this work through a favored bank, to concentrate more fees with it and thereby give the company more leverage over the bank in regard to lending arrangements.

- *Have multiple lenders.* One lender may be forced by circumstances to tighten credit, but this does not mean that *all* lenders will do so. Consequently, it is best to arrange loans with several lenders. Do not take this concept too far, since giving a small slice of a company's business to a large number of banks means that no single bank has an overwhelming interest in continuing to do business with the company.
- *Renew credit facilities early.* Begin the refinancing of existing debt agreements well in advance of their termination dates. By doing so, replacement agreements will be in place before there is any risk of a last-minute credit tightening that might cause a scramble for new sources of debt.
- *Have a balanced redemption schedule.* Do not schedule all loans to be repaid within a short period of time, since this puts too much pressure on the company to come up with alternative financing within a short period of time, especially during periods when there are liquidity shortfalls in the market. Instead, stagger redemptions across a broad range of dates.

- *Build relations*. The CEO and CFO of the company should seek out their lender counterparts, and engage in regular discussions. By building close relations between the upper ends of both organizations, it is more likely that lenders will continue to offer credit facilities to the company.

The CFO should continually monitor changes in interest rates and be willing to restructure the company's debt on short notice, if this could result in a substantial savings. Most lenders require the formal approval of the board of directors before they will extend loans to a company, so being able to alter lending arrangements on short notice requires the rapid approval of the board. To obtain their approval, it is useful to keep the board apprised of ongoing financing strategies, and to install a streamlined board approval process for various debt scenarios.

Deleveraging

If a company has accumulated a large amount of cash, does it make sense to use some portion of this cash to pay down any remaining debt? The key decision factors are:

- *Cost of debt*. Itemize the debt by interest cost, and pay down the debt having the highest interest cost. Convertible debt may also be ranked for immediate pay down, if the company wants to avoid the conversion of debt into stock.
- *Use of cash*. If cash is simply being invested at the best possible interest rate, rather than being employed for operational purposes, it may be better to use it to pay down debt.
- *Differential cost*. If the interest rate on invested cash is lower than the interest rate on debt, pay down the debt.

Even if the preceding criteria point strongly in the direction of deleveraging, also consider the benefits of retaining a cash hoard for downturns in the economic cycle. It is entirely possible that the company can snap up assets or competitors at bargain-basement prices during a downturn – but that is only possible if there is sufficient cash on hand to do so.

Summary

Most of the forms of debt financing noted in this chapter can only be accessed in limited amounts that are defined by the amount of collateral, after which lenders will be extremely unwilling to advance additional funds. For really high debt levels, it will be necessary to obtain personal guarantees from the company owners, or the sale of stock to increase the amount of equity on hand.

If a business has extremely variable earnings, it may not make sense to have *any* debt, since it may be difficult to pay back the lender. In such a situation, it makes more sense to stockpile cash during periods when the company is flush with cash, or to rely primarily on the sale of stock to raise cash. For the latter alternative, we discuss fund raising with equity in the next chapter.

Chapter 13
Fund Raising with Equity

Introduction

Selling stock can be a major source of cash for a company. However, doing so can seriously reduce the ownership percentages of existing shareholders, as well as introduce a veritable plague of new shareholder privileges. In this chapter, we describe the alternatives available to a company that wants to raise funds through the sale of an equity interest in the business, some potential sources of capital, and regulatory issues that can impact the sale of stock.

Related Podcast Episodes: Episodes 89, 90, and 93 of the Accounting Best Practices Podcast discuss Regulation D stock sales, Regulation A stock sales, and stock registrations, respectively. The episodes are available at: **accounting-tools.com/podcasts** or **iTunes**

Overview of Equity Funding

The first source of funding that most CFOs turn to is debt financing, since interest expense is tax deductible and it does not change the ownership of a business. However, lenders are risk-averse, and will only lend a certain amount of cash. When that point is reached, the main alternative for fund raising is to sell shares in the business.

Though there is no legal obligation for a company to make regular payments to its investors, there is an expectation by investors of substantial returns, which they can achieve either through dividend payments or the appreciation in value of the company's stock. This expectation for returns is higher than the interest cost associated with debt, which is why the average CFO is reluctant to advocate the sale of stock when there are still opportunities for other types of fund raising.

When the decision is made to issue stock, a privately-held business may find that there are few investors willing to buy its shares, on the grounds that the shares cannot be easily resold to other investors. Also, since there is no market for its stock, there is no easy way to determine the value of the shares. As just noted, stock appreciation is one of the primary means by which an investor gains a return on shares held – but with no way to value the shares, appreciation cannot occur. Given these issues, a privately-held company has three options for selling equity:

- *Sell shares at a discount.* Investors may be interested in buying shares if the shares are being sold at a substantial discount, and especially if warrants are attached to the shares that give the right to buy additional shares at a certain strike price. Of course, this means that the ownership percentages of existing shareholders could decline dramatically.

- *Sell preferred shares*. More sophisticated investors will want to purchase preferred shares, which may carry a variety of features, such as dividends, conversion privileges to common stock, liquidation rights ahead of common stockholders, and/or the right to approve the sale of the business.
- *Go public*. Many stock sale agreements include a provision that requires the company to register the shares with the Securities and Exchange Commission (SEC) within a certain period of time. This means that the business must go public specifically so that the shareholders can be placed in a position to more easily sell their shares.

In addition to the issues associated with each alternative for selling equity, there is also the problem that shares bought by more sophisticated investors may come with the additional price of a board seat, monthly reporting packages, and possibly even control over the management of the business. In short, fund raising with equity is particularly unpalatable for privately-held businesses.

The situation is less dire for larger publicly-held companies, which can have new shares registered for sale within a short period of time and sell them on a stock exchange. Smaller publicly-held companies may face a considerably more prolonged review period before their shares can be registered for sale; further, the trading market for their stock may be so small that it takes some time to sell new shares.

In short, only larger public companies can easily sell shares within a reasonable time period and at a reasonable price. Most other entities must offer discounts or some sort of preference rights to convince investors to buy their shares. These issues should make it clear why so many smaller businesses actively avoid fund raising with equity.

Restricted Stock

Restricted stock carries a restriction statement on the face or back of the certificate, stating that there are restrictions on its transfer, purchase, or resale. This restriction is usually because the issuing company has not yet registered the shares with the SEC. It can be quite difficult for the holder of restricted shares to move the shares to a different owner. An example of the restriction verbiage shown on a stock certificate is:

> "These securities may not be sold, offered for sale, or pledged in the absence of a registration statement."

Unrestricted stock does not contain a restriction legend, and so can be sold or transferred. Because of the issues with restricted stock, the typical investor is much more interested in buying unrestricted stock from a company.

245

Unrestricted Stock

Investors are always the most interested in buying unrestricted stock, which is also known as registered stock. A company that wants to sell registered stock must file a Form S-1 registration statement with the SEC. The Form S-1 is an extremely detailed document that describes a company's financial and operational condition, as well as other matters. Among the more important categories of information in the form are:

- *Risk factors*. States the risks that may impact the company.
- *Use of proceeds*. Notes how the cash garnered from sale of the stock will be used.
- *Selling security holders*. Lists any current shareholders whose shares in the company are being sold.
- *Registrant information*. Describes the company, its financial results, management's discussion and analysis of the company, legal proceedings, and many other matters.

Completing the form properly requires the services of the company's auditors and attorneys, as well as their assistance when the SEC sends back several iterations of questions about the information in the form. It is likely that a number of months will pass before the SEC declares the form effective, which means that the stock listed in the form is now registered, and can be sold without restriction.

Once a Form S-1 has been declared effective, the company having made the filing is now considered a publicly-held company, which means that it must file regular reports with the SEC about its financial results and material changes in its business.

If a company is already publicly held, it can use a *shelf registration* to pre-register stock that it does not necessarily plan to sell immediately. This still involves the difficult registration process, but the company is in less of a rush to complete it, since there is not an immediate need to sell shares. Under SEC rules, shelf registration requirements are eased for larger public companies.

In general, a privately held company will want to stay that way, since the costs of registering stock and making subsequent filings with the SEC as a public company are substantial. If the owners and/or managers of the company do not wish to issue registered stock, then there are several exemptions from the SEC rules that may provide a reasonable alternative. In later sections, we describe the concept of the accredited investor and the Regulation D stock sales to this special type of investor. We also cover another popular exemption, the Regulation A stock sale, which does not require accredited investors, but which is limited in terms of the amount of cash that can be raised.

The Accredited Investor

An accredited investor qualifies under SEC rules as being financially sophisticated. The SEC definition of an accredited investor is:

1. A bank, insurance company, registered investment company, business development company, or small business investment company;
2. An employee benefit plan, within the meaning of the Employee Retirement Income Security Act, if a bank, insurance company, or registered investment adviser makes the investment decisions, or if the plan has total assets in excess of $5 million;
3. A charitable organization, corporation, or partnership with assets exceeding $5 million;
4. A director, executive officer, or general partner of the company selling the securities;
5. A business in which all the equity owners are accredited investors;
6. A natural person who has individual net worth, or joint net worth with the person's spouse, that exceeds $1 million at the time of the purchase, excluding the value of the primary residence of such person;
7. A natural person with income exceeding $200,000 in each of the two most recent years or joint income with a spouse exceeding $300,000 for those years and a reasonable expectation of the same income level in the current year; or
8. A trust with assets in excess of $5 million, not formed to acquire the securities offered, whose purchases a sophisticated person makes.

This definition comes from Rule 501 of the SEC's Regulation D.

The accredited investor can be of considerable importance when a company is interested in the sale of unregistered securities, as described in the next section.

Regulation D Stock Sales

Regulation D provides an exemption from the normal stock registration requirement, and is most useful when a company is still privately held. There are different rules and allowed funding amounts available under Regulation D, which are described in its Rule 504, 505, and 506. In general, to sell shares under Regulation D, a company must follow these rules:

- Only sell shares to accredited investors.
- Investors cannot be contacted through a general solicitation, such as advertising or free seminars open to the public.
- If shares are sold over a long time period, prove that all sales are covered by Regulation D. This can be proven by documenting a financing plan, selling the same type of stock to all investors, showing that all shares are sold for the same type of consideration, *and* by proving that the sales are being made for the same general purpose.

Because of the inability to advertise a stock sale, companies usually have to turn to investment bankers, who contact their clients to see who is interested in buying shares. The bankers impose a fee for this service, which is a percentage of the amount of funds generated.

If prospective investors are interested in buying shares, the company sends them a boilerplate questionnaire to fill out, in which they state that they are accredited investors. This form provides the company with legal protection, in case the SEC questions whether the stock issuance is protected by Regulation D.

Investors then send their money to an escrow account that is maintained by a third party, until such time as the total amount of funding meets the minimum requirement set by the company. The investment banker extracts its fee from the escrowed funds, the company collects its cash, and the company's stock transfer agent sends stock certificates to the investors.

Shares issued under Regulation D are not initially registered, which means that a restriction statement appears on the back of each certificate. This statement essentially prohibits the shareholder from selling to a third party.

This restriction on the resale of stock is usually a major concern for all but the most long-term investors. Accordingly, investors like to see one or more of the following guarantees being offered by a company:

- *Piggyback rights*. The company promises to include their shares in any stock registration statement that it may eventually file with the SEC. This is a near-universal inclusion in a Regulation D offering, since it does not impose an immediate obligation on the company.
- *Registration promise*. The company promises to file a registration statement with the SEC by a certain date. If the company is currently privately held, this promise essentially requires it to become publicly held, along with the various ongoing SEC filing requirements that are part of being a public company. A more onerous agreement will even require the company to issue additional stock if it does not obtain SEC approval of the registration statement by a certain date.

The downside of using a Regulation D stock sale is that investors typically want something extra in exchange for buying unregistered stock. This may take the form of a reduced price per share or the issuance of warrants (see the next section).

An even more serious downside of using Regulation D is when prospective investors insist upon buying preferred stock, rather than common stock. Preferred stock may include a number of oppressive terms, such as favorable conversion rights into common stock, the payment of dividends, and perhaps even override voting privileges concerning the sale of the company or other matters.

Given the number of rights that investors may demand in a Regulation D stock sale, it is best to only use this approach when the company is operating from a position of strength, where it does not have an immediate need for cash.

Warrants

A warrant is a call option issued by a company on its own shares. The recipient has the right, but not the obligation, to buy the company's shares at a certain price during a specific period of time, which is usually at least five years. It may be tempting to issue warrants as part of a package deal under which investors buy company stock and warrants. The value of a warrant to an investor is that any future uptick in the price of the company's stock can be converted into an immediate profit by exercising the warrant at the price stated in the warrant agreement, and then selling the shares for a profit at the market price.

The value of the arrangement is not so clear from the perspective of the company, since it will be forced to sell its shares at a reduced price if warrants are eventually exercised. Because of this possible watering down of the shareholder base in exchange for a relatively small cash inflow, it is better to negotiate hard for the issuance of a reduced number of warrants. The worst-case scenario is *100% coverage*, where one warrant is issued for every share sold. A *50% coverage* scenario is better, since only one warrant is issued for every two shares sold. It is certainly worthwhile to negotiate an even lower warrant coverage, if the circumstances allow for it.

EXAMPLE

Hammer Industries sells 10,000 shares of its common stock for $10.00, along with 10,000 warrants to buy additional shares of the company for the next three years at $10.00 per share. The price of the company's stock later rises to $17.00, at which point the investor uses his warrant privileges to buy an additional 10,000 shares at $10.00 each. If he can then have the shares registered and sells them at the $17.00 market price, he will pocket a profit of $70,000 on his exercise of the warrants.

The best way to consider the impact of warrants is that they allow warrant holders to profit from any upside in the stock price, at the expense of existing shareholders whose percentage of ownership will decline if the warrants are exercised.

Regulation A Stock Sales

The preceding discussion of Regulation D was oriented toward stock sales to accredited investors. What if a company does not have access to this group of wealthy investors, or cannot find any who are willing to invest? An alternative is available under the Regulation A exemption.

Under Regulation A, a company can issue securities under two tiers. The more essential requirements associated with each tier are noted in the following table.

Regulation A Tiers

	Tier 1	Tier 2
Amount raised per year	$20 million maximum	$50 million maximum
Investment limitations	None	For non-accredited investors, 10% of the greater of income or net worth, per offering
Non-accredited investors allowed	Yes	Yes
Audited financials required	No	Yes
Registration required with SEC	Yes	Yes
Shares freely tradable	Yes	Yes
Ongoing reporting requirements	No	Yes (semi-annual)

The Regulation A exemption is not available to a number of types of companies. They are investment companies, foreign companies, oil and gas companies, public companies, and companies selling asset-backed securities.

If a company qualifies for this exemption, the basic process flow is to issue an SEC-reviewed offering circular to attract investors, then file a Form 1-A with the SEC, then sell shares, and then file a Form 1-Z to document the termination or completion of the offering. If the company is in Tier 2, it must then file a Form 1-K annual report that includes audited financial statements, a discussion of its financial results, and information about its business and management, related-party transactions, and share ownership. A Tier 2 company must also file a Form 1-SA semi-annual report that includes interim unaudited financial statements, as well as a discussion of the company's financial results. Finally, a Tier 2 company must file a Form 1-U within four business days of certain events, such as a bankruptcy, change in accountant, or change in control.

A key feature of Regulation A stock sales is that shares are freely tradable. This might initially appear to be an exceedingly valuable feature for investors. However, because the shares are not being traded on a public exchange, it still may be difficult for investors to sell their shares.

In short, Regulation A is designed to be a moderately streamlined way to raise a reasonable amount of cash. If there is a need to raise larger amounts of cash without going public, the Regulation D exemption is a better choice.

Angel Investors and Venture Capital

When a business is in its startup phase and the owners want to grow it quickly, they may initially turn to an angel investor for funding. An angel investor is a wealthy individual who usually invests between $25,000 and $1,000,000 in a business, in exchange for a significant minority ownership position. This is an extremely risky investment for the investor, since the business is unproven and could quite possibly fail. Given the high risk, expect to issue a disproportionate number of shares for this investment.

After a business has developed a proof of concept, or has perhaps issued its first products or services, it may again be in need of cash to ramp up its rate of growth. The cash requirement at this point will be larger, so funding from angel investors will no longer be sufficient. Instead, a venture capital fund (VC) is a possible source of capital. A VC is a corporate entity that pools the cash contributions of multiple investors and institutions for investments in startup companies. Typical investments made by a VC are in the range of $500,000 to $10,000,000.

It can be quite difficult to obtain funding from VCs, since they are looking for those few companies that have the potential for an extremely high rate of growth. Their basic business model is to invest in a number of companies that have superstar potential, knowing that most will fail or become substandard investments, while a few will have stratospheric returns that offset the losses in the rest of their portfolios.

To obtain funding from a VC, create a short presentation and business plan, and present it to a VC partner. This presentation is critical, since venture funds see an enormous number of proposals every year, and only select a few for investment. If the VC partner is interested, expect a considerable amount of due diligence investigation before any funding offer is made.

Venture firms want some level of control over their investments. This may call for majority ownership, perhaps the issuance of preferred stock, a change in key management positions, and/or board seats. They want this level of control in order to be closely involved in how the company is managed. This can mean that company founders are pushed out or relegated to non-critical management positions.

Tip: Consider accepting a lower valuation in order to attract a higher-quality VC that can bring expertise and a strong network to the company. Bargaining for a higher valuation may turn away these firms, since their prospective returns will be reduced. In short, think about the long-term value of working with a VC as a partner in the business.

A strong case can be made that most businesses should not even attempt to gain VC funding. A VC firm will push a company to expand extremely rapidly in order to increase its valuation as quickly as possible. As noted in our discussion of pacing in the strategy chapter, an excessively rapid pace of growth can severely damage a company and increase its long-term risk of failure. Instead, it may make more sense to adopt a slower-growth stance with more traditional forms of equity and debt funding.

Debt for Equity Swaps

In some cases, it may be possible to swap company shares for outstanding company debt securities. This is most common when a company issues convertible bonds that allow bond holders to convert their bonds into company stock at certain predefined exchange ratios. This option is only available to publicly-held companies.

In a privately-held company, a debt for equity swap usually occurs only when a company is in such dire financial straits that it is unable to repay its debt. If so, taking an equity interest in the company may be the only option remaining to the lender, other than writing off the debt as being uncollectible. This conversion to equity is more likely when the lender is an individual, rather than a bank, since banks may be constrained by their own lending rules from engaging in debt for equity swaps. A company that succeeds in converting debt to equity under these difficult financial circumstances may find that it can issue stock at such a low valuation that it is required by the accounting standards to book a profit on the conversion of debt to equity.

When a large public company issues convertible debt, any resulting conversions to equity are unlikely to be large enough to alter the debt-equity ratio of the business to a significant extent. The reverse is the case when a private company succeeds in converting debt to equity; it may be eliminating much of its debt, and had such little equity to begin with that it switches from having a dangerously unbalanced debt-equity ratio to one that gives the appearance of being solidly well-funded. Of course, the operational profitability of such a company is still questionable, but the debt for equity swap can repair its balance sheet.

Crowdfunding

The concept of crowdfunding is authorized under the Jumpstart Our Business Startups (JOBS) Act. Crowdfunding uses the Internet and social media to raise small amounts of capital from a large number of people. The basic provisions of crowdfunding in the JOBS Act are:

- A company is limited to raising $535,000 per year (as of 2017) through crowdfunding, or $1,070,000 (as of 2017) if it provides investors with audited financial statements.
- If the purchasers of these securities agree to hold the securities for at least one year, the offering is exempt from registration with the SEC. Also, the securities can be sold to anyone, even if they are not accredited investors. Further, the company has no ongoing information delivery requirements to investors.
- Individual investors are limited to investing 10% of their annual income or net worth, which is capped. A smaller percentage applies to those investors with smaller annual incomes.
- An initial filing with the SEC is required.

Though the concept is interesting, the lack of information reporting means that crowdfunding could be subject to abuse. Also, the annual fund raising limitation for a business is so small that crowdfunding is likely to be a viable alternative only for the smallest companies.

Summary

It can be quite difficult to obtain equity funding in a privately-held company, since an investor's prospects for reselling the shares are not especially good. In order to obtain such investments, expect a negotiating battle with prospective investors, who will want a variety of extremely favorable terms. If the company needs successive rounds of equity funding, expect the terms to change for each round, depending upon relative changes in the negotiating power of the company and its investors. The result may well be a tangle of different types of preferred stock, each with different rights. If such a company is ever in a position to go public, it will then be necessary to clean up these different classes of stock by converting them to common stock at whatever conversion ratios were built into the original stock agreements. The situation is substantially different for a large public company, which can routinely issue new common stock whenever the market price is reasonable. Thus, the decision to raise funds through the sale of stock is substantially different for a private company and a public company.

Chapter 14
Credit Rating Agencies

Introduction

When a company is large enough to issue debt instruments into the marketplace, it usually must obtain a credit rating from a credit rating agency. In this chapter, we discuss why credit ratings are necessary, the major rating agencies, and the process used to obtain a credit rating.

The Credit Rating Environment

A credit rating agency is an entity that assigns credit ratings to either the issuers of certain kinds of debt, or directly to their debt instruments. Some of these agencies also offer credit rating advisory services, under which they advise clients regarding how to structure their debt issuances in order to achieve a particular credit rating. The larger agencies earn most of their income from fees levied against the issuers of debt instruments; this can result in a conflict of interest, since a debt issuer could possibly influence a rating decision by shopping among the rating agencies for the best rating.

There are several fee structures used by the rating agencies. The more common fees are as follows:

- One-time fee based on a percentage of the nominal value of the underlying transaction
- Recurring base fee

If a fee is based on a percentage of nominal value, it may be subject to a cap to avoid an excessive charge.

There are three major credit rating agencies that provide ratings for the bulk of all debt issuances. They are authorized for ratings work as Nationally Recognized Statistical Rating Organizations (NRSROs) by the Securities and Exchange Commission (SEC). Since there are only a few authorized rating agencies, the ratings industry is essentially a closed oligopoly, and so probably charges higher fees than would be the case in a more competitive environment. The three agencies that collectively control most of the market are:

- Moody's Investor Service
- Standard & Poor's
- Fitch Ratings

In addition, the following agencies are also authorized as NRSROs, but have much smaller market shares:

- Kroll Bond Rating Agency
- A. M. Best Company
- Dominion Bond Rating Service, Ltd.
- Japan Credit Rating Agency, Ltd.
- Egan-Jones Rating Company
- Morningstar, Inc.

The ratings issued by these agencies are used by investors to determine the price at which to buy debt (usually bonds). In addition, the investment policies of many entities require them to limit their investments to debt issuances having certain minimum credit ratings. It is difficult to issue debt without a credit rating, since the issuance may be undersubscribed or can only be sold at a high effective interest rate.

The rating classifications used by the agencies vary from each other to some extent. The following table presents a comparison of the credit rating classifications of the three largest agencies. Debt issuances rated as investment grade in the table are considered suitable for investment purposes. The ratings classified as speculative are generally avoided by those entities looking for safe investments.

Credit Rating Comparison

Risk Level	Moody's	Standard & Poor's	Fitch
Investment grade:			
(highest investment grade)	Aaa	AAA	AAA
	Aa1	AA+	AA+
	Aa2	AA	AA
	Aa3	AA-	AA-
	A1	A+	A+
	A2	A	A
	A3	A-	A-
	Baa1	BBB+	BBB+
	Baa2	BBB	BBB
(lowest investment grade)	Baa3	BBB-	BBB-
Speculative grade:			
(highest speculative grade)	Ba1	BB+	BB+
	Ba2	BB	BB
	Ba3	BB-	BB-
	B1	B+	B+
	B2	B	B
	B3	B-	B-
	Caa1	CCC+	CCC+

Note: There are additional lower speculative grades than those listed in this table.

Only a large company with a stable business model and conservative financial practices can hope to qualify for one of the top-tier investment grades. Indeed, so few AAA ratings are issued that the recipients tend to use them as marketing tools to impress customers, suppliers, and employees. Since the AAA rating is well out of reach for most companies, the primary goal is simply to obtain a mid-level investment grade rating. By doing so, investors will not demand an excessively high interest rate on bond issuances. Companies certainly do not want their debt instruments to be classified as speculative, since investors will not buy them unless the company is willing to pay a very high interest rate.

A debt issuer may find that the credit rating agencies assign different credit ratings to different bond issuances, even though the bonds are all being issued by the same entity. This variation is caused by differences in the amount of collateral (if any) assigned to the debt, the level of subordination to other debt instruments of the issuer, and other debt terms.

The Rating Process

The CFO should be aware of the process flow that results in a credit rating, particularly in regard to the amount of time required to complete the process. The key process steps are:

1. The agency assigns a primary analyst to the company, as well as a senior analyst specializing in the company's industry.
2. The agency issues a questionnaire to the company, asking for responses in a number of areas, as well as for the provision of financial information. The company may need a full week to prepare a complete response to the questionnaire. The types of information that the agency will want to see include:

    *   Overview of the business and its objectives
    *   Historical and forecasted financial information for the past five years and next five years, respectively
    *   Key manager biographies
    *   Market analysis

3. Representatives of the company and the agency meet to go over the requested information, as well as for the company's management team to make a presentation regarding the financial condition of the business and future plans. There will be an extensive question-and-answer session where the agency team attempts to gain insights into how the company operates.
4. The agency's ratings team spends several weeks reviewing the information and developing a detailed report, which is then critically reviewed by the agency's ratings committee. If the ratings committee wants additional information before reaching a decision, it can send the proposed rating package back for further review. The resultant rating will be based on a combination of the finances of the business, the market in which it competes, and its estimated future prospects.

5. The primary analyst presents the rating to the company's senior management team. If there is a rush to complete the process, this notification may be by phone.
6. The agency releases its rating to the major news services, possibly including a brief description of the reason(s) for the rating assignment.
7. The primary analyst continues to monitor the condition of the company, and may alter the assigned rating based on any number of financial, operational, and/or industry-related factors. If there is a rating change, the agency will release this information to the major news services.

The time required for an agency to issue a rating varies, because the development of a rating is an iterative process that requires input from both the issuer and the agency. The issuer must provide a significant amount of detailed information, and then respond to several additional requests from the agency. Thus, a fast rating requires the cooperation of both parties. If it is necessary to obtain a rating in short order, it is helpful if the CFO, treasurer, *and* controller can empty their calendars to the greatest extent possible, in order to deal with any information requirements. If both sides have adequate resources and are willing to make the effort, it should take between six and eight weeks to obtain a rating.

Tip: Given the amount of time required to obtain a rating, it can make sense to obtain the rating as early as possible, so the CFO can allocate more time to marketing the debt issuance and negotiating its terms.

If a company is a small one or issues debt relatively infrequently, it can make sense to obtain ratings from more than one agency. Though doing so is expensive, it shows that multiple entities have given their seal of approval to the financial condition of the business. Also, the cost is reduced somewhat for additional ratings, since the agencies base their analyses on approximately the same information, which the company only has to compile once. It is possible to obtain more than one rating during the same evaluation period.

If a business pursues multiple ratings, do not be surprised if the ratings awarded by each agency are not equivalent to each other. Each agency has its own rating system, and may give different weightings to a variety of company obligations, the quality and tenure of management, the consistency of earnings and cash flow, adherence to risk management principles, and the size of the business. However, these should not be significant differences that are many ratings apart.

If a company is not experienced with the rating process, it can make sense to hire the services of a ratings advisor, possibly from the company's investment banker. Though expensive, these advisors are experienced in every aspect of the rating review process, and so can assist with the production and presentation of information to the agencies.

> **Tip:** The amount of effort required to obtain a rating is significant, so try to schedule it away from a quarterly review or annual audit of the financial statements. Otherwise, the accounting department will be overloaded.

There may be cases where the CFO disagrees with the rating assigned by a rating agency. If so, there is no formal appeal process, nor will an agency suppress its rating. The only scenario under which an agency will consider changing its opinion is when new information is made available that was not presented as part of the initial rating review.

If the management team wants to obtain an improved credit rating at some point in the future, it may need to reposition the financial structure of the business to make it more conservative. For example, shares in the business could be sold and the proceeds used to reduce the amount of debt outstanding. However, doing so may reduce the amount of cash available for other purposes, which can impact the company's growth plans.

Ratings agencies may alter a rating subsequent to its initial issuance. The CFO can impact these rating changes to some extent by discussing with the primary analyst any major changes being contemplated to the finances or operations of the business. The feedback given by the analyst may convince the CFO to alter the company's plans, thereby leading to a rating enhancement or at least the avoidance of a rating downgrade.

Though the CFO should be involved in the rating process, the primary company representative may be the treasurer, thereby offloading what can be a substantial amount of work.

Summary

Credit ratings and the objectives of a business are intertwined. If senior management wants to achieve rapid growth, it may need to issue more debt than a rating agency might consider prudent, resulting in a lower credit rating. Conversely, if it is considered more important to maintain a high credit rating, doing so will mandate a level of fiscal prudence that cannot support a rapid rate of growth. In short, it is difficult to obtain both a high growth rate and a stratospheric credit rating – management has to choose which objective is more important.

Chapter 15
Going Public and Going Private

Introduction

Many company owners and managers believe that taking a company public is the capstone of their careers, since being involved with a publicly-held company is considered to be not only prestigious, but also a superior way to raise capital. While such involvement may indeed be prestigious, it is also expensive, massively time-consuming, and quite possibly not such a superior way to raise capital.

In this chapter, we discuss the pros and cons of going public, note the standard process flow for an initial public offering, and describe the alternative approach of using a reverse merger to go public. And in case running a public company turns out to be less enthralling than expected, we reveal how to take a public company private.

> **Related Podcast Episodes:** Episodes 33 and 84 of the Accounting Best Practices Podcast discuss the acquisition of a shell company and taking a company private, respectively. The episodes are available at: **accountingtools.com/podcasts** or **iTunes**

Reasons for and Against Going Public

There are several reasons why the owners of a business may want to take it public through an initial public offering (IPO). The first is the perception that the owners can more easily sell their shares, or at least have the option to do so through a stock exchange. Second, being publicly held makes it easier to raise funds with which to operate the business or pay for acquisitions. Third, the absence of restrictions on the sale of shares tends to increase their price. Fourth, the increased ease with which a company can sell shares tends to reduce its proportion of debt to equity, which can reduce the risk of its financial structure. Another reason is prestige – taking a company public is considered by some to be the capstone of one's professional career. Also, the awarding of stock options has more meaning in a public company, since they can eventually be converted to shares that can be sold on a stock exchange. Finally, there is some evidence that the management team of a public company receives higher compensation than they would in a similar private company, so managers tend to be in favor of going public.

While these reasons may seem compelling, there are a number of other excellent reasons for *not* going public. First, it requires significant new expenditures for the services of auditors and securities attorneys, as well as additional in-house accounting, internal audit, and investor relations personnel. The cost of directors and officers liability insurance will also increase (possibly by several multiples of the prior amount). These incremental expenses may be large enough to eliminate the profits of a smaller company. Also, the multitude of public company activities will take up some of the time of the management team, such as attendance at shareholder meetings, analyst meetings, earnings calls, and road shows. Further, the new owners of the business may demand that the company focus more attention on the immediate generation of profits, rather than the pursuit of longer-term goals. Also, there is a risk that required public disclosures might shift some competitive advantage to other players in the industry. In addition, there is some risk that the original owner will be forced out as part of an unfriendly takeover, which would have been impossible if the company had remained private. Further, investment bankers charge a high fee for raising capital through stock offerings, which a smaller business might find exorbitant. Finally, there are always alternatives to selling stock on the open market to raise funds, and which may be less expensive than doing so through an initial or secondary stock issuance.

In addition to the problems just pointed out with being public, smaller firms may also suffer from stock manipulation. When there are few registered shares outstanding, it is relatively easy for dishonest shareholders to create transactions that rapidly alter the stock price and allow them to sell out at a profit.

In short, there are a number of arguments both in favor of and against going public. Smaller companies will likely find that the cost of compliance with securities laws will erase a large part of their profits, and so may elect to remain private. A larger firm with more revenues will probably find that these costs only reduce profits by a relatively small amount, so that the overall benefits of being public outweigh those of being private.

The Initial Public Offering

The following discussion of the IPO process represents the *approximate* flow of activities. In reality, there is some timing overlap between events. We have also clustered together some actions to improve the narrative flow. The intent is to give a sense for how the process works, rather than an exact series of perfectly sequenced steps.

When the board of directors believes that a company is ready to take the step from being a private company to a public company, it hires a legal firm that specializes in SEC filings to complete a *registration statement*. This form is mandated by the SEC, and contains a detailed review of the company's financial and operational condition, risk factors, and any other items that it believes investors should be aware of before they buy the company's stock. The primary categories of information in a registration statement are:

- Summary information and risk factors
- Use of proceeds
- Description of the business
- Financial statements
- Management's discussion and analysis of the business

- Compensation of key parties
- Related party transactions

There are a large number of additional categories of information, as well. As a result, the registration statement can be a massive document. Since the company's auditors and attorneys must review it several times, and in great detail, it is also a very expensive document to create.

Once the SEC receives the form, its staff has 30 days in which to review the document – which it will, and in excruciating detail. The SEC's in-house accountants and attorneys look for inconsistencies and errors in the registration statement, as well as unclear or overblown statements, and summarize these points in a comment letter, which it sends to the company. Some of the comments made by the SEC involve substantive issues, such as the nature of the revenue recognition methodology used by the company, and which may call for a restatement of the company's financial statements. Other comments may note minor typographical issues, such as a missing middle initial in the name of a board member. The SEC does not impose a materiality convention on its staff for reviews – all parts of the registration statement are subject to review, no matter how minor the resulting changes may be.

The company responds to all of the SEC's questions and updates its registration statement as well, and then sends back the documents via an amended filing for another review. The SEC is allowed 30 days for each iteration of its review process. The SEC staff is in absolutely no hurry to assist a company with its IPO; consequently, this question-and-answer process may require a number of iterations and more months than the management team would believe possible.

> **Tip:** High-end securities attorneys are extremely expensive, and totally worth the money, since they can minimize the number of question-and-answer iterations with the SEC, thereby accelerating the process of going public.

While the registration statement is being reviewed and revised, the company is also negotiating with one or more *underwriters* to assist the company in going public. The choice of which investment bank to use as an underwriter depends upon a number of factors, such as the prestige of the bank, whether it has prior experience in the company's industry, the number of its contacts within the investor community, and its fee. A larger and more prestigious firm usually charges a higher fee, but also has a greater ability to sell the entire amount of a company's offering of securities.

> **Tip:** Obtain references from candidate underwriters and call the CFOs of those companies to obtain an understanding of the actual level of support that each candidate provides, as well as its expertise and willingness to continue to support the company.

The company negotiates the terms of a letter of intent with its preferred underwriter. The following are among the key elements of the letter of intent:

- *Fee.* The primary fee of the underwriter is a percentage of the total amount of funds collected. In addition, there are a variety of legal, accounting, travel, and other costs that it may pass through to the company for reimbursement.
- *Firm commitment or best efforts.* The underwriter will either agree to a *firm commitment* or a *best efforts* arrangement. Under a firm commitment deal, the underwriter agrees to buy a certain number of shares from the company, irrespective of its ability to sell those shares to third parties. This is preferable if the company is targeting raising a certain amount of cash. Under a best efforts deal, the underwriter takes a commission on as many shares as it can sell. If an underwriter insists on a best efforts deal, it indicates that there is some risk of not being able to sell the targeted number of shares.
- *Overallotment.* The underwriter may want the option to purchase additional shares from the company at a certain price within a set time period after the IPO date, which it can then sell to investors at a profit.

The underwriter supervises the creation of a road show presentation, in which the senior management team is expected to present a summary of the company and its investment prospects to prospective investors. These investors are likely to be mostly institutional investors. The bankers and management team will go through a number of iterations to polish the presentation.

The management team and its investment bank advisors embark on a road show, which spans several weeks and takes them to a number of cities to meet with investors. If investors are interested in buying the company's stock, they tell the banks how many shares they want to buy, and at what price.

At this time, the company also files an application with the stock exchange on which it wants its stock to be listed. The stock exchange verifies that the company meets its listing requirements (see the Stock Exchanges chapter) and then assigns it a ticker symbol. In addition, if it does not already have one, the company hires a stock transfer agent to handle the transfer of shares between parties. The company's legal staff will also submit filings to the securities agencies of those states in which the company anticipates selling shares.

When the SEC is satisfied with the latest draft of the registration statement, it declares the filing to be "effective." The management team and its bankers then decide upon the price at which the company will sell its shares. A key determinant is the price at which institutional investors are most likely to buy shares, since they usually comprise a large part of the initial block of shares sold. Underwriters want to set the initial share price slightly low, so that there is more likely to be a run-up in the first trading day that they can publicize. Also, a slightly low price makes it easier to create an active aftermarket in the stock, since other investors will be interested in obtaining and holding the stock to realize additional gains.

Tip: The underpricing of shares is most common in an IPO. If management wants to obtain the highest price per share, consider selling fewer shares during the IPO and more shares in a secondary offering, when the amount of underpricing is less extensive.

The underwriter traditionally likes to set the initial price of a share at somewhere between $10 and $20. Doing so may require a stock split or reverse stock split, depending on the number of shares currently outstanding. For example:

- A company has an initial valuation of $100 million, and has one million shares outstanding. To offer shares at an initial price of $20, there must be a five-for-one stock split that brings the number of shares outstanding to five million shares. Thus, a $100 million valuation divided by five million shares equals $20 per share.
- A company has an initial valuation of $80 million, and has 20 million shares outstanding. To offer shares at an initial price of $16, there must be a four-for-one reverse stock split that brings the number of shares outstanding to five million. Thus, an $80 million valuation divided by five million shares equals $16 per share.

The company then sends the registration statement to a financial printer. The printer puts the final stock price in the document, and uploads it to the SEC.

In those cases where there is more demand for shares than are to be sold, the underwriter is forced to allocate shares among its customers. The bankers will likely allocate more shares to their best customers, and may be somewhat more inclined to reduce allocations to those customers who are less likely to hold the stock for a reasonable period of time.

The underwriter sells the shares to the investors that it has lined up. The underwriter collects cash from the investors, subtracts its commission, and pays the remaining proceeds to the company at a closing meeting. The underwriter is typically paid about five percent of the amount of the total placement, though this can involve a sliding scale where a larger placement results in an aggregate fee that is substantially lower. Conversely, bankers may not be interested in handling a smaller placement without charging a correspondingly higher fee.

The company is now listed on a stock exchange, has registered shares that are being traded among investors, and has presumably just received a large amount of cash for its efforts. However, the IPO process is expensive, both in terms of costs and the time required by management to complete it. A simpler approach to going public is described in the next section.

The Reverse Merger Concept

A company uses a reverse merger when it wants to avoid the expense of an initial public offering, and instead buys a company that is already publicly-held. In most cases, the company being purchased is nothing more than a shell company that has been inactive for several years. By owning the public company, the buyer can now register stock for sale to the public, though it must now have its financial statements audited and issue regular reports to the SEC. Its shares will probably initially be available for trading on the over-the-counter (OTC) market, though it can apply to have its shares traded on a formal stock exchange.

The basic transaction flow for a reverse merger is that a private company gains control of a public shell company, with the shell structured to be the parent company and the buyer's company becoming its subsidiary. The owners of the private company exchange their shares in the private company for shares in the public company. They have now gained control over a majority of the stock of the shell.

The legal structure used for this merger is called a reverse triangular merger (see the Mergers and Acquisitions chapter). The process flow for a reverse triangular merger is:

1. The shell company creates a subsidiary entity.
2. The newly-formed subsidiary merges into the private company that is buying the shell.
3. The newly-formed subsidiary has now disappeared, so the private company becomes a subsidiary of the shell company.

The reverse triangular merger is used to avoid the cumbersome shareholder approval process that is normally required for an acquisition. Though the shareholders of the private company must still approve the deal, it is only the shareholder of the new subsidiary that must approve the deal on behalf of the shell company – and the only shareholder of the new subsidiary is its parent company.

The reverse triangular concept is particularly useful, because it allows a private company to continue operating as a going concern and without a change in control of the entity. Otherwise, the business might suffer from the loss of any contracts that would automatically expire if either of those events were to occur.

> **Note:** It is easier to complete a reverse merger with a shell company whose shares only trade on the over-the-counter market, rather than on a formal exchange. The reason is that stock exchange rules typically require the approval of the shareholders of the shell company. Thus, it may make sense for a shell company to delist from an exchange prior to engaging in a reverse merger.

Other than the use of the reverse triangular merger concept, the reverse merger follows the normal set of steps used for any acquisition. The acquirer conducts due diligence on the shell, and the attorneys for both sides negotiate a purchase agreement. However, there is one additional requirement, and it is an onerous one – the filing of a Form 8-K with the Securities and Exchange Commission within four business days of the reverse merger. This filing contains many of the items found in a full-scale prospectus for an initial public offering, and so is a major production. It includes several years of audited financial statements, a comparative analysis of results over several periods, related party transactions, and so forth. This Form 8-K filing should be the source of considerable dread by the CFO of the acquiring business, since the four-day filing requirement makes it difficult to issue this document with the complete suite of required information.

Advantages and Disadvantages of the Reverse Merger

There are a number of advantages associated with the reverse merger concept, which are:

- *Speed.* A reverse merger can be completed in just a few months.
- *Time commitment.* If a company were to follow the tortuous path of an initial public offering, the management team would be so distracted that there would be little time left to run the business. Conversely, a reverse merger can be accomplished with such minimal effort by anyone outside of the accounting department that management barely notices the change.
- *Timing.* If the buyer is not immediately intending to use the shell to raise money from the public, it can take the reverse merger path even in weak stock market conditions.
- *Tradable currency.* Being public means that the stock issued by the combined entity is a more tradable form of currency than the stock of a private company, which makes it easier for an acquirer to engage in stock-for-stock transactions (see the Mergers and Acquisitions chapter). Also, the shares of a public company are frequently valued higher than those of a private one (because the stock is more tradable), so the public company that engages in stock-for-stock purchases can do so with fewer shares. However, issued shares must still be registered if the recipient wants to sell them, which can be an involved process. Also, if the market for the company's stock is not large, it may be difficult for the recipients of its shares to sell them over a relatively short period of time.

- *Liquidity.* The reverse merger path is sometimes pushed by the current shareholders of a business, because they want to have an avenue for selling their shares. This is a particular concern for those shareholders who have been unable to liquidate their shares by other means, such as selling them back to the company or selling the entire business.
- *Dilution.* In an IPO, the underwriter wants the company to sell more stock than it really needs to, since the underwriter earns more money by collecting more cash from stock sales on behalf of the company. This dilutes the ownership of the original shareholders. In a reverse merger situation, the company typically raises only the amount of cash it needs, thereby limiting the amount of shareholder dilution.
- *Stock options.* Being public makes the issuance of stock options much more attractive to the recipients. If they elect to exercise their options, they can then sell the shares to the general public, while also obtaining enough cash to pay for taxes on any gains generated from the options.

Against these advantages are arrayed a number of disadvantages, which are:

- *Cash.* A company may not achieve an immediate cash inflow from the sale of its stock, as would be the case if it had taken the path of an initial public offering. Instead, a stock offering may be delayed until a later date.
- *Cost.* Even the lower-cost reverse merger approach still requires a large ongoing expenditure to meet the requirements of being public. It is difficult for an active business to spend less than $500,000 per year for the auditors, attorneys, controls, filing fees, investor relations, and other costs needed to be a public entity. In the author's experience, the actual figure is closer to $800,000 for the first year of operations, after which annual costs can be reduced into the $400,000 to $500,000 range.

> **Tip:** Do not engage in a reverse merger unless senior management is fully committed to making the necessary expenditures needed for a public company, such as extra accounting staff and more attention to control systems. Otherwise, the CFO and controller will be so harried that they will be rendered ineffective for all normal activities.

- *Liabilities.* There is a risk associated with buying the liabilities that still attach to the old public company shell. This risk can be ameliorated by acquiring only a shell that has been inactive for a number of years. The seller is rarely willing to personally commit to any representations and warranties regarding liabilities, so the acquirer is taking on these risks.
- *Stock price.* When a company goes public through a reverse merger, the sudden rush of selling shareholders puts immediate downward pressure on the price of the stock, since there are more sellers than buyers. When the stock price drops, this makes any stock options issued to employees less effective, since they will not profit from exercising the options. Also, if the

company intends to use its stock to make acquisitions, it will now have to issue more shares to do so.

- *Thinly traded.* There is usually only a minimal amount of trading volume in the stock of a public shell company – after all, it has been sitting quietly for several years with no operational activity, so why should anyone trade its stock? Also, immediately following the purchase of the shell, the only stock that is trading is the original stock of the business, since no other shares have yet been registered with the SEC. It takes time to build trading volume, which may require an active public relations and investor relations campaign, as well as the ongoing registration of additional stock (see the Trading Volume section).

> **Tip:** A good way to keep too much downward pressure from impacting the stock price is to impose waiting periods on the holders of company stock, so that there are no surges of sell orders hitting the market as soon as the company becomes publicly-held.

This lengthy list of problems with reverse mergers keeps many companies from engaging in them. In particular, take note of the annual cost of being public, and the issue with thinly-traded stock. The cost should completely block smaller companies from taking this path, while the lack of a market for the stock offsets the main reason for being publicly-held, which is having tradable stock.

The Price of a Shell

If a company wishes to purchase a public shell company, it should contact the local legal community to determine who has shells for sale. Shell companies are frequently acquired or fronted by attorneys who are responsible for maintaining them, usually for a number of years.

The price of a shell will certainly vary based on supply and demand, but the following factors also impact its price:

- *Assets.* Most shells have a small cash balance to pay for accounting and legal fees, but some have larger cash balances that will boost the price.
- *Liabilities.* If there are liabilities on the books of the shell, the buyer needs to take them into account. Some are valid, and will reduce the purchase price. Other liabilities are so old that no one is actively trying to collect them.
- *Legal and other issues.* If there have been legal issues in the past or other unresolved liabilities, and especially environmental liability problems, then these issues will seriously impact the price. However, a price reduction is not worth the risk associated with these issues, so a buyer would be better served by spending more to buy a cleaner shell.
- *Reporting status.* If the shell has continued to report its results to the SEC on a regular basis, this calls for less work by the acquirer to bring the reporting

status of the entity up-to-date, so current reporting yields a more valuable shell.

- *Shareholders*. The foundation of an active market in a company's stock is a large number of shareholders, so if the shell has several thousand shareholders, it is considered more valuable than one with just a few. However, depending on the age of the shell, many of these shareholders may be inactive or have bad addresses, which makes them less valuable to the buyer.

Tip: If there are potential legal issues or liabilities, the buyer can ask for an indemnification clause in the purchase agreement, so that the seller must reimburse the buyer for any liabilities settled after the purchase date.

These factors make it difficult to pin down a price for a shell. Generally, most shells sell for well under $1,000,000, with some clean shells selling for less than half that amount. The seller usually wants some stock in the acquiring company, as well.

Shell Due Diligence

Even though there may appear to be nothing about a shell company to review, the acquirer must *always* engage in due diligence, especially if there are to be no representations and warranties associated with the deal. There are admittedly fewer due diligence tasks to pursue than in a normal acquisition, since the shell has no operations. Nonetheless, the acquirer should investigate the following items:

- *Assets*. Though unlikely, there may be some non-cash assets still owned by the shell. If so, review them to see if they have any value, or can be profitably disposed of.
- *Auditors*. Have the financial statements of the shell been audited, and has the audit been conducted by auditors who are registered with the Public Company Accounting Oversight Board?
- *Board minutes*. Review the board minutes to search for any issues that may require additional investigation.
- *Contracts*. Are there any contracts that the company entered into when it was an operating entity that are still in force?
- *Historical business*. What was the original business of the company underlying the shell? Is there any reason to believe that the nature of the business makes it more likely that there will be undocumented liabilities?
- *Liabilities*. Search for any undocumented liabilities of the shell.
- *Litigation*. Have any lawsuits been filed against the shell, or has anyone threatened to do so?
- *Personnel*. Review the histories of anyone currently involved with the management or sale of the shell. Any prior lawsuit relating to shells is a major red flag.
- *SEC filings*. Review the shell's most recent filings with the SEC to see if it is a current filer.

- *SEC investigations.* See if the SEC has ever conducted investigations of the company, and the results of those investigations.
- *Shareholders.* Review the list of current shareholders. If there are many small shareholders, the acquirer may need to engage in a reverse stock split to flush them out of the shareholder records.
- *Shares.* Pay particular attention to the records of stock issuances and repurchases, and verify that the net amount outstanding matches the detailed stockholder list.
- *Structure.* Examine the certificate of incorporation and bylaws.
- *Trading patterns.* Has there been much trading volume recently in the shell's tradable stock? If so, it may indicate the presence of insider trading in anticipation of selling the shell to the acquirer.

This list is far shorter than the due diligence list needed for an operating entity, because it is targeted at those few aspects of a shell company that can cause problems for the acquirer. The acquirer should investigate all of the items noted here, since any one of them could uncover a serious issue.

Nearly every item in this due diligence list is related to legal issues. Therefore, it would be appropriate to have an all-lawyer team conduct the due diligence. These attorneys should have specific experience in due diligence investigations. Also, give the team sufficient time to investigate the shell thoroughly; mandating a one-day investigation presents a considerable risk of missing a problem.

A strong indicator of problems in a shell is missing documentation. This could simply be sloppy record keeping by the shell administrator, but a true professional understands that there has been plenty of time to "scrub" the shell and have everything laid out perfectly for an acquirer. Consequently, if contracts, shareholders votes, board minutes, and so forth are missing, it is time to look at other shells.

Trading Volume

One of the larger problems with a reverse merger is that the acquirer wants to use its publicly-traded stock to acquire other businesses, but there is only a minimal market for the stock. The trouble is that the shell company was not reporting its results for years, so no one has any interest in the stock. Also, the only trading has been in the shares that were tradable prior to the reverse merger, and there may be few of those shares in circulation. Further, institutional investors are usually barred by their own internal investment rules from buying stock in companies that are not listed on a stock exchange, or which sell below a certain minimum price point. This means that an acquisition target may not accept a stock payment because it would then be nearly impossible to sell the shares. In short, an acquirer who has bought a shell company needs to build the trading volume of its stock in order to make stock-for-stock purchases attractive to its acquisition targets.

It is not easy to increase trading volume. Here are several techniques for improving the situation:

- *Analyst coverage.* It is nearly impossible to gain analyst coverage of a new reverse merger company. It is possible, however, to pay for such coverage (as long as the payment is disclosed). The resulting analyst reports may generate some interest in the stock.
- *Investor relations.* The company should hire an investor relations firm and its own investor relations officer. They are both responsible for spreading news about the company throughout the investor community.
- *Road shows.* The senior management team should periodically go on road shows, where they talk about the firm to brokers and investors. If there is no immediate intention to raise money through these trips, they are called *non-deal road shows.*
- *Create a message.* The investor relations people need to craft a message about the company that investors understand, and which they are willing to buy into. This message should be consistently applied over time, with the company's actions adhering to its statements.
- *Report consistent results.* The company does not want to startle the investment community with unexpected jumps and drops in its reported results. Instead, the senior management team and its advisors must use all of the communication tools at its disposal to convey its expectations for the company's results in the near term, so that actual reported results are usually close to the expectations that the company has established in the marketplace.
- *List on an exchange.* Gaining a listing on any stock exchange will probably increase trading volume, with higher volumes being associated with larger and more reputable stock exchanges. Each exchange has its own listing requirements, which typically involve some mix of shareholder, revenue, profit, and asset volumes that may be difficult for a smaller business to achieve in the near term. However, if the company has a consistent pattern of growth, it may eventually gain entry into a stock exchange. See the Stock Exchanges chapter for more information.

A company may engage heavily in all of the preceding activities and still see little improvement in its trading volume. This is particularly likely when a company is in an industry that the investment community does not feel is "hot" at the moment. If so, the company can elect to either continue on the same path, reposition itself with a new company strategic direction, or go private. Going private is covered in a later section.

Other Reverse Merger Issues

If a company engages in a reverse merger, there are a number of issues that it may be faced with. There is a strong likelihood that investors will want to sell their shares in the near future, in which case the company's senior managers should be aware of the SEC's Rule 144, which allows investors to make their shares tradable under certain circumstances. Also, it may be necessary to clean up the shareholder list by eliminating smaller shareholdings; this can be accomplished with a reverse-forward split. Both issues are addressed in this section.

Rule 144

The new owner of a public shell may find that the process of registering shares with the SEC is cumbersome, expensive, and time-consuming. In some cases, the better part of a year may pass before the SEC allows stock to be registered. There will be pressure from shareholders to register their stock, since stock certificates bear a restrictive legend that prevents their sale until they are registered. If the company finds the registration process to be too difficult, it can point out to its shareholders that they can use the SEC's Rule 144 to register the shares themselves.

Under Rule 144, investors can sell their stock holdings if all of the following conditions have been met:

- *Holding period.* A shareholder must hold the shares for at least six months.
- *Reporting.* The company must be complying with its SEC reporting requirements.
- *Trading volume.* If the stockholder is in a control position at the company, then he or she can only sell the greater of 1% of the outstanding shares of the same class being sold or 1% of the average weekly trading volume in the four weeks preceding a notice to sell shares.
- *Trading transaction.* The sale of stock must be handled as a routine trading transaction, with the broker receiving a normal commission.
- *Notice of sale.* If the stockholder is in a control position at the company, he or she must file a Form 144 with the SEC, giving notice of intent to sell. This requirement is not applicable if the sale is for fewer than 5,000 shares or the aggregate dollar amount will be less than $50,000.

Following completion of the applicable conditions, shareholders must apply to the company's stock transfer agent to have any restrictive legends removed from their stock certificates. The stock transfer agent will only remove the legend with the written approval of the company's designated attorney. Once the legend has been removed, a shareholder can sell the stock.

Though Rule 144 appears to give investors a reasonable means for selling their stock, its practical application is limited by the volume of trading in the stock. Thus, even though investors may be allowed to sell their stock, it does not mean that there will be a sufficient number of interested buyers to allow for their sale.

The Reverse-Forward Split

When a private company acquires a public shell, it may find that the shell has been operationally inactive for so long that many of its shareholders no longer have valid addresses. These shareholders tend to have very small stock holdings; this makes sense, since investors with larger shareholdings will go out of their way to ensure that the company has the correct contact information for them. There are shareholder research firms that can locate some of these shareholders, but it may be impossible to find them all. This can be a problem, because the company is still responsible for sending annual reports, proxy statements, and dividends to them, and this cost will accumulate over time.

A possible method for eliminating some of these shareholders is the reverse-forward stock split. Under this approach, the company declares a hefty reverse stock split, such as 100 current shares for one new share, and then immediately flips this around and declares the reverse of the first split. Thus, to extend the example, a reverse stock split of 100 to 1 is followed by a forward split of 1 to 100. The end result of these gyrations is that the larger shareholders see no change at all, while the smaller shareholders are eliminated. For example, if a shareholder holds 99 shares of company stock, and the company declares a 100 to 1 reverse-forward stock split, then the shareholder ends up with less than one share as part of the reverse stock split, and is sent a cash payment for that partial share.

While it may appear excessively convoluted, the reverse-forward stock split is an effective way to clean up the shareholder records and eliminate those shareholders who are most likely to be inactive.

Going Private

It is quite likely that a smaller business that has gone public will find that the cost and liability associated with doing so is too great, and so wants to take the company private. When a company deregisters its equity securities, this is called *going private*.

> **Note:** Technically, the act of stopping filings with the SEC is called *going dark*. Going private is a more specific situation where some shareholders are bought out *and* a company stops filing reports with the SEC.

A company can go private when:

- There are no more than 500 shareholders of record who are not accredited, or 2,000 persons; and
- The company has not exceeded $10 million of assets as of the end of the last three fiscal years.

A *shareholder of record* is a person or entity listed in the shareholder records of a business as owning its stock. A brokerage can be the shareholder of record on behalf of its clients. Thus, it is possible to have many more actual shareholders than is indicated by the number of shareholders of record.

Under the preceding circumstances, going private involves filing the very simple Form 15 with the SEC. Only the approval of the board of directors is required to go private; there is no shareholder vote. In addition, if a company's shares are listed on a stock exchange, the exchange should be notified. The type of notification varies by exchange.

In short, if senior management is at all uncertain about a company's ability to continue as a public company, it should try to keep the number of shareholders as low as possible. This means not handing out a few extra shares to employees, or issuing warrants, or any other action that will result in a scattering of a small number of shares amongst a large number of new shareholders.

If there are too many shareholders, the company will have to find a way to reduce the number, such as through a stock buyback program or a reverse stock split. It then documents its intentions in the much more elaborate Schedule 13e-3, which it files with the SEC. Schedule 13e-3 requires a discussion of the purposes of the stock buyback or reverse split, any alternatives considered by the company, and whether the transaction is unfair to unaffiliated shareholders.

The SEC views going private transactions with suspicion, on the grounds that they must be one-sided transactions in favor of those buying existing shares. Consequently, expect the SEC to review and comment on the Schedule 13e-3, possibly several times, which can result in a multi-month delay between filing the form and taking any of the actions noted in it. Once the company then takes steps to reduce the number of shareholders that were outlined in the Schedule 13e-3, it can file a Form 15 and take itself private.

A company that is trying to go private must be careful not to undertake share repurchases in a manner that would be construed as a tender offer, since the filing of a tender offer requires substantial documentation. A repurchase is considered a tender offer if most of the following conditions are present:

- There is active and widespread solicitation of shareholders for their shares
- The solicitation is made for a substantial percentage of company stock
- The offer to purchase is for a premium over the current market rate
- The terms of the offer are firm, rather than negotiable
- The offer is contingent upon the tendering of a fixed number of shares
- The offer is open only for a limited period of time
- The offeree is subjected to pressure to sell stock
- There is publicity concerning the repurchase program

Thus, the avoidance of a tender offer may mandate occasional stock repurchases in small numbers over a period of time, where contacts are made with individual shareholders. To avoid the condition regarding a substantial percentage of company stock, consider only buying back the shares of odd lot shareholders, which should constitute a very small proportion of total shares outstanding. It is best to involve the company's securities attorneys in this process, to mitigate the risk of having a formal tender offer.

> **Tip:** A company that has gone private needs to continually monitor the number of shareholders of record. If the number ever exceeds the 500-person limit for non-accredited shareholders or the 2,000-person limit, the company must resume its public company filings with the SEC. This event can arise when there is a *broker kick out*, which is when a broker no longer wants to serve as the official shareholder for its clients, and shifts the official share ownership back to the shareholders, thereby increasing the number of shareholders of record.

Much of this discussion has been about ways to avoid the filing requirements associated with going private. However, there is a risk of shareholder lawsuits if a company goes private without a formal tender offer to buy back shares, since it will be very difficult for shareholders to liquidate their holdings once the company has gone private. Thus, the risk of lawsuits must be weighed against the ease of using a Form 15 filing to go private.

Summary

It may have become apparent in this chapter that the author is not wildly enthusiastic about taking a company public and then issuing the never-ending series of disclosures that are required of public companies. The amount of work required of the CFO is so severe that it is mandatory to invest in enough support staff to handle SEC disclosures and controls analyses. And even with this investment, the CFO will still find that a considerable amount of time will be required for perusing filings, meeting with investors, and monitoring controls. Further, the ongoing outlays for auditors, attorneys, controls specialists, and other fees will consume a significant chunk of company profits. Consequently, before committing to go public, take a very hard look at all other alternatives to see if it is possible to remain private for as long as possible. At a minimum, go public while keeping all options open for going private again if the rewards associated with being publicly-held do not materialize.

Chapter 16
Stock Exchanges

Introduction

Any publicly-held company should strive to have its shares listed on a stock exchange, since doing so makes it much more likely that there will be regular trading in its stock. The CFO is typically responsible for maintaining relations with the chosen exchange, as well as ensuring that its filing requirements are met. In this chapter, we note the reasons why stock exchanges can be so useful, as well as the listing requirements of the primary stock exchanges.

> **Related Podcast Episode:** Episode 69 of the Accounting Best Practices Podcast discusses listing on a stock exchange. The episode is available at: **accounting-tools.com/podcasts** or **iTunes**

Stock Exchange Overview

A stock exchange is a physical location or an electronic system, on which investors buy and sell securities. A stock exchange creates an orderly market, which makes it easier for transactions to be completed. They also impose listing requirements that keep the securities of less financially stable companies from being listed. Thus, investors use stock exchanges for their transactional efficiency and the supposition that the securities being traded come from issuing companies that have passed minimum financial benchmarks.

From the perspective of a publicly-held company, why bother with a stock exchange listing? There are numerous reasons for doing so, including:

- *Trading volume.* Many investors only trade securities that are listed on an exchange, so moving onto a stock exchange makes it much more likely that daily trading volumes will increase.
- *Price volatility.* When there are only occasional trades, share prices are usually quite volatile. With the increased trading volume associated with a stock exchange, it is much more likely that prices will stabilize.
- *Acquisition currency.* The increased trading volume of a stock exchange makes it easier to convince the owners of an acquisition target to accept stock in exchange for their company, since they can sell the shares with relative ease.
- *Prestige.* There is a distinct difference in the prestige level of public companies that are listed on a national exchange, and those that are not. This can have an impact on the decisions of lenders, customers, and suppliers to do business with a company.

- *Reduced bid-ask price spread.* When there are a larger number of buyers and sellers, the difference between the bid price and ask price for a stock are reduced. This means that the transaction cost associated with buying or selling shares on an exchange is reduced. The CFO can use this argument to attract new investors.

If a company wants to be traded on a stock exchange, it must first qualify under the standards set by the exchange. Generally speaking, the qualification standards are easiest for the American Stock Exchange and the most difficult for the New York Stock Exchange. These standards focus on a variety of factors, such as net income, cash flow, market capitalization, shareholders' equity, and total assets. All of the stock exchanges offer multiple alternative sets of criteria under which a company can qualify for listing. For example, a company with strong cash flow but little net income can qualify under one set of criteria, while another business with less income or cash flow can still qualify if it has a large market capitalization. The different sets of criteria are designed to allow the securities of a variety of types of businesses to be listed.

If a company's owners decide to list its securities on a stock exchange, they must apply to the exchange. The steps for doing so vary somewhat by exchange, but generally follow these steps:

1. *Alter bylaws.* The company alters its bylaws to comply with the governance requirements of the stock exchange. This usually requires that the board establish audit, nominating, and compensation committees.
2. *File application.* The company completes the exchange's listing application and submits it, along with a filing fee.
3. *Investigation.* The stock exchange assigns an analyst to the company, who investigates the application and asks additional questions on a variety of topics. This may result in a comment letter that points out changes the company must make before its application will be approved.
4. *Reserve ticker symbol.* The stock exchange reserves a ticker symbol for the company, in anticipation of the successful completion of the application process.
5. *Set trading date.* If the listing application is approved, the parties agree on a date when trading in the company's stock on the exchange will begin.
6. *Begin trading.* Depending on the exchange, the CEO of the company may be asked to appear at the stock exchange at the beginning of the first day of trading in the company's stock.

Tip: Though it should not be a primary consideration in selecting a stock exchange, there are differences in the fees charged by the various stock exchanges, with higher fees being charged by those exchanges having more rigorous listing requirements.

A publicly-held company is not necessarily listed on a stock exchange. If a company is still submitting timely filings to the SEC, but either does not qualify to be listed on a stock exchange or does not choose to do so, then it is listed on the over the counter market. A trading symbol for a company that trades on the over the counter market is OTB:[ABCD]. See the Over the Counter Bulletin Board section for more information.

At the most minimal level, a company can stop its periodic reporting to the SEC, in which case it cannot be listed on a stock exchange or the over the counter market. Instead, the most recent trades are listed on the Pink Sheets. A trading symbol for a company that trades on the Pink Sheets is PINK:[ABCD]. See the Pink Sheets section for more information.

In the next few sections, we cover the initial listing requirements imposed by several of the larger stock exchanges, to show how different exchanges are oriented toward different types and sizes of companies.

The New York Stock Exchange

The stock exchange that has the most prestige and sets the most difficult listing standards is the New York Stock Exchange (NYSE). The standards are set high in order to limit the exchange to a smaller group of securities whose issuers are the most qualified by being financially stable. It is less common for a company to initially list its shares on the NYSE, because it takes time to build sufficient mass to justify being on this exchange.

Some institutional investors are only allowed by their internal investment rules to invest in the shares of companies listed on the NYSE, which is why growing companies tend to start with other stock exchanges, and later switch to the NYSE when they are large enough to qualify for it.

The listing standards of the NYSE involve meeting minimum standards in multiple areas, which are noted in the following table.

NYSE Initial Listing Financial Criteria

Required to meet *one* of the following financial standards:

Financial Standards	Earnings Test	Global Market Capitalization Test	Real Estate Investment Trusts	Closed-end Management Investment Companies	Business Development Companies
Adjusted pre-tax income	Aggregate for last 3 years ≥ $10 million; each of the 2 most recent years ≥$2 million				
Global market capitalization		$200 million			$75 million
Shareholders' equity			$60 million		
Market value of publicly held shares	See next table	See next table	See next table	$60 million	$60 million

277

Required to meet *all* of the following distribution standards:

Distribution Standards	IPOs, Spin-offs, Carve-outs	Transfer or Quotation			All Other Listings
Shareholders	400 round lot	400 round lot	2,200 total	500 total	400 round lot
Publicly held shares	1.1 million	1.1 million	1.1 million	1.1 million	1.1 million
Market value of publicly held shares	$40 million	$100 million	$100 million	$100 million	$100 million
Minimum share price	$4	$4	$4	$4	$4
Average monthly trading volume (shares)		100,000	100,000	1 million	--

The NYSE MKT

The New York Stock Exchange purchased the American Stock Exchange, and now calls this exchange the NYSE MKT. This exchange is designed for much smaller companies than those found on the NYSE. The listing standards of the NYSE MKT are noted in the following table.

NYSE MKT Initial Listing Standards

Criteria	Standard 1	Standard 2	Standard 3	Standard 4
Pre-tax income	$750,000	N/A	N/A	N/A
Market capitalization	N/A	N/A	$50 million	$75 million or at least $75 million total assets and $75 million revenues
Market value of public float	$3 million	$15 million	$15 million	$20 million
Minimum price	$3	$3	$2	$3
Operating history	N/A	2 years	N/A	N/A
Shareholders' equity	$4 million	$4 million	$4 million	N/A
Public shareholders / Public float (shares)	Option 1: 800 / 500,000 Option 2: 400 / 1,000,000 Option 3: 400 / 500,000			

Note how the initial listing standards are designed to accept many types of smaller businesses. A company can qualify by having a moderate amount of pre-tax income, or with a moderate amount of shareholders' equity, or if it has one of several measures of business mass, such as assets or market capitalization. None of the requirements are especially difficult to meet, which means that many smaller firms find the NYSE MKT to be a reasonable starting place in which to list their shares. Later, as a company presumably grows, it may want to move to an exchange with higher minimum standards, in order to obtain access to a larger group of investors.

The NASDAQ

The NASDAQ is a computerized system that provides price quotations and facilitates the purchase and sale of securities. The NASDAQ operates several exchanges, each with different listing standards that are designed to attract different types and sizes of companies. The listing standards of three of these exchanges are described in the remainder of this section.

The NASDAQ Global Select Market

The Global Select Market has the most rigorous standards, because it is designed to compete with the NYSE. Its listing standards are noted in the following table.

NASDAQ Global Select Market Initial Listing Standards

Criteria	Standard 1	Standard 2	Standard 3	Standard 4
Pre-tax earnings	≥ Aggregate $11 million in prior three fiscal years*			
Cash flows	N/A	≥ Aggregate $27.5 million in prior three fiscal years**	N/A	N/A
Market capitalization	N/A	≥ $550 million 12-month average	≥ $850 million 12-month average	$160 million
Revenue	N/A	≥ $110 million	≥ $90 million	N/A
Total assets	N/A	N/A	N/A	$80 million
Stockholders' equity	N/A	N/A	N/A	$55 million
Bid price	$4	$4	$4	$4
Round lot / total shareholders	450 / 2,200	450 / 2,200	450 / 2,200	450 / 2,200
Publicly held shares	1,250,000	1,250,000	1,250,000	1,250,000
Market value of publicly-held shares***	$45 million	$45 million	$45 million	$45 million

* And with pre-tax profits of ≥ $2.2 in each of the two most recent fiscal years, with no losses in any of the three years
** With no losses in any of those three years
*** The stated market value is for initial public offerings. The figure is $110 million for seasoned companies.

The NASDAQ Global Market

The NASDAQ Global Market has listing standards that sandwich it between the NASDAQ Global Select Market and the NASDAQ Capital Market. Its listing standards are noted in the following table, where a company must meet all of the requirements under at least one of the standards.

NASDAQ Global Market Initial Listing Standards

Criteria	Income Standard	Equity Standard	Market Value Standard	Total Assets / Total Revenue Standard
Income from continuing operations*	$1 million	N/A	N/A	N/A
Stockholders' equity	$15 million	$30 million	N/A	N/A
Market value of listed securities	N/A	N/A	$75 million	N/A
Total assets and total revenue	N/A	N/A	N/A	$75 million and $75 million
Publicly held shares	1.1 million	1.1 million	1.1 million	1.1 million
Market value of publicly held shares	$8 million	$18 million	$20 million	$20 million
Bid price	$4	$4	$4	$4
Round lot shareholders	400	400	400	400
Market makers	3	3	4	4
Operating history	N/A	2 years	N/A	N/A

* In the latest fiscal year or in two of the last three fiscal years

The NASDAQ Capital Market

The NASDAQ Capital Market imposes the easiest listing standards, which makes it a direct competitor to the NYSE MKT. Its listing standards are noted in the following table, where a company must meet all of the requirements under at least one of the standards.

NASDAQ Capital Market Initial Listing Standards

Criteria	Equity Standard	Market Value Standard	Net Income Standard
Stockholders' equity	$5 million	$4 million	$4 million
Market value of publicly held shares	$15 million	$15 million	$5 million
Operating history	2 years	N/A	N/A
Market value of listed securities	N/A	$50 million	N/A
Net income from continuing operations*	N/A	N/A	$750,000
Bid price	$4	$4	$4
Publicly held shares	1 million	1 million	1 million
Round lot shareholders	300	300	300
Market makers	3	3	3

* In latest fiscal year or in two of the last three fiscal years

The Toronto Stock Exchange

The major stock exchanges described in the preceding sections are by no means the only ones on which a company can list its shares. In this section, we note the listing standards of one of the more active smaller exchanges, the Toronto Stock Exchange. The following table shows that this exchange has found a number of alternative ways to allow a company to list its securities, with different categories for businesses engaged in technology, research and development (R&D), and industrial activities. There is even a category for businesses that are not yet profitable, but forecast that they will be in the near future. Its listing standards are noted in the following table.

Toronto Stock Exchange Listing Standards

Criteria	Technology Issuer	R&D Issuer	Forecasting Profitability Issuer	Profitable Issuer	Industrial Issuer
Earnings or revenue	N/A	N/A	Evidence of pre-tax earnings for current or next year of at least $200,000	Pre-tax earnings from operations of at least $300,000 in the last year	Pre-tax earnings from operations of at least $300,000 in the last year
Cash flow			Evidence of pre-tax cash flow for current or next year of at least $500,000	Pre-tax cash flow of $700,000 in the last year, $500,000 average for the past two years	Pre-tax cash flow of $700,000 in the last year, and an average of $500,000 for the past two years
Net tangible assets			$7,500,000	$2,000,000	$7,500,000
Working capital and capital structure	Funds to cover all planned development, capital, and administrative expenditures for one year	Funds to cover all planned R&D, capital, and administrative expenditures for 2 years	Sufficient working capital to carry on the business, plus an appropriate capital structure	Sufficient working capital to carry on the business, plus an appropriate capital structure	Sufficient working capital to carry on the business, plus an appropriate capital structure
Cash on hand	At least $10 million cash on hand, with the majority raised through a prospectus offering	At least $12 million cash on hand, with the majority raised through a prospectus offering			
Products and services	Evidence of advanced stage of development for products, or management has expertise to develop the business	2+ year operating history with R&D activities; evidence of technical expertise to advance the R&D program			

Criteria	Technology Issuer	R&D Issuer	Forecasting Profitability Issuer	Profitable Issuer	Industrial Issuer
Public distribution	1 million shares and 300 round lot shareholders	1 million shares and 300 round lot shareholders	1 million shares and 300 round lot shareholders	1 million shares and 300 round lot shareholders	1 million shares and 300 round lot shareholders
Market capitalization	$10 million market capitalization, $50 million total capitalization	$4 million market capitalization	$4 million market capitalization	$4 million market capitalization	$4 million market capitalization
Minimum operating history	Advanced stage development		N/A	One year	

Note: All monetary requirements are stated in Canadian dollars.

The Toronto Stock Exchange, and other exchanges like it, have designed their listing requirements to make it relatively easy for a smaller company to be listed. This type of exchange can be a good starting point for a company, after which it can graduate to an exchange with tougher listing requirements (which has a larger pool of investors).

There are dozens of stock exchanges on which a company could list its shares. Many exchanges are designed for the listings of businesses located in the same country as the exchange, but the following exchanges tend to attract a broader clientele:

- Australian Securities Exchange
- Deutsche Bourse
- Hong Kong Stock Exchange
- London Stock Exchange
- Shanghai Stock Exchange
- Tokyo Stock Exchange

Delisting from an Exchange

Thus far, we have noted the initial listing requirements that stock exchanges impose. There are also *ongoing* listing standards that companies must meet in order to continue to be listed. These ongoing standards vary by stock exchange, but are always less than the initial listing requirements. Ongoing standards may include the maintenance of minimum amounts for a combination of:

- The number of publicly traded shares
- Total market value
- Stock price
- The number of shareholders

If a company does not meet an ongoing listing standard, the exchange on which its securities are listed will contact it regarding the issue, and will give the company a certain amount of time in which to rectify the matter. If the company does not resolve the issue, then the stock exchange will delist the applicable securities.

When a company is delisted, it may also lose its market makers. A *market maker* is a broker-dealer that facilitates trading in a security by displaying buy and sell quotations for the issuing company's shares, for which it may sell from its own inventory. Once a company is delisted, its stock trading volumes will likely decline precipitously, while the variability of its stock price will increase. Market makers will then be at risk of incurring losses on their holdings of a company's stock, and so will terminate their roles as market makers.

The Over the Counter Bulletin Board

The over the counter market is known as the Over the Counter Bulletin Board, or OTCBB. It is a stock listing service that shows real-time quotes, last-sale price, and volume information for all securities listed on the OTCBB.

This is not a formal stock exchange, but rather the default designation given to a company that is not listed on a stock exchange but which is current in its filings with the SEC. There are no other requirements for being listed on the OTCBB. If a company is not current with its filings, it is instead classified as being listed on the Pink Sheets (see the next section).

Companies that are current with their SEC filings but not listed on an exchange are likely to have small amounts of revenue and/or assets, and may have irregular earnings. As such, investments in OTCBB companies are considered to be risky. Also, because there is not much trading activity in these stocks, there tends to be a large spread between bid and ask prices, which makes investments in these stocks especially risky for investors.

It is very difficult for an investor relations officer to interest investors in acquiring company stock if the company is languishing on the OTCBB. Rather than wasting time trying to attract investors, it is more productive to convince management to apply to and be listed on *any* stock exchange. Once such a listing has been obtained, it is much easier to find an interested audience.

The Pink Sheets

If a company is remiss in its SEC filings or has gone private, its shares will be listed on the Pink Sheets. This is essentially the default listing for the securities of a company that does not expend any effort to make its financial results known to the public. The Pink Sheets are administered by OTC Markets Group, Inc. Share prices will be listed on the Pink Sheets even if a company no longer has *any* interest in the trading of its shares. If a business finds that its stock has fallen into the Pink Sheets category, OTC Markets Group will likely contact the company to see if it is interested in moving the stock listing into a different listing category that contains recent financial information about the company – which requires an ongoing fee.

A company that has dropped into the Pink Sheets classification clearly has little interest in maintaining an investor relations function, since the business is only in this category if it has stopped filing the mandatory reports with the SEC that investors rely upon to make share purchase and sale decisions.

Summary

If a company is publicly held, then it should be listed on a stock exchange. Doing so confers the benefits of a higher volume of stock trading, though this comes at the cost of annual listing fees and some changes to the governance structure of a business. Once a company is listed on an exchange, the CFO should have an ongoing interest in advancing the business to an exchange that is used by a larger number of investors, thereby increasing the volume of trading in company stock.

A large part of this chapter contained summaries of the listing standards required by the various stock exchanges. Please note that these were only *summaries* – the more critical requirements were listed, but a large number of variations and qualifications were excluded. Also, we did not include governance requirements, which usually call for modifications to a company's bylaws, and perhaps to the committees reporting to the board of directors. Thus, refer to the official listing requirements of an exchange to obtain a comprehensive view of *all* requirements.

Chapter 17
Investor Relations

Introduction

In a privately-held company, there will probably be few investors for the CFO to deal with. In a public company, however, there is an ongoing need to deal with investors, outside analysts, and members of the business media. In this chapter, we address those aspects of investor relations in which the CFO is directly involved, with particular emphasis on the earnings call and the road show. For a much more detailed discussion of the investor relations specialty, please refer to the author's *Investor Relations Guidebook*.

> **Related Podcast Episodes:** Episodes 63, 74, 99, 102, and 110 of the Accounting Best Practices Podcast discuss guidance, short sellers, the non-deal road show, the fund raising road show, and the National Investor Relations Institute, respectively. These episodes are available at: **accountingtools.com/podcasts** or **iTunes**

Investor Relations Overview

Investor relations is a function almost exclusively found within publicly-held companies. It provides information about the financial and operational performance of a company to members of the investment community. In addition, it maintains relations with those investors who may be interested in making additional investments in the company in the future. Thus, the function maintains a two-way line of communications with the investment community. These capabilities can be translated into the following investor relations goals:

- *To maintain an active market in the company's stock.* Investors want to have confidence that they can easily move in and out of stock positions, which is only possible if there is a large and active market for a company's stock.
- *To obtain a fair valuation.* By adopting an understandable story for a business and managing expectations around that story, a company should achieve a reasonable stock price valuation.
- *To enhance the company's ability to cost-effectively raise capital as needed.* There should be investors who are sufficiently cognizant of a company's capabilities and results to be willing to invest in it at a reasonable share price.

The investor relations function disseminates a mix of information that is required under financial regulations, or which it voluntarily issues. The information released is intended to give recipients a detailed knowledge of how a company operates, its financial performance, governance, and future prospects. The intent is to give someone enough information to make an informed decision to invest (or not) in a business.

Investor relations should be an ongoing activity, rather than something that a business only engages in when it goes public or needs to raise additional funds. There are thousands of publicly-held companies, and they are all clamoring for the attention of investors and the business media. If a company does not allocate sufficient resources to ensure that it is heard, it will attract little investor interest, and its stock price and trading volume will both likely linger at a low level.

The Earnings Call

Many public companies schedule periodic conference calls with the investment community, in which a presentation team discusses recent financial results, issues guidance regarding expected future performance, and responds to questions. The CFO is deeply involved in the scheduling, preparation for, and operation of this conference call, which is known as an *earnings call*. In this section, we describe how these calls are scheduled and operated, and their content.

The primary participants in the earnings call are the CEO and CFO. They discuss all of the financial and operational results and projections (if any) of the business. The investment community likes to hear the CEO on the earnings call, since it implies that this individual is actively involved in the financial management of the company. However, it may be acceptable for the CFO to lead the earnings call instead of the CEO, as long as the CFO has an excellent all-around knowledge of the company and is trusted by the investment community.

The earnings call is normally scheduled for a date immediately following the release of a company's quarterly Form 10-Q or annual Form 10-K filing. It is customary to schedule earnings calls one week in advance. A shorter notice period may result in fewer attendees, since they may have already scheduled time during the earnings call for other activities. The best time of day in which to hold an earnings call and issue an accompanying press release is after the financial markets have closed for the day. This scheduling means that investors and analysts have the time to analyze the contents of both the press release and the earnings call before making any injudicious trades that might increase the volatility of the stock price.

Earnings calls are usually handled by third party conference calling services that set up phone lines and handle the queue of callers who have questions for the management team. They also typically provide a recording of the entire call; consider posting this recording in the investor relations section of the company website, so that those unable to attend the call can still listen to it at a later date.

The earnings call is normally divided into two sections, with the first part being a prepared set of remarks about the company's results, while the second part is set aside for a question and answer session with whomever is listening to the call. The first part of the call follows a baseline script that is used repeatedly for all of a company's earnings calls. It is more efficient to use the same detailed format for each call, so the latest updates on the company's earnings can be dropped into the script. Using the same format also ensures that the company does not inadvertently miss mentioning information during a call, which listeners might otherwise consider to be an intentional avoidance of information. The use of a script does not mean that the company's presentation team always states exactly the same types of information – it is only a baseline. Also, the baseline script will change incrementally over time, as the operations of the business and the company's message to investors gradually evolve.

Tip: If a difficult question is anticipated for an upcoming conference call, such as the departure of a key employee, always address it in the scripted part of the earnings call. By doing so, management can make a thorough answer, rather than the "off the cuff" response it might otherwise make if the issue comes up during the question and answer session.

The scripted part of the earnings call should not last longer than 30 minutes, with 20 minutes being sufficient for most companies to state their results and guidance. Since the entire earnings call is expected to last no more than one hour, having a longer presentation cuts into the limited amount of time set aside for the question and answer session. If the prepared statements run overly long, and especially if the management team has a history of continually running long, then expect listeners to drop off the call or have subordinates take notes in their place.

Following the prepared statements in the first section of the earnings call, participants in the call state their questions. It is possible to achieve a considerable amount of scripting even in the question and answer session. This is done by anticipating which questions are most likely to be asked during the earnings call, and then constructing a list of talking points to reference when answering a question. This level of preparation is extremely useful, since it makes the management team appear to be well prepared.

Some of the questions asked are ones that the company encounters on an ongoing basis, such as asking for an update on the sales levels for stores that have been open for at least one year. Other possible questions may be gleaned from the questions that were asked recently during road shows or during meetings with analysts. In addition, assume that questions will be asked about any variances from historical results that appeared in the most recent set of the company's financial statements.

Tip: Consider scheduling the company's earnings call to be a few days later than the earnings calls of other companies in the same industry. Then listen to their earnings calls to see which questions are being asked, and prepare for the same questions in the company's earnings call.

It is better to list the scripted answers to anticipated questions on the walls of the room in which the earnings call is taking place. This allows participants to quickly focus on the set of points they want to make in response to a particular question. It also avoids the interminable delays associated with shuffling a set of question and answer cards.

> **Tip:** Have a staff person write down each question on a white board as it is asked, so that the CEO and CFO do not have to worry about providing an answer to a question that they did not hear correctly.

It is impossible to anticipate all questions that may be asked, though the CEO and CFO should still follow a set of rules for how they answer *all* questions. For example:

- If a question is a vague one, do not answer the question that you *think* was asked; continually ask for clarification until you are sure of the question. Otherwise, listeners may be quite startled by a seemingly odd answer.
- If a question is multi-part, answer only the first part. Doing so keeps one person from hogging the question and answer period. If a caller wants to continue asking questions, he can re-enter the queue of callers, and will have an opportunity to ask his next question in due time.
- If a question is speculative, such as "what would you do if an earthquake toppled your main production facility," refuse to speculate. Instead, answer with factual information only, such as "we carry earthquake insurance for all of our facilities."

It is customary to shut down the earnings call after one hour has passed, even if there are additional callers waiting to ask a question. This makes sense when the management team or listeners have only set aside one hour for the earnings call in their schedules. If the management team wants to restructure the call to permit more questions to be asked, consider the following options:

- *Single question rule.* Allow each caller one question, after which they go to the back of the queue if they want to ask additional questions. This tends to limit the number of inconsequential questions.
- *Time monitoring.* If the CEO and CFO tend to run over their allotted time in the first part of the call, have a staff person warn them when they exceed their scheduled time allotments.
- *Extend call.* The CEO and CFO can block out additional time in their schedules for the period immediately following the earnings call, in case they want to extend the call to take extra questions.
- *Additional session.* Consider scheduling an additional conference call that is set aside entirely for questions and answers.

Guidance

It is worthwhile to consider the information environment from the perspective of the investor. This person receives information about a business a minimum of four times per year, when the quarterly and annual financial statements are released. These documents are almost entirely oriented toward the historical results of a business, so the investor has little information to use as the basis for future projections. Also, a business may release information at random intervals during the year in the Form 8-K about various material events, such as major agreements entered into or terminated, or the sale or purchase of a business. While this additional information makes note of specific events, it does little to inform the investor about changes in the basic income-generating capabilities of a business. In short, the standard reporting structure mandated by the Securities and Exchange Commission (SEC) does little to keep investors apprised of the likely *future* results of a business.

If analysts are following a company, they will periodically issue estimates of future results. Each analyst has his or her following of investors, so there will be some aggregation of investors around the opinions of their favorite analysts. If there are no analysts following a company, then individual investors must arrive at their own estimates of company performance, which can be wildly divergent from each other. The result is a potentially broad range of estimates regarding what the correct share price should be. Also, as more time passes between the release of the last set of financial statements and the arrival of the next set, there is a greater divergence in views regarding the proper stock price.

The result is a fairly large amount of stock price volatility. This is caused by a continuing series of stock purchases and sales at different price points. Each price point is based on the diverging views of what buyers and sellers believe the stock is worth. Thus, it is reasonable to state that a lack of information about the future prospects of a business increases the volatility of its stock price.

Guidance can be given to reduce investor uncertainty about a company's future prospects. If you elect to issue guidance, do so on a consistent schedule. Many businesses prefer to do so once a quarter, usually immediately following the release of the quarterly financial statements, as part of the earnings call. This schedule helps analysts, who can then combine the company's future estimates with the "hard" numbers shown in the quarterly financial statements to arrive at their own estimates of the company's prospects. This also allows analysts to issue their own recommendations to their followers on a consistent schedule.

Tip: If the decision is made to issue guidance, the investment community will assume that the most recent guidance given is still relevant. Consequently, if the company's outlook changes to a sufficient extent to make the existing guidance incorrect, consider issuing new guidance. This should only be necessary if there is a substantial change from the existing guidance.

In addition to the normally scheduled release of guidance, consider some unscheduled guidance. This may be necessary when some or all of the analysts following the stock are issuing projections that clearly diverge from the company's internal projections. In these cases, there will be an inevitable (and potentially large) correction when the company issues its regularly-scheduled quarterly guidance. If the divergence appears to be unusually large, the CFO may elect to issue unscheduled guidance, thereby keeping the price of the stock from becoming too volatile.

The minimum amount of information to include in guidance is the projected earnings per share. Investors may expect other information taken from the income statement, such as revenues and net income. The gross margin number is also sometimes included in guidance, as well as the order backlog. It is generally not advisable to issue a massive amount of information, for investors will come to expect it, and generating this material on an ongoing basis may prove to be time-consuming and expensive.

It is impossible to tell investors in advance what the exact performance of any business will be, so instead give them a range of likely outcomes. This range should be relatively narrow for guidance covering the next quarter, and widen for periods further in the future, to reflect the increased level of uncertainty that accompanies more distant projections. There is no standard guidance range, since the possible outcome will vary by industry, company, and forecasting system. For example, a government contractor with a portfolio of long-term contracts may be able to give guidance within a tight range of possible outcomes, since its revenue stream is highly predictable. Conversely, a developer of software apps for a smartphone may not know from day to day what its results will be, and so must report guidance within an extremely broad range.

An example of guidance that uses an expanding range for more distant time periods is:

> We have reduced our guidance for the fiscal year ended September 30. We now expect the year's revenues to be in the range of $200 to $225 million, resulting in net profits of between $19 and $22 million, and diluted earnings per share of between $1.90 and $2.20. For the following year, we expect sales to be in the range of $210 to $250 million, resulting in net profits of between $21 and $27 million, and diluted earnings per share of between $2.10 and $2.70.

In the example, notice that the revenue range for the current fiscal year was $25 million, which expanded to cover a range of $40 million in the following year. Similarly, the net profit range expanded from $3 million in the first year to $6 million in the second year. This reflects the increased uncertainty of the guidance as a company projects further into the future.

Tip: If guidance is issued within an excessively narrow range, you will be more likely to keep issuing updated guidance whenever it appears that actual results will fall outside of the original range. If there are too many updates, you probably need to widen the guidance range.

An overly enthusiastic CEO might be tempted to issue aggressive guidance, where projected revenue and profit levels are higher than has historically been the case. The benefit of doing so is that the investment community will then assume that the company is more valuable than it had previously estimated, and bid up the stock price. However, aggressive guidance is not such a good idea when the CEO continues to use it over the long term, for the following reasons:

- *Inability to meet targets.* It is extremely difficult to report actual results that come anywhere near aggressive guidance over a long period of time. Eventually, actual results will lag, which creates a credibility problem for the CEO. If there are a series of missed projections, the investment community will eventually give little credence to any guidance given.
- *Price variability.* If a business is always struggling to meet the guidance targets that its CEO has issued, the result will likely be initial increases in the stock price when guidance is announced, followed by sharp price declines when the company cannot make its numbers, and so on. Thus, aggressive guidance tends to create more stock price volatility. Lots of stock price volatility tends to attract short sellers, who drive down the price of the stock.
- *Ethical breaches.* A more pernicious issue with aggressive guidance is that the management team will find itself under increasing pressure to deliver the results that the CEO has promised, which creates pressure to bend the accounting rules. If so, and those ethical lapses are reported to the public, the impact on the company's stock price may be catastrophic.

A vastly better alternative to aggressive guidance is to develop projections that are squarely within the comfort zone of the management team. The intent is not to issue projections that are too easy for the company to meet, since this does not create any pressure to improve the business. Instead, the CEO needs to follow a fine line of setting reasonable stretch goals for the business, without making managers so desperate to achieve their assigned goals that the only practical way to do so is through fraudulent financial reporting.

This comfortable level of guidance is appreciated by the investment community, since they will find that the company can nearly always deliver on its promises – and a business that reports reliable results is one for which more analysts are willing to provide coverage.

We have just built a case for why a public company should provide guidance to the investment community, and what the form and timing of that information may be. However, there are several situations in which guidance may not be appropriate, or where it may even be counterproductive. They are:

- *Inadequate forecasting.* If a company's forecasting systems are unable to generate reliable guidance that the company can meet, it is best not to issue any guidance until the systems are improved. Otherwise, continually issuing guidance that the company does not attain reflects poorly upon the management team. It is better to not even mention that the company is having trouble with its forecasting. Instead, simply state that the company continues to evaluate whether it should provide guidance, and does not choose to do so at this time.
- *New markets.* A company may have just entered new markets where it is uncertain of revenue and profit levels, or the ability of the business to grow.

If so, any guidance issued has a high probability of being wrong, and so is worthless to investors. In this case, the management team can either issue guidance with very wide estimated ranges, or forego guidance until results become more predictable.

- *Many acquisitions.* The strategy of a company may be to grow through acquisitions. It is very difficult to provide guidance under this strategy, since the ability of a company to complete an acquisition has a binary outcome – either an acquisition is completed, or it is not. If guidance assumes the completion of an acquisition, and the deal falls through, then the guidance could be wrong by a substantial amount. This is a particular problem when acquisitions are quite large, and so contribute to a large proportion of a company's projected financial results.

- *Development stage company.* A small number of companies go public when they are still quite small, and do not yet have a clear idea of the size of their markets, market share, profitability, and so forth. In these cases, it makes sense to resolve the informational uncertainties and *then* issue guidance.

With the exception of the inadequate forecasting situation, explain to investors the reasons for not issuing guidance, and promise to periodically re-examine the situation to see if the company's results have become sufficiently predictable to use as the basis for guidance.

The situations noted here are in the clear minority for public companies. Usually, a company has been in business for a number of years and reached a certain critical mass before going public, so it should have adequate systems and a sufficient knowledge of its markets and financial results to be able to provide reasonably accurate guidance.

Earnings Smoothing

The CFO may feel pressure to report a predictable level of earnings for the foreseeable future. Doing so may require that certain discretionary expenses (such as research expenditures) be curtailed, which can impede long-term performance. Alternatively, it may be necessary to recognize somewhat higher or lower than normal expenses, such as for bad debts or obsolete inventory reserves, in order to "make the numbers." There will also be pressure to engage in financial statement fraud by recording sales that have not really occurred. Given all of these issues, one should question the need for reporting a predictable stream of earnings.

Instead, it is much easier to simply take a hands-off attitude when preliminary profit figures are generated, and only alter them when the numbers are clearly in error. Doing so will likely produce a higher degree of earnings volatility. This should not be a problem for the investment community, as long as the company fully informs them of the reasons for major changes in earnings from prior periods. If anything, a more sophisticated investor will be suspicious of a perfectly predictable earnings growth path, and will assume that management is altering the numbers.

The Road Show

A road show involves traveling to meet with a number of investors, in order to present an overview of the company to them. A road show may involve a general discussion of the business, or a more tightly-defined fund raising pitch. In either case, the road show is one of the key tasks of the CFO. In this section, we will describe road shows oriented toward fund raising, road shows used to build investor familiarity with a company, and the structure of a road show presentation.

The Fund Raising Road Show

As the name implies, a fund raising road show is a series of meetings with investors, with the specific intention of raising funds from them. During a road show, the presentation team will likely be accompanied by an investment banker, who has arranged all of the meetings with potential investors. These investors are likely to be fund managers, who are responsible for investing the funds with which they have been entrusted by clients. Because any one fund manager could potentially invest a very large amount in a company, each one deserves a private presentation.

When a company plans to raise money through an investment banker, the banker typically issues a notification to his or her contacts throughout the country. If any investors are interested, the banker schedules them so that the presentation team can visit several investors in a row in one city, and then move on to the next city and present to the next cluster of interested parties. In some cities where there are large numbers of prospective investors, such as New York and Chicago, the presentation team will probably schedule an entire trip to just that one city, and then continue with their road show to other cities in the following week.

The typical road show presentation is for about 90 minutes. A prospective investor may bring several associates or aides, but expect the total group size to be quite small. The investment banker attends all meetings, but mostly confines his or her comments to introductions at the beginning of a meeting, and inquiries about the investor's interest in the company at the end of a meeting. The typical meeting format is for the presentation team to walk through a handout that describes the company, its need for cash, and how it plans to use the cash (see the Presentation section for more information). The investor's team then peppers the presenters with questions. There is usually no need for a projector, since the group size is so small.

Before each meeting, the investment banker should brief the CEO and CFO about the types of investments that each investor prefers, so that they can tailor their presentations to address the issues that the investors want to learn about. Also, it is useful to determine at the start of each meeting how much an investor knows about the company's industry; it may be necessary to adapt the presentation to add or subtract information to make it match the knowledge of the investor.

Always assume that this meeting belongs to the investor, not the company. Therefore, if the investor wants to immediately ask questions, or set aside the formal presentation entirely, then go ahead and do whatever the investor wants. After all, the entire point of the meeting is for the investor to learn about the company and the safety of any investment made in it – so let the investor determine how to acquire that information.

The fund raising road show is critical for obtaining debt and equity funding. Given its importance, the presentation team should be willing to customize its presentation for each investor meeting, as well as to meet wherever and whenever investors want. This is not the case for a non-deal road show, which we address next.

The Non-Deal Road Show

As the name implies, a non-deal road show is one in which there is no attempt to raise money. Instead, the intent is to educate the investment community about the company. By doing so, they may be more inclined to investigate the company further, and perhaps buy its stock.

A non-deal road show is normally conducted shortly after a company has released its quarterly results in a Form 10-Q or its annual results in a Form 10-K. By doing so, the presenters on the road show will be at little risk of disclosing any information that is not already public knowledge, since the most recent information should have just been issued to the SEC. Conversely, the longer the time interval between the public release of financial statements and a road show, the greater the risk that someone will make an inadvertent disclosure of material, non-public information (see the Regulation FD section).

Conversely, road shows are never scheduled during the weeks immediately following the end of a reporting quarter, since the presenting team will likely know the details of how the company performed, and may let slip information about those results that has not yet been made available to the public.

As just noted, the purpose of a non-deal road show is to educate the investment community. More specifically, it is about educating a *large proportion* of the investment community, and preferably people who have not come into contact with the company in the past. This means that the presentation team should continually target new geographic locations, to gain exposure to a larger number of new investors. Conversely, the team should avoid revisiting the same investor groups over and over again, since they already have an in-depth knowledge of the company, and are unlikely to invest in the company now if they had not already done so in the past.

The typical company does not have a sufficient number of contacts to set up its own non-deal road shows. Instead, rely upon an investment banker or an investor relations firm, which likely has an extensive contacts list. These firms make contacts on behalf of the company and arrange for meeting space, so that the management team only has to appear at the designated time and make its presentation. The exact routing of a road show will be driven to some extent by where the investment banker or investor relations firm has clients.

It is possible that some road show attendees will be individual investors. However, since you want to educate a large proportion of the investment community about the company, it is better to present to stockbrokers to a considerable extent. Stockbrokers advise many clients, so there is a multiplier effect when presenting to them. Ideally, presentations to a few hundred stockbrokers during a road show equates to putting company information into the hands of several thousand investors. However, the presentation needs to be a good one, or else that multiplier effect will work in reverse – the stockbroker will be more inclined to steer his clients *away* from your company.

When dealing with stockbrokers, it is best to present to them during a lunch meeting, when they are most likely to be available. This means offering them a free meal (with drinks), and keeping the presentation short. If the presentation can be limited to 20 minutes, this gives them time for questions. Otherwise, if the team drones through a boring presentation, expect the stockbrokers to leave early. If you are giving a massive hour-long presentation, there will probably not be many people left in the room by the end of it; and the people remaining are likely to be the least productive stockbrokers who have the fewest clients.

Stockbrokers rarely engage in any preliminary research about a company before attending a road show presentation, so expect a broad range of questions – some of them downright odd. Nonetheless, nearly all questions will be repeated as you proceed through a road show, so the team will eventually become comfortable with answering many types of questions.

Since a non-deal road show is intended to address a large audience, use a projector and projection screen. Given the size of some audiences, which may exceed 50, it is not workable to only issue a handout to participants. It is difficult to lead a large audience through a handout, and they will also be less attentive.

If the presentation team is comfortable with doing so, they can even turn off the projector, walk into the audience area, and make comments without notes. This can greatly increase audience interest in the presentation, but is only recommended when presenters are extremely comfortable with their material and have an engaging speaking style.

Though we do not recommend a handout as the primary form of presentation, there should be a brief handout that succinctly states the main points of the presentation. It should also prominently state the investor relations officer's contact information, as well as the name of the company and its ticker symbol.

The Road Show Presentation

There must be a formal presentation document for any road show, both to ensure that the team covers all speaking points and to form the basis for a handout. The document is almost always created using PowerPoint, which is the standard presentation software. A road show presentation usually encompasses the following points:

- *Introduction.* State what the company does on a single slide.
- *The company as an investment.* State why the company is a good investment.
- *Strategy.* In just a few points, describe the company's competitive strategy, such as franchising, expanding into new product lines, and so forth.

- *Competitive stance.* Describe how the company is competitively positioned within its industry, and how the company protects that position. Be sure to mention "hard" defenses, such as patents and regulatory approvals.
- *Market size.* Note the size of the market in which the company competes. Consider putting the source of this information in a handout, since investors may want to verify this information.
- *Customers.* If the company has large, well-known customers, state who they are and the portion of the company's total business that they represent. Also, note the general types of customers.
- *Financial statements.* Include a condensed income statement and balance sheet that shows the company's results and financial position for the past few years.
- *Resumes.* On a single slide, note the names, titles, and areas of responsibility of the most senior company executives.
- *Summarization.* On one slide, note the key points about the company that will be of importance to a prospective investor.

When creating the presentation, consider the following points:

- *Minimize the number of slides.* Do not burden the audience with an overwhelming number of slides. Instead, tighten the message being presented to focus on only the most important aspects of the business. Otherwise, a prolonged presentation will leave the audience so muddled that they will not have a clear idea of what the company does or how it creates value. A presentation that contains 100 slides is far too large; there is no perfect number of slides, but something closer to 20 slides will be more cogent.
- *Minimize the information on each slide.* As was the case with the number of slides, do not bury the audience with too much information on each slide. Try extending this concept to not just the number of words on a slide, but also to the length of the words. Ideally, the word count per slide should be short, as should the syllable count. Perhaps as few as a dozen words could be sufficient. Keep in mind that slides should contain only enough information to highlight the points being made by the presenter.
- *Minimize introductions.* Do not waste a great deal of time on introductions. Simply state the name and position of each presenter, without waxing lyrical about their accomplishments.

In addition to the presentation itself, spend some time addressing questions that are likely to arise. If the company has had road shows in the past, this is simply a matter of looking back through the notes taken concerning questions asked by attendees. Common questions are likely to be in the general areas of:

- Threats to the business
- Barriers to entry

- Actions of competitors
- Trends in financial results

The team should agree upon the best response to each question. Also, it may make sense to designate someone to answer a certain group of questions, if that person has the best background for doing so. For example, the CFO usually handles all questions of a financial nature.

Tip: If the presentation team wants to work out the bugs in its presentation, consider presenting to a less-important audience first, so that the team can make changes before going in front of a more important audience.

Regulation FD

Regulation FD was created in response to a number of situations in which companies were found to have given material non-public information, such as advance notice of earnings results, to a select few outsiders. The outsiders were able to use the information to make trades that placed them in an unfair competitive position in relation to other, less well-informed investors. Company managers were also allegedly able to manipulate analysts by giving advance information to those who portrayed the company favorably in their research reports.

To combat these issues, the SEC issued Regulation FD, which mandates that a company immediately release to the general public any material non-public information that it has disclosed to certain individuals outside of the company.

The following text from Regulation FD has been heavily edited to compress a large amount of legalese into a format that states the essence of the Regulation:

a. Whenever an issuer, or any person acting on its behalf, discloses any material nonpublic information regarding that issuer or its securities to [a broker, dealer, investment advisor, investment company, or holder of the issuer's securities], the issuer shall make public disclosure of that information:

   1. Simultaneously, in the case of an intentional disclosure; and
   2. Promptly, in the case of a non-intentional disclosure. Promptly means as soon as reasonably practical after a senior official of the issuer learns that there has been a non-intentional disclosure. In no event shall this public disclosure be later than the longer of 24 hours or the commencement of the next day's trading on the New York Stock Exchange.

b. Paragraph (a) of this section shall not apply to a disclosure made:

   1. To a person who owes a duty of trust or confidence to the issuer (such as an attorney, investment banker, or accountant);
   2. To a person who expressly agrees to maintain the disclosed information in confidence;
   3. In connection with a securities offering registered under the Securities Act, if the disclosure is by a registration statement, or an oral communi-

cation made in connection with the securities offering after filing the registration statement.

Note that the regulation is triggered by disclosures only to those individuals who are either investors or who work in the investment industry. There is no mention of disclosures to spouses or other family members, since such a requirement would call for a truly oppressive amount of information tracking by the investor relations staff.

Regulation FD states that "public disclosure" of material non-public information is considered to be a Form 8-K filing, or disseminating the information "through another method of disclosure that is reasonably designed to provide broad, non-exclusionary distribution of the information to the public." Most companies deal with the situation by issuing a Form 8-K. The expectation is that the 8-K will be released within 24 hours of a disclosure event coming to the attention of a senior official of the company.

Tip: A possible alternative form of dissemination of material nonpublic information is a press release that is broadly distributed through a newswire service.

A small number of public companies update their company blogs with information that would normally be found in distributed press releases. We do not recommend the use of blogs for meeting the dictates of Regulation FD, since they might be construed as not providing sufficiently broad distribution to the public.

There are a number of ways to mitigate the risk that there will be a material non-public disclosure of information. Most of the following possibilities require either the adoption of policies and procedures that govern the release of information, or the active participation of the investor relations staff. Compliance best practices include:

- *Quiet period.* Mandate that there will be *no* communications with the investment community from the period when the company's results become reasonably apparent, until quarterly earnings are released in the Form 10-Q or the annual results in the Form 10-K. The quiet period could be quite long when annual results are being released, since the company must wait for the outside auditors to complete their audit of its financial records.
- *Post everything.* The company could make a standard practice of posting all of its presentations to the investor relations section of its website. At a minimum, this would mean posting the presentation PowerPoint slides and any written script that goes along with it. However, since a presenter could depart from the script, an even better approach is to make a video recording of every presentation and the following question-and-answer sessions, and make these videos available on the website. This latter approach ensures that all presenter commentary is made available to the investment community.
- *Standard Q&A list.* Compile a list of standard questions that are being asked of the company, along with the standard answers to those questions. A problem with this approach is that the information in the list can become stale

within a short period of time, so have a mechanism in place for refreshing the list with new information and distributing it on a regular basis.

- *Standard forbidden topics list*. If there are some aspects of the company that should only be discussed with outsiders by a few well-trained individuals, make sure that all other employees know they are prohibited from discussing those topics.

- *Impose employee non-disclosure agreements*. Wherever possible, have employees sign a non-disclosure agreement, in which are stated a number of topics which they are not allowed to discuss with outsiders. The agreement should state the penalties for revealing this information, such as immediate termination, so that employees will understand the seriousness of any violation.

Tip: Insist that all presentations to the investment community be heavily scripted, since this reduces the risk of making a stray comment that contains material non-public information.

Short Sellers

A short seller is someone who expects a company's stock price to decline in the near term; he sells borrowed stock with the expectation of earning a profit later, when he buys back the stock at a lower price.

What type of company is an ideal target for a short seller? Any company can be targeted, but here are some characteristics for companies that are more likely to be impacted:

- *Smaller float*. If a company has a small number of shares outstanding, it is easier for a relatively small number of trades to create large changes in the price of the stock.

- *Available shares*. If investors have placed large amounts of the company's stock in their margin accounts, these shares are probably available to be loaned to short sellers by the brokerages managing those accounts.

- *Earnings variability*. If a business has a recent history of large fluctuations in its reported earnings, its stock price has also probably bounced around in conjunction with the earnings. High stock price variability attracts short sellers, who are more likely to experience price drops that they can take advantage of.

- *Aggressive guidance*. If the CEO has a habit of stretching the credulity of the investment community with aggressive guidance, it is more likely that there will be an earnings shortfall at some point, which will yield a drop in the stock price.

Conversely, there are some situations that are *less* likely to attract short sellers. A company that has a well-defended market position and which faces minimal competitive pressure can be reasonably assured of consistent profitability. A high level of earnings consistency (especially if buttressed by a reliable and long-term dividend payout) will keep the stock price from fluctuating very much, and which in turn tends to deflect the attention of short sellers.

What can a company do about short sellers? The CEO may be tempted to force them out by issuing guidance for better-than-expected earnings results. This kind of publicity may initially increase the stock price, which creates an untenable situation for short sellers. In the short term, such guidance may quite possibly drive them away.

The problem is that the more aggressive guidance will make it very hard to meet investor expectations. If the CEO keeps issuing higher and higher guidance numbers, all the short sellers have to do is wait quietly until the stock price is clearly much too high, and then sell short in even greater quantities and turn a massive profit when the stock price inevitably craters. In short, the CEO's own actions have manufactured profits for short sellers.

So obviously, increasing guidance is a bad idea. There are several other actions to consider that are more workable. They are:

- *Never issue aggressive guidance.* Increasing the expected results of the business only raises the stock price to an unsustainable level. Instead, issue conservative guidance which the company can comfortably meet on a long-term basis. This approach reduces stock price volatility; with minimal stock volatility, short sellers will see little point in targeting the company.

- *Issue press releases.* Monitor the larger investor message boards to see if there are sudden increases in negative discussions about the company. Those increases may coincide with short selling. If there appears to be a smear campaign going on, then consider issuing a press release that addresses the substance of the allegations.

- *Issue all bad news at once.* Issue every scrap of bad news to the investing public at one time. For example, if the company reports a bad quarter, short sellers may start monitoring the company, and possibly selling short, because they expect that the business will issue a string of more bad news that will drive the stock price down even further. Thus, when you know there is bad news, dump *all* of it on the market at once, so there will be no additional bad news for short sellers to feed on. The result should be a one-time drop in the stock price – and no further.

- *Limit road shows.* Limit the number of people who are aware of any plans to sell more company stock. Since a stock issuance can drive down earnings per share, and therefore the stock price, short sellers are more likely to sell short if they know stock is about to be issued.

- *Shift company stock out of margin accounts.* Company insiders may keep their stock in margin accounts. If so, they have probably signed a hypothecation agreement with their broker, under which the broker can extend a margin loan in exchange for lending out any security in the account as collateral to raise the capital needed to fund the loan. This means that shares in the company held by company insiders may be used for a short seller attack on the company. To avoid this situation, have all insiders move their company shares to a cash account with their brokerages.

Summary

The CFO is the financial "face" of a company, and so is expected to be highly visible to the investment community. In particular, the CFO takes part in earnings calls and road show presentations. There are many other mechanics involved in the investor relations function that are best left to an investor relations officer, such as arranging for shareholder votes, road show and shareholder meeting logistics, maintaining an investor relations website, and so forth. In a public company environment where there are many investors, the CFO must be careful to limit his or her role to those activities noted in this chapter – all other investor relations work should be left to a support team. If the company is not profitable enough to pay for an investor relations team, it is better to scale back investor relations activities than to overload the CFO with too many tasks.

Chapter 18
Public Company Financial Reporting

Introduction

The CFO is certainly expected to know about the contents of the traditional set of financial statements and their accompanying disclosures. However, not that many CFOs have been involved with a publicly-held company, for which additional financial reports are required. In this chapter, we address the quarterly and annual reports that must be filed with the Securities and Exchange Commission (SEC) by all publicly-held companies, as well as several conceptual issues related to these reports. We also make note of the Form 8-K, which must be filed whenever one of a large number of material events occurs. These three reports comprise the bulk of all SEC filings that a CFO is likely to be involved with.

Interim Reporting

If a company is publicly-held, the Securities and Exchange Commission requires that it file a variety of quarterly information on the Form 10-Q. This information is a reduced set of the requirements for the more comprehensive annual Form 10-K. The requirement to issue these additional financial statements may appear to be simple enough, but you must consider whether to report information assuming that quarterly results are stand-alone documents, or part of the full-year results of the business. This section discusses the disparities that these different viewpoints can cause in the financial statements, as well as interim reporting issues related to inventory.

The Integral View

Under the integral view of producing interim reports, the assumption is that the results reported in interim financial statements are an integral part of the full-year financial results (hence the name of this concept). This viewpoint produces the following accounting issues:

- *Accrue expenses not arising in the period.* If you know that an expense will be paid later in the year that is incurred at least partially in the reporting period, accrue some portion of the expense in the reporting period. Here are several examples:
    - *Advertising.* If payment is made in advance for advertising that is scheduled to occur over multiple time periods, you can recognize the expense over the entire range of time periods.
    - *Bonuses.* If there are bonus plans that may result in bonus payments later in the year, the expense is accrued in all accounting periods.

Only accrue this expense if the amount of the bonus can be reasonably estimated, which may not always be possible during the earlier months covered by a performance contract.

o *Contingencies.* If there are contingent liabilities that will be resolved later in the year, and which are both probable and reasonably estimated, then accrue the related expense.

o *Profit sharing.* If employees are paid a percentage of company profits at year-end, and the amount can be reasonably estimated, then accrue the expense throughout the year as a proportion of the profits recognized in each period.

o *Property taxes.* A local government entity issues an invoice to the company at some point during the year for property taxes. These taxes are intended to cover the entire year, so accrue a portion of the expense in each reporting period.

- *Tax rate.* A company is usually subject to a graduated income tax rate that incrementally escalates through the year as the business generates more profit. Under the integral view, use the expected tax rate for the entire year in every reporting period, rather than the incremental tax rate that applies only to the profits earned for the year to date.

EXAMPLE

The board of directors of Hammer Industries approves a senior management bonus plan for the upcoming year that could potentially pay the senior management team a maximum of $240,000. It initially seems probable that the full amount will be paid, but by the third quarter it appears more likely that the maximum amount to be paid will be $180,000. In addition, the company pays $60,000 in advance for a full year of advertising in *Construction Times* magazine. Hammer recognizes these expenses as follows:

	Quarter 1	Quarter 2	Quarter 3	Quarter 4	Full Year
Bonus expense	$60,000	$60,000	$30,000	$30,000	$180,000
Advertising	15,000	15,000	15,000	15,000	60,000

The accounting staff spreads the recognition of the full amount of the projected bonus over the year, but then reduces its recognition of the remaining expense starting in the third quarter, to adjust for the lowered bonus payout expectation.

The accounting staff initially records the $60,000 advertising expense as a prepaid expense, and recognizes it ratably over all four quarters of the year, which matches the time period over which the related advertisements are run by *Construction Times.*

One problem with the integral view is that it tends to result in a significant number of expense accruals. Since these accruals are usually based on estimates, it is entirely possible that adjustments should be made to the accruals later in the year, as the company obtains more precise information about the expenses that are being accrued. Some of these adjustments could be substantial, and may materially affect the reported results in later periods.

The Discrete View

Under the discrete view of producing interim reports, the assumption is that the results reported for a specific interim period are *not* associated with the revenues and expenses arising during other reporting periods. Under this view, record the entire impact of a transaction within the reporting period, rather than ratably over the entire year. The following are examples of the situations that can arise under the discrete method:

- *Reduced accruals.* A substantially smaller number of accruals are likely under the discrete method, since the assumption is that you should not anticipate the recordation of transactions that have not yet arisen.
- *Gains and losses.* Do not spread the recognition of a gain or loss across multiple periods. If you were to do so, it would allow a company to spread a loss over multiple periods, thereby making the loss look smaller on a per-period basis than it really is.

Comparison of the Integral and Discrete Views

The integral view is clearly the better method from a theoretical perspective, since the causes of some transactions can span an entire year. For example, a manager may be awarded a bonus at the end of December, but he probably had to achieve specific results throughout the year to earn it. Otherwise, if you were to adopt the discrete view, interim reporting would yield exceedingly varied results, with some periods revealing inordinately high or low profitability.

However, the integral view could be adopted from the perspective of accounting *efficiency*; that is, it is very time-consuming to maintain a mass of revenue and expense accruals, their ongoing adjustments, and documentation of the reasons for them throughout a year. Instead, use the integral view only for the more material transactions that are anticipated, and use the discrete view for smaller transactions. Thus, the expense for property taxes could be accrued throughout the year if the amount was significant, or it could be recorded in the month when the invoice is received, if the amount is small.

Interim Reporting Issues

When reporting interim results, there are several issues involving the recordation of inventory that vary from the normal handling of inventory for the year-end financial statements.

One issue is the method you are allowed to use for calculating the cost of goods sold. Normally, a periodic or perpetual inventory tracking system is used to derive the on-hand quantities of inventory. However, this can be too burdensome for interim reporting, so it is acceptable to estimate it instead. A good method for doing so is the gross profit method, under which the cost of goods sold is estimated based on the expected gross profit.

Another issue concerns the use of the last in, first out (LIFO) method for calculating the cost of inventory. A key issue when using LIFO is that an inventory layer cannot be recovered that was liquidated as of year-end. However, such a layer *can* be recovered if it is liquidated during an interim period and there is an expectation that the layer will be replaced by year-end. If that is the case, add the expected inventory replacement cost to the cost of sales for the interim period.

Yet another issue is the recognition of any losses that may have been caused by the lower of cost or market (LCM) rule. If LCM losses are recognized during an interim period, it is acceptable to offset the full amount of these losses with any gains in subsequent periods within the same year on the same inventory items. Further, you can simply avoid recognizing these losses in an interim period if there are seasonal price fluctuations that are expected to result in an offsetting increase in market prices by the end of the year.

Segment Reporting

A publicly-held company must report segment information, which is part of the disclosures attached to the financial statements. This information is supposedly needed to give the readers of the financial statements more insights into the operations and prospects of a business. In this section, we describe how to determine which business segments to report separately, and how to report that information.

Primary Segment Reporting Issues

The primary issue with segment reporting is determining which business segments to report. The rules for this selection process are quite specific. Only report segment information if a business segment passes any one of the following three tests:

1. *Revenue*. The revenue of the segment is at least 10% of the consolidated revenue of the entire business; or
2. *Profit or loss*. The absolute amount of the profit or loss of the segment is at least 10% of the greater of the combined profits of all the operating segments reporting a profit, or of the combined losses of all operating segments reporting a loss (see the following example for a demonstration of this concept); or
3. *Assets*. The assets of the segment are at least 10% of the combined assets of all the operating segments of the business.

Some parts of a business are not considered to be reportable business segments under the following circumstances:

- *Corporate overhead.* The corporate group does not usually earn outside revenues, and so is not considered a segment.
- *Post-retirement benefit plans.* A benefit plan can earn income from investments, but it has no operating activities, and so is not considered a segment.

- *One-time events*. If an otherwise-insignificant segment has a one-time event that boosts it into the ranks of reportable segments, do not report it, since there is no long-term expectation for it to remain a reportable segment.

If the preceding tests are run and you arrive at a group of reportable segments whose combined revenues are not at least 75% of the consolidated revenue of the entire business, then add more segments until the 75% threshold is surpassed.

If there is a business segment that used to qualify as a reportable segment and does not currently qualify, but which is expected to qualify in the future, then continue to treat it as a reportable segment.

If there are several smaller segments that would normally be considered too small to be reported separately, combine them for reporting purposes if they have similar regulatory environments, types of customers, production processes, products, distribution methods, *and* economic characteristics. The number of restrictions on this type of reporting makes it unlikely that you would be able to aggregate smaller segments.

Tip: The variety of methods available for segment testing makes it possible that a business will have quite a large number of reportable segments. If so, it can be burdensome to create a report for so many segments, and it may be confusing for the readers of the company's financial statements. Consequently, consider limiting the number of reportable segments to ten; the information for additional segments can be aggregated for reporting purposes.

EXAMPLE

Hammer Industries has six business segments whose results it reports internally. Hammer's CFO needs to test the various segments to see which ones qualify as being reportable. He collects the following information:

Segment	(000s) Revenue	(000s) Profit	(000s) Loss	(000s) Assets
Anvils	$120,000	$10,000	$--	$320,000
Cutters	85,000	8,000	--	180,000
Hammers	29,000	--	-21,000	90,000
Multi-tools	200,000	32,000		500,000
Pliers	15,000	--	-4,000	4,000
Vises	62,000	--	-11,000	55,000
	$511,000	$50,000	-$36,000	$1,149,000

In the table, the total profit exceeds the total loss, so the CFO uses the total profit for the 10% profit test. The CFO then lists the same table again, but now with the losses column removed and with test thresholds at the top of the table that are used to determine which segments are reported. An "X" mark below a test threshold indicates that a segment is reportable. In addition, the CFO adds a new column on the right side of the table, which is used to calculate the total revenue for the reportable segments.

Segment	(000s) Revenue	(000s) Profit	(000s) Assets	75% Revenue Test
Reportable threshold (10%)	**$51,100**	**$5,000**	**$114,900**	
Anvils	X	X	X	$120,000
Cutters	X	X	X	85,000
Hammers				
Multi-tools	X	X	X	200,000
Pliers				
Vises	X			62,000
			Total	$467,000

This analysis shows that the anvil, cutter, multi-tool, and vise segments are reportable, and that the combined revenue of these reportable segments easily exceeds the 75% reporting threshold. Consequently, the company does not need to separately report information for any additional segments.

The Segment Report

The key requirement of segment reporting is that the revenue, profit or loss, and assets of each segment be separately reported. In addition, reconcile this segment information back to the company's consolidated results, which requires the inclusion of any adjusting items. Also disclose the methods by which you determined which segments to report. The essential information to include in a segment report includes:

- The types of products and services sold by each segment
- The basis of organization (such as by geographic region or product line)
- Revenues
- Interest expense
- Depreciation and amortization
- Material expense items
- Equity method interests in other entities
- Income tax expense or income
- Other material non-cash items
- Profit or loss

EXAMPLE

The CFO of Hammer Industries produces the following segment report for the segments identified in the preceding example:

(000s)	Anvils	Cutters	Multi-tools	Vises	Other	Consolidated
Revenues	$120,000	$85,000	$200,000	$62,000	$44,000	$511,000
Interest income	11,000	8,000	28,000	8,000	2,000	57,000
Interest expense	--	--	--	11,000	39,000	50,000
Depreciation	32,000	18,000	50,000	6,000	10,000	116,000
Income taxes	4,000	3,000	10,000	-3,000	-7,000	7,000
Profit	10,000	8,000	32,000	-11,000	-25,000	14,000
Assets	320,000	180,000	500,000	55,000	94,000	1,149,000

Earnings per Share

If the company is publicly-held, there is a requirement to report two types of earnings per share information within the financial statements. In this section, we describe how to calculate both basic and diluted earnings per share, as well as how to present this information within the financial statements.

Basic Earnings per Share

Basic earnings per share is the amount of a company's profit or loss for a reporting period that is available to the shares of its common stock that are outstanding during a reporting period. If a business only has common stock in its capital structure, it presents only its basic earnings per share for income from continuing operations and net income. This information is reported on its income statement.

The formula for basic earnings per share is:

$$\frac{\text{Profit or loss attributable to common equity holders of the parent business}}{\text{Weighted average number of common shares outstanding during the period}}$$

In addition, subdivide this calculation into:

- The profit or loss from continuing operations attributable to the parent company
- The total profit or loss attributable to the parent company

When calculating basic earnings per share, incorporate into the numerator an adjustment for dividends. Deduct from the profit or loss the after-tax amount of any dividends declared on non-cumulative preferred stock, as well as the after-tax amount of any preferred stock dividends, even if the dividends are not declared; this

308

does not include any dividends paid or declared during the current period that relate to previous periods.

Also, incorporate the following adjustments into the denominator of the basic earnings per share calculation:

- *Contingent stock.* If there is contingently issuable stock, treat it as though it were outstanding as of the date when there are no circumstances under which the shares would *not* be issued.
- *Issuance date.* Include shares under any of the following circumstances:
  - A liability is settled in exchange for shares
  - An acquisition paid for with shares is recognized
  - Any shares related to a mandatorily convertible instrument as of the contract date
  - Cash is receivable for sold shares
  - Dividends are reinvested
  - Interest stops accruing on convertible debt instruments on which shares can be issued
  - Services are paid for with shares
- *Weighted-average shares.* Use the weighted-average number of shares during the period in the denominator. Do this by adjusting the number of shares outstanding at the beginning of the reporting period for common shares repurchased or issued in the period. This adjustment is based on the proportion of the days in the reporting period that the shares are outstanding.

EXAMPLE

Hammer Industries earns a profit of $1,000,000 net of taxes in Year 1. In addition, Hammer owes $200,000 in dividends to the holders of its cumulative preferred stock. Hammer calculates the numerator of its basic earnings per share as follows:

$1,000,000 Profit - $200,000 Dividends = $800,000

Hammer had 4,000,000 common shares outstanding at the beginning of Year 1. In addition, it sold 200,000 shares on April 1 and 400,000 shares on October 1. It also issued 500,000 shares on July 1 to the owners of a newly-acquired subsidiary. Finally, it bought back 60,000 shares on December 1. Hammer calculates the weighted-average number of common shares outstanding as follows:

Date	Shares	Weighting (Months)	Weighted Average
January 1	4,000,000	12/12	4,000,000
April 1	200,000	9/12	150,000
July 1	500,000	6/12	250,000
October 1	400,000	3/12	100,000
December 1	-60,000	1/12	-5,000
			4,495,000

Hammer's basic earnings per share is:

$800,000 Adjusted profits ÷ 4,495,000 Weighted-average shares = <u>$0.18</u> per share

---

Diluted Earnings per Share

Diluted earnings per share is the profit for a reporting period per share of common stock outstanding during that period; it includes the number of shares that would have been outstanding during the period if the company had issued common shares for all potential dilutive common stock outstanding during the period.

If a company has more types of stock than common stock in its capital structure, it must present both basic earnings per share and diluted earnings per share information; this presentation must be for both income from continuing operations and net income. This information is reported on the company's income statement.

To calculate diluted earnings per share, include the effects of all dilutive potential common shares. This means that the number of shares outstanding is increased by the weighted average number of additional common shares that would have been outstanding if the company had converted all dilutive potential common stock to common stock. This dilution may affect the profit or loss in the numerator of the dilutive earnings per share calculation. The formula is:

(Profit or loss attributable to common equity holders of parent company
<u>+ After-tax interest on convertible debt + Convertible preferred dividends)</u>
(Weighted average number of common shares outstanding during the period
+ All dilutive potential common stock)

Two adjustments should be made to the numerator of this calculation. They are:

- *Interest expense.* Eliminate any interest expense associated with dilutive potential common stock, since the assumption is that these shares are converted to common stock. The conversion would eliminate the company's liability for the interest expense.
- *Dividends.* Adjust for the after-tax impact of dividends or other types of dilutive potential common shares.

It may be necessary to make several adjustments to the denominator of this calculation. They are:

- *Contingent shares dependency.* If there is a contingent share issuance that is dependent upon the future market price of the company's common stock, include the shares in the diluted earnings per share calculation, based on the market price at the end of the reporting period; however, only include the issuance if the effect is dilutive. If the shares have a contingency feature, do not include them in the calculation until the contingency has been met.
- *Contingent shares in general.* Treat common stock that is contingently issuable as though it was outstanding as of the beginning of the reporting

period, but only if the conditions have been met that would require the company to issue the shares.

- *Anti-dilutive shares*. If there are any contingent stock issuances that would have an anti-dilutive impact on earnings per share, do not include them in the calculation. This situation arises when a business experiences a loss, because including the dilutive shares in the calculation would reduce the loss per share.

In addition to these three adjustments to the denominator, also apply all of the adjustments to the denominator already noted for basic earnings per share.

Tip: The rules related to diluted earnings per share appear complex, but they are founded upon one principle – that you are trying to establish the absolute worst-case scenario to arrive at the smallest possible amount of earnings per share. If you are faced with an unusual situation involving the calculation of diluted earnings per share and are not sure what to do, that rule will likely apply.

If there is a share issuance that is contingent upon certain conditions being satisfied, and those conditions were met by the end of the reporting period, then include them in the calculation as of the beginning of the period. However, if the conditions were not met by the end of the period, then include in the calculation, as of the beginning of the period, any shares that would be issuable if:

- The end of the reporting period were the end of the contingency period; and
- The result would be dilutive.

If the number of contingent shares issued is based on a certain amount of earnings, and the company achieved those earnings during the reporting period, then include the contingent shares in the calculation; but only if the effect is dilutive.

In addition to the issues just noted, here are a number of additional situations that could impact the calculation of diluted earnings per share:

- *Most advantageous exercise price*. When the number of potential shares that could be issued is calculated, do so using the most advantageous conversion rate from the perspective of the person or entity holding the security to be converted.
- *Settlement assumption*. If there is an open contract that could be settled in common stock or cash, assume that it will be settled in common stock, but only if the effect is dilutive.
- *Effects of convertible instruments*. If there are convertible instruments outstanding, include their dilutive effect if they dilute earnings per share. Consider convertible preferred stock to be anti-dilutive when the dividend on any converted shares is greater than basic earnings per share. Similarly, convertible debt is considered anti-dilutive when the interest expense on any

converted shares exceeds basic earnings per share. The following example illustrates the concept.

EXAMPLE

Hammer Industries earns a net profit of $2 million, and it has 5 million common shares outstanding. In addition, there is a $1 million convertible loan that has an eight percent interest rate. The loan may potentially convert into 500,000 of Hammer's common shares. Hammer's incremental tax rate is 35 percent.

Hammer's basic earnings per share is $2,000,000 ÷ 5,000,000 shares, or $0.40/share. The following calculation shows the compilation of Hammer's diluted earnings per share:

Net profit	$2,000,000
+ Interest saved on $1,000,000 loan at 8%	80,000
- Reduced tax savings on foregone interest expense	-28,000
= Adjusted net earnings	$2,052,000
Common shares outstanding	5,000,000
+ Potential converted shares	500,000
= Adjusted shares outstanding	5,500,000
Diluted earnings per share ($2,052,000 ÷ 5,500,000)	$0.37/share

- *Option exercise.* If there are any dilutive options and warrants, assume that they are exercised at their exercise price. Then, convert the proceeds into the total number of shares that the holders would have purchased, using the average market price during the reporting period. Then use in the diluted earnings per share calculation the difference between the number of shares assumed to have been issued and the number of shares assumed to have been purchased. The following example illustrates the concept.

EXAMPLE

Hammer Industries earns a net profit of $200,000, and it has 5,000,000 common shares outstanding that sell on the open market for an average of $12 per share. In addition, there are 300,000 options outstanding that can be converted to Hammer's common stock at $10 each.

Hammer's basic earnings per share is $200,000 ÷ 5,000,000 common shares, or $0.04 per share.

Hammer's CFO wants to calculate the amount of diluted earnings per share. To do so, he follows these steps:

1. *Calculate the number of shares that would have been issued at the market price.* Thus, he multiplies the 300,000 options by the average exercise price of $10 to arrive at a total of $3,000,000 paid to exercise the options by their holders.
2. *Divide the amount paid to exercise the options by the market price to determine the number of shares that could be purchased.* Thus, he divides the $3,000,000 paid to exercise the options by the $12 average market price to arrive at 250,000 shares that could have been purchased with the proceeds from the options.
3. *Subtract the number of shares that could have been purchased from the number of options exercised.* Thus, he subtracts the 250,000 shares potentially purchased from the 300,000 options to arrive at a difference of 50,000 shares.
4. *Add the incremental number of shares to the shares already outstanding.* Thus, he adds the 50,000 incremental shares to the existing 5,000,000 to arrive at 5,050,000 diluted shares.

Based on this information, the CFO arrives at diluted earnings per share of $0.0396, for which the calculation is:

$$\$200,000 \text{ net profit} \div 5,050,000 \text{ common shares}$$

- *Put options.* If there are purchased put options, only include them in the diluted earnings per share calculation if the exercise price is higher than the average market price during the reporting period.
- *Call options.* If there are purchased call options, only include them in the diluted earnings per share calculation if the exercise price is lower than the market price.

Tip: There is only a dilutive effect on the diluted earnings per share calculation when the average market price is greater than the exercise prices of any options or warrants.

- *Compensation in shares.* If company employees are awarded shares that have not vested or stock options as forms of compensation, then treat these grants as options when calculating diluted earnings per share. Consider these grants to be outstanding on the grant date, rather than any later vesting date.
- *Repurchase agreements.* If there is a contract that requires a business to reacquire its own shares, *and* the repurchase price is higher than the average market price during the past period, *and* there is a dilutive effect, then include them in the calculation of diluted earnings per share. To do so, assume that a sufficient number of shares were issued at the beginning of the reporting period to raise the funds needed to repurchase the shares. Then include the difference between the number of shares issued to raise funds and the number of shares retired in the calculation of diluted earnings per share.

- *Dilutive shares.* If there is potential dilutive common stock, add all of it to the denominator of the diluted earnings per share calculation. Unless there is more specific information available, assume that these shares are issued at the beginning of the reporting period.

Always calculate the number of potential dilutive common shares independently for each reporting period presented in the financial statements.

Presentation of Earnings per Share

Basic and diluted earnings per share information is normally listed at the bottom of the income statement, and should be stated for every period included in the income statement. Also, if diluted earnings per share information is reported in *any* of the periods included in the company's income statement, it must be reported for *all* of the periods included in the statement. The following sample illustrates the concept.

Sample Presentation of Earnings per Share

Earnings per Share	20x3	20x2	20x1
From continuing operations			
Basic earnings per share	$1.05	$0.95	$0.85
Diluted earnings per share	1.00	0.90	0.80
From discontinued operations			
Basic earnings per share	$0.20	$0.17	$0.14
Diluted earnings per share	0.15	0.08	0.07
From total operations			
Basic earnings per share	$1.25	$1.12	$0.99
Diluted earnings per share	1.15	0.98	0.87

The Public Company Closing Process

A publicly-held company is required by the SEC to file a large report concerning its financial condition at the end of each quarter. These are the Form 10-Q (for quarterly filings) and Form 10-K (for annual filings). The contents of both reports are discussed in the following sections.

The additional steps needed to close the books for a publicly-held company include all of the following:

1. *Auditor investigation.* The company's outside auditors must conduct a review of the company's financial statements and disclosures for its quarterly results, and a full audit of its annual results. This is the most time-consuming of the public company requirements. The company can reduce

the amount of time required for a review or audit by providing full staff support to the audit team, as well as by having all requested information available as of the beginning of the audit or review work.

2. *Legal review.* It would be extremely unwise to issue the financial statement package without first having legal counsel review the statements and (especially) the disclosures to ensure that all required disclosures have been made, and to verify that all statements made are correct and fully supportable. This review is usually completed near or after the end of the work done by the auditors, but can be scheduled slightly sooner if you believe the disclosures to be substantially complete at that time.

3. *Officer certification.* Depending upon what type of Form is being issued, different company officers are required to certify that the information in the financial statements presents fairly the financial condition and results of operations of the business. Since there are substantial penalties and jail time involved if an officer were to make a false certification, it should be no surprise that the signing officers will want to spend time reviewing the complete set of financial statements and disclosures. This review can be done before the auditors have completed their work, so officer certification does not usually increase the duration of the closing process.

4. *Audit committee and board approvals.* The audit committee must approve every Form 10-Q, and the board of directors must approve every Form 10-K. Given the number of people involved, schedule review and approval meetings well in advance, to be conducted a few days prior to the required filing date of the applicable Form. Scheduling the review slightly early leaves some time to make adjustments, in case anyone expresses concerns during the review, and wants changes to be made prior to filing.

   Issue the complete set of financial statements and disclosures to the audit committee or board member at least one full day in advance of a review and approval meeting, so that they have sufficient time to examine the material.

5. *EDGARize and file.* Once the Form 10-Q or Form 10-K is complete and fully approved, it must be filed with the SEC. The filing is done using the Electronic Data Gathering, Analysis, and Retrieval (EDGAR) system that is operated by the SEC. This information can be submitted in various formats, but it will almost certainly be necessary to convert it from the format in which the documents were originally prepared. This means hiring someone to convert the reports to the applicable format, which is a process known as *EDGARizing.* Not only is the conversion specialist responsible for converting the financial statements, but this person also files the statements with the SEC on behalf of the company. The conversion process usually takes one or two days, but factor in additional time for the auditors to review the converted format – the auditors must give their approval before the document can be filed with the SEC.

The closing process described here is very slow, so be sure to have the financial statements prepared as soon as possible after the end of the applicable reporting period. Doing so should leave enough time to prepare the statements for filing by the designated due date.

The Form 10-Q

A publicly-held company is required to issue the Form 10-Q to report the results of its first, second, and third fiscal quarters. The Form 10-Q includes not just the financial statements, but also a number of disclosures. The following table itemizes the more common disclosures:

Selection of Form 10-Q Disclosures

Item Header	Description
Part I	
Item 1. Financial statements	Make all disclosures required by GAAP, including descriptions of: • Accrued liabilities • Acquisitions • Discontinued operations • Fixed assets • Income taxes • Related party transactions • Segment information • Stock options
Item 2. Management's discussion and analysis (MD&A)	Describe opportunities, challenges, risks, trends, future plans, and key performance indicators, as well as changes in revenues, the cost of goods sold, other expenses, assets, and liabilities.
Item 3. Quantitative and Qualitative Disclosures about Market Risk	Quantify the market risk at the end of the last fiscal year for the company's market risk-sensitive instruments.
Item 4. Controls and Procedures	Generally describe the system of internal controls, testing of controls, changes in controls, and management's conclusions regarding the effectiveness of those controls.
Part II	
Item 1. Legal Proceedings	Describe any legal proceedings currently involving the company, and its estimate of the likely outcome of those proceedings.
Item 1A. Risk factors	A thorough listing of all risks that the company may experience. It warns investors of what could reduce the value of their investments in the company.

Item Header	Description
Item 2. Unregistered sales of equity securities and use of proceeds	Describe any equity securities sold during the period that were not registered.
Item 3. Defaults upon senior securities	Describe any material default in the payment of principal, interest, or any other material default not cured within 30 days.
Item 4. Mine safety disclosures	If applicable, discuss mine safety laws, and the types of warnings and penalties that occurred during the reporting period.
Item 5. Other information	Any information required to be disclosed under the Form 8-K during the period, but not otherwise reported in this Form.
Item 6. Exhibits and financial statement schedules	Item 601 of Regulation S-K requires that a business attach a number of exhibits, including (but not limited to): <ul><li>Code of ethics</li><li>Material contracts</li><li>Articles of incorporation</li><li>Bylaws</li><li>Acquisition purchase agreements</li></ul>

Before filing, the Form 10-Q must be signed by an authorized officer, as well as the principal financial or chief accounting officer.

The Form 10-Q must be filed within 40 days of the end of the fiscal quarter if the company is either a large accelerated filer or an accelerated filer. If that is not the case, file it within 45 days of the end of the fiscal quarter. A *large accelerated filer* is a company having an aggregate market value owned by investors who are not affiliated with the company of a minimum of $700 million. This measurement is as of the last business day of the most recent second fiscal quarter. An *accelerated filer* is a company having an aggregate market value owned by investors who are not affiliated with the company of less than $700 million, but more than $75 million. This measurement is as of the last business day of the most recent second fiscal quarter.

The Form 10-K

A publicly-held company is required to issue the Form 10-K to report the results of its fiscal year. The Form 10-K includes not just the financial statements, but also a number of additional disclosures. The following table itemizes the more common disclosures.

Selection of Form 10-K Disclosures

Item Header	Description
Item 1. Business	Provide a description of the company's purpose, history, operating segments, customers, suppliers, sales and marketing operations, customer support, intellectual property, competition, and employees. It should tell readers what the company does and describe its business environment.
Item 1A. Risk factors	A thorough listing of all risks that the company may experience. It warns investors of what could reduce the value of their investments in the company.
Item 1B. Unresolved staff comments	Disclose all unresolved comments received from the SEC if they are material. (only applies to written comments from the SEC received at least 180 days before the fiscal year-end by an accelerated or large accelerated filer)
Item 2. Properties	Describe the leased or owned facilities of the business, including square footage, lease termination dates, and lease amounts paid per month.
Item 3. Legal proceedings	Describe any legal proceedings currently involving the company, and its estimate of the likely outcome of those proceedings.
Item 4. Mine safety disclosures	If applicable, discuss mine safety laws, and the types of warnings and penalties that occurred during the reporting period.
Item 5. Market for company stock	Describe where the company's stock trades and the number of holders of record, as well as the high and low closing prices per share, by quarter.
Item 6. Selected financial data	For the last five years, state selected information from the company's income statement and balance sheet (should be in tabular comparative format).
Item 7. Management's discussion and analysis (MD&A)	Describe opportunities, challenges, risks, trends, future plans, and key performance indicators, as well as changes in revenues, the cost of goods sold, other expenses, assets, and liabilities.
Item 7A. Quantitative and qualitative disclosures about market risk	Quantify the market risk at the end of the last fiscal year for the company's market risk-sensitive instruments.
Item 8. Financial statements and supplementary data	Make all disclosures required by GAAP, including descriptions of: • Accrued liabilities • Acquisitions • Discontinued operations • Fixed assets • Income taxes

Item Header	Description
	• Related party transactions • Segment information • Stock options
Item 9. Changes in and disagreements with accountants on accounting and financial disclosure	Describe any disagreements with the auditors when management elects to account for or disclose transactions in a manner different from what the auditors want.
Item 9A. Controls and procedures	Generally describe the system of internal controls, testing of controls, changes in controls, and management's conclusions regarding the effectiveness of those controls.
Item 10. Directors, executive officers and corporate governance	Identify the executive officers, directors, promoters, and individuals classified as control persons.
Item 11. Executive compensation	Itemize the types of compensation paid to company executives.
Item 12. Security ownership of certain beneficial owners and management and related stockholder matters	State the number of shares of all types owned or controlled by certain individuals classified as beneficial owners and/or members of management.
Item 13. Certain relationships and related transactions, and director independence	If there were transactions with related parties during the past fiscal year, and the amounts involved exceeded $120,000, describe the transactions.
Item 14. Principal accountant fees and services	State the aggregate amount of any fees billed in each of the last two fiscal years for professional services rendered by the company's auditors for: • Reviews and audits; • Audit-related activities; • Taxation work; and • All other fees.

Item Header	Description
Item 15. Exhibits and financial statement schedules	Item 601 of Regulation S-K requires that a business attach a number of exhibits, including (but not limited to): • Code of ethics • Material contracts • Articles of incorporation • Bylaws • Acquisition purchase agreements

Before filing, the Form 10-K must be signed by *all* of the following:

- Principal executive officer
- Principal financial officer
- Controller
- A majority of the board of directors

The Form 10-K must be filed within 60 days of the end of the fiscal year if the company is a large accelerated filer or an accelerated filer, or within 75 days of the end of the fiscal year if the company is an accelerated filer. If the company does not have either designation, then file it within 90 days of the end of the fiscal year.

The Form 8-K

The Form 8-K is by far the most commonly-issued SEC filing. A public company uses it to disclose a broad range of material events that impact the business. The following table itemizes the types of disclosures that can appear in a Form 8-K.

Types of Form 8-K Disclosures

Item Header	Description
Item 1.101. Entry into a material definitive agreement	Refers to an agreement not made in the ordinary course of business. Disclose the agreement date, the names of the parties, and the general terms of the agreement.
Item 1.102. Termination of a material definitive agreement	Refers to the non-standard termination of an agreement not made in the ordinary course of business. Disclose the termination date, the general terms of the agreement, the circumstances of the termination, and any termination penalties.
Item 1.103. Bankruptcy or receivership	If the business enters bankruptcy or receivership, identify the proceeding, the name of the court, the date when jurisdiction was assumed, and the identity of the receiver. There are additional disclosures regarding reorganization plans.

Item Header	Description
Item 1.104. Mine safety – reporting of shutdowns and patterns of violations	Disclose the receipt of an imminent danger order issued under the Federal Mine Safety and Health Act, noting the date of receipt of the order, the category of the order, and the name and location of the mine involved in the order.
Item 2.01. Completion of acquisition or disposition of assets	Disclose the date of asset acquisition or disposition, describe the assets, and identify the counterparty. Also note the nature and amount of consideration involved. Further, note the source of funds for an acquisition, if there is a material relationship between the company and the source of funds.
Item 2.02. Results of operations and financial condition	Disclose material non-public information regarding the company's results of operations or financial condition if it was publicly announced or released by someone acting on behalf of the company.
Item 2.03. Creation of a direct financial obligation	If the company enters into a material, direct financial obligation, disclose the date when the obligation began, describe the transaction, note the amount and terms of the obligation, and other material issues. If the company becomes directly or contingently liable for a material amount under an off-balance sheet arrangement, disclose the same information, as well as the material terms whereby it may become a direct obligation, the nature of any recourse provisions, and the undiscounted maximum amount of any future payments.
Item 2.04. Triggering events that accelerate or increase a direct financial obligation	If there was a triggering event that altered a direct financial obligation and the effect is material, disclose the date of the event, describe it, note the amount of the obligation, and the payment terms.
Item 2.05. Costs associated with exit or disposal activities	If the company commits to an exit or disposal plan, disclose the date of the commitment, describe the course of action, and estimate the range of costs for each major type of cost and in total.
Item 2.06. Material impairments	If the company concludes that there is a material impairment charge, disclose the date of this conclusion, describe the impaired assets, and the facts and circumstances leading to the conclusion. Also note the estimated amount of the impairment charge.
Item 3.01. Notice of delisting or failure to satisfy a continued listing rule	If the company has received notice that it does not satisfy a rule for continued listing on an exchange, disclose the date when any notice was received, the applicable rule not being satisfied, and actions the company will take in response to the notice. If the company has submitted an application to delist from an exchange, disclose the action taken and the date of the action.

Item Header	Description
Item 3.02. Unregistered sales of equity securities	If the company sells unregistered securities, state the date of sale and the title and amount of the securities sold. Also name the principal underwriters and the names of the persons to whom the securities were sold. Also note the aggregate offering price and the amount of any discounts or commissions paid. Also describe any terms under which the securities are convertible into company stock.
Item 3.03. Material modifications to rights of security holders	If there has been a material modification to the rights of security holders, disclose the modification date, the name of the affected class of securities, and the effect on the rights of the security holders.
Item 4.01. Changes in registrant's certifying accountant	Disclose whether the company's existing independent accountant has resigned or been dismissed. Also disclose whether a new independent accountant has been engaged.
Item 4.02. Non-reliance on previously issued financial statements or a related audit report or completed interim review	If the company concludes that previously issued financial statements contain errors and so should not be relied upon, disclose the date when this conclusion was reached and identify the financial statements and periods that cannot be relied upon. Also note the facts underlying this conclusion, and state whether the issue has been discussed with the company's independent accountant.
Item 5.01. Changes in control of registrant	If there is a change in control of the company, disclose the identity of the persons who acquired control, the date of the change in control, the basis of the control, the amount of consideration used by the acquiring person, the sources of funds used, the identity of the persons from whom control was assumed, and any arrangements between the old and new control groups.
Item 5.02. Departure of directors or certain officers; election of directors; appointment of certain officers; compensatory arrangements of certain officers	If a director has resigned or will not stand for re-election due to a disagreement with the company, disclose the date of the resignation or refusal to stand for election, the positions held by the director, and describe the circumstances. If the director has sent written correspondence to the company concerning this matter, attach it to the Form 8-K. If a senior manager of the company resigns from the company or is terminated, disclose the date of the event. If a new senior manager is hired, disclose the person's name, position, and date of appointment, and compensation arrangements.
Item 5.03. Amendments to articles of incorporation or bylaws; change in fiscal year	If the company amends its articles of incorporation or bylaws, disclose the effective date of the amendment, and describe the alteration. If the company changes its fiscal year, disclose the change date, and the date of the new fiscal year end.

Item Header	Description
Item 5.04. Temporary suspension of trading under registrant's employee benefit plans	When a director or officer of the company is subject to a blackout period for an equity security, disclose the reasons for the blackout period, a description of those transactions to be suspended, the class of securities subject to the blackout, and the expected beginning and ending dates of the blackout period.
Item 5.05. Amendments to the registrant's code of ethics, or waiver of a provision of the code of ethics	If there has been an amendment to or waiver of the company's code of ethics, disclose the date and nature of the event. If a waiver is involved, also state the name of the person to whom the waiver was granted.
Item 5.06. Change in shell company status	If the company was a shell company, and has ceased being classified as a shell, disclose the material terms of the transaction.
Item 5.07. Submission of matters to a vote of security holders	If any matters have been submitted to shareholders for a vote, disclose the date of the meeting, whether it was a special or annual meeting, the names of the directors elected, and a summarization of each matter voted upon at the meeting. Also state the number of votes cast for, against, and withheld on each voting matter, as well as by individual director (if there is a director election).
Item 5.08. Shareholder director nominations	If the company did not hold an annual meeting in the preceding year, or if the date of this year's meeting is more than 30 days from the date of the preceding year's meeting, disclose the date by which a nominating shareholder must submit notice on Schedule 14N, so that the company can include any director nominations by shareholders in its proxy materials.
Item 6.01. ABS informational and computational material	Disclose any informational and computational material for asset-backed securities.
Item 6.02. Change of servicer or trustee	If a servicer or trustee has resigned or been replaced, or if a new servicer has been appointed, disclose the date and nature of the event. For a new servicer, describe the material terms of the agreement and the servicer's duties.
Item 6.03. Change in credit enhancement or other external report	If the depositor becomes aware of any material enhancement or support that was previously applicable for any class of asset-backed securities, and which has been terminated other than by contract expiration or the completion by all parties of their obligations, disclose the date of termination, the identity of the parties providing enhancement or support, the terms and conditions of the enhancement or support, the circumstances of the termination, and any early termination penalties.

Item Header	Description
Item 6.04. Failure to make a required distribution	If distributions are not made to the holders of asset-backed securities by the required date, disclose the nature of the failure.
Item 6.05. Securities Act updating procedure	If any material pool characteristic of an offering of asset-backed securities differs by more than five percent from the prospectus description at the time of issuance, disclose the characteristics of the actual asset pool.
Item 7.01. Regulation FD disclosure	The company may elect to disclose information under the provisions of Regulation FD (Fair Disclosure).
Item 8.01. Other events	The company can, at its option, disclose any information that is not specifically identified elsewhere in the Form 8-K. This is typically only done if the company believes that the information will be of importance to the holders of its securities.
Item 9.01. Financial statements and exhibits	Attach the financial statements, pro forma financial information, and any other exhibits filed along with the Form 8-K.

Every Form 8-K must be filed within four business days of the event being disclosed. When a reportable event occurs on a weekend or holiday, the four-day rule begins on the next business day.

Summary

For the CFO of a publicly-held company, it may sometimes appear as though the *only* responsibility involves the filing of the Forms 10-Q and 10-K, because they take so much time to prepare. Never underestimate the workload associated with public company financial reporting – it is downright oppressive. We recommend that you conduct a thorough review of the time required to prepare the necessary filings, including a discussion of any concerns the auditors may have about the timeliness of work completion and errors found, and present these findings to senior management along with a request for additional resources. Otherwise, you may find that there is not sufficient time to engage in all of the other responsibilities of the CFO position.

Chapter 19
Share Management

Introduction

One of the primary goals that the CFO of a publicly-held company pursues is to attract liquidity; liquidity entails a high volume of trading in a company's stock. The liquidity goal is much easier to achieve if there are a large number of registered shares available for trading, which is known as *float*. The CFO can influence the management of a company's shares to improve the probability that liquidity will be achieved.

In this chapter, we describe many of the considerations involved in managing a company's shares to increase its float. We also address several techniques for selling small amounts of additional shares, discuss the advantages and disadvantages of dividends and stock buyback plans, and other similar issues.

Float Management

A large float creates a significant level of liquidity, which means that investors can easily buy and sell shares without any undue delays to find counter parties. Also, a large float means that investors can buy and sell large blocks of stock without having their actions impact the stock price, which is of particular importance to institutional investors, which routinely invest large amounts in a company's securities.

The CFO can have an impact on a company's float by paying attention to the following float management activities:

Activities to Increase the Float

- *Issue more shares.* When a company has the option of raising funds through a debt or equity issuance, the finance staff usually favors obtaining a loan, since it is (usually) quicker and less expensive to obtain than funds raised through a stock offering. However, if the company has an unusually small float, it could make quite a difference from a stock liquidity perspective to obtain funds through selling stock, and then registering those shares as soon as possible. Going to the trouble of issuing new shares may be less worthwhile if the company already has a sufficient float.

- *Register stock (company initiative).* If a company has a large amount of unregistered stock, consider having the company's securities attorneys file with the SEC for a stock registration. This will take a number of months to accomplish, as well as a significant amount of legal fees, but can be worthwhile if the result is a large amount of registered shares. Indeed, some shareholders may have *required* the company to register their shares as part of a private placement of the company's stock. Since these investors are likely to sell their shares immediately following registration, it increases the amount of readily available stock.

- *Register stock (employee initiative)*. If employees hold unregistered stock and the company has no plans to register the shares for them, then inform the employees of their right under the SEC's Rule 144 to have their shares automatically registered after a six month holding period. This can include the recommendation of brokerages to employees who can sell the shares for the employees once the holding period has been completed.

- *Only issue common stock*. When a company issues a wide range of securities, only some may be registered for trading. Alternatively, each type may be registered, but the volume of securities of each class represents too small a float to create an active market. Accordingly, consider simplifying the capital structure of the business, so that it is only comprised of a large pool of common stock. At a minimum, keep an offer open to the holders of all other types of securities to swap them for whatever number of common shares appears appropriate, so that the common stock float gradually increases over time.

- *Minimize stock repurchases*. When a company has an excess amount of cash, a common use is to repurchase some of the outstanding stock. Doing so tends to prop up the stock price, and also increases the earnings per share for the remaining shares. However, a stock repurchasing initiative also reduces the float. This is a minor issue when a company already has a large float. Nonetheless, if the amount of the repurchase is expected to be large, or if the existing float is small, it may not be a good idea to repurchase shares.

- *Break up stock blocks*. A company may have a large number of registered shares outstanding and yet have a relatively small float, if some investors have accumulated large positions in the company's stock. These large holdings have effectively withdrawn stock from circulation, leaving a vastly smaller effective float. It may be worthwhile to contact these investors about selling off at least a portion of their holdings, which may represent a substantial increase in the size of the available float.

Activities to Delay Stock Sales

If a company has issued large amounts of shares as payment for acquisitions, it may be faced with potentially massive stock sales when the holders of those shares want to convert their holdings to cash. This intense selling pressure can seriously depress the stock price, especially when shareholders want to sell so many shares that it may take days or weeks of selling to liquidate their positions. This aggravation can be ameliorated to some extent by imposing *lock-up agreements* on the new recipients of company stock. Under a lock-up agreement, shareholders are constrained from selling their shares for a certain period of time, such as six months. Alternatively, the agreement may state that a shareholder can only sell in certain volumes per time period, such as 10,000 shares per month. Thus, the lock-up agreement spreads the downward price pressure over a longer period of time; during that time, a company can work on increasing its float, which thereby shrinks the proportional impact of the shares being sold.

In short, the CFO should pay continual attention to the size of the float, and take steps to keep it as large as possible. This is especially important in a smaller firm, where there is a tendency for the float to shrink over time, reducing the ability of investors to easily move in and out of ownership positions.

The Direct Stock Purchase Plan

A company may set up a direct stock purchase plan (DSPP), under which shareholders can buy shares directly from the company's stock transfer agent without going through a stockbroker. This approach avoids paying a stockbroker commission. To encourage buying through a DSPP, a company may offer a discount to the current market price of the stock.

There is usually a maximum purchase amount built into a DSPP in order to control the amount of shares purchased through the plan. However, if a company wants to raise a significant amount of new capital, it can waive the maximum purchase limitation to bring in more cash. Conversely, if the market price of the stock drops too low, the company can freeze the DSPP and not allow any additional purchases until such time as the stock price increases again.

A DSPP is attractive to the CFO, because it tends to attract long-term investors. Other investors move in and out of stock positions more quickly, and so would have little interest in a DSPP that may require a long period of time to acquire a significant number of shares.

The Employee Stock Purchase Plan

A public company can create an employee stock purchase plan (ESPP), under which employees make regular payments (usually through payroll deductions) to purchase shares of the company's stock at regular intervals. The shares do not involve a stockbroker commission, and may be offered at a modest discount to the current market price.

A company can file a Form S-8 with the SEC to register the shares issued to employees under an ESPP; this is an inexpensive and quick registration method, and allows employees to sell their shares relatively quickly.

An ESPP does not usually generate a great deal of cash for a company, and requires a modest amount of administrative overhead. However, it *does* improve the level of employee engagement with the business, and can be considered part of the employee benefits package.

Dividend Reinvestment Plans

Dividends are a distribution of a company's earnings, and are paid from a company's retained earnings. A company can set up a dividend reinvestment plan

(DRIP), under which shareholders can elect to reinvest their dividends in the purchase of additional company shares. The company can purchase shares through the plan on the open market, which has the advantage of ensuring that the stock is already registered. Alternatively, the company can issue new shares and have them registered, thereby increasing the float.

From the perspective of an investor, a DRIP reduces the cost of acquiring shares, since no stockbroker is involved, and therefore no stockbroker commission. Also, since cash from dividends is being reinvested, a DRIP is essentially a long-term savings plan.

From the perspective of the company, dividends are being retained within the business, which increases the amount of cash available for a variety of other purposes.

Stock Splits

If a company enjoys a continuing run-up in the price of its stock, the price may eventually be so high that it prevents individual investors from buying large blocks of stock. The resulting reduction in demand is not large, and is unlikely to have a significant impact on the price of the stock. Nonetheless, companies occasionally choose to split their stock, so that one share is converted into two or more shares. The result is a reduction in the stock price to a level that is presumably more affordable for investors.

EXAMPLE

An investor holds 100 shares of stock that are currently trading at $100 each. The market value of these shares is $10,000 (calculated as 100 shares × $100 each). The issuing company decides to initiate a 1-for-5 stock split. This means that the investor swaps out his old certificate for 100 shares for a new one for 500 shares. The market price should drop to $20 to reflect the increased number of shares, which means that the investor should still have holdings worth $10,000 (calculated as 500 shares × $20 each).

The board of directors should be cautious about authorizing excessively large stock splits, since the result drops the stock price substantially lower; any additional decline in the price of the stock could classify it as a penny stock, at which point institutional investors may be required by their investment rules to sell the stock.

If a lower share price will increase trading volume, then the CFO should certainly be in favor of a stock split. However, if the price drops so low that some investors are selling off their positions, the CFO might instead recommend a *reverse stock split*, where the company exchanges a larger number of shares for a smaller number of shares. Doing so should increase the stock price to the point where investors will feel more comfortable investing in the stock.

EXAMPLE

An investor holds 100 shares of stock that are currently trading at $2 each. The market value of these shares is $200 (calculated as 100 shares × $2 each). The issuing company decides to initiate a 10-for-1 reverse stock split. This means that the investor swaps out his old certificate for 100 shares for a new one for 10 shares. The market price should increase to $20 to reflect the reduced number of shares, which means that the investor should still have holdings worth $200 (calculated as 10 shares × $20 each).

In general, there is no real advantage to a stock split from the perspective of benefits experienced by the investor. However, there is a definite cost associated with a stock split from the perspective of the company, since there are a number of legal, accounting, and stock recordkeeping issues that must be addressed whenever a split is authorized.

Dividend Payments

The decision to issue dividends to shareholders is made by the board of directors. If a company is planning to issue a dividend for the first time, it is worthwhile for the CFO to discuss the issue with the board before they approve the transaction. When a company has followed a consistent revenue and earnings growth path, a reasonable proportion of its investors are probably investing in the company to take advantage of the increases in its stock price that are caused by company growth. A rapidly growing company is presumed to need all of its cash to fund growth, so no dividend is expected. Once the company issues a dividend, these growth-oriented investors will assume that the company is not planning to grow as fast, and so will sell the stock. They will be replaced by a different group of investors who are more interested in earning dividend income.

The change in the type of investor is neither good nor bad, but it does mean that there will be an increased amount of turnover among shareholders for a period of time. During this transition period, it is possible that the share price will be somewhat more volatile than usual.

If the board wants to find a use for the company's excess cash, but does not want to turn away its growth-oriented investors, then alternative uses for the cash are making acquisitions or paying off liabilities.

If the board of directors elects to go forward with an initial dividend payment, it is important to signal to the marketplace that the company intends to continue to issue dividends at regular intervals. Otherwise, a one-time distribution to shareholders via a dividend will merely send the growth investors to the exits without creating an incentive for income investors to take their place, thereby creating downward pressure on the stock price.

Tip: When initially announcing a dividend, point out the timing and expected size of future dividends, so that the investment community can properly value the shares on which dividends are being paid.

When embarking on a strategy of issuing ongoing dividends, it is of some importance to begin with a small dividend that the company can easily support from its current resources and expected cash flows. By doing so, the board can comfortably establish a gradual increase in the size of the dividend that the investment community can rely upon, which should result in a slow increase in the price of the company's stock. Conversely, the worst type of dividend is one that is so large that the company has a difficult time scraping together the cash needed to pay it, which can endanger the ability of the company to operate on an ongoing basis.

It is also useful for the board of directors to consider the negative implications of not having sufficient cash to continue paying a dividend. If this were to happen, the income-oriented investors who are holding the stock precisely because of those dividends will sell their shares; this will trigger a supply and demand imbalance that will lower the price of the stock. Eventually, value-oriented investors will buy the stock when it has dropped by a sufficient amount, in hopes of a recovery in the stock price. Nonetheless, a dividend cancellation almost always triggers a steep stock price decline.

In summary, the board of directors should think long and hard about the decision to begin issuing dividends. Dividends work best when followed consistently over a long period of time, but doing so requires rock-solid cash flows. Any inability to meet a dividend obligation will trigger a rapid stock price decline. Thus, always consider a vote to issue dividends as a long-term strategic issue, not just a short-term payout.

The Stock Buyback Option

Companies sometimes engage in stock buybacks, where the board of directors authorizes that a certain amount of cash be set aside for a repurchase program. There are three reasons why a company may engage in a buyback:

- To reduce the number of shares outstanding; this should increase the amount of earnings per share, and therefore provide pressure to increase the share price.
- Because management believes that the share price is currently too low, and does not adequately reflect the true market value of the business. Thus, if a buyback plan is announced that the company will buy back shares whenever the share price falls below a certain price point, there will be a tendency for the stock price to stay above that trigger point.
- To mop up excess shares that have been created through the issuance of stock options and warrants.

EXAMPLE

Hammer Industries has 5,000,000 shares of its common stock outstanding. These shares currently trade at $20. In the fiscal year just ended, Hammer reported net profits of $2,000,000, which results in reported earnings per share of $0.40 (calculated as $2,000,000 profits ÷ 5,000,000 shares).

Hammer's board of directors approves a $10,000,000 stock buyback. At the current $20 market price, this means the company can acquire 500,000 shares. By doing so, there will now be 4,500,000 shares outstanding. The altered share total changes the earnings per share figure to $0.444.

Tip: In any press release mentioning a stock buyback, be sure to mention how long the company has been buying back shares and the amount of cash still reserved for more repurchases, so that investors get the impression that the company has a long-term commitment to supporting its stock price.

There are multiple problems with a stock buyback. One is certainly float management, since there will be fewer shares in circulation after the buyback has been completed, which reduces the liquidity of the stock. If a company already suffers from an excessively small float, this is a valid objection to a buyback.

Another problem is that companies have a strong tendency to acquire shares when they are flush with cash, which is usually at a point in their life cycles when they have a very high stock price. Thus, they are converting a relatively small number of shares to treasury stock in exchange for a large amount of cash, which does little to boost the earnings per share for the remaining shares outstanding. This is the reverse of what would be considered prudent behavior for an investor, who attempts to buy low and sell high. If a company were as prudent as an investor, it would only buy back shares when its stock price was very low.

Yet another issue is that a buyback signals to the investment community that a company has more cash than it needs for its operations, so growth-oriented investors suspect that the company will not grow as fast in the future as it has in the past. This signal may cause growth investors to sell the stock. Conversely, the company has not used its cash to issue dividends, so it has *not* sent a signal that will attract income-oriented investors who are in search of a reliable dividend stream. Thus, a buyback tends to create selling pressure among one group if investors, while not attracting any new investors.

When a company has excess cash, it should consider a stock buyback to be one of the last potential uses for that cash. Instead, the sequence of possible uses should roughly follow this series of decision options:

1. *Invest in company operations.* This is assumed to be the best profit generator.
2. *Acquire related companies.* This approach is riskier than internal growth, but still focuses the company on its primary markets.
3. *Pay down debt.* This reduces the risk of not paying back loans. The approach can be extended to paying off leases and even reducing the amount of accounts payable.
4. *Build a reserve.* There is nothing wrong with building a large cash reserve to guard against a downturn in the company's fortunes.

5. *Buy back stock.* If all of the preceding steps have been taken, only then is a buyback warranted, and only if the stock is trading at a reasonably low price.

The Stock Repurchase Safe Harbor Provision

Under the Securities Exchange Act, a company is not allowed to enter into any transactions related to its securities that will affect their prices or trading volumes. A stock buyback program is very likely to breach this provision, so the SEC promulgated Rule 10b-18 to create a safe harbor provision for companies engaged in stock buybacks.

To qualify for the safe harbor provision, a company must ensure that its stock buyback program complies with the following four conditions on a daily basis:

- *Purchase centralization.* Buyback purchases made on behalf of the company must be made by a single broker/dealer on any given day.
- *Time of purchases.* A buyback purchase must not be the opening purchase of the day or within the last 30 minutes before the close of trading. However, a company with a public float of at least $150 million and an average daily trading volume of at least $1 million can purchase shares until 10 minutes before the close of trading.
- *Price of purchases.* Buyback purchases must be at prices that do not exceed the higher of the highest independent bid or the last independent transaction price. If the shares are not quoted on an organized exchange, then the price cannot be higher than the highest bid obtained from three independent dealers.
- *Volume of purchases.* The total volume of buyback purchases in a single day cannot exceed 25% of the average daily trading volume for that security. The SEC does allow one block trade per week that is not subject to this 25% limitation, but only on the condition that the company makes no other buyback trades that day.

> **Tip:** The Rule 10b-18 safe harbor provision only applies to buybacks of common stock. It does not apply to any other types of securities.

In short, the SEC's trading rules for a buyback program are designed to dampen the impact of buyback trades on the price of a company's stock, using a combination of controls over the centralization, timing, price points, and volume of purchases made.

Odd Lot Shareholders

The CFO normally has an intense interest in increasing the number of shares in circulation, as well as the number of shareholders. However, it is not cost-effective to maintain a large number of odd lot shareholders. An odd lot shareholder is an investor who holds less than 100 shares of a company's stock. The annual cost of issuing proxy statements and annual reports to odd lot shareholders is not considered cost-effective, so many CFOs take the position that they should either be eliminated or encouraged to increase their share holdings.

An additional factor favoring the elimination of odd lot shareholders arises when a public company wants to go private. Doing so requires a steep reduction in the number of shareholders, and one of the least expensive ways to achieve this reduction is the elimination of odd lot shareholders, since the company must buy back so few shares from them.

Odd lot shareholdings tend to form an unusually large proportion of the shareholder base in a public shell company (see the Going Public and Going Private chapter). If a company goes public through the purchase of a shell entity, it may find that it is saddled with a large number of odd lot shareholders who are completely inactive.

There are three ways to mitigate the odd lot shareholder conundrum, which are as follows:

- *Buy back shares*. The company could contact odd lot shareholders and offer to buy back their shares. This requires a certain amount of labor, so a case can be made that it is even less cost-effective to buy back these shares than it is to leave them alone. Also, buying back shares can run afoul of the SEC's rules regarding tender offers, the avoidance of which requires widely-spaced transactions with individual shareholders.
- *Offer direct stock purchase plan*. The company can go out of its way to contact odd lot shareholders to make them aware of the company's direct stock purchase plan (see the Direct Stock Purchase Plan section). A few of the shareholders may take advantage of it to increase their shareholdings, thereby boosting them out of the odd lot classification.
- *Reverse stock split*. A company can conduct a reverse stock split, where a large number of shares are exchanged for a smaller number of shares. For example, a 100-to-1 reverse split would reduce the holdings of a shareholder who owns 99 shares to a fraction of one share, which allows the company to cash him out. Once the smaller shareholders have been cashed out in this manner, the company can conduct a forward stock split (such as a 1-to-100 split) to return the remaining shareholders to their pre-existing shareholding levels. The disadvantage of this approach is that it requires shareholder approval, some administrative effort, and the cash needed to pay off the fractional share holdings.

The odd lot shareholding issue never really goes away, because there are always methods by which someone might come into ownership of just a few shares. For example, the estate of a large shareholder may distribute his holdings among many relatives upon his death, or a reverse stock split may convert a large share holding into a small one, or employees may be issued small stock grants. Thus, the CFO should periodically review the number of odd lot shareholdings and decide whether steps should be taken to reduce their number.

Summary

Whenever a public company makes a decision that will impact its float, the CFO should make those recommendations needed to ensure that a sufficient number of registered shares are available for trading. Otherwise, institutional investors will be less likely to take stock positions in the company, and the firm may struggle to attract interest from other investors who may also be concerned about holding a potentially illiquid stock.

When a company makes a change to any part of its stock management program, the CFO should reconsider the entire marketing message being sent out to the investment community, to ensure that the message continues to reflect the actions of the company. For example, issuing a dividend may bring investors to question whether a company is still in growth mode, or if it has now become a mature business. Similarly, a stock buyback implies that a company can no longer find an in-house use for its available cash, which also implies a lack of growth prospects.

Chapter 20
Information Technology

Introduction

The information technology (IT) area may provide a company with a large part of its competitive advantage, as well as the ability to reduce costs. Even if IT does not contribute in these areas, it may still comprise a large part of the capital expenditures of a business. Given these factors, the CFO should have a considerable interest in how funds are spent in the IT area, and on the types of systems in which a company invests.

In this chapter, we review the various classifications of information technology and which ones confer a competitive advantage, as well as additional detail on certain of the more common types of software that a company may consider installing.

Types of Information Technology

One of the larger competitive advantages that a business can have is its technology infrastructure. The advantage is more pronounced in some industries than others, but every industry can benefit to some extent from having a well-defined technology strategy that is closely adhered to.

The investment in technology is usually managed by the chief technology officer (CTO), but the CFO can have significant input into what that investment will be. Not all CFOs have a deeply ingrained knowledge of (or love for) technology, but it is useful to understand how general technology concepts can be applied to a business. In particular, note that technology investments can be divided into three areas, not all of which have the same strategic impact on a business. These areas are:

- *Transaction processing.* Almost every business has a system for recording business transactions and aggregating the information for financial reporting and other purposes. This is a "nuts and bolts" application that underlies all other technology investments. It can range from a simple accounting system with one user to a comprehensive enterprise resource planning system that encompasses the entire business. Other examples of transaction processing systems are customer relationship management systems, just-in-time manufacturing systems, and employee payroll self-service systems.
- *Analytical applications.* These are systems that aggregate information in different ways and present it for analysis. Analytical applications give a company important clues about how to shape its strategic and tactical actions in the marketplace. For example, analysis might reveal that a company is generating large losses in a particular sales region, which triggers the withdrawal of the company from that region.

- *Transformational applications.* These are the small number of carefully targeted applications that drive a company's business. For example, it may be the reservation system used by an airline or the product search capability used by an online retailer. This type of application is more likely to be custom-made, and may require significant cultural and process changes within a business to make it fully operational.

The CFO should be aware of the amount of funding proposed for each of these three categories of IT investment. In all too many cases, the IT department wants to spend the bulk of its funds on the transaction processing area, either for the replacement or extension of the existing IT infrastructure. While these investments are important, they do not provide a major competitive advantage to a business, since competitors likely have similar systems. Instead, more attention should be paid to transformational applications, as well as to the effort required to fully integrate these applications into the business. By doing so, a company can build a large market share lead over its competitors that will take them years to overcome.

There are many types of transformational applications. If a company has not closely examined its operations and those of its competitors, it may not even be aware that any transformational applications exist. The following is a list of such applications. Note that they are radically different from the transaction processing or analytical applications.

- *Computer aided design systems.* The intent is to speed up the product design process.
- *Rapid prototyping systems.* The intent is to build product prototypes at high speed.
- *Product design system for customers.* Customers can mix and match from various components to create their own products.
- *Customer purchasing trends.* A system tracks what customers have bought in the past and uses this information to suggest additional purchases to them.
- *Order completion status.* Customers can track the status of their orders to see if they have been completed yet, as well as the anticipated delivery date.

While transformational applications are of the most importance to a business, it is also useful to have a broad range of analysis applications, since they provide clues to how operations can be improved, and may also indicate areas in which transformational applications should be installed. Here are several examples of analytical applications:

- Activity-based costing
- Complaint analysis
- Deduction analysis
- Measurement of profitability at the customer level
- Product and process quality analysis
- Regulatory compliance analysis

- Scenario planning
- Throughput analysis

In addition to these investments in applications, the CFO should be aware of the physical IT infrastructure that a business must continually invest in, which includes the following items:

- Firewalls
- Local area networks
- Physical security
- Server farms
- User-level computer equipment

In short, the CFO needs to look at the general allocations of funds and other resources amongst the categories of IT expenditures noted here, and ensure that a sufficient proportion is being expended in areas that extend the competitive advantage of the business. In many cases, *no* funds are being allocated to transformational applications, which may require massive persuasive efforts by the CFO to correct. The CTO may not even be aware of these issues, being more deeply involved at the tactical level with the costs and implementation plans for each individual project.

Tip: If most IT resources are being used to maintain existing systems, it may be time to replace custom-developed systems with commercial off-the-shelf software. Doing so shifts the maintenance burden to software suppliers.

Technology Ranking Methods

It is quite likely that more IT projects have been requested than can be paid for with the amount of funds available. The CFO will likely be involved in the decisions to proceed with some projects and hold back on others. The standard financial analysis approach to this conundrum is to only invest in those projects having the highest net present value (NPV) or internal rate of return. However, doing so substitutes a highly quantitative approach for what should be the consideration of many other factors – few of which can be resolved with an NPV calculation. Consider instead the following approach to ranking projects, presented in declining order of priority:

1. *Set aside operational costs.* A large part of the IT budget must be reserved for ongoing maintenance of the existing system, which includes the re-placement of hardware at regular intervals, department staffing, and the annual maintenance fees on packaged software. This one step will take away a large part of the available funding.
2. *Set aside transformation funds.* Set aside a percentage of the remaining funding for use solely on transformational projects. If this is not done up front, it is quite likely that a variety of other projects will soak up all remaining cash, leaving nothing for these key projects.

3. *Bottleneck funding.* If the company could immediately increase its sales by investing in a bottleneck activity, it makes sense to do so. This decision should be subject to an analysis of exactly how much additional capacity is needed, since there is a risk of investing too much and then having excess capacity.

4. *Forced ranking.* All of the key needs having now been met, remaining projects can be compared to each other to determine which are most likely to improve the company's efficiency, competitive stance, data gathering capabilities, and other factors. This ranking can be refined to the point where there is general agreement regarding which residual projects will not be funded.

Note that the suggested ranking system does not mention net present value. At most, NPV can be used to decide between two projects that are otherwise considered equal. In most cases, strategic considerations should trump the use of NPV in selecting IT projects for funding.

Technology Usage Based on Strategy

The preceding discussion of strategy makes it appear as though the types of IT investments will vary radically by company. This is true to some extent, since each business in an industry uses IT to seek out and defend its own niche. However, there will also be a baseline set of applications that every company will probably need to install in order to remain competitive, on top of which additional transformational IT investments can be made. Consider the following industry-specific situations:

- *Automobile manufacturing.* In order to be competitive, a company must have a manufacturing planning or just-in-time system, as well as on-line linkages with its suppliers to coordinate the flow of components to automobile assembly areas. A transformational investment in this area could be an on-line ordering system for customers, so that they can configure what they want to buy.

- *Consulting company.* In order to be competitive, a business must have a time tracking system that can be used to bill customers, as well as an employee productivity tracking tool to monitor billable hours. A transformational investment is a community knowledge base that allows employees to post questions regarding their client projects, and obtain answers from internal subject matter experts.

- *Consumer products company.* In order to be competitive, a business must be able to manufacture products with a specific set of features and within a designated price point, which could be achieved by outsourcing production to a low-cost manufacturing area. A transformational investment would be an investment in software that allows for rapid prototyping, so the company can drastically shrink its product development cycle.

338

- *Retail store.* In order to be competitive, there must be a sales tracking system that also updates available inventory as items are sold. A transformational investment could be an app that allows customers to order items online and have them waiting in the customer service area for pickup.

In short, the baseline IT investment varies by industry, as do the possible transformational investments. These differences are caused by variations in the flow of goods and services, how companies deal with customers, how products are developed, and a variety of other factors.

We now turn to a discussion of several IT systems that are likely to rank high in the discussions for a company's future IT infrastructure.

Cloud Computing

The general concept of cloud computing is that a company moves its data to a location outside of the company. More specifically, it usually means that an outside service provider is selling software as a service (SaaS), so that someone else provides the software, updates the software, manages server farms, and basically takes over large swathes of a company's IT function. The result can be a substantial reduction in costs, as well as an extraordinarily fast ramp-up time on a new system.

The cloud computing concept is a tempting one for those companies that seem unable to achieve a well-managed IT department in-house, or one whose costs are spiraling out of control. If this is the situation, a business may elect to try cloud computing more out of exasperation with its own systems than the features and benefits of the SaaS being contemplated.

Indeed, the SaaS concept has reached the point where entire enterprise-wide systems can now be supported elsewhere, typically for a monthly charge per user. This approach may be quite appealing for newer businesses that cannot afford the significant expenditures required for in-house IT systems. Also, a newer business has not yet implemented its own policies and procedures, and so can easily adapt to the requirements of whatever SaaS system it chooses.

The concept is less appealing for a company with a number of legacy systems, since the level of in-house customization may be so great that it is not possible to entirely switch to a cloud-based system. Also, such a company will probably need custom interfaces between its remaining systems and those systems it has been able to outsource. These interfaces may require periodic custom adjustments over time, as the outsourced or internal systems are modified. Also, switching to a new system may require procedural changes, which the employees of an older company may be less willing to accept.

Despite the issues just noted, cloud computing can provide a singularly large cost-reduction benefit. In addition, moving the technical aspects of IT to a supplier means that the CFO can focus on the cost-benefit of the monthly payments required for an SaaS system, rather than muddling through a discussion about the need for technical upgrades to outmoded systems.

339

GRC Software

A larger organization might consider investing in governance, risk, and compliance (GRC) software. This software is designed to show if a company is properly managed, takes appropriate risks, meets its compliance obligations, and properly disseminates its policies and procedures to employees.

A GRC system integrates a variety of governance, risk, and compliance objectives into an integrated set of software modules that may, in turn, be linked to various company databases. These systems can include the following features:

- *Environment, health, and safety*. The software tracks air emissions, waste discharge, greenhouse gas emissions, chemicals inventory, permitting, and performance metrics.
- *Financial controls*. The system can monitor controls compliance.
- *Internal audit*. The software supports any audit methodology in creating a framework for managing audits.
- *Risk management*. The system identifies risks, aggregates them across departments, provides incident tracking, and documentation of corrective actions.
- *Risk modeling*. The software can be used to monitor and model operational risks.
- *Rules engine*. The software accepts a download of a company's general ledger, and uses investigative rules to pinpoint areas of the financial results and financial position that could pose material hazards to the business.
- *Survey publishing*. If a compliance organization requires that employees answer a specific set of questions, a questionnaire module can issue questions to designated employees regarding policies and procedures, which the system then aggregates and issues in a standardized report format.

GRC software is expensive enough to be out of range for smaller businesses, which must rely upon an assemblage of smaller, possibly home-grown systems for their GRC needs. Even larger organizations will find that the multi-month implementation and training time required for a GRC system may result in a lengthy payback period.

> **Tip:** A GRC system will not necessarily prevent a governance, risk, or compliance issue from occurring. The system can flag a likely problem, but an employee can still choose to ignore the issue.

Enterprise Resource Planning Systems

Enterprise resource planning (ERP) is an integrated software package that supports all of a company's functional areas. Thus, it can handle the transactional requirements of the accounting, customer service, manufacturing, sales, warehousing, and other departments. Many ERP systems also accept data from a company's customers and suppliers for supply chain management purposes, so that the system surpasses the traditional boundaries of a corporation.

The great advantage of an ERP system is that *all* corporate data is integrated, so data is only entered into the system once (as opposed to the "silo" approach, where information is entered into the separate software packages used by each department). With an integrated ERP system, companies find that their transaction error rates decline, while many tasks that formerly required manual effort are now entirely automated. Also, subject to security issues, employees can access information in other departments that was previously difficult to obtain, or only with the help of special programming by the IT department.

The downside of an ERP system is its extreme complexity. The software requires a great deal of time to set up, as well as to convert a company's existing data into it. Also, because ERP systems can only be configured in a limited number of ways, most companies will find that they must alter their operating procedures to fit the software, rather than altering the software to fit their procedures. These changes call for a large training expenditure, and may result in resistance from those employees accustomed to the old system. These issues call for an implementation budget in the millions of dollars, and several years of intensive effort to complete.

A less-expensive alternative to an ERP system is to assemble only those software modules from various software vendors that are considered most crucial to company operations, and create custom interfaces to transfer information between the modules. This approach does not provide a comprehensive, company-wide solution and usually requires the updating of interfaces whenever a software upgrade is installed. However, it allows for the use of industry-specific modules that closely fit the needs of a business. This approach works best for smaller businesses that cannot afford a comprehensive ERP solution.

Sales Force Automation Software

From the perspective of the CFO, perhaps the most important element of software that tracks sales activities is the sales pipeline. Investors are typically clamoring for insights into a company's future sales, and if the CFO responds with predictions, they must be founded upon detailed information, not wild guesses. For a public company, missing an earnings forecast can lead to a serious stock price decline, which makes the sales pipeline feature especially important. Furthermore, missing an earnings forecast creates a notable increase in the odds that a CFO's employment will be terminated.

A sales pipeline system should identify the number of initial contacts, presentations made, proposals made, final deal negotiations, and so forth, along with deal closing probabilities. The CFO can compare this information to historical outcomes to develop success percentages at each stage of the sales process, which are then used to derive revenue forecasts.

A crucially important factor in the success of sales force automation software is its usage level by the sales staff. The sales manager must periodically reinforce the need for this tool, so that sales information is updated and reviewed continually.

Otherwise, information pertaining to sales leads will never be entered, or will not be updated, resulting in incorrect forecasts.

Tip: Sales forecasting is not a good place in which to use electronic spreadsheets, since format variations will proliferate, making it difficult to aggregate sales information.

Summary

The CFO is one of the primary drivers of strategy in a business. In this role, it is of critical importance to understand which types of information technology are of most use in creating a competitive advantage, and which other investments are primarily intended to maintain existing systems. It is all too common for a company to invest all of its excess funds in enhancements or replacements of existing systems, without reserving any cash for transformational IT projects.

In this chapter, we have not dealt with the hands-on management of the IT function by the CFO, since we assume that the CFO deals with information technology primarily from a strategic investment perspective. The deepest level of detail to which the CFO should go is in ascertaining whether the IT department and the company as a whole have the ability to implement an IT project. If the company does not have the correct mix of subject matter experts, software developers, trainers, and so forth, it is necessary to determine whether additional resources should be brought in to assist, or whether the odds of success are simply too low to proceed. Thus, the CFO remains in the position of allocating resources, rather than managing the IT function.

Glossary

A

Accredited investor. An investor who is defined by the Securities and Exchange Commission as being financially sophisticated.

ACH debit. An electronic transaction initiated by the payee to shift funds from the payer's account to the payee's account.

Automated control. A control that is built into the computer systems used to operate a business.

Average daily trading volume. The average daily trading volume reported for a security during the preceding four calendar weeks.

B

Block. A quantity of stock that either has a purchase price of $200,000 or more, or is at least 5,000 shares and has a purchase price of at least $50,000, or is at least 20 round lots of the security and totals 150 percent or more of the trading volume for that security.

Borrowing base. The total amount of collateral against which a lender will lend funds to a business.

Breakeven. The sales level at which a business earns a profit of exactly zero, and is computed by dividing all fixed costs by the average gross margin percentage.

Budgetary slack. When the people involved in creating a budget deliberately under-estimate the amount of revenue to be generated, or over-estimate the amount of expenses to be incurred.

C

Capital expenditure. A payment made to acquire or upgrade an asset. It is recorded as an asset, rather than charging it immediately to expense.

Call option. An agreement giving the buyer the right to buy an investment instrument at a certain price and within a certain time period.

Capital lease. A lease in which the lessor only finances the lease, and all other rights of ownership transfer to the lessee.

Chief operating decision maker. A person who is responsible for making decisions about resource allocations to the segments of a business, and for evaluating those segments.

Cloud computing. The use of remote servers to store and process data over the Internet.

Collateral. An asset that a borrower has pledged as security for a loan.

Control. A means by which we gain a reasonable assurance that a business will operate as planned, that its financial results are fairly reported, and that it complies with laws and regulations.

Control premium. The additional value associated with shares that will give the purchaser control over a business.

Cost of capital. The cost of debt and equity used by a business. It is comprised of debt, preferred stock, and common stock.

Cloud computing. The use of remote servers to store and process data over the Internet.

Counterparty. The other party that engages in a financial transaction. For example, if a company sells an asset, there is a counterparty that buys the asset.

Covenants. Conditions related to company operations and practices that are imposed by lenders.

Credit rating agency. An entity that assigns ratings to debt issuers or directly to debt instruments.

D

Detective control. A control designed to spot control breaches after they have already occurred.

Discount rate. The interest rate used to discount a stream of future cash flows to their present value.

Dividend. The distribution of cash or other assets to a class of company shareholders by the company in which they hold shares, as authorized by its board of directors.

E

Earnings call. A conference call between the senior management team of a public company and the investment community, to discuss the company's financial results.

Earnings credit. The interest paid on the funds in a bank account, to be used to offset account fees.

Earnings per share. A company's net income divided by the weighted-average number of shares outstanding.

Earnout. An additional payment made to the shareholders of an acquired company if it can meet certain performance objectives.

EBITDA. The earnings before interest, taxes, depreciation, and amortization. It is a rough measure of the cash flows of a business.

Effective interest rate. The actual interest rate earned, based on actual proceeds divided by the amount of the initial investment.

Employee stock purchase plan. A company program under which employees can buy company shares, sometimes at a discount, through ongoing payroll deductions.

Enterprise resource planning. An integrated software package that supports all of a company's functional areas.

Expected loss. The probability that a loss will occur, multiplied by the potential size of the loss.

Expiry date. The expiration date of a contract.

F

Float. The number of shares in a public company that are currently available for trading by the public. This does not include restricted stock.

Form 10-K. A document filed annually with the SEC by a publicly-held company, containing its audited financial statements and supporting commentary.

Form 10-Q. A document filed quarterly with the SEC by a publicly-held company, containing its audited financial statements and supporting commentary.

Form 8-K. A document filed with the SEC by a publicly-held company, to announce a variety of pre-defined significant changes impacting the company.

Form S-1. The initial registration form required by the SEC for the issuance of securities by publicly-held companies.

Form S-8. A document filed with the SEC by a publicly-held company, to register shares issued to employees through benefit or incentive plans.

Functional currency. The currency that an entity uses in the majority of its business transactions.

G

Goodwill. The difference between the purchase price of an acquisition and the amount of the price not assigned to the assets and liabilities obtained in the acquisition.

Guidance. Estimates of future earnings that a business makes to the investment community.

H

Hedging. Actions taken to reduce the volatility of cash flows, earnings, and/or the value of investments.

Held-to-maturity security. A security having a fixed maturity, for which the holding entity has both the ability and the intention to hold it to maturity.

Hypothecation. The pledging of assets as loan collateral; usually refers to the debit balance in a margin account.

Glossary

I

Incremental cost. The extra cost associated with manufacturing one additional unit of production.

Initial public offering. The first offering of the stock of a privately-held business to the investing public.

Institutional investor. An entity that buys and sells securities in sufficiently large quantities to obtain reduced commissions and other preferential treatment.

Insurance. A contract under which an insurance company agrees to provide financial protection against certain losses.

Investment banker. A person who raises capital on behalf of businesses, and who may also engage in brokering the sale of businesses.

L

Laddering. The strategy of investing in a set of securities having different maturities.

Last in, first out method. A method of inventory valuation that operates under the assumption that the last goods purchased are the first goods sold.

Lease. An agreement under which the lessee makes periodic payments to the lessor for the use of an asset, while the lessor owns the asset associated with the lease.

Line of credit. A commitment from a lender to pay a company whenever it needs cash, up to a pre-set maximum limit. A line of credit is generally secured by company assets.

Lockup agreement. A legal agreement under which an individual (usually a company insider) cannot sell shares in a business for a specific period of time.

London interbank offered rate. An interest rate at which banks borrow funds from each other in the London interbank market. LIBOR is based on the deposit rate for loans between the most financially-secure banks.

Lower of cost or market rule. A rule requiring inventory to be recorded at the lower of its cost or the current market price.

M

Manual control. A control that requires a person to perform it.

Marginal cost. The cost to create one more unit of a product.

Mark to market. The revaluation of a security to reflect its current market price, rather than the cost at which it was purchased.

Market maker. A broker-dealer that facilitates trading in a security by displaying buy and sell quotations for the issuing company's shares, for which it may sell from its own inventory.

Markup percentage. A percentage increase in the cost of a product to arrive at its selling price.

N

NASDAQ. A computerized system that provides price quotations and facilitates the purchase and sale of securities.

Notional amount. The face amount used to calculate payments on a financial instrument, such as an option or interest rate swap.

O

Odd lot shareholder. A shareholder who holds less than 100 shares of the stock of a company.

Operating lease. The rental of an asset from a lessor.

Over the counter bulletin board. A stock listing service that shows real-time quotes, last-sale prices, and volume information for securities that are not listed on a stock exchange, but which are current in their SEC filings.

Overdraft. A bank loan to cover checks that would otherwise be rejected due to a lack of funds.

P

Paydex. A score issued by Dun & Bradstreet to businesses, indicating the promptness of their payments to creditors.

Penny stock. A stock that trades at a price below $5. The resulting low capitalization of companies whose shares are classified as penny stock makes them speculative investments.

Piggyback rights. An investor's right to have his unregistered shares included in a share registration.

Pink sheets. Bid and ask prices published by OTC Markets Group, Inc. for over-the-counter stocks. The name is derived from the pink color of the paper on which this information was originally printed.

Preferred stock. A financial instrument that has characteristics of both debt and equity, and which may contain preferential features.

Preventive control. A control designed to keep a control breach from occurring.

Profit center. A business unit or department within a company, for which both revenues and expenses are recorded.

Put option. An agreement giving the buyer the right to sell an investment instrument at a certain price and within a certain time period.

R

Receipts and disbursements method. The use of specific cash expenditure and receipt information to derive a cash forecast.

Reference rate. An interest rate used as the basis for an interest rate swap, floating rate security, interest rate option, or forward rate agreement.

Registration statement. A detailed form that must be completed and filed with the Securities and Exchange Commission before the initial offering of securities to the investing public.

Restricted stock. Shares in a company that cannot be traded without first being registered with the SEC or qualifying under an exemption.

Road show. A series of presentations by an issuer of securities to potential buyers, with the intent of creating interest in the securities it intends to sell.

Rolling forecast. The recasting of a company's financial prospects on a frequent basis.

Round lot. A grouping of 100 shares of a stock, or any grouping that can be evenly divided by 100.

S

Segment. A distinct component of a business that produces revenue, and for which the business produces separate financial information that is regularly reviewed internally by a chief operating decision maker.

Shareholder of record. A person or entity listed in the shareholder records of a business as owning its stock.

Shell company. A company with minimal operations or assets, or assets that are solely in cash.

Software as a service. A software delivery model by which software and data are centrally hosted by the software provider and accessed over the Internet.

Spot price. The price at which a currency can currently be purchased.

Stock exchange. A physical or electronic financial market in which securities are bought and sold.

Strike price. The price at which an option or other similar contract can be exercised.

Sunk cost. A cost that has been incurred, and which can no longer be recovered by any means.

T

Target balance. A designated minimum amount of cash to keep on hand, to meet short-term cash requirements.

Target costing. The process of projecting the costs expected to be incurred to create a new product and how this will impact product profitability levels. By doing so, managers can determine how they should alter product designs before they enter the manufacturing process to ensure that the company earns a reasonable profit on new products.

Tender offer. An offer to buy the shares of a company from its shareholders.

Throughput. Revenues minus totally variable costs.

Ticker symbol. A grouping of characters that uniquely identify a publicly-traded security. Investors use ticker symbols to place trade orders for securities.

Transaction exposure. The risk of loss from a change in exchange rates during the course of a business transaction.

Translation exposure. The risk of a reported change in value of a company's assets and liabilities, if they are denominated in a foreign currency.

U

Underwriter. An entity that administers the issuance of securities by another business.

W

Warrant. The right to purchase an issuing company's securities from the issuer at a designated price and within a certain period of time.

Wire transfer. The direct transfer of funds from the payer's account at one bank to the payee's account at another bank.

Y

Yield curve. A line that plots the interest rates associated with an investment having different durations. A normal yield curve reveals a gradual increase in interest rates as maturity dates increase. An inverted yield curve reveals declining interest rates as maturity dates increase.

Z

Zero balance account. A bank account in which a zero balance is automatically maintained by only transferring sufficient funds into it to cover presented checks, and to transfer out funds that are not immediately needed.

Index

Printed in Great Britain
by Amazon

56729442R00210